INSIGHT GUIDES

BURMA
MYANMAR

DISCOVERY CHANNEL

APA PUBLICATIONS

Part of the Langenscheidt Publishing Group

INSIGHT GUIDE
BURMa

Editorial

Project Editor
Francis Dorai
Managing Editor
Clare Griffiths
Editorial Director
Brian Bell

Distribution

UK & Ireland
GeoCenter International Ltd
The Viables Centre, Harrow Way
Basingstoke, Hants RG22 4BJ
Fax: (44) 1256 817988

United States
Langenscheidt Publishers, Inc.
46–35 54th Road, Maspeth, NY 11378
Fax: 1 (718) 784 0640

Canada
Thomas Allen & Son Ltd
390 Steelcase Road East
Markham, Ontario L3R 1G2
Fax: (1) 905 475 6747

Australia
Universal Publishers
1 Waterloo Road
Macquarie Park, NSW 2113
Fax: (61) 2 9888 9074

New Zealand
Hema Maps New Zealand Ltd (HNZ)
Unit D, 24 Ra ORA Drive
East Tamaki, Auckland
Fax: (64) 9 273 6479

Worldwide
Apa Publications GmbH & Co.
Verlag KG (Singapore branch)
38 Joo Koon Road, Singapore 628990
Tel: (65) 6865 1600. Fax: (65) 6861 6438

Printing

Insight Print Services (Pte) Ltd
38 Joo Koon Road, Singapore 628990
Tel: (65) 6865 1600. Fax: (65) 6861 6438

©2005 Apa Publications GmbH & Co.
Verlag KG (Singapore branch)
All Rights Reserved
First Edition 1980
Eighth Edition 2000
Updated 2005

CONTACTING THE EDITORS
We would appreciate it if readers
would alert us to errors or out-
dated information by writing to:
Insight Guides, P.O. Box 7910,
London SE1 1WE, England.
Fax: (44) 20 7403 0290.
insight@apaguide.co.uk

www.insightguides.com

ABOUT THIS BOOK

This guidebook combines the interests and enthusiasms of two of the world's best-known information providers: Insight Guides, whose titles have set the standard for visual travel guides since 1970, and Discovery Channel, the world's premier source of non-fiction television programming.

The editors of Insight Guides provide both practical advice and general understanding about a destination's history, culture, institutions and people. Discovery Channel and its website, www.discovery.com, help millions of viewers explore the world from the comfort of their own homes and also encourage them to explore it first-hand.

This fully updated edition of *Insight Guide: Burma (Myanmar)* is carefully structured to convey an understanding of the country and its culture as well as to guide readers through its sights and activities:

◆ The **Features** section, indicated by a yellow bar at the top of each page, covers the history and culture of the country in a series of informative essays.

◆ The main **Places** section, indicated by a blue bar, is a complete guide to all the sights and areas worth visiting. Places of interest are coordinated by number with the maps.

◆ The **Travel Tips** listings section, with an orange bar, provides a handy point of reference for information on travel, hotels, shops, restaurants and more.

The contributors

This edition of *Insight Guide: Burma* was commissioned by **Francis Dorai,** Insight's Singapore-based managing editor in charge of its Asia Pacific titles. Assisting him in the picture selection and text editing was managing editor **Clare Griffiths** from Insight's London office. The book has been completely restructured and updated with the invaluable help of a number of people.

Andrew Forbes, of the Chiang Mai-based CPA Media, updated all the essays in the Features section and wrote new chapters on history, festivals, temple architecture and the poppy trail, as well as picture stories on Burma's ethnic minorities and Buddha images. In addition, Forbes contributed biographies on Thibaw and Supalayat and Aung San Suu Kyi. Food and travel writer **Wendy Hutton** wrote the chapter on Burmese cuisine. CPA'S **David Henley,** in addition to providing many of the new images for this edition, assisted Forbes in the update of the sections on the Plains of Bagan, and Northwestern and Southeastern Burma.

The sections on Yangon and the Ayeyarwady Delta, Mandalay and Environs and Northeastern Burma were updated by **Tan Chung Lee**, editor of a travel magazine based in Singapore and a frequent traveller to Burma. Tan also wrote the picture stories on Burmese *thanaka* and transport, and updated the Travel Tips section.

Kachin State was updated and photographed by **Oliver Hargreave** from CPA while respected Burma commentator and journalist **Bertil Lintner** provided CPA with invaluable help in updating remote Naga Hills.

Thanks also go to **Joe Cummings** for help with the cartography and toponyms for this guide, and for his collaboration with CPA on the updating of the Myeik (Mergui) Region chapter. **Ron Renard** of CPA improved the language section of the Travel Tips at the back of the book. In 2005, the guide was updated by the aforementioned **Joe Cummings**.

This edition builds on the work of **Wilhelm Klein** and photographer **Günter Pfannmüller** who put together the first edition of the book at a time when most regions in Burma were closed to foreigners.

New photography was provided by **Marcus Braun, Blaine Harrington, Hans Hayden, Paul Beiboer, Mark Downey** and CPA.

Picture research was done by **Hilary Genin** and **Britta Jaschinski;** proofreading by **Mandi Gomez** and indexing by **Penny Phenix.**

Map Legend

▬ ▪ ▬ ▪	International Boundary
▬ ▬ ▬	State Boundary
▪ ● ▪ ●	National Park/Reserve
▬ ▬ ▬	Ferry Route
✈ ✈	Airport: International/Regional
🚌	Bus Station
❶	Tourist Information
✉	Post Office
✝ ✝	Church/Ruins
✝	Monastery
☾	Mosque
✡	Synagogue
🏰	Castle/Ruins
∴	Archaeological Site
∩	Cave
1	Statue/Monument
★	Place of Interest

The main places of interest in the Places section are coordinated by number with a full-colour map (e.g. ❶), and a symbol at the top of every right-hand page tells you where to find the map.

INSIGHT GUIDE
BURMA

CONTENTS

Maps

Burma **112–13**

Yangon **116–17**

Shwedagon Pagoda **118**

Delta Region and Bago **144**

Pathein **146**

Bago **156**

Mandalay **174**

Mandalay Environs **190**

Bagan **212**

Bagan Environs **236**

Northeastern Burma **252**

Kachin State **262**

Mrauk-U **282**

Northwestern Burma **296**

Southeastern Burma **306**

Mawlamyaing **309**

Inside front cover:
Burma
Inside back cover:
Yangon

Introduction

An Eternal Beauty **15**

History

Decisive Dates **18**

From Earliest Times **21**

The Loss of Independence **27**

Independence and Military Rule **35**

Features

Land of Rice and Rivers **45**

The Poppy Trail **53**

People **61**

Burmese Buddhism **70**

Festivals **76**

A Feast of Flavours **80**

Arts and Crafts..................... **85**

The Performing Arts **91**

Temple Architecture **99**

The view over
Mandalay
Hill.

Insight on ...

Ethnic Minorities **68–9**
Buddha Images **96–7**
Transport **168–9**
Thanaka and Longyi **244–5**

Information panels

Thibaw and Supayalat **33**
Aung San Suu Kyi **41**
Rubies and Jade **48**
The Path of Life **67**
Shin-Pyu **73**
The Legend of Shwedagon .. **124**
Train Ride **207**
The Naga Hills **293**
Rakhaing Yoma **299**

Travel Tips

Getting Acquainted .. **322**
Planning the Trip **323**
Practical Tips **328**
Getting Around **332**
Where to Stay **337**
Where to Eat **344**
Nightlife **347**
Culture **348**
Sport **351**
Shopping **353**
Language **354**
Further Reading **356**
◆ **Full Travel Tips index
is on page 321**

Places

Introduction **111**
Yangon & Ayeyarwady Delta 115
Yangon **119**
Delta Region **145**
Bago Division **151**
Mandalay & Environs **173**
Mandalay **175**
Around Mandalay **189**
The Plains of Bagan **211**
Bagan Archaeological Zone .. **213**
Around Bagan **235**

Northeastern Burma **249**
Shan and Kayah States **251**
Kachin State **261**
Northwestern Burma **275**
Mrauk U and Chin State **277**
The Northwest Coast **295**
Southeastern Burma **303**
Mon and Kayin States **305**
Myeik Region **315**

AN ETERNAL BEAUTY

Visiting Burma has always been a magical experience,
but now there is also an ethical dimension

Travellers contemplating a trip to Burma will be aware that it is regarded by a large section of the global community as a pariah because of the human rights abuses of the Burmese people by the ruling military junta. The burning question is this: does visiting Burma endorse the current regime or, in a small way, reduce the country's isolation from the outside world and constrain the junta's actions? Both views have convincing advocates, and informed travellers must make up their own minds.

The essence of Burma lies in its atmosphere, its varied scents and colour, its ambience recalling past ages. This book, first published in 1980, aims to present that eternal beauty, which will remain after today's political repression has become part of history, and we hope that keeping the book up to date may play a part in ensuring that the country and its deeply religious and dignified people will not be forgotten or ignored.

Today, even the country's name is contentious. In 1989, the Burmese authorities implemented a series of name changes replacing colonial names with equivalents closer to actual Burmese usage. The most important change was to the name of the country, officially changed from the "Union of Burma" to the "Union of Myanmar". The same is true with "Rangoon", which became "Yangon", a name given to the city as far back as 1755 by Alaungpaya when he captured and renamed the city of Dagon. The river Irrawaddy is now the Ayeyarwady, the Sittang changed to Sittoung, the Chindwin to Chindwinn, and the Salween to Thanlwin.

Of the cities, Pegu became Bago, Pagan changed to Bagan, Tavoy to Dawei, Prome to Pyay, Moulmein to Mawlamyaing, Maymyo to Pyin-U-Lwin, Magwe to Magway, Bassein to Pathein, Mergui to Myeik, and Sandoway to Thandwe. Tenasserim is now Tanintharyi and Arakan has become Rakhaing. Burmans are now called Bamar, the Karen are called Kayin, and the Arakanese are called Rakhaing. In this book we use the new names, with the old names in parentheses in the first reference of each chapter.

The name of the country, however, will remain Burma and that of the language Burmese, since this is derived from the internationally-accepted term "Tibeto-Burman". We have made a distinction between the Bamar (Burman) people, the country's majority ethnic group, and the Burmese, a term that represents all the peoples of Burma. Indigenous terms used are from the Burmese language, except for Pali language words in religious contexts. ❑

PRECEDING PAGES: pensive monks looking through the oval windows of the *thein* (consecration hall) of Shwe Yaunghwe Monastery in Nyaungshwe; faces of monks; a young monk at Kyaik-tiyo; standing room on a local ferry.
LEFT: lobster catch at Ngapali beach, Rakhaing State.

Decisive Dates

THE EARLY EMPIRE

3000–5000 BC The Anyathian culture flourishes in northern Burma.

circa 500 BC The Pyu enter the upper part of the Ayeyarwady (Irrawaddy) River basin.

3rd century BC Mon settle in the Sittoung Valley.

AD 832 Pyu state of Thayekhittaya (Sri Ksetra) founded. Pyu capital of Halin is captured by the Tai-Shan of Nan-Chao.

9th century AD The Myanmar people, known as the Bamar, come from the China-Tibet border area, over-

run the Kyaukse plain and establish themselves as a major power in the rice-cultivation region. From Bagan, they controlled trade routes between China and India.

THE BURMAN DYNASTIES

AD 1057 Anawrahta founds first Burmese empire.

1084–1113 Golden Age of Bagan. Under Kyanzittha, the great era of pagoda-building begins.

1287 Fall of first Burmese empire following Mongol invasion. Mons establish state at Mottama (Martaban).

1364 Inwa (Ava) founded as capital of a Shan-Bamar dynasty in northern Burma.

1369 Mon capital transferred to Bago.

1385–1425 War between Mon and Shan.

1519 Portuguese establish trade station at Mottama.

1531 Second Burmese empire established.

1600–13 A Portuguese, de Brito, rules at Thanlyin.

1635 Burmese capital is moved to Inwa. British, French and Dutch develop trade with Burma.

1752 Mon conquer Inwa, bringing to an end the second Burmese empire.

1755 Alaungpaya founds new dynasty and third Burmese empire at Shwebo.

1767 Burmese conquer Thai capital of Ayutthaya.

1785 King Bodawapaya conquers Rakhaing (Arakan).

COLONIAL PERIOD TO WORLD WAR II

1824–26 First Anglo-Burmese war; under Treaty of Yandabo, Britain gains the regions around Rakhaing and Tanintharyi (Tenasserium).

1852 Second Anglo-Burmese war; Britain annexes Southern Burma including Yangon (Rangoon).

1861 King Mindon (1853–78) transfers his court to the new city of Mandalay.

1886 Third British annexation includes all Burma.

1886–95 Burmese wage guerrilla warfare against British in northern Burma.

1937 Burma is separated from India.

1939 Communist Party of Burma (CPB) is founded.

1941 Japanese military enters Burma.

1942–45 Burma under Japanese occupation.

1943 Declaration of Burma's independence under the Japanese military.

1945 The Burma National Army starts anti-Japanese uprising. Allies reconquer all of Burma.

1947 Aung San-Attlee agreement is signed. Panglong agreement is signed. Constituent assembly elections are held. Aung San and six other members of interim government are assassinated. Constituent assembly adopts new Burmese constitution. The Nu-Attlee agreement is concluded.

INDEPENDENCE

1948 Burma regains independence as Union of Burma and leaves British Commonwealth. CPB goes underground and civil war begins. Kayin rebellion breaks out.

1951 First parliamentary elections in post-independence Burma are held.

1956 Second parliamentary elections.

1958 The ruling party splits into two factions. A caretaker government, headed by General Ne Win, assumes office.

1960 Border agreement and treaty of friendship and non-aggression concluded between Burma and the People's Republic of China. U Nu's Pyidaungsu Party wins in parliamentary elections.

1961 Union Parliament makes Buddhism the official state religion.

MILITARY RULE

1962 Military coup brings to power the Revolutionary Council (RC) of General Ne Win, who declares the "Burmese Way of Socialism". The Burma Socialist Programme Party (BSPP) is founded.

1963 Peace talks between the RC and various rebel organisations and groups are held in Yangon.

1964 All legal political parties and organisations except BSPP are banned. Nationalisation of all export trade and commodity distribution is implemented.

1967 Anti-Chinese riots in Yangon.

1969 Former Prime Minister U Nu founds Parliamentary Democracy Party to fight RC from abroad.

1971 First BSPP Congress is held and the Twenty-Year Plan (1974–94) announced. Ne Win's state visit to China marks the normalisation of official relations.

1974 New constitution becomes effective, creating the Socialist Republic of the Union of Burma.

1979 Burma withdraws from Non-Aligned Movement.

1980 U Ne Win announces retirement from Presidency. U San Yu elected as President of the country.

1987 The UN General Assembly approves Least Developed Nation status for Burma.

1988 Major demonstrations at Yangon University campuses. On 26 July, Brigadier-General Sein Lwin elected as BSPP's new chairman and chairman of state council (President of the State). On 3 August, martial law declared in Yangon. Five days later, general strike and demonstrations in Yangon. Dr Maung Maung replaces Sein Lwin on 12 August. Largest demonstration in Yangon occurs on 28 August and martial law lifted. U Nu sets up League for Democracy and Peace.

SLORC TAKES POWER

1988 U Nu proclaims Burma's "parallel government" with himself as Prime Minister. After a military coup on 18 September, the State Law and Order Restoration Council (SLORC), headed by General Saw Maung, is formed. Aung Gyi, Tin U and Daw Aung San Suu Kyi found the National League for Democracy (NLD). BSPP is now the National Unity Party (NUP).

1989 On 17 April, rebellious Wa troops capture CPB's headquarters at Panghsang, ending a 41-year-long communist insurgency in Burma. The English name of the country is officially changed to Myanmar. Some Western governments refuse to recognise the change.

1990 While Aung San Suu Kyi is confined under house arrest, general elections are held and the NLD gains over 80 seats in the Assembly.

1991 SPDC refuses to recognise election results till a new constitution is drafted. Aung San Suu Kyi is awarded the Nobel Peace Prize.

1992 The UN Human Rights Commission unanimously condemns Burma for serious human rights violations. General Saw Maung resigns and is succeeded by General Than Shwe (Vice-Chairman of SLORC), who becomes new prime minister. Burma is readmitted to Non-Aligned Movement. Two decades of martial law end.

1993 Myanmar's biggest ethnic rebel group, the Kachin Independence Organisation (KIO), signs ceasefire agreement with the Yangon government, ending a 30-year war in north of the country. This is followed by agreemns with 14 other insurgent groups.

1995 In July, Aung San Suu Kyi is temporarily freed from six years of house arrest but cannot leave Yangon. Soon she is returned to effective house arrest.

1998 Burma is admitted to the Association of Southeast Asian Nations (ASEAN).

2002 Aung San Suu Kyi is again released from house arrest and allowed to travel to Mandalay. General Ne Win, accused of plotting to overthrow the military regime, dies while under house arrest.

2003 Khin Nyunt becomes Prime Minister.

2004 The SPDC reconvenes a national convention to write a new constitution. The NLD refuses to participate as Aung San Suu Kyi is barred from it. In October, Khin Nyunt is ousted by Soe Win, a more conservative member of the ruling military junta.   ❏

PRECEDING PAGES: elegant Burmese festival dress.
LEFT: King Mindon (1853–78), founder of Mandalay.
RIGHT: Aung San Suu Kyi.

FROM EARLIEST TIMES

Settlement by the Mon, the Pyu, the Tai and the Bamar eventually led to a
Burmese empire that would in turn fall prey to European imperialism

According to *The Glass Palace Chronicle of the Kings of Burma (see box below)*, the first kingdom on Burmese soil was founded in pre-Christian times by Sakyan immigrants from India. However, ethnologists generally agree that the present Bamar (Burman) inhabitants of Burma are the descendants of people who originally migrated south from the Sino-Tibetan borderlands.

The "land of gold"

The Mon may have been the first historic group to occupy Burma, possibly several centuries before the birth of Christ. These people, whose language belongs to the Mon-Khmer family and who are still to be found in parts of Thailand and Cambodia today, may have come from Central Asia or from eastern India. They settled on the estuaries of the Thanlwin (Salween) and Sittoung (Sittang) rivers, and their civilisation, which Indian chronicles call *Suvannabhumi* ("Land of Gold"), is also mentioned in ancient Chinese and Arab chronicles.

Legend says it was the Mon who laid the foundation stone of the Shwedagon Pagoda as far back as 2,500 years ago. While this is difficult to prove, it is known that the Mon first established the Buddhist tradition in Burma. By the 3rd century BC, the Mon already enjoyed close ties with the realm of King Ashoka in India through their port of Thaton.

About 2,000 years ago, the Pyu settled in Upper Burma. Unlike the Mon, they belonged to the Tibeto-Burman language family. The Pyus set up their first capital at Thayekhittaya (Sri Ksetra), near present-day Pyay (Prome). The brick ruins of Thayekhittaya still clearly show extensive evidence of their brand of religious architecture – mainly Buddhist in style, but with a noticeably strong Brahman influence. In about the 8th century AD, the Pyu relocated their capital north to Halin, in the region of Shwebo. At about the same time, the Tai were pressing southward from their ancestral home in Yunnan. As a part of the Nan Chao Kingdom, the Tai subjugated Upper Burma in the 9th century, capturing Halin in 832, and assimilating the population.

It was also in the 9th century that the Bamar first made their appearance. Coming from the

LEFT: Yun Bayin Nat, from Sir Richard Temple's *The Thirty-seven Nats* (1906).
RIGHT: Nagzishig Nat from the same source.

THE GLASS PALACE CHRONICLE

In 1829, King Bagyidaw of Burma appointed a committee of scholars to write a chronicle of the Burmese monarchy, which became a 19th century history and mythology of the entire country. The committee consisted of "learned monks, learned brahmans and learned ministers" who compiled a record "which they sifted and prepared in accordance with all credible records". The resultant chronicle, which takes its name from Bagyidaw's Palace of Glass where the compilation was made, recounts the story of Buddhism and of the Buddhist kings of ancient India, as well as the history of the early Burmese kingdoms to the fall of Bagan.

China-Tibet border area, they moved down the Ayeyarwady (Irrawady), overran the Kyaukse plain, and established themselves as the major power in the rice-cultivating region of Upper Burma. From the fortified town of Bagan (Pagan), they controlled the Ayeyarwady and Sittoung river valleys and the trade routes between China and India.

VINCENZO SANGERMANO

An Italian missionary who spent many years in Burma at the end of the 18th century, Father Sangermano wrote an important reference work called *The Burmese Empire.*

The First Burmese Empire

Anawrahta established the First Burmese Empire in 1057 when he suddenly and over-

this new influence, especially that of the monk Shin Arahan, Anawrahta became a devout Theravada Buddhist. He commissioned the building of the Shwezigon Pagoda in Nyaung U (near Bagan), as well as other shrines on the dry plain.

Bagan's golden age

It was under the reign of Anawrahta's second successor, Kyanzittha (1084–1113), that the golden age of pagoda building began. Kyanzittha, whose name means "soldier lord", came to power after

whelmingly conquered the Mon capital of Thaton. He returned to Bagan with 30,000 prisoners, including the Mon royal family and many master builders. Other Mon and Pyu settlements submitted to Anawrahta's dominance over Burma, and the king reigned for 33 years.

Ironically, despite the Mon's defeat, their culture became dominant in the Bamar capital. The Mon language replaced Pali and Sanskrit in royal inscriptions, and the Theravada Buddhist religion became the state religion. Through the close relations maintained by the Mon with Sri Lanka, at that time the centre of Theravadin culture, "the way of the elders" spread throughout most of mainland Southeast Asia. Under

his troops had crushed a Mon rebellion during which Anawrahta's son and successor, Sawlu, was killed. Like Anawrahta, Kyanzittha was a deeply religious man. He ordered the construction of the Ananda Temple, and sent a ship filled with treasures to India to assist in the restoration of the Mahabodhi Temple in Bodhgaya, the place of Buddha's enlightenment. Kyanzittha gave his daughter away in marriage to a Mon prince, and chose their son, Alaungsithu, as successor to preserve the unity of the Burmese Empire.

Bagan's golden age came during the 12th century, when it acquired the name "city of the four million pagodas". This civilisation was supported by rice cultivation, made possible by a highly developed system of irrigation canals. But in the middle of the 13th century, the empire began to crumble. The culturally sustaining power of Buddhism quickly abated, and the Tai – known to the Bamars as Shan – threatened from the northeast.

The end of the empire

Then, to hasten the end of the empire, the Mongol armies of Kublai Khan appeared. The Mongols had supplanted the Nan-Chao Empire in Yunnan, China, and Kublai Khan now demanded payment of tribute by the Bagan emperors. King Narathihapate, overestimating the strength of his own forces, refused.

When the Mongol forces invaded Burma in a series of battles, advancing as far as present-day Bhamo, it is said that, in desperation, Narathihapate pulled down 6,000 temples to fortify Bagan's city walls. Despite his attempts to defend his empire, Narathihapate was branded *Tarok-pyemin*, which means "the king who ran away from the Chinese". The unfortunate king died soon after, poisoned by his own son, the ruler of Pyay. The end result was the conquest of Bagan by the Mongols in 1287.

The Mon, supported by the Shan leader Wareru, withdrew from the First Burmese Empire, and the Rakhaing (Arakanese) on the Bay of Bengal did the same. After the fall of Bagan, Burma was divided into several small states for almost 300 years.

In Lower Burma, the Mon founded a new kingdom centred on Bago (Pegu). Although they lost their grip on Tanintharyi (Tenasserim) during a mid-14th century invasion by the Thai (Siamese) from Ayutthaya, they managed to hold the rest of their realm together. In Upper Burma, meanwhile, the Shans established sovereignty over a Burmese kingdom with its capital at Inwa (Ava). And in the west, along the Bay of Bengal, the Rakhaing spread north to Chittagong in what is now Bangladesh.

The Portuguese period

It was in the 15th century that Europeans first appeared in Burma. In 1435, a Venetian merchant named Nicolo di Conti visited Bago and remained for four months. Six decades later, in 1498, the Portuguese seafarer Vasco da Gama discovered the sea route from Europe to India, and his countrymen were very quick to take advantage of his great success. Alfonso de Albuquerque conquered Goa in 1510, and within a year Malacca, the spice centre of the Orient, was in his grasp.

It was from these two ports that the Portuguese sought to establish a monopoly over the commerce of the Indian Ocean. Antony Correa arrived in Mottama (Martaban) in 1519 and signed a trade and settlement treaty with the town's viceroy. The treaty gave the Portuguese a port of trade with Siam without

making the long sea journey through the Straits of Malacca. Bago's King Tabinshweti, however, would not tolerate a Portuguese presence in his vassal state. In 1541, he laid siege to Mottama, and surprisingly was joined by 700 Portuguese who opposed their countrymen's decision to side with the viceroy of Mottama. While Tabinshweti was successful and solidified his grip on the Second Burmese Empire, the Portuguese maintained their hold on Mottama as a trading settlement until 1613.

Meanwhile, the Portuguese also allied themselves with the king of Mrauk U (Myohaung) in Rakhaing, thereby controlling the sea routes of the Bay of Bengal for 100 years.

LEFT: Bagan in the 13th century.
RIGHT: the Burmese invasion of Ayutthaya (1767).

The most remarkable character from the Portuguese era in Burma was Philip de Brito y Nicote. He came to Asia as a cabin boy and later accepted a post in the court of King Razagyi of Rakhaing, who had conquered Bago.

De Brito was entrusted with the job of running the customs administration in Thanlyin (Syriam). Before long, de Brito had built forts and placed the town under Portuguese sovereignty. After a trip to Goa, during which he married the viceroy's daughter, he returned to Thanlyin with supplies and reinforcements to withstand native sieges – which had already been attempted by Bamar and Rakhaing – and

1527. The Bamar population withdrew to the town of Taungoo, where Tabinshweti established his empire before moving it to Bago.

After his victory over Mottama, Tabinshweti extended his control down the Tanintharyi coast to Dawei (Tavoy), and then west to Pyay on the central Ayeyarwady. His son-in-law and successor, Bayinnaung, overwhelmed the Shan and conquered the Tai kingdoms of Lan Na and (briefly) Ayutthaya, thus extending Burma's boundaries to the maximum.

During the 17th century, the Dutch, British and French set up trading companies in Burma's coastal ports. When the country's cap-

proclaimed himself as king of Lower Burma.

De Brito's superior naval power forced all seagoing trade through his port of Thanlyin. In his 13-year reign, 100,000 native people are said to have converted to Christianity. But his religious beliefs were most intolerant. He displayed utter contempt for Buddhist beliefs and destroyed and plundered monuments. Buddhist leaders condemned him to eternal damnation.

In 1613, Anaukhpetlun of Taungoo stormed Thanlyin with 12,000 men. Around 400 Portuguese defended the town for 34 days but de Brito was captured and impaled: it took him three days to die. In north Burma, meanwhile, hill tribes razed the Shan capital of Inwa in

ital was transferred back to Inwa, it was retaken by the Mon in 1752 with the help of French arms. As a result, the Second Burmese Empire foundered and dissolved. Soon afterwards, however, Alaungpaya, a Bamar from Shwebo, founded the Third Burmese Empire. He defeated the Mon, deported the French to Bayingyi, and got rid of British trading posts. Mon resistance ceased entirely, and the Mon people either fled to Siam or submitted to Bamar rule.

British control

Alaungpaya's second successor, Hsinbyushin, attacked Ayutthaya in 1767 and returned to Inwa with artists and craftsmen who gave a fresh cultural impetus to the Burmese kingdom. Bodawpaya, who took the throne in 1782, conquered Rakhaing, bringing the borders of his kingdom right up against the British sphere of influence in Bengal. On the advice of his soothsayers, he moved his capital to Amarapura, not far from Inwa. Because Burma and British India now shared a common boundary, the number of border incidents increased.

Serious conflict was sparked after King Bagyidaw came to the throne in 1819. The Raja of Manipur, who had previously paid tribute to the Burmese crown, did not attend Bagyidaw's coronation. The subsequent punitive expedition took the Burmese into the Indian state of Cachar, and this intrusion was used by the British as a reason for what is now called the First Anglo-Burmese War.

The Burmese underestimated the strength of the British, and were soundly defeated. In the Treaty of Yandabo (1826), the Burmese were forced to cede Rakhaing and Tanintharyi, plus Assam and Manipur border areas taken in 1819, to the European victors. The British thereby succeeded in making secure their exposed flank on the Bay of Bengal.

The Burmese were without a capable ruler through the first half of the 19th century and since this weakened the kingdom during the period of rapid European colonial expansion, when British and French interests collided in Southeast Asia, Burma's independence was rapidly nearing an end. In 1852, two British sea captains registered a complaint about unfair treatment in a Burmese court. The British Empire responded by sending an expeditionary force to Burma. In the Second Anglo-Burmese War, this force quickly conquered Lower Burma.

Mindon's Mandalay

It was about this time that King Mindon (1853–1878) came to power in Amarapura. His was a relatively enlightened rule. Mindon was the first Burmese sovereign to attempt to bring the country more in line with Western ideas. In 1861, commemorating the 2,400th anniversary of the Buddha's first sermon, Mindon transferred his court to the new city of Mandalay.

Mandalay was sacred to the Buddhist faith, and in 1872 Mindon hosted the Fifth Great

Synod of Buddhism, during which the great Buddhist scripture, known as the *Tipitaka*, was committed to stone. Mindon wanted the sacred scriptures to be conserved in a way that they would be available until the coming of the Maitryea Buddha.

Hence, some 2,400 scribes worked on the text, which was then chiselled onto 729 tablets of stone and a pagoda was built over each of the tablets at the base of Mandalay Hill. But even this appeal for a return to the values of Buddhism, which would thereby sustain the Burmese state and people, could not alter the course of history. ❑

KING MINDON

The king of Burma between 1853 and 1878, Mindon deposed his brother Pagan Min in 1852, occupying Amarapura in 1853. In 1857, he transferred his capital to Mandalay. Sources characterise Mindon as a man of high moral standards who did his best, in difficult circumstances, to preserve Burmese independence while maintaining relations with Britain. A pious Buddhist, he welcomed Christian missionaries to his country and sent missions to the courts of Britain, France and Italy. In 1861, he introduced coinage and reorganised the tax system, greatly improving Burmese state finances. He died at the age of 64, without choosing a successor.

LEFT: a typical 16th-century Portuguese galleon.
RIGHT: the First Anglo-Burmese War (1824–26).

THE LOSS OF INDEPENDENCE

In the late 19th century, Burma was annexed as a province of British India,
a move that still has repercussions today

King Mindon was succeeded by Thibaw, who wasted little time in alienating the British. The French, meanwhile, were negotiating an agreement with Thibaw for shipping rights on the Ayeyarwady. They sought a direct trade route to China, but this was clearly contrary to the interests of the British. When a British timber company became embroiled in a dispute with Thibaw's government, the king was given an ultimatum which he chose to ignore. In no time, British troops had invaded Upper Burma, and with virtually no resistance, easily overwhelmed the capital.

British Burma

On 1 January 1886, Burma ceased to exist as an independent country. Thibaw and his queen, Supayalat, were sent into exile, and Burma was annexed as a province of British India.

To facilitate their exercise of power over all of Burma, the British permitted the autonomy of the country's many racial minorities. As early as 1875, they had enforced the autonomy of the Kayin (Karen) states by refusing to supply King Mindon with the arms he needed to put down a Kayin revolt. The repercussions of this and other similar political moves by the British are still influencing Burma today. Throughout Upper and Lower Burma, the British assumed all government positions down to district officer level. In the bordering states where Chin, Kachin, Shan and various other minorities predominated, the British relied on indirect rule, permitting the respective chieftains to govern in their place. Military forces were largely recruited from India and the northern hill tribes. During most of the colonial period the Bamar were barred from admission to the armed forces.

British interest in Burma was principally of an economic nature. So it is understandable that an economic upswing took place after 1886. The Ayeyarwady Delta had been opened up for rice cultivation and colonised following the

LEFT: 19th-century mural of the Burmese army.
RIGHT: a British soldier at the Shwedagon Pagoda.

British occupation of Lower Burma in 1852.

A generation later, this move began to pay large dividends. Economic growth was to the advantage both of the British, who controlled the rice exports, and Indian moneylenders and merchants, who were far more sophisticated than the Burmese in their familiarity with a

money economy. In particular, the *chettyars*, a caste of moneylenders from south India, profited greatly from Burma's agricultural expansion.

In the five years following annexation of Upper Burma, a quasi-guerrilla war tied up some 10,000 Indian troops in the country's regions. The guerrillas were led by *myothugyis*, local leaders of the old social structure. This resistance declined after 1890, however, and from this time on the Burmese attempted to adjust to the far-reaching social and economic changes that were taking place.

Following World War I, India was granted a degree of self-government by its British rulers but Burma remained under the direct control of the Colonial Governor. This led to extensive opposition within the country, highlighted by a lengthy boycott of schools beginning in December 1920. Eventually, in 1923, the same concessions granted to India – known as the "dyarchy reform" – were extended to Burma.

The rise of nationalism

A major revolt took place in the Tharrawaddy region north of Yangon between 1930 and 1932. Saya San, a former monk, organised a group of followers called *galon*

SHIKOE

In Burmese the term *shikoe* means the act of touching one's head to the floor before the presence of an honoured person, a Buddha image or a Buddhist monk.

autonomy, the underground nationalist movement was gaining momentum. In 1930, at the University of Yangon, the All Burma Student Movement emerged to defy the British system. The young men who spearheaded this group studied Marxism and called each other *Thakin* ("master"), a term generally used to address Europeans. In 1936, the group's leaders – Thakin Aung San and Thakin Nu – boldly led another strike of university and high school classes in opposition to the "alien" educational system.

(after the mythical bird Garuda), and convinced them that British bullets could not harm them. In a subsequent battle, 3,000 of his supporters were killed and another 9,000 were taken prisoner, of whom 78, including Saya San, were executed.

Throughout the early 1930s, opinion was split in Burma as to whether the country should be separated from British India or not. The question was resolved in 1935 when the "Government of Burma Act" was signed in London. Two years later, Burma became a separate colony with its own legislative council. This council dealt only with "Burma Proper", however, and not with the indirectly administered border states. However, as Burma was gaining greater

The success of their movement in bringing about major reforms helped to give these men the confidence in the following decade to come to the forefront of the nationalist movement.

Meanwhile, however, war was brewing. The "Burma Road" made that inevitable. Built as an all-weather route in the 1930s to carry supplies and reinforcements to Chinese troops attempting to repulse the Japanese invasion, it was of extreme strategic importance. As Allied forces moved to defend the road, Japan planned an all-out attack on the Burmese heartland.

The colonial government unexpectedly played into Japanese hands when it arrested several leaders of the Thakin group in 1940. Aung San escaped by disguising himself as a Chinese crewman on a Norwegian boat. He arrived in Amoy seeking contact with Chinese communists to help in Burma's drive for independence. But the Japanese arrested him, and although his movement was opposed to Japan's war on China, his release was negotiated on the grounds that he and other members of the Thakin organisation would collaborate with the Japanese.

In March 1941, Aung San returned to Yangon aboard a Japanese freighter. He secretly picked out 30 members of the Thakin group (the "Thirty Comrades") – to be trained by the Japanese on Hainan Island in guerrilla warfare.

fighting was nowhere more bitter as in the jungles of Southeast Asia. Hand-to-hand combat was a frequent necessity, and tens of thousands of Allied soldiers were killed, along with hundreds of thousands of Burmese. The 27,000 Allied graves in the Htaukkyan cemetery near Yangon are but one testimony to the horror of the war. Survivors of this conflict emerged from the jungle with stories of suffering, sacrifice and heroic deeds. They made household names out of such warriors as "Vinegar Joe" Stilwell, "Old Weatherface" Chennault, Wingate's Chindits and Merrill's Marauders.

In February 1942, Joseph Warren Stilwell, a

A brutal battlefield

In December 1941, the Japanese landed in Lower Burma. Together with the "Burmese Liberation Army" led by Aung San, they overwhelmed the British, drove them from Yangon four months later, then convincingly won battle after battle. British, Indian, Chinese and American troops suffered heavy casualties and were forced to retreat to India. While World War II raged in fury in Europe and the Pacific, the

LEFT: an 19th-century postcard of the Shwedagon Pagoda. **ABOVE:** Dr Ba Maw, head of state in 1943. **RIGHT:** Bogyoke Aung San, the founding father of the Burmese nation.

three-star lieutenant general, was sent by the US government as the senior military representative to the China-Burma-India theatre. Within two months of his arrival, Stilwell was struggling through Upper Burma, a mere 36 hours ahead of Japanese troops, trying desperately to reach the safety of the British lines in India.

Stilwell's retreat

There were 114 soldiers, mainly Chinese, in Stilwell's party. "Vinegar Joe" promised each one of them they would reach India. His retreat – which he called "eating bitterness," citing a Chinese proverb – involved 1,500 km (930 miles) of trekking through formidable jungles and over arid plains with no hope of outside assistance. At about the same time, 42,000 members of the British-Indian army began to withdraw. The Japanese were right on the tail of the Allied retreat, burning every major town along the escape route. There were hundreds of thousands of civilian casualties, and only 12,000 British-Indian troops reached Assam safely. Some 30,000 perished.

All 114 of Stilwell's charges reached the haven of India, just as the general had pledged. But "Vinegar Joe" was riled. "I claim we got run out of Burma," he told a press conference in Delhi some days later. "It is humiliating as hell.

I think we ought to find out what caused it, go back and retake it." Stilwell's words helped guide the Allied war effort in Burma from that point on. He and British General William Slim retraced their steps along the same difficult route – out of Assam, across the Chindwin River to Myitkyina, and down the Ayeyarwady River to Mandalay. Yangon was finally recaptured on 3 May 1945.

Wingate's Chindits

While Stilwell is perhaps best remembered for his retreat, others gained their greatest fame on the offensive. One of these men was General

SCOTT OF THE SHAN HILLS

Sir James George Scott, who is also known by his Burmese pseudonym Shway Yoe, was a prominent British administrator, soldier, explorer and writer who lived in Burma during the latter half of the 19th century. Scott was chiefly remarkable for his ability to assimilate Burmese customs and language, as well as for his love of the country and its people. The founder of Taunggyi (a place of respite for the British from the tropical heat) and one of the most respected colonial officers in the history of British Burma, Scott was a personal friend of King Thibaw, but later became a colonial administrator following the annexation of the Shan States in 1890. Scott is credited with introducing the game of football to Burma, as well as for such major academic endeavours as producing the multi-volume *Gazetteer of Shan State*. His most famous work, *The Burman: His Life and Notions* (1882), published under the pseudonym "Shway Yoe – Subject of the Great Queen", presented so authentic an image of Burma that some contemporary reviewers mistakenly believed it to be the work of a prominent Bamar scholar. Scott went on to serve as British Commissioner of India in 1897. His book *The Burman* has been republished many times, and still remains an invaluable sourcebook for all those wishing to understand Bamar life cycles, society, religion and culture.

Orde Charles Wingate, a Briton whose deep penetration teams used guerrilla tactics to slip behind the Japanese lines and block supplies. Known as Chindits – after the mythological *chinthe*, the undefeatable lions guarding temples throughout Burma – the troops were an amalgam of British, Indian, Chin, Kachin and Gurkha soldiery.

An eccentric scholar, Wingate himself did not live to see the end of the war. His plane crashed into a mountain near Imphal, Manipur, on 24 March 1944.

The return to Burma of a large land force to combat the Japanese depended very much on a usable road. US Army engineers undertook the task with a unit consisting mostly of black Americans. Called the Ledo Road, the new route was to reach from Assam to Mong Yo, where it would join the Burma Road and then continue into Chinese Yunnan.

For more than two years, several thousand engineers and 35,000 native workers laboured in one of the world's most inaccessible areas. The war was almost over by the time the 800-km (500-mile) road was completed. Japanese snipers killed 130 engineers, hundreds more lost their lives through illness and accidents, and the Ledo Road became known as "the man-a-mile road". Built down deep gorges and across raging rapids, it traversed a jungle where no road had passed before.

Despite the immense effort that went into the building of this vital link between India and Southeast Asia, today it is overgrown and virtually impassable to motor traffic.

Flying "The Hump"

Until the Ledo Road was completed, supplies had to be flown to the Allied forces in western China. The air link over "The Hump", as it came to be known, was one of the most hazardous passages of the war. Between Dinjan air base in Assam and the town of Kunming in Yunnan lay 800 km (500 miles) of rugged wilderness. Planes had to fly over the Himalayan range with its 6,000-metre (20,000-ft) peaks, as well as the 3,000-metre (9,843-ft) high Naga Hills, the 4,500-metre (14,764-ft) high Santsung range, and the jungle-covered gorges of the

Ayeyarwady, Thanlwin (Salween) and Mekong rivers. Yet the Air Transport Command flew it with alarming regularity, carrying 650,000 tons of cargo to China.

About 1,000 men and 600 planes were lost during the operation. In fact, so many planes went down on one of the many unnamed peaks of "The Hump" that it was nicknamed the "Aluminum Plated Mountain".

The C-46, the workhorse of the transport operation, was often overloaded, and its pilots, flying up to 160 hours a month, were overworked. During 1944, three men died for every 1,000 tons of cargo flown into Yunnan.

LEFT: Merrill's Marauders move towards Myitkyina via the Ledo Road in February 1944.
RIGHT: a member of Wingate's Chindits.

ROYAL PALACE OF MANDALAY

The palace is located at the centre of a royal enclosure within Mandalay City, built by King Mindon in 1857. The former royal city is a mile square, surrounded by a moat 70 metres (225 ft) wide and 3 metres (11 ft) deep. The surrounding walls are 8.5 metres (27 ft) high and 3 metres (10 ft) thick. After annexation by the British, it was renamed Fort Dufferin, and parts of the wall were demolished to permit railway tracks to pass through the enclosure. In March 1945, the palace buildings were badly damaged by fire during fighting between Allied and Japanese forces. Now restored, the former royal palace is set amid lands used by the Burmese Army.

Chennault's "Flying Tigers"

Another air unit which achieved fame in the Burma war were the "Flying Tigers" of "Old Weatherface" Chennault. Volunteer pilots from the US Army, Navy and Marine Corps fought for only seven months under Chennault. But during that period they became so feared by the Japanese that a Tokyo radio broadcaster called them "American guerrilla pilots" for their unorthodox tactics.

These same tactics, masterminded by Chennault, put him in head-on conflict with General Stilwell. While Stilwell pressed for an infantry-led reconquest of Burma, Chennault

offensive in Burma, there was only one US ground unit involved in the theatre. It had an unmemorable name: the 5307th Composite Unit. But behind this title was one of the toughest volunteer fighting teams the US Army has ever assembled.

Merrill's Marauders

The troops called themselves "Galahad Force." However, they were better known as "Merrill's Marauders", after their commander General Frank Merrill. Originally intended to join Wingate's Chindits, General Stilwell designated them for his own deep-penetration operations.

intended to win the war through air superiority. Ironically, both men had to leave the Asian theatre before the war had ended, but not before Chennault had left his unforgettable mark.

During their brief offensive, the "Flying Tigers" destroyed as many as 1,900 Japanese aircraft, while losing 573 planes themselves. Before they were incorporated into the 14th US Air Force, this band of heroic volunteers – who made their planes look like airborne sharks and who painted Japanese flags on their planes' bodies for every enemy aircraft shot down – built a legend which lingers on even today.

While the US provided an estimated 50 percent of the air strength to the Allied counter-

From the border of Assam to Myitkyina, these soldiers went head-to-head with Japanese forces. It was a formidable task. By the time the unit was disbanded in the summer of 1944, there were 2,394 casualties out of an original 2,830 men.

As the first American fighting force on the Asian mainland since the Boxer Rebellion at the turn of the 20th century, "Merrill's Marauders" fought bravely. But their casualty figure tells a gruesome story, one that helped make the name of "Burma" synonymous with the brutality of war.   ❏

ABOVE: a British soldier's grave – one of the 27,000 in the Htaukkyant Allied War Cemetery north of Yangon.

Thibaw and Supayalat

Writing in his journals in 1882, Sir James George Scott described his contemporary and sometime acquaintance King Thibaw of Burma in these less than flattering terms: "His most Glorious, Excellent Majesty, the present ruler of the City of Mandalay... Ruler of the Sea and Land, Lord of the Rising Sun... King of all the Umbrella-Bearing Chiefs... Lord of the Mines of Gold, Silver, Rubies, Amber and Serpentine... possessor of Boundless Dominions and Supreme Wisdom... has a very bad character. He killed his brothers and sisters and he drinks gin".

In retrospect Scott might be accused of *lèse-majesté*, but his evaluation of Thibaw's character was nonetheless painfully close to the truth. King Mindon, the last great Alaungpaya monarch, had no fewer than 48 sons, but failed to appoint a designated successor. On his deathbed in October 1878, Mindon sent for the most popular of his sons, Nyaungyan Min, with a view to naming him heir. Before he could do this, however, Mindon's chief queen, Sinpyumashin, who had borne him two daughters but no sons, seized control of the palace and environs. It was customary for Burmese kings to marry their half-sisters, so Sinpyumashin arranged the marriage of her second daughter, Supayalat, to an almost unknown and politically powerless son, Thibaw Min. The new king was completely dominated by his wife and mother-in-law, both of whom had strong personalities.

Thibaw's reign began badly, with the execution, in February 1879, of no fewer than eighty possible royal rivals to the throne, including eight of his brothers. The victims were blindfolded and clubbed to death, before being thrown into a ditch, covered with earth and trampled by elephants. Shaw, the British resident in Mandalay, managed to prevent further massacre by threatening to haul down the British flag and break off relations. Reports soon reached the British in Yangon, arousing widespread revulsion and lending weight to those businessmen and politicians who favoured a forward policy.

In the event, Thibaw was temporarily saved as Britain was already engaged in wars elsewhere. Over the next few years things went from bad to worse. The authority once enjoyed by King Mindon rapidly disintegrated, while by 1882 Supayalat reportedly exercised all real power and acted as

royal treasurer. Peter Camaratta, a Portuguese in the service of Thibaw, secretly informed the British that "no single payment, however small, can be paid without her order". Thibaw and his queen restricted themselves to small back rooms in the palace; he was forbidden to leave her side for more than a few moments, and if other ladies of the court caught the king's eye, the queen reportedly made short work of them.

By 1885, relations between Thibaw and the British had deteriorated to such an extent that the latter launched the Third Anglo-Burmese War, resulting in the seizure of Mandalay on 29 November. Supayalat reportedly caught a first glimpse of

the arrival of British warships from the palace watchtower; a day later Thibaw and his queen were taken aboard a vessel with little ceremony and at night. The long voyage into exile had begun.

Thibaw never saw his palace again. He lived out he rest of his life at Ratnagiri in India, supported by a government pension and with Supayalat at his side. When he died in 1916, the former queen was permitted to return to Yangon where she lived in a small private house. A contemporary report in *The Times* describes her as "a pathetic old lady strangely different from the feline personality who had dominated Thibaw in the tragic days before the Burmese monarchy came to its sudden and inglorious end". ❑

RIGHT: a portrait of King Thibaw.

INDEPENDENCE AND MILITARY RULE

Post-war independence in Burma has led to growing militarisation,
economic hardships and an uneasy peace between rival factions

By 1943, it was evident that the Japanese wanted to see Burma's government, which they had helped establish, become subordinate to the Imperial Japanese Army. Burma was declared "independent" in August of that year, with Dr Ba Maw, former education minister, as head of the puppet state, Thakin Aung San was named minister of defence, and Thakin Nu was chosen as foreign secretary.

The Burmese nationalists, however, were not pleased with the arrangement. In December 1944, Aung San established contact with the Allies, and in March 1945 he transferred his 10,000-man army to the side of the Allies. His troops were now called the "Patriotic Burmese Forces" – and they helped the Allies recapture Yangon. The Japanese surrender was signed in Burma's capital on 28 August.

Results of war

The war had completely devastated Burma. That which had not been destroyed during the Japanese attack was laid to waste during the Allied reconquest. There were however, two positive results of war for the Burmese: their experience of nominal self-government, and the weakening of British power and prestige. It was clear Burma could no longer remain under the former colonial constitution.

But the British, climbing back into the driver's seat after the wartime hiatus, had other ideas: they had planned a three-year period of direct rule for Burma.

Meanwhile, Aung San was quietly building up two important nationalist organisations. One of these was the Anti-Fascist People's Freedom League, a Marxist-oriented group better known by its acronym (AFPFL). As the military wing of this political league, Aung San founded the People's Volunteer Organisation (PVO), which, as early as 1946, claimed 100,000 (mostly unarmed) members.

LEFT: a statue of Bogyoke Aung San, near Yangon's Royal Lake.
RIGHT: U Nu, Prime Minister (1948–58, 1960–62).

Despite the growth of nationalist sentiment behind the AFPFL, the British remained firmly in control of Burma until September 1946. Then, a general strike, first by the police, then by all government employees plus railway and oil workers' unions, brought the country to a standstill. The colonial government turned to

the AFPFL and other nationalist groups for help. A moderate national council was formed, and the strike ended in early October.

The AFPFL took advantage of the weakened position of the British to seize the political initiative. Aung San presented a list of demands to the British Labour government, which included the granting of total independence to Burma by January 1948.

A conference was promptly called in London in January 1947. Burma was awarded its independence as demanded, but there were several difficult questions to resolve in negotiations, especially concerning ethnic minorities. The AFPFL representative insisted upon complete independence for all of Burma, including the minority regions; the British were concerned about the consequences of continual friction between the Bamar and other groups.

In February, however, Aung San met with minority representatives at Panglong in Shan State. The result was a unanimous resolution that all the ethnic groups would work together with the Burmese interim government to achieve independence for the minority regions in a shorter space of time. After a period of 10 years, each of the major groups that formed a state would be permitted to secede from the Union if they so desired.

National Independence

National elections for a Constituent Assembly were held in April 1947 and Aung San and his AFPFL won an overwhelming majority of seats. But on 19 July, as the new constitution was still being drafted, tragedy struck. A group of armed men burst in on a meeting of the interim government and assassinated nine people, including Aung San and six of his ministers. U Saw, right-wing prime minister of the last pre-war coslonial government, was convicted of instigating the murders and later executed.

Thakin Nu, one of the early leaders of the All Burma Student Movement, and later of the

GENERAL NE WIN

The strongman of Burmese politics for over 30 years, and a powerful force behind the SPDC, Ne Win was born at Pyay in 1910. Originally styled Thakin Shu Maung, he took the name Bo Ne Win or "Sun of Glory General" at the time of the formation of the association of the "thirty comrades". Educated at Yangon University, he left without a degree in 1930. He worked for the post office while becoming an early member of the "Our Burma" Association. In 1943, he became commander of the Burma National Army with the rank of Japanese colonel, and in 1945 became commander of the Patriotic Burmese Forces. After the war Ne Win became second in command and later CO of the 4th Burma Rifles. He became an MP in 1947, advanced to the rank of Brigadier-General in 1948, and then to Major-General and Commander-in-Chief of the Burmese Army in 1949. In the 1950s he served as Minister for Defence and Home Affairs, before seizing power in a military coup in 1958. In 1960 he was replaced by U Nu in general elections, but in 1962 he seized power again through a military coup. Since that time the military grip on Burma has remained absolute. Ne Win resigned the presidency in 1981 and stepped down as BSPP chairman seven years later. However, till his death in 2002 from natural causes, Ne Win retained a baleful influence over the Burmese military junta.

AFPFL, was asked by the British colonial government to step into Aung San's shoes. U Nu became prime minister when on 4 January, 1948, at the astrologically auspicious hour of 4.20am, the "Union of Burma" became an independent nation. In so doing, Burma became the first former British colony to sever ties with the Commonwealth.

No sooner had Burma been thrust into solving its own problems than it came face-to-face with the bitter realities of nationhood. The first three years of independence were marked by violent domestic confrontations and a militarisation of daily life. No less than five separate

Kayin were discharged from active service. Under Ne Win, the army gained an upper hand in the early 1950s.

Economic disaster

In economic terms, the first few years of independence were disastrous for Burma. Income from rice exports plummeted and tax revenue diminished, yet the expenditure that was needed to maintain the oversized military machine continued to grow.

U Nu and the AFPFL kept a firm grip on power during the 1951 national elections. But a schism within the party soon disrupted the gov-

groups, including the Kayin, opposed to membership in the "Union of Burma" took up arms against the newly founded state.

Lieutenant General Ne Win was appointed commander-in-chief of the armed forces, and soon thereafter minister of defence. The Bamar, who had not been allowed in the armed forces since the British took over in 1886, assumed all the high-ranking military posts, and all mutinous

LEFT: Japanese officers at Yangon, August 1945 during the signing of their surrender to the Allied Forces.
ABOVE: General Ne Win, head of the Revolutionary Council in 1963.
RIGHT: General Saw Maung, Chief of Staff.

ernment's programme of economic development. The Eight-Year Plan of 1953, produced by a team of US experts and called Pyidawtha (Happy Land), had to be abandoned in 1955 due to the increasing intra-party disputes.

In 1958, the squabbling had become so serious that the government was virtually paralysed. U Nu was forced to appoint a caretaker government, with General Ne Win at its helm. The 18-month administration was stern, but made progress in cleaning up the cities, modernising the archaic bureaucracy and establishing free and fair elections.

The elections were held in February 1960, and the U Nu faction of the AFPFL, renamed the

Pyidaungsu (Union) Party, regained power. U Nu's campaign promises inspired scepticism, however. He sought to have Buddhism recognised as the state religion. He also promised the Mon and Rakhaing people semi-autonomy. The promises spurred the Shan and Kayah to demand the right of secession granted them in the 1948 constitution, and again the U Nu government was thrown into turmoil. There was little resistance when Ne Win swept into power in a nearly bloodless coup on 2 March 1962.

> **SINO-BURMESE RELATIONS**
>
> Over the past two decades China, which until 1980 backed the CPB's attempts to overthrow the Burmese regime, has emerged as Yangon's political supporter in the region.

(NULF), an alliance between his followers, the Mon and Kayin, as well as a smattering of Shan and Kachin. He claimed to have an army of 50,000, although that figure may well have been exaggerated. In 1971, the rebels launched successful raids from the Thai border, and for a while, held territory inside Burma.

In Burma, meanwhile, Ne Win was reforming the government structure and introducing a constitutional authoritarianism. First, in an effort to "civilianise" the system, he dropped his military title.

The road to Socialism

Ne Win's first move was to appoint a Revolutionary Council made up entirely of military personnel. On 30 April, the council published its manifesto, which was titled: *The Burmese Way to Socialism*.

For 12 years, Ne Win ruled by decree, with all power vested in the Revolutionary Council. Foreign businesses were nationalised, and the state took control of all businesses, including banks. The army was put in charge of commerce and industry. A foreign policy of self-imposed isolation and neutrality was pursued.

In May 1970, U Nu announced the formation of a National United Liberation Front

On 2 March 1974, the Revolutionary Council was officially disbanded and the "Socialist Republic of the Union of Burma" was born. Ne Win became president of the nation and chairman of the Burma Socialist Program Party; various leaders of the armed forces filled 16 of the 17 ministerial posts.

In foreign affairs, Burma shocked much of the world in September 1979 when it became the first country to withdraw from the 88-member Non-Aligned Movement. Impatience with "big powers engaged in a behind-the-scene struggle for exerting their influence on the movement" was the official government explanation for the decision to pull out.

Ne Win stepped down from the presidency in November 1981. U San Yu, a loyal disciple, was elected to succeed him. Ne Win, then already 71, continued as Burma Socialist Program Party (BSPP) Chairman, and retained behind-the-scenes power. In December 1987, the United Nations general assembly approved LCD (Least Developed Country) status for Burma.

A year of turmoil

Students started to stage demonstrations, which soon escalated, prompting the flight of thousands of students across the Thai border. In June of 1988, a curfew was imposed in Yangon. In July, while proposing a referendum on a multi-party system, Ne Win announced his retirement as BSPP chairman. Sein Lwin became, for a short while, chairman of the Council of State.

On 8 August, a huge popular demonstration was crushed by the *tatmadaw* (military), with thousands of demonstrators shot dead on the streets of Yangon. Sein Lwin was succeeded by Dr Maung Maung, a civilian, who was then made president and BSPP chairman. However, after huge country-wide demonstrations, he lifted martial law and promised a referendum.

At an emergency session on 10 September, however, the BSPP instead proposed general elections under a multi-party system. Soon after, Aung San Suu Kyi, daughter of the national hero Aung San, proposed the formation of an interim government. But this was not to be.

The SLORC in power

On 18 September, the Chief of Staff, General Saw Maung, announced over the radio that the military had assumed power and set up the State Law and Order Restoration Council (SLORC), with himself as prime minister. The next day the Pyithu Hluttaw and other organs of power were dissolved. Opposition leaders formed the National League for Democracy (NLD). The general strike collapsed and thousands of students crossed the borders into neighbouring countries, later forming the Democratic Alliance of Burma (DAB) in which 10 ethnic resistance armies and 12 underground student groups united under the leadership of the Kayin leader Bo Mya.

LEFT: anti-government demonstrations in 1988.
RIGHT: the military keeps a tight lid over the country, making protests against the regime impossible.

In 1990, the English name of Burma was officially changed to that of Myanmar and the SLORC promulgated a new election law for the Pyithu Hluttaw. Aung San Suu Kyi, who had assumed the leadership of the NLD (National League for Democracy), was barred from participating in the elections and was placed under house arrest (she received the Nobel Peace Prize in September 1991 while still in captivity).

When the general elections finally took place on 27 May 1990, the NLD captured 82 percent of the vote. However, the military demanded that a new constitution should first be drafted in which different groups, including the military,

should have a say. In spite of the free elections and the clear democratic vote, the Pyithu Hluttaw could not be convened and the military remained in control of the government. In 1993, under pressure from China, the Kachin Independence Organisation (KIO) signed a cease-fire agreement with the Yangon government, thus ending a 30-year war in the north of the country. This was soon followed by agreements with 14 other insurgent groups. Another factor was the disintegration of the BCP, once an eminent contender for power and the best-armed foe of the *tatmawdaw*.

As if to underline these successes, and in a cosmetic bid to improve its overseas image, in

1997 the SLORC reconstituted itself as the State Peace and Development Council (SPDC).

The wait for democracy

Despite the quasi-boycott of Western nations barring Burma from World Bank loans and International Monetary Fund assistance, the SPDC managed to speed up the economy by attracting Southeast Asian, Chinese, Japanese and French capital, often in form of joint ventures channelled through the regime. In the 1990s GDP grew by around 4 to 5 percent a year, but by 2003 there was negative growth of a half percent per year. The per capita GDP runs US$1,800 (measured by

sible for spawning the most repressive regime in Asia, died in disgrace while under house arrest. He had been accused of supporting a plot to overthrow the government.

The SPDC frequently undermines the position of the main opposition party, the NLD and its secretary general Aung San Suu Kyi. In early 2002, after lengthy negotiations with the UN, she was released from house arrest and permitted to travel around the country, but a 2003 attack on her convoy in Kyaukse – during which Suu Kyi may have endured a minor head wound – prompted the government to order her activities confined to Yangon. The attack appears to

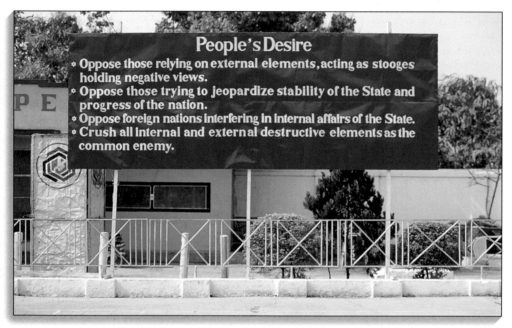

the purchasing power parity method), or about one-third that of neighbouring Thailand.

Meanwhile, the opposition looks fractured and weak. Armed resistance is in total disarray, with the Kayin divided into mutually hostile Buddhist and Christian factions. The Thai government – long discreet supporters of the Kayin cause – were angered by the actions of "God's Army", a breakaway Kayin faction led by child soldiers, who in 1999 seized the Burmese Embassy in Bangkok, and in 2000 hit international headlines when they took more than 400 Thai nationals hostage at a hospital in Ratchaburi.

In December 2002, General Ne Win, founder of military rule in Burma in 1962 and respon-

have been perpetrated by a government-supported political action group. NLD supporters claim dozens of Burmese were killed during the clash. The government denied orchestrating the violence, which it blamed on Suu Kyi, and said four people were killed.

Political analysts believe that Burma's military regime is deeply entrenched as ever, while the ASEAN policy of "constructive engagement" with Yangon continues apace. Within Burma, many opponents of the SPDC have abandoned hope of real change in the near future.   ❑

ABOVE: a government propaganda poster at the Thai border crossing with Burma.

Aung San Suu Kyi

Also known by her supporters as "The Lady", Aung San Suu Kyi has come to be seen both in Burma and abroad as a symbol of implacable but peaceful resistance to military oppression. She was awarded the Nobel Prize for Peace in 1991, while under house arrest.

Born in 1945, Suu Kyi is the daughter of the late Burmese nationalist leader, General Aung San, whose resistance to British colonial rule culminated in Burma's independence in 1948. After attending school in Yangon, Suu Kyi lived in India before going to Britain for her higher education. There she met and married her late husband, Michael Aris, an Oxford University professor specialising in Tibetan Studies. Aris accepted that his wife's destiny might ultimately lie in Burma. "Before we were married I promised my wife that I would never stand between her and her country," he said. Suu Kyi first came to prominence when she returned to Burma in August 1988, with her husband to visit her ailing mother. She became the leader of a burgeoning pro-democracy movement in the aftermath of the brutal repression of a pro-democratic uprising in the summer of 1988. Inspired by the non-violent campaigns of the American civil rights leader Martin Luther King and India's Mahatma Gandhi, Suu Kyi organised rallies after her return to Burma, and travelled the country, calling for peaceful democratic reforms and free elections. She campaigned for change through dialogue.

The movement quickly grew into a political party that went on to win a majority 82 percent in national elections in 1990, by which time she had already been under house arrest for a year. The military regime, however, refused to relinquish power and stepped up intensified repression of her party, the National League for Democracy (NLD).

After her release from house arrest in 1995, she defined her position as follows: "The great majority of people in Burma want democracy. We as the National League for Democracy and as part of the forces for democracy, are always ready to work together with the authorities to achieve national reconciliation. We would like to think that the strength of our goodwill and the very strong desire of the people for democracy will bring positive results."

Despite Suu Kyi's official release from house arrest, the Burmese authorities maintain strong de facto restrictions on her freedom of movement and speech. She is severely restricted in her movements and slandered by the pro-government media as a political opportunist and a "genocidal prostitute". This last unlikely phrase is a product of the military regime's obsession with Suu Kyi's marriage to Michael Aris, who died of cancer in Oxford in 1999, at the age of 53. Throughout Aris's final illness, the Yangon authorities denied Aris permission to visit Burma. Fearing that she would be refused permission to return to Burma, Suu Kyi declined the option of leaving the country and remained separated from her husband and two sons at the time of his death.

At the start of the new millennium, Suu Kyi remains effectively isolated in Yangon while the SPDC is busy creating a new national charter using a hand-picked selection of constitutional convention delegates. With the NLD barred from participating, the party has become increasingly unable to serve the aspirations and needs of the average Burmese citizen. Meanwhile, the military's stranglehold on Burma has become even more absolute. Continuing "constructive engagement" with ASEAN; the military support from China and financial backing from Singapore, Malaysia and Taiwan; and the ousting of Prime Minister Khin Nyunt in October 2004 have all combined to maintain the army's grip on power. ❑

RIGHT: Nobel laureate Aung San Suu Kyi.

LAND OF RICE AND RIVERS

*Burma is roughly kite-shaped: a diamond with the long Tanintharyi as its tail
and the Ayeyarwady as the kite's controlling string*

As the centre of the rice culture on which Burma's economy has always been based, the Ayeyarwady (Irrawaddy) is the lifeblood of the land. Rising in the Himalayas, the river crosses the country from north to south for 2,170 km (1,350 miles), emptying into the Andaman Sea through a nine-armed delta. Called "the Road to Mandalay" by British colonialists, the broad river has traditionally been Burma's major transportation route, though during the colonial and post-independence periods both road and rail have played an increasingly important role.

Travellers following the Ayeyarwady's entire course may experience the full range of Burma's climatic zones. Beginning at the far north, the river runs through the rugged Kachin Hills, foothills of the Himalayas. At Bhamo, the furthest point to which the Ayeyarwady is navigable by steamer (1,500 km/930 miles from the delta), it enters the Shan Plateau. Further downstream, it emerges on the broad dry plain of central Burma, the centre of classical Burmese civilisation. The Ayeyarwady then flows past sandbars to the ruins of Bagan and Thayekhittaya (Sri Ksetra), and enters the more fertile southern stretch of its course. In the vast delta, 240 km (150 miles) wide and 290 km (180 miles) long the river irrigates rice paddies.

With a surface area of 676,577 sq km (261,228 sq miles), Burma is the largest country in mainland Southeast Asia. Its population is estimated at about 49 million, of whom about 75 percent live in rural villages. After Yangon, with its population of 4 million plus, the major population centres are Mandalay (pop 1 million), Mawlamyaing (Moulmein; pop 400,000) and Pathein (Bassein; pop 215,000).

Bounded by Bangladesh and India on the northwest, China on the northeast, Laos and Thailand on the east, the Andaman Sea on the south, and the Bay of Bengal on the southwest,

PRECEDING PAGES: rain-saturated paddy fields in central Burma. **LEFT:** climbing a golden mountain of harvested paddy. **RIGHT:** a boat in the Bay of Bengal.

Burma is located between 10°N and 28°N. The Tropic of Cancer traverses the country 160 km (100 miles) north of Mandalay.

Three season cycle

The most agreeable season is winter. From November through February, the average mean

temperature along the Ayeyarwady plain is between 21°C and 28°C (70°F and 82°F), although in the northern Kachin mountains and on the Shan Plateau the temperature can drop below freezing point.

March and April are the hottest months, with the temperature in central Burma reaching 45°C (113°F). In May, the rainy season begins. It is also a time of high humidity, somewhat more bearable in Mandalay than in Yangon. From May through October, there are almost daily afternoon and early evening showers.

Burma's central river system is ringed by peaks which create profound effects on the climate. There are the Rakhaing, Chin, Naga and Patkai hills in the west, the Kachin hills in the north, and the Shan Plateau, extending to the Tanintharyi Coast ranges, in the east.

The coasts of Rakhaing (Arakan) and Tanintharyi receive 300 to 500 cm (120 to 200 inches) of rain a year, with the Ayeyarwady Delta getting 150 to 250 cm (60 to 100 inches). On the leeward sides of the mountain ranges and on the Shan Plateau, annual precipitation ranges from 100 to 200 cm (40 to 80 inches), while central Burma's Dry Zone varies from 50 to 100 cm (20 to 40 inches). It is largely due to the protection of the 2,000-metre (6,500-ft) peaks of the Rakhaing Yoma (mountain range)

that central Burma is Southeast Asia's driest region – and that Bagan's ancient buildings have remained so well preserved.

The seasonal monsoons nourish Burma's rice crops with abundant rainfall but it is the melting snows of the Himalayas, far to the north, which feed Burma's great rivers.

Inland navigation

Two rivers besides the Ayeyarwady are important to Burma's inland navigation and irrigation. One, the Chindwin, is a tributary of the Ayeyarwady, joining the larger river about 110 km (70 miles) downstream from Mandalay.

WHAT'S IN A NAME?

In 1989, the Burmese military authorities announced that Burma would change its name to Myanmar on the grounds that the former name was a relic of the colonial past. The opposition refused to acknowledge the change and continues to use the name Burma. But which is most appropriate for the visitor?

In fact, according to linguistic experts, both are correct. *Myanmar* is the formal, royal term for the country, while *Bama* – from which Burma is derived – is a more colloquial term. In historical records, both forms have been used interchangeably. It is worth noting that the founding fathers of independent Burma, including Bogyoke Aung San, called

their movement "Doh-Bama Asiayone", or "The Our-Burma Association", rather than "Doh-Myanmar Asiayone". This was because they considered the term Bama to implicitly include every nationality in the state, whereas Myanmar tended to imply only the Bamar majority – people living in the country's heartland.

For this reason, the Burmese opposition, as well as various national minorities such as the Mon, Shan, Kayin, Kachin, Chin and Kayah, refuse to acknowledge the change of name. They fear it is the intention of the Burmese military authorities to subsume all Burma's diverse nationalities within a single Bamar-Myanmar identity.

Readily navigable for 180 km (110 miles) upstream from its confluence – and for 610 km (380 miles) during the rainy season – it opens up remote stretches of the Sagaing Region.

In eastern Burma, the Thanlwin (Salween) River slices through Shan State in a series of deep gorges. Like the Mekong, which comprises the Burma–Laos border, the Thanlwin flows for long stretches through areas still held or contested by rebel forces. It has few tributaries between its source in the Himalayas and its exit to the Andaman Sea at Mawlamyaing (Moulmein), despite a 2,816-km (1,749-mile) course. It is navigable only for about 160 km (100 miles) upstream due to its fast current and 20-metre (65-ft) fluctuations in water level. It used to play an important role in the economy – as the route by which teak was rafted from the Shan Plateau to Mawlamyaing, its export harbour – but now teak is exported via Yangon.

Disparate zones

Geographically, Burma can be divided up into several zones. In the far north, are the Kachin Hills, reaching heights of 3,000 metres (10,000 ft). On the Tibetan border is Hkakabo Razi, the highest peak in Southeast Asia at 5,887 metres (19,314 ft). Deep valleys, many of them with subtropical vegetation and terraced rice fields, separate the mountain ridges. The chief inhabitants are the Kachin; Lisu are also common in the Chinese border region. The administrative centre of Myitkyina is the terminus of the railway from Yangon and Mandalay.

The Kachin Hills link with the Shan Plateau in the south, a vast area averaging 1,000 metres (3,200 ft) in elevation. Deep valleys intersect the undulating surface of the plateau, and the Thanlwin (Salween) flows through it like an arrow. Once popular as a site for hill stations, the region still offers the flavour of a bygone era in its administrative centres of Taunggyi, Pyin-U-Lwin (Maymyo), Kalaw and Lashio. A tourist centre has been developed around Inle Lake in the southwestern part of the plateau. With a European-like climate, fruit, citrus crops and vegetables thrive on the Shan Plateau, as does timber. Burma is the world's leading exporter of teak, most of which is harvested in the Shan

State. Other crops include rice, peanuts, potatoes, tea, tobacco, coffee, cotton and opium. The "Golden Triangle" encompasses much of the eastern part of the Shan Plateau. East of the Gulf of Mottama (Martaban), the Shan Plateau narrows into the Tanintharyi coastal range which forms the natural border between southern Burma and Thailand. The coastland which follows this range down to the Isthmus of Kra is not easily accessible, but the coastal areas of Mawlamyaing, and Dawei (Tavoy) have densely populated farming settlements.

Scattered off the Tanintharyi coast are the isles of the Myeik (Mergui) Archipelago, one of

LEFT: a boat laden with lake weed, used as fertiliser for floating gardens.
RIGHT: a fig tree on the banks of the Ayeyarwady.

Rubies and jade

The first image many foreigners have of Burma is of precious, sparkling gems. The reputation is deserved. The northern mines of Mogok (now open to visitors) and Mogaung boast large quantities of rubies, jade and sapphires.

Ludovico di Varthema, an Italian who visited Burma in 1505, was the first European to report this wealth to the West. "The sole merchandise of this people is jewels," wrote di Varthema. "Large pearls and diamonds are worth more there than with us, and also emeralds."

Di Varthema was also the first Westerner to prosper by dealing in gems in Burma. He presented the King of Bago with corals, and was rewarded with 200 rubies – worth about 100,000 ducats (about US$150,000) in Europe at that time.

Today, it is not so easy to get rich in the gem market but each February for some decades now, hundreds of gem dealers from all over the world have gathered in Yangon for the "Gems and Pearls Emporium" at the Inya Lake Hotel.

Most prized of all Burmese gems is the ruby, the stone in which Burma virtually holds a world monopoly. Stones the colour of pigeon blood, apparently unique to Burma, fetch the highest prices. However, it doesn't require an alchemist's recipe to produce a fake. False rubies can be made in a flame-fusion process from purified ammonia alum and small amounts of chrome alum, with a dash of chrome oxide tossed in for the deep colour. These synthetic stones, deceptively labelled, are popular attractions at tourist markets.

Mogok, where Burma's largest ruby mines are situated, lies about 110 km (70 miles) northeast of Mandalay. In earlier times, the kings of Burma appropriated much of the wealth recovered here, leaving the miners with only the smaller stones.

When the British annexed Upper Burma in 1886, a year of frenzied digging ensued, as the Burmese were now unhindered by royalty. But the colonials were able to occupy the Mines District in 1887, and the London firm of Messrs Streeter & Co received sole buying rights for whatever the ground yielded. It made the company's shareholders and the government revenue office significantly rich. Today, however, the mines have been nationalised.

In the far north, west of Myitkyina in Kachin State, is the town of Mogaung, the centre of a jade-mining district. The riches of this region were well known to the Chinese as long ago as 2000 BC.

As most of Burma's natural wealth is found where minority ethnic groups live, how this wealth is distributed is of crucial importance to the country's future. For decades, these natural resources have been the main source of income for various ethnic rebel groups. If an appropriate way to share this wealth between the regions and central government can be found, then there is a chance for peace in these areas. Rubies, jade and teak are in huge demand on the world market; Burma could supply them so that currently strife-torn regions may prosper. But this has yet to happen.

Since peace has come to Kachin State, the jade mining district has been experiencing what California saw during the gold rush years. Burmese from all over the country have flocked there in search of instant wealth. Some have succeeded, but most end up as day labourers in the larger pits that are often controlled by ethnic Chinese. Stories of lawlessness and exploitation are rife in this "off limits" area.

Rubies and jade are the most evident examples of Burma's precious mineral wealth, but sapphires, Oriental aquamarine and emeralds, topaz, amethysts and lapis lazuli are among other stones which attract international buyers to the "Gems and Pearls Emporium". ❑

LEFT: a handful of precious stones.

Southeast Asia's least developed island groups. Due to Taninthayi's isolation, the region is the centre of a large smuggling trade between Thailand and Burma. For security reasons it is still off-limits to most Burmese and foreign visitors, though it has begun, slowly, to open up.

West of the Ayeyarwady, on the seaward side of the Rakhaing Yoma, is the state of Rakhaing. This flat, fertile coastal strip is broken by small rivers flowing out of the east-lying mountains, the highest of which is Mount Victoria at 3,053 metres (10,016 ft). Several as yet undeveloped, long and sandy beaches grace the coastline.

The central belt of the nation extends around

and dry cultivation in rice-growing. A complicated system of lakes and canals allowed the earliest Burmese civilisations to exist here. Today, 607,000 hectares (1.5 million acres) of land are devoted to irrigated rice farming. Crop failures occur at least once a decade, and before rice was available from Lower Burma, famine was common. As the delta is now Burma's rice bowl, an impressive 1.5 million hectares (3.7 million acres) of irrigated land in the Dry Zone is devoted to the farming of cotton, tobacco, peanuts, grain sorghum, sesame, beans and corn.

If Upper Burma's agricultural area is impressive, that of Lower Burma is astounding. The

the Ayeyarwady. With its tributary the Chindwin, and the Sittoung, it is the settlement area of the dominant Bamar (Burman) people. The region is subdivided into two parts – Upper Burma, the area surrounding Mandalay, north of Pyay (the former Prome, also called Pyi) and Taungoo; and Lower Burma, which focuses on Yangon, and south of the Pyay-Taungoo line.

Burma's rice bowl

Upper Burma is a region of low rainfall, with farmers using traditional methods of irrigated

ABOVE: elephants are the main form of transport in the roadless jungles.

Ayeyarwady Delta contains 3.6 million hectares (9 million acres) of irrigated rice farms, with a yield great enough to feed the whole population of Burma. The delta is expanding into the Andaman Sea at a rate of about 5 km (3 miles) a century as a result of silt deposits.

When the British arrived here in the mid-19th century, the delta was uncultivated jungle and tall grass. The monsoon rains attracted colonists from the Dry Zone, who cleared the jungle and planted it with wet-rice fields. For the most part of the 20th century, until 1962, Burma was the world's largest exporter of rice. The population, though, has grown faster than production, so that the annual amount exported – more than 3 million tons in the pre-war years – dropped to 600,000 tons by 1976. In 1994/95 exports had passed the 1 million ton mark, and with the introduction of high-yield strains, land reclamation and improved irrigation, the figure continues to rise.

Minerals and forests

Burma also has huge, untapped mineral reserves. Oil, found in the Ayeyarwady basin, is most important; in recent years, test drilling for natural gas in the Gulf of Mottama has resulted in a US$2 billion investment by the French/American Total/Unocal group. Further con-

cessions for gas, oil and gold should bring badly needed foreign currencies into Burma.

Iron, tungsten, lead, silver, tin, mercury, nickel, plutonium, zinc, copper, cobalt, antimony and gold are found in significant quantities around the country. The famed rubies and sapphires are mined in Mogok in western Shan State, and fine jade is extracted near Mogaung in Kachin State.

Burma's vegetation varies according to regional rainfall. Almost half of the country is covered by vast unexploited forests; 15 percent is given over to teak and other hardwoods. In wetter districts, tropical rainforests climb the hills to 800 metres (2,625 ft) above sea level;

bamboo, used in house construction, is common here. From this elevation to the snow line at about 3,000 metres (9,842 ft), oaks, silver firs, chestnuts and rhododendrons thrive. In the central Dry Zone, cacti and acacia trees are common.

Taunggya (slash-and-burn) cultivation used through much of upland Burma has resulted in the depletion of the original forest cover, now replaced by a second growth of scrub forest. In *taunggya* agriculture, large trees are felled and the jungle burned to prepare for planting – often with 40 or more different crops.

When crops and torrential rains have depleted soil fertility (within a year or two), the clearing is abandoned and the land left to fallow for 12 to 15 years. Villages, therefore, often change sites when the accessible land has been exhausted. About 2½ million inhabitants still follow this agricultural method.

Burmese wildlife

The remaining virgin forests are home to a rich variety of wild animals. Elephants, tigers, leopards, wild buffalo and red deer are often hunted, along with the Himalayan black bear, Malayan sun bear, civet cat, wild boar, several species of monkeys, mountain goats, flying squirrels, porcupines, and even rhinoceri. There is a great variety of birds, insects and reptiles, including many snakes.

The Burmese do not go in for domestic pets as such, although they do keep beasts of burden – oxen in the Dry Zone, buffalo in the wet regions, and elephants in the mountains. Devout Buddhists do not kill animals, though most will eat meat killed by someone else – often a Muslim or Christian butcher. The Mon people in the southeast, however, do keep some domestic animals, such as dogs, cattle, swine and poultry. Some tribes, especially the Kayah, specialise in the breeding of horses.

The famous Burmese cat, noted for its short brown hair, is actually from Thailand, and not from Burma at all. In fact, the so-called "fixed" characteristics of this pedigreed feline, according to Western cat breeders, was established only after a period of experimental cross-breeding with the more established Siamese cats. ❑

LEFT: water buffalo.
RIGHT: gem merchants at the jade market in Mandalay display their wares.

THE POPPY TRAIL

Despite the toxic nature of the opiates business, the Golden Triangle retains
an irresistible fascination for many travellers

During the past half century the remote and often lawless region where Burma, Laos and Thailand meet has become known and widely romanticised as the "Golden Triangle". Originally a Western designation applied to the region due to its wealth in gems, lumber and, above all, opium, the name has stuck and is today widely accepted. The area is home to drug warlords, arms dealers, insurgent armies and old-fashioned bandits. It is currently the source of about half the world's illicit opiates, as well as a major production centre for amphetamines and other drugs. Recently, opium production in Laos has seen something of an increase, while in Thailand it has been cut back to almost nothing. Burma, however, remains by far the largest producer in the Golden Triangle, and illicit Burmese opiates, most notably heroin, continue to poison hundreds of thousands of addicts from the hills of Shan State to the streets of New York City.

Ancient medicine

Opium has been recognised as a narcotic for at least 2,000 years. It is thought to have grown wild in the mountains of the eastern Mediterranean from Neolithic times, and was known to both the early Greeks and Romans. It was probably introduced to both China and India by Arab traders about a thousand years ago, and soon came to be widely valued for its medicinal properties. Although it flourished in the cool hills of southwest China, it did not become a serious problem until the 18th century when Britain, seeking a way to pay for Chinese tea shipments other than with silver, began to export opium from India to China on a massive scale. The situation was compounded as both Britain and France established colonies in Southeast Asia during the latter half of the 19th century. The British encouraged and then prohibited opium consumption in the Burman heartland, but permitted unrestricted usage in indirectly administered areas such as the Shan States. The French, for their part, encouraged cultivation in their Indochinese colonies, making opium a state monopoly. As a consequence opium production, consumption and export boomed in the Golden Triangle region, as well as in the neighbouring Chinese province of Yunnan.

From opium to heroin

The medicinal properties of opium have long been appreciated in many diverse societies. In its raw state, opium acts as an antidote for pain, diarrhoea and coughing, and it has been widely used as an anaesthetic. Set against these beneficial qualities, however, the drug is addictive and rapidly becomes dangerous when used for recreational rather than medicinal purposes. This is still more true of the opium derivatives morphine and heroine. Morphine was first refined from raw opium in 1805. Taken orally, it soon became an important medical anaesthetic, but it was not until 1858, when American doctors first injected morphine directly into the

LEFT: a late 19th-century muleteer in the Shan State smoking an opium pipe.
RIGHT: opium poppies in bloom.

human bloodstream, that the full potency of the drug was realised. At about this time the true perils of opiate addiction began to become clear. For almost a century the basic pharmacoepia of Europe and the US had relied on opium in various solutions to treat common such as headaches and the common cold. As a consequence, addiction had become increasingly commonplace, though the subject was not properly discussed until 1821, when the British writer Thomas de Quincey drew attention to the problem through his essay, *Confessions of an English Opium-Eater*. By the late 19th century, Western pharmacologists began to search for a non-addictive painkiller which might replace morphine.

At the end of the 19th century, scientists working for the Bayer Corporation in Eberfeld, Germany, thought they had made a major breakthrough when they boiled a mixture of morphine and acetic anhydride to distil diacetylmorphine. They tested the new drug and found that it was an excellent treatment for such respiratory ailments as bronchitis, chronic coughing, asthma and tuberculosis. Diacetylmorphine was a bit of a mouthful to pronounce, however, so they marketed the new drug under the brand name of "heroin". Bayer then launched an

TRADERS OF THE GOLDEN TRIANGLE

The rugged, indomitable Chinese muleteers known to the Burmese as Panthay were – and to some extent still are – the masters of the Golden Triangle. In the 19th century, they made the remote settlement of Panglong in the Wa region of Shan State their base. From here, their caravans laden with precious stones, jade and guns, but above all opium, traded as far as Mawlamyaing in Burma, Luang Prabang in Laos, Dali and Kunming in Yunnan, and Chiang Mai in northern Thailand. Wherever they went they were protected with the best weapons money could buy, and they used these to good effect – to ensure the respect of the law-abiding and the fear of the lawless. When the British first arrived in Shan State in 1886, they were amazed to discover the Panthay armed with Remington repeater rifles better, in most cases, than those of their own troops.

During World War II, Panglong was looted and burned by marauding Japanese soldiers, but the Panthay – now armed with newer AK47s – survived to help generations of drug-smugglers transport their opium.

Today, most Panthay are respectable and increasingly prosperous, having settled in the larger towns of Shan State and in Mandalay. Their reputation as traders survives, however, and they are still considered to be the hard men of the Golden Triangle.

aggressive advertising campaign in a dozen languages, hailing heroin as a non-addictive patent medicine and cure-all. By 1924, the unrestricted use of heroin had resulted in addiction throughout the West. It was estimated that there were 200,000 addicts in the US alone, and that heroin abusers committed 94 percent of drug-related crimes in New York. As soon as the extent of the problem was grasped, legislation was passed in the West which caused legal heroin production to plummet from a peak

THE OPIUM EXPLOSION

By the late 19th century, opium was widely established in Shan State and exported to neighbouring Yunnan, Laos, Vietnam and Siam. Within 50 years the traffic had grown to encompass the world.

Growth of the Golden Triangle

By 1948, when Burma finally attained independence from Britain, the stage was already set for an explosion of narcotics in the region. Riven by years of fighting during World War II, Burma was soon to face another invasion as the defeated remnants of China's Nationalist government, the Kuomintang (KMT), withdrew south across the frontier. Within a few short months, the KMT had established themselves as a major force in Shan State.

LEFT: a mule in a Yunnan caravan.
ABOVE: an 19th-century postcard of the people of the Shan State.

of 9,000 kg (19,842 lbs) in 1926 to just over 1,000 kg (2,205 lbs) in 1931.

But it was already too late. Criminal syndicates that stood to make a fortune from the illicit production and distribution of heroin shifted manufacture from the legal pharmaceutical factories in Europe and the US to clandestine laboratories in the Far East, most notably in Shanghai and Tianjin. A new breed of illicit Chinese heroin technicians was about to inherit the manufacturing side of the business.

Following the assassination of Aung San in 1947, and as discontent and rebellion spread across Burma, the KMT were joined by a dozen disparate armed groups, communist, separatist and warlord. All had one thing in common – the need to finance their continuing struggle against the authorities. The obvious source of finance was smuggling, and in the Golden Triangle opium was both a readily available and highly profitable form of contraband.

During the early years of the Cold War period many of the KMT soldiers became front-line paramilitary forces for the anti-communist Thai and Lao governments. Armed, and to some extent protected by the CIA, they mounted two unsuccessful counter-invasions of Yunnan, only to be forced back to their mountain strongholds in Shan State. Here, as anti-communism waned and the bitterness of isolation and defeat crept in, the KMT remnants turned increasingly to the opium business to finance not just their way of life, but life itself. Armed with sophisticated weaponry, they soon developed a stranglehold on the trade. Speaking in 1967, General Tuan Shi-wen, commander of the KMT 5th Army, made no bones about where the money came from. "Necessity knows no law," he informed a visiting journalist. "We have to continue to fight the evil of communism. To fight you must have

an army, and an army must have guns, and to buy guns you must have money. In these mountains the only money is opium."

The growing influence of renegade KMT soldiers over the opium business in the Golden Triangle was mirrored by a sustained offensive against drug trafficking and manufacture within China. After the communist seizure of power in 1949, illicit heroin manufacture in Shanghai or Tianjin became all but impossible. It made sense for the heroin technicians to relocate in Hong Kong, or better yet in KMT-controlled sectors of the Golden Triangle itself.

By manufacturing heroin in the hills where the opium was actually grown, costs could be cut appreciably – refined heroin takes up less than 5 percent the space of raw opium and is therefore easier to both transport and conceal. The trade received another major boost during the first and second Indochina Wars, as both the French and subsequently the Americans used opium and its derivatives to fund anti-communist armies in Laos and Vietnam, while more than half-a-million US troops in Indochina were encouraged both by miserable circumstances and communist enemies to use hard drugs. Many US servicemen who were first exposed to heroin in Indochina took their habit home with them. This in turn led to increased demand in Southeast Asia, and especially in the key production areas of Burma's Shan State.

Papaver somniferum

Opium is the latex-like sap from the *papaver somniferum* – literally "the poppy of sleep", a plant which grows best at altitudes of 900 to 2,000 metres (3,000 to 7,000 ft) and which prefers a relatively dry climate. It flourishes on well-drained mountain slopes with a western exposure, preferring acidic red earth with a high limestone content. These specifications make the hills of eastern Burma, especially the Wa and Kokang regions of Shan State, an ideal location for opium cultivation.

The opium poppy is usually grown on a crop rotation basis, alternating with maize or other foodstuffs. It is sown in October, at the end of the rainy season, and harvested during January and February. Harvesting takes place after the petals have fallen, when the pod is scored with a sharp, triple-bladed knife, allowing the sap to seep through and oxidise on the pod. The next day the resultant brown gum is scraped off,

---

BAMAR DISAPPROVAL

Despite Burma's infamous reputation as a major illicit opium-producing nation, most ordinary Bamar view opiates and all intoxicants with strong disapproval. A 19th-century observer noted that "opium use among the better class of Burmese is extremely rare" and that "a respectable Burman would hesitate to be seen around a government liquor shop". He adds that "Burmans have no taste for *ganja* (cannabis)". This disapproval is based on long-standing Buddhist injunctions against taking intoxicants. Perhaps as a result of these injunctions, tea drinking became popular among Buddhist Burmese from around the 14th century.

rolled into balls, and wrapped in banana leaves ready for sale to the buyers – often Yunnanese Chinese, known locally as Haw – who roam the hills. The buyers in turn carry the opium by mule or lorry to clandestine laboratories where expert chemists, usually Chinese, convert it into heroin and package it for distribution throughout Southeast Asia, China, India and the West.

A lucrative industry

While a favoured cash crop of certain hill tribes – notably, the Hmong, Akha, Mien, Lahu and Lisu – opium has not greatly benefited these peoples; their reward has been government suspicion, widespread addiction and social disruption. Instead, most profits from the drug trade accrue to international syndicates and major traffickers. In the 1950s and 1960s, the KMT controlled the Golden Triangle drug business. During the 1970s and 1980s, they were replaced by private warlords, such as the notorious Shan-Chinese "freedom fighter" Khun Sa and allies of the Burmese junta like Lo Hsing Han. Today, the Wa National Army – heavily armed and with an estimated 20,000 troops – rules the roost. At secret locations in eastern Shan State, raw

opium is collected and boiled in oil drums over wood fires. At the right moment, lime is added, causing waste matter to precipitate and leaving impure morphine suspended near the surface. This is collected, filtered and boiled again, at which point concentrated ammonia is added, causing the morphine to solidify and fall to the bottom. Once dried and packed this morphine is around 10 percent of the weight of the raw opium from which it was extracted. The next stage of production is far more complex and requires the skills of an experienced chemist. The morphine passes through five processes – including that known as No. 3 heroin (brown sugar) which can only be smoked – before the No. 4 heroin, a fluffy white powder suitable for injecting, is obtained. It is this last, pure form which is destined for the First World. On reaching its destination the heroin is usually "cut" with a substance such as talcum or milk powder to increase its volume. By the time it reaches an end-user, an average dose of No. 4 heroin has been diluted to less than 5 percent pure. The best time to see the poppies is December–January, just before harvest – but it's better to do so legally in Thailand, and certainly not in Burma. Those wishing to learn more are advised to visit official centres where poppies are grown for research and medicinal purposes. ❏

LEFT: a scored opium poppy. **ABOVE:** Wa National Army soldiers at the Thai-Burmese border.

PEOPLE

*No fewer than 67 indigenous racial groups inhabit Burma, and
as many as 242 languages and dialects are spoken*

"Burma... is peopled by so many races that truly we know not how many; nor who they are, nor whence they came. In no other area are the races so diverse, or the languages and dialects so numerous..."
– CM Enriquez, *Races of Burma* (1933)

The Burmese are not a homogeneous people. This simple fact has caused many problems over the years, but it also enriches the cultural life of the country and enhances Burma's appeal to visitors.

Burma's present population is approximately 49 million, the majority of which live in the fertile Ayeyarwady delta region, in Rakhaing, and along the southern Taninthayri coastline. The Burmese authorities presently recognise no fewer than 135 separate nationalities living within the union. Of this number the Bamar (Burman) majority, taken together with the six main ethnic minority groups – each of which has its own state – constitute about 92 percent.

Ethnologists divide Myanmar's indigenous population into four main groups, Tibeto-Burman, Mon-Khmer, Austro-Tai and Karennic. The Tibeto-Burman group, which includes the predominant Bamar, the Rakhaing, Kachin and Chin constitute around 78 percent of the total. Mon-Khmer peoples include the Mon, the Wa and the Palaung, while the major Austro-Tai group are the Shan. Karennic peoples include the Kayin (Karen) and the closely-related Kayah. Major non-indigenous groups, who are predominantly urban-based, are relatively recent migrants (in the past 150 years) from South Asia and China.

The Bamar

Traditional holders of power in Burma since they displaced the Mon more than a thousand years ago, the Bamar – also known as Burmans – today constitute around 68 percent of the total

PRECEDING PAGES: a spice vendor at Myitkyina.
LEFT: *cheroot* smoker. **RIGHT:** a Rakhaing woman carrying water home from the Kaladan River.

population. Originally migrants from the Tibetan Plateau, they are a wet-rice farming people, Theravada Buddhist by religion, whose tonal, Tibeto-Burman tongue – Burmese – has long been the national language. As the majority racial group and predominant landholder, as well as the group holding the reins of govern-

ment, the Bamar are often viewed with suspicion and even hostility by other groups. Their main areas of settlement are in the predominantly lowland divisions of Yangon (Rangoon), Ayeyarwady, Pathein (Bassein), Bago (Pegu), Magway (Magwe), Mandalay and Sagaing, as well as the Rakhaing (Arakan) State, Mon State and Taninthayri (Tenasserim).

Most of the cultural forms described in later sections of this book are broadly representative of the Bamar, who live typically in thatched dwellings and work as wet-rice farmers. Perhaps their greatest distinguishing trademark is the pale yellow powder, made from *thanaka* bark *(see pages 244–5)*, which Bamar women apply to their faces as protection against the sun. Their traditional dress is the wrap-around *longyi*, which is similar to the Malaysian sarong.

The Shan

At just over 9 percent of the population, the Shan – close relatives of the Thai – are the second largest nationality in Burma. Inhabitants of the upland plateau and rolling hills of northeast Burma, the Shan – or Tai Yai, as they call themselves – are wet-rice farmers and Theravada Buddhists.

From the 15th century – when they were pushed back onto the Shan Plateau after early success in establishing an Ayeyarwady kingdom – until 1959, 34 *sawbwas* (hereditary princes) ruled separate feudal principalities in medieval splendour, with serfs, slaves and mistresses. Their alliance of small states was recognised by the 1948 constitution, and granted the right to withdraw from the "Union of Burma" after 10 years of membership.

But in 1959, the *sawbwas* sold out: they signed an agreement with the Ne Win caretaker government, renouncing all their hereditary rights and privileges. In exchange, they accepted a payment of 25 million kyat (over US$4 million at 1991 exchange rates), a sum

roughly equal to their income over a 15- to 25-year period.

Some of the *sawbwas* and their followers founded the Shan Independence Army, and in the ensuing years attempted to wrest Shan territory away from the government. Because of U Nu's apparent inability to deal with this problem, Ne Win staged his military coup in 1962, subsequently imprisoning some Shan leaders who failed to flee Burma. They were released in 1968, but by that time their era had passed. Some are now in self-imposed exile; others, highly educated scholars, teach at universities in Yangon; while those who responded to the 1980 amnesty have returned to Shan State.

HILL TRIBE ETIQUETTE

There are 10 commandments for trekkers. These protect hill tribe sensibilities and promote good relations. They are common sense, and should be accompanied by a friendly smile. First, always ask permission before entering any building or before taking a photo. Avoid photographing old people, pregnant women and babies. Avoid touching, photographing or sitting beneath village shrines. Avoid stepping or sitting on doorsills as according to custom this brings bad luck. Avoid changing clothes in public and always dress modestly. Avoid public displays of overt affection and excessive wealth. Always try to speak calmly and quietly.

Most Shan are Buddhists. This distinguishes them from animist or Christian hill peoples, who generally occupy the mountaintops and steep slopes. Burma's 3.9 million Shan make their homes in valleys and on high plains.

Shan are recognisable by the turbans worn by their men and their married women. Men usually dress in baggy, dark-blue trousers rather than in Bamar-style *longyi*. Girls wear trousers and blouses until the age of 14, at which time they don colourful dresses. As they get older, their costumes get less colourful, until – at about the age of 40 – the women start to wear sober black clothing for the rest of their lives.

Closely related groups are the Kayah and the "long-neck" Padaung of Kayah State.

At 2.5 percent of the population and the dominant minority of northern Burma, the Kachin are skilled dry-rice farmers and hunters. Like the Kayin, they were widely employed as soldiers by the British and have fought a long struggle for independence. Sometimes called the "Gurkhas of Southeast Asia", the Kachin are renowned for their military prowess. They have been widely Christianised, chiefly by American Baptist missionaries, but retain a complex and wide-reaching kinship system. The most numerous of the six main Kachin

The Kayin and Kachin

The fiercely independent Kayin (Karen), who constitute about 7 percent of the Burmese population, live scattered throughout central and southern Burma, but especially in their own Kayin State, which they call Kawthoolei. Many Kayin are Christian, and this – together with the favoured status they enjoyed over the majority Bamar during the British period – has exacerbated their already poor relations with the Bamar-dominated Yangon government.

LEFT: Shan children.
ABOVE: painting of a Padaung woman.
RIGHT: a Kachin woman puffs on a *cheroot.*

groups are the Jinghpaw; the language of whom has become the de facto lingua franca of the Kachin people. At war with the military authorities from the early 1960s, the Kachin Independence Organization (KIO) has proved perhaps the most intractable of Yangon's opponents. Since 1994, however, the KIO has observed a ceasefire agreement, by and large, with the Burmese authorities.

The Rakhaing and the Chin

The Rakhaing (Arakanese), also known as Rakhine, inhabit Rakhaing State and constitute about 4 percent of the total population. Closely related to the Bamar, the Rakhaing are about 75 percent Buddhist and 25 percent Muslim, the latter known as Rohingya. Ever since King Bodawpaya swept south from his capital at Inwa (Ava) and annexed the kingdom of Rakhaing two centuries ago, the Bamar have had their hands full dealing with this coastal race. The Rakhaing still look back with pride on the many centuries of independence they enjoyed.

Although of the same Tibeto-Burman stock as the Bamar, the Rakhaing are slightly darker in complexion, an indication of the region's 2,000-year history of contact and intermarriage with Indian traders, sailors and Brahman settlers. There are several significant differences

between the lifestyles of the coastal Rakhaing and the Ayeyarwady basin Bamar.

Rakhaing gets far more rain and has higher humidity than does the inland regions, due to its exposure to the monsoons. Thus, Rakhaing's entire transportation system is dependent on boats. Cultivated land is always situated only a short distance from navigable rivers, creeks, channels and tidal waters.

Most Rakhaing are devout Buddhists. But a fairly large number of people in the capital city of Sittwe (Akyab), and along the northern coast, are Muslims of mixed Rakhaing-Bengali descent. The ancestors of many of these people settled in Rakhaing during the British colonial era, when movement between India and Burma was not restricted.

In both city and country areas, Muslim and Buddhist Rakhaing have little to do with one another. In Sittwe, many Muslims live along the Kaladan River and work as fishermen – a profession no devout Buddhist would choose because it involves the taking of life.

The Chin, together with the related Naga people, make up about 2 percent of Burma's population. They live in Burma's far Northwest, where they spill over the international frontier into India and Bangladesh. Most Chin are animists who practice slash-and-burn agriculture to grow dry rice.

The Mon

Possessors of a proud, ancient civilisation which precedes that of the Burmans, the Mon – at about 2 percent of the population – have their own state centred on Mawlamyaing (Moulmein), but have long been largely assim-

THE WILD WA

The Wa are a Mon-Khmer people inhabiting the remote northeast Shan State along Burma's frontier with China. Although there are about 300,000 Wa in this wild region, little was known about them until about 65 years ago. The main reason for this was that the Wa were head hunters, so sensible strangers stayed away.

In the 1930s, G.E. Harvey, the Commissioner of Shan State, visited the Wa hills. He found the Northern Wa living in heavily stockaded villages, protected by 20-metre (66-ft)-thick walls of thorn, entered only by narrow winding tunnels to protect against attacks. He also found that the Wa placed a scale of sliding values on heads, which were

taken and displayed at the entrance of villages to ensure a good harvest. Bamar, Chinese and Shan heads were fairly commonplace – worth the trouble of taking, certainly, but of no great power. Wa heads, especially those of a rival clan, had more power and were highly desirable.

Better still was a European head – especially one with mutton-chop whiskers. Harvey's Wa had only three European heads, but they were thought to be powerful and had brought the villages who owned them great prosperity. Most valued of all, Harvey was assured, was the bearded, turbaned head of a Sikh… worth many ordinary heads, and at least those of a couple of Europeans.

ilated into Burman culture. Living mainly around the cities of Mawlamyaing and Bago, before the Bamar came, they were the most powerful group in the region. Today, the Mon – who number just over 1 million – have been largely assimilated into mainstream Burmese culture, although they continue to use their own distinct language, and have retained their own state within the Burmese union.

The Mons are at home in the monsoonal plains of the southeast. Traditionally, they have preferred to live in rainy lowland areas to pursue wet-rice growing. As Buddhists, they observe their own calendar of Theravadin festivals.

However, it was not until the 19th century, when Burma became a part of the British Raj, that they began to settle in such large numbers.

Some Indians were well-educated, and occupied middle and higher levels of administration and business during the colonial era. Those with less education came to Burma as contract labourers for government construction projects.

Many of the immigrants were from southern India, and brought with them their beliefs and regional village social structure, which included the caste system, Hindu deities and professional moneylenders *(chettyars)*, who quickly became so entrenched in Burmese society that they

The Indians

Burma has an influential migrant Indian community, particularly in Yangon and Mandalay. At one time, during the British period, the population of Yangon was almost 60 percent Indian, though this figure has since declined drastically as a result of re-migration due to ethnic discrimination and economic mismanagement. Today, the Indian population of Burma is down to about 2 percent. The Indians and their culture have a 2,000-year history in Burma, predating the presence of the Bamar majority.

LEFT: a Wa man with traditional tattoos.
ABOVE: a woman with *thanaka* bark make-up.

bought up more than half of the arable land in the Ayeyarwady Delta region.

Many were, however, forced to return to India during the Japanese occupation of Burma, and those who remained faced the land reforms of the new independent government of the "Union of Burma". Businessmen who stayed during the U Nu years staged a mass migration when Ne Win installed his nationalisation programme.

Besides Hindus, there is a small South Asian Muslim population in major towns. Many trace their ancestry back to areas that now form part of Pakistan, Nepal and Bangladesh Others, known as *zerbadi*, are the result of unions between migrant Muslim men and Bamar women.

The Chinese

Many Chinese left the major cities following independence, and especially after the vicious anti-Chinese riots at Yangon in 1967. Recently, however, Chinese migrants have been entering Burma in large numbers. They live mainly in the northeast, close to Yunnan province from where many originated. In the Kokang area of northern Shan State they form more than 80 percent of the population, so that Kokang is known as Burma's "Little China".

For millennia, the Chinese have travelled overland into Burma, down the northeastern trade routes and along the great rivers. In cen-

sities, they soon occupied the middle and higher strata of modern society. Far from being "overlanders" from Yunnan, most were Overseas Chinese originating from the coastal provinces of Guangdong, Fujian and Hainan Island.

Another Chinese group found in remote parts of Shan State, as well as in large towns like Yangon and Mandalay, are the Panthay. This group is essentially identical with the Hui minority in Yunnan. The descendants of Uzbek soldiery who fought for the Mongol dynasty, their ancestors settled in Yunnan over six centuries ago and intermarried with local Han Chinese. Today, there is little to distinguish them

turies past, many Chinese settlements were established along these routes. In broad terms, there are two groups of Chinese who inhabit Burma today, with very different histories and lifestyles. The first is mainly rural, comprising the Shan Tayok and the Kokang Chinese. They came across the border of Yunnan during the time when the Shan principalities were under British administration.

The urban Chinese, on the other hand, have an entirely different background. Many came to Yangon by sea to work as merchants or restaurant owners during the colonial era. By working hard and sending their children to be educated in Western-type schools and univer-

from other Chinese except for their Muslim faith. Despite nationalisation under Ne Win, the urban Chinese remained strong commercially, and with a market economy now becoming established in the country, many are once again in business. Estimates of the number of Chinese in Burma today range from 100,000 to 400,000. At the height of Mao's Cultural Revolution, many young Chinese in Yangon undertook to import the revolution to Burma. The Bamar reacted violently, rampaging through the city's Chinese sector. Since then, the Chinese have kept a much lower profile in Burma. ❑

ABOVE: guests at a Chinese Christian wedding party.

The Path of Life

There are few countries in the world today in which tradition has such a strong influence on everyday life as it has in Burma. The colonial period did not pass without affecting the Burmese; rationalism, science and realism profoundly altered commerce and national affairs. But daily life is still dominated by old values, and the path of life that a typical Burmese goes through has undergone little change over the generations.

Seven days after birth, the baby's parents invite friends to a naming ceremony. The baby is given a name based on astrological calculations, which need bear no relation to that of the parents.

Children are sent to school at the age of five. However, despite a system of compulsory education and strenuous efforts by the government since independence to ensure education for all, there are still areas with no state schools. In these places, the local *kyaung* (monastery) takes charge of elementary education.

When a boy is nine years old, his *shin-pyu* takes place. This is an initiation ceremony marking the end of childhood and the start of a period of monkhood. Girls of the same age participate in an ear-piercing ceremony called the *nahtwin*, which also symbolises a farewell to the unburdened life of the child.

As two-thirds of the population still work on the arable land, the transition from school to adult life is relatively easy for most young people: during their school years, they help out with the harvest in their parents' fields.

Women, despite their lower status in Buddhist doctrine, have a secure place in society. Their rights are almost always equal to those of men, guaranteed by simple divorce laws. Burmese tend to get married relatively young, women do not change their name when married. If the marriage fails, women can return to their parents.

The Burmese emphasise their national identity through the clothes they wear. Most evident is the *longyi*. Similar to the Malaysian sarong, it consists of a kilt-like piece of cloth worn from the waist to the ankle. Together with the *eingyi*, a transparent blouse which is worn with a round-collared, long-sleeved jacket, the *longyi* still takes precedence over Western-style garments. Today, the traditional headgear of the men, the *gaung-baung*, is worn

only on special occasions. During the colonial period, it was wrapped around the head like a turban, with different styles and colours according to one's social position. These days it is superseded by a ready-made cap.

Burmese women attach great importance to jewellery. As rubies, sapphires, jade and pearls are found in Burma, it is common at festivals to see peasant women richly adorned with precious stones and elaborate pieces of jewellery. The Burmese still regard the purchase of gem stones as the safest form of investment.

Few young Burmese remain in the monkhood (*sangha*) for more than a few months after their

shin-pyu. Some become *pongyis* and devote their entire lives to meditation and the teachings of the Buddha. To most adult Burmese, however, the *sangha* is not merely a religious brotherhood – it is also an institution which provides social insurance and a support network in old-age.

When the Burmese die they are either buried or cremated. A coin is put in the mouth of the deceased so they can pay the "ferryman" who will transport them "across the river" into the next life. Relatives and friends of the dead person are invited to the funeral. It is generally accepted that the dead person takes part in these rites, and that their spirit remains in the family's house for a week after the ceremony. ❑

RIGHT: a tightly swaddled Burmese child contemplates her world.

A LAND OF ETHNIC DIVERSITY

The majority ethnic Bamar dominate the central heartlands. Much of the hinterland, however, is inhabited by astonishingly diverse ethnic groups

The Burmese authorities presently recognise no fewer than 135 separate nationalities living within the union. Most numerous are the Bamar, who make up 68 percent of the population. Originally migrants from Southwest China, they are a wet rice-farming people and Theravada Buddhist by religion. Their tonal Tibeto-Burman tongue – Burmese – has long been Burma's national language. At just over 9 percent of the population the Shan are the second largest nationality in Burma and are also Theravada Buddhists. Closely related to the Thai they inhabitant the upland plateau and rolling hills of Northeast Burma where they practice wet rice farming. The fiercely independent Kayin (Karen), who constitute about 7 percent of Burmese, live in their own state and are scattered throughout central and southern Burma. The Rakhaing, of Rakhaing State, make up 4 percent of the population. They are closely related to the Bamar and are mostly Buddhist. The Kachin are the dominant minority people of northern Burma and are skilled dry rice farmers and hunters, while the Chin, together with the related Naga people, make up about 2 percent of the population. The Chin live in Burma's far Northwest and spill over the frontier into India. The Mon – at about 2 percent of the population – have their own state and are inheritors of a proud, ancient civilization preceding that of the Bamar. Today, the Mon have been largely assimilated into Bamar culture.

△ **LISU STYLE**
A young Lisu couple at Manhkring, Kachin State. Much time and money is invested in traditional clothing, which is designed to display status and tribal identity.

▷ **KACHIN WOMAN**
A young Kachin woman from Myitkyina, the capital of Kachin State, wearing traditional clothing and elaborate headdress.

▷ **A GROUP OF PALAUNG**
Scene at a market in Pindaya, Shan State. Both male and female Palaung, an upland Mon-Khmer minority, wear turbans.

◁ GURKHA WOMEN
Originally from central Nepal, many Gurkhas who served in the British Army settled in Burma where their descendants work as guards, as restaurateurs or run small businesses.

▽ KAYINS AND CABBAGES
Kayin, or Karen, working in a market garden near Myawadi. Kayin women still favour traditional clothing, but many Kayin men have adopted Bamar or Western dress.

▽ PANTHAY ELDER
A Chinese Muslim wearing prayer cap at a mosque in Tachileik. The Panthay, originally from Yunnan, are called Hui in Chinese.

THE CRYSTAL SONS OF THE SHAN

One of the more extravagant celebrations that visitors to Burma can witness is the Shan festival of Poy Sang Long, when young Shan boys are ordained as novice monks in the Buddhist *sangha*. The occasion usually falls in March and is best seen in Shan State, though it can be witnessed anywhere where sizeable communities of Shan are settled, from the frontiers of Assam to Mae Hong Son in Thailand. During Poy Sang Long, the novices are elaborately arrayed in make-up, jewellery and traditional Shan clothing to resemble celestial princes. They are then carried to the temple on the shoulders of their fathers or elder brothers, or sometimes on horseback. The ceremony is performed with much pomp and circumstance: golden umbrellas are used to shield the novices-to-be from the sun while proud, and sometimes tearful family members look on. The *samanera* (novice monks) will remain at the temple for between one and two weeks, though nine days – nine being an auspicious number – is popular.

BURMESE BUDDHISM

The ancient faith permeates the everyday lives of the people, placing
great emphasis on individual achievement

It has often been said that Burma is the most profoundly Buddhist country in the world. That may well be true, but the brand of Buddhism practiced in this isolated land is unique. Burmese Buddhism, theoretically, is Theravada or Hinayana Buddhism, that ancient sect of Buddhism adhering most closely to the

This southern island is the only place where future Buddhas can be born. This is because Jambudvipa is a place of misery compared to the other abodes of this universe. There are, in fact, 31 planes of existence on, above and below Mount Meru. They can be divided into three main groups: the 11 planes of *Kama-*

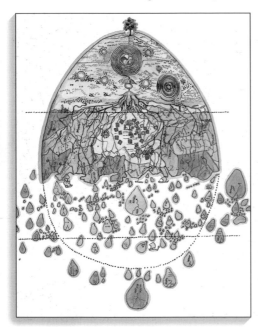

Buddha's original teaching, and which is the dominant form of Buddhism found throughout much of Southeast Asia. It was preceded in Burma, however, by the animistic beliefs of the hill tribes and by the Hindu-Brahmanism of early traders, which has had a profound effect on the cosmological concept of the land.

Strictly speaking, Burmese cosmology is Buddhist cosmology, but it has been shaped by millennia of influences from other cultures, particularly that of the Brahmans. According to the Burmese, the European-Asian continent is called Jambudvipa. It is the southern of four islands situated at the cardinal points surrounding Mount Meru, the centre of the world.

Loka, the realm of the sensuous world; the 16 planes of *Rupa-Loka*, the realm of subtle material matter; and finally, the four planes of *Arupa-Loka*, the realm of formlessness.

Simplifying Buddhism

King Anawrahta, founder of the first Burmese empire, devoted his attention to simplifying spiritual beliefs. When he introduced Theravada Buddhism into Upper Burma as the national religion, he was unable to eliminate the animistic beliefs of his people. Despite radical

LEFT: a diagram of Burmese cosmology. **ABOVE:** an ancient Buddha's head. **RIGHT:** young novices.

measures, 36 of the countless *nat* survived in the people's daily activities. For the Burmese, these 36 *nat* serve nearly the same purpose as the saints of the Catholic Church. In both cases they are called upon in times of need. So Anawrahta introduced a 37th figure – Thagyamin – and made him king of the *nat*. He thereafter tolerated the popular worship of these 37 *nat*, once it had been established that they were also followers of the Buddha's teachings.

Beatitudes of Buddhism

Theravada Buddhism is recognised as the principal religion of about 80 percent of all Burmese people. While there are significant numbers of Hindus, Muslims, Christians and primitive animists (especially among the northern hill tribes), it is safe to say that over 99 percent of the Bamar (Burman), Mon, Shan and Palaung are Theravadins.

The division between the Theravada and Mahayana styles, while already developing for some time, actually occurred in 235 BC when King Ashoka convened the Third Buddhist Synod at Pataliputra, India. The Buddhist elders (Theravada means "the way of the elders") held tight to their literal interpretation of the Buddha's teaching. They were opposed by a

THREE JEWELS, FOUR NOBLE TRUTHS AND THE EIGHTFOLD PATH

As there is no true form of worship in the Theravada style of Buddhism, the only true ritual to which both monks and laity submit themselves is the recitation – three times a day – of the "Three Jewels," or the *Triratna*: "I take refuge in the Buddha. I take refuge in the Dhamma. I take refuge in the Sangha."

The formula of the "Three Jewels" offers solace and security. These are needed for strength, if one understands the "Four Noble Truths" expounded upon by Gautama Buddha In his first sermon:

● Life always has in it the element of suffering
● The cause of suffering is desire

● In order to end the suffering, give up desire and give up attachment
● The way to this goal is the Noble Eightfold Path

The Noble Eightfold Path consists of right view, right intent, right speech, right conduct, right means of livelihood, right endeavour, right mindfulness and right meditation. This "path" is normally divided into three areas: view and intent are matters of wisdom; speech, conduct or action, and livelihood are matters of morality; and endeavour, mindfulness and meditation are matters resulting from true mental discipline.

group which sought to understand the personality of the historical Buddha, and its relationship to one's salvation. The Theravada branch of Buddhism is actually a more conservative, more orthodox form of Buddhist thought. The latter group became known as the Mahayana school. It established itself in Tibet, Nepal, China, Korea, Mongolia, Japan and Vietnam, where its further development varied greatly from region to region. The Theravada school, meanwhile, has thrived in Sri Lanka, Burma, Thailand, Laos and Cambodia.

The Buddha denied the existence of a soul. There is no permanence, he explained, for that

which one perceives to be "self". Rather, one's essence is forever changing. The idea of rebirth, therefore, is a complicated philosophical question within the structure of Buddhism. When a Buddhist (or any person, for that matter) is reincarnated, it is neither the person nor the soul which is actually reborn. Rather, it is the sum of one's karma, the balance of good and evil deeds. One is reborn as a result of prior existence. A popular metaphor used to explain this transition is that of a candle. Were a person to light one candle from the flame of another, then extinguish the first, it could not be said that the new flame was the same as the previous one. Rather, in fact, its existence would be due to that of the previous flame. The Noble Eightfold Path, therefore, does not lead to salvation in the traditional Judeo-Christian sense. By pursuing matters of wisdom, morality and mental discipline, one can hope to make the transition into *nibbana* (nirvana), which can perhaps best be defined as the extinction of suffering, the cessation of desire. It is not heaven, nor is it annihilation. It is simply a quality of existence.

The monk

There are no priests in Theravada Buddhism. But the faithful still need a model to follow on the path to salvation and this is provided by monks. In Burma, there are about 800,000 monks. Most of these are students and novices who put on the monk's robe only temporarily; nearly all male Burmese devote a period – from just a few weeks to several years – to the monkhood *(sangha)*.

There are three fundamental rules to which the monk must subscribe. First, the renunciation of all possessions, except eight items: three robes, a razor for shaving, a needle for sewing, a strainer (to ensure that no living thing is swallowed), a belt, and an alms bowl. Second, a vow to injure no living thing and to offend no one. Finally, the vow of complete sexual celibacy. The monk must make his livelihood by seeking alms, setting out two hours before dawn and going door to door. The food received is the monk's only meal of the day. A young Burmese begins his novitiate at around the age of nine. For the majority of Burmese, the novitiate does not last long. Most would have left the monkhood before their 20th birthday. ❑

BURMESE BUDDHIST TERMINOLOGY

Gyo-daing – small Buddha shrines found in temples.
Kyaung – a Buddhist monastery; also *pongyikyaung*.
Parabaik – folded palm-leaf manuscript.
Paya – generic term for Buddha images and stupas.
Pongyi – a Buddhist monk.
Pyat-that – multi-roofed pavilions, usually made of wood.
Samsara – cycle of birth and death (rebirth).
Sayadaw – Abbot of a Burmese monastery.
Tazaung – a Buddhist shrine.
Thabeiq – a monk's bowl.
Thilashin – a Buddhist nun.
Zedi – a stupa.

LEFT: a *dasasila* ("Ten-Precept" nun).

Shin-Pyu

The most important moment in the life of a young Burmese boy is his *shin-pyu* – his initiation as a novice in the order of monks. Until a Buddhist has gone through the *shin-pyu* ceremony, he is regarded as being no better than an animal. To become "human", he must for a time withdraw from secular life, following the example set forth by the Buddha when he left his family to seek enlightenment.

Unlike his illustrious predecessor, the novice will probably carry his alms bowl for a short period, then return to his normal lifestyle. But his time spent studying scriptures and strictly following the code of discipline makes him a dignified human being.

During the period between his ninth and twelfth birthdays, a boy is deemed ready to don the saffron-coloured robes of the *sangha* and become a "son of the Buddha". If his parents are very pious, they may arrange to have the *shin-pyu* staged on the full moon day of Waso (June/July), the start of the Buddhist Lent. This arrangement ensures that the novice can remain in the monastery throughout the entire rainy season, until Lent ends in October.

Once the ceremony has been arranged, the boy's sisters announce it to the whole village or neighbourhood. Everyone is invited, and contributions are collected for a festival which will dig deep into the savings of the boy's parents.

Traditionally, a *shin-pyu* is a time of extravagance. The boy is dressed in princely garments of silk, wears a gold headdress and has a white horse. These objects are meant to symbolise the worldly goods that the novice monk must renounce.

The night before a *shin-pyu* is a busy one. A feast is prepared for all the monks whose company the young boy will join, and they are elaborately fed early on the morning of the ceremony. Next, all male guests are fed, then the women.

Later in the morning, the novitiate's head is shaved in preparation. The boy's mother and eldest sister hold a white cloth to receive the falling hair, and later bury it near a pagoda. This head-shaving is a solemn moment; when completed, the boy looks appropriately like a "son of the Buddha".

In the weeks before the ceremony, the boy would have been familiarised with the language and behaviour befitting a monk. He would have learned

---

RIGHT: a boy gets his head shaved at his *shin-pyu* (initiation ceremony) to the monkhood.

how to address a superior; how to walk with decorum, keeping his eyes fixed on a point 2 metres (6 ft) in front of him; and how to respond to the questions put to him at the ceremony.

His instruction serves him well when it is time to ask to be admitted to the *sangha*: "Reverend Sir, I request admission to the novicehood in view of the perfect liberation from the cycle of suffering transmigration. Reverend Sir, I request for the 10 Precepts to be observed by a novice..."

During his novicehood, he will not take any food after noon, sing or play, use cosmetics, sit on any elevated seat, possess any money, interfere in the business of other monks or abuse them. He must

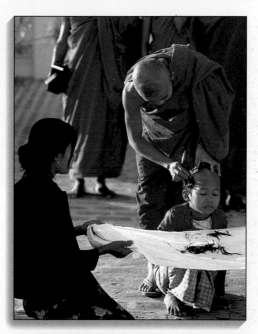

not kill, steal, lie, get drunk or have sex. He must not blaspheme or listen to heretical doctrines.

When the boy's request to enter the monkhood is approved, he prostrates himself three times. He is robed, and now he is ready to walk the path of perfection first trodden by the Buddha. If he is steadfast enough, he might even reach nirvana.

Once the *sayadaw* – the abbot who has presided over the ceremony – hangs the novitiate's *thabeit* (alms bowl) over his shoulder, the boy's childhood is left behind. He has been accepted as a monk.

During his time in the monastery, his parents must address him in honorific terms. He will call them "lay sister" and "lay brother", the same names he calls others not in the monkhood. ❑

FESTIVALS

Solemn Buddhist Lent in July is flanked by the frivolous water dousing of the New Year in April and the incredible Festival of Lights in October

The traditional Burmese year is based on a 12-month lunar calendar. Traditional festivals and Buddhist holidays revolve around this lunar year, which begins with Thingyan, the Burmese New Year, in March or April. Secular Burma, by contrast, revolves around the solar year and starts on 1 January.

Whenever the full moon waxes, it's time for a *pwe*, or festival of one sort or another. Some *pwe* are solemn, others are occasions for fun and frivolity. All are worth experiencing. The most important festivals in the Burmese calendar follow.

The Htamein (rice harvest festival) takes place between January and February. This is a joyous occasion, when rice is offered to the monasteries and elaborate meals are cooked. A special dish, made of rice, sesame, peanuts, ginger and coconut is eaten.

The last month of the Burmese year, March, is considered a time of romance and tranquillity. On the full moon day of the festival of Tabaung, Burmese travel to lakes or rivers where they play music, singing and recite poetry, often in the company of a loved one.

Festivals of fun

March to April brings Thingyan ("changing over") water festival, Burma's biggest party, marking the traditional New Year's Day held at full moon during the lunar month of Tagu. The festival goes on for three or four days, the length of the celebration determined by *ponna* or Brahman astrologers. Water is poured from delicate silver vessels, sprayed from water pistols, hurled from buckets, and even blasted from fire hydrants to wash away the old year and welcome the new. The drenching stops each day at 6.30pm, and is followed by an evening of feasting and partying. For the duration of the festival, government buildings and businesses are closed.

Thingyan also celebrates the descent to earth of Thagyamin, the king of the 37 *nat*, to bring blessings for the new year. He brings two books with him: one bound in gold to record the names of children who have been well-behaved in the past year, and one bound in dog skin to record the names of any naughty children. Thagyamin rides a winged golden horse and bears a water jar, symbolic of peace and prosperity. Households greet Thagyamin with flowers and palm leaves at the front door. Guns are fired and music is played in salute. Gaily-decorated floats parade up and down the streets of the cities and larger towns. But there are also moments of tranquillity in the midst of this exuberance. Most revellers find time to make offerings at pagodas and at the homes of their elders, and Buddha images are washed by the devout.

Kason (the birthday of Lord Buddha) is celebrated between April and May. Lustral water is poured over the roots of sacred Banyan trees, beneath the branches of which the Buddha

PRECEDING PAGES: offerings at a *pwe*.
LEFT: in festival dress.
RIGHT: preparing a balloon for Tazaungmone.

attained enlightenment. Kason is a time of anticipation – the monsoon could break at any time. At the full moon, the birth, enlightenment and death of the Buddha are celebrated. The devout join a procession of musicians and dancers to the local pagoda.

During the full moon of Nayon (May to June), after the rains have begun and the hot, dry months are at an end, Burmese students are tested on their knowledge of the *Tripitaka* (the Buddhist scriptures). Abbots lecture before large crowds, schools operated by monasteries are opened to the public, and eminent scholars exhibit their knowledge to public acclaim.

Buddhist Lent

Dhammasetkya (the beginning of Buddhist Lent), held during June–July, is a solemn religious occasion, during which all monks go into a period of deep retreat for study and meditation. This is an auspicious time for young men to have their *shin-pyu* initiation into the monkhood *(see page 73)*. For the next three months the country is soaked in water as the monsoons gain strength. During this time monks are not permitted to travel, and the devout will enter a period of fasting.

Between the months of July and August the Wagaung ("Draw-a-Lot" Festival) is held.

PERFORMING PWE

Pwe is a generic Burmese term for theatrical performances and dramatic shows. It embraces all kinds of plays, dramas and musical operas. Dancing is inevitably part of a *pwe*, and performances generally last for at least eight hours, and often right through the night. It's possible to make a loose classification of different types of *pwe*, thus a *zat pwe* is a religious performance based on the various *Jataka*, or Buddha life-cycle stories, while a *yama zat pwe* is based on the great Hindu epic, *Ramayana. Anyein pwe* are plays without plots, usually accompanied by clowning, ironic repartee and dancing. Finally, *yein pwe* feature group singing and dancing.

Since no marriage or other secular celebration is permitted during Buddhist Lent, the full moon of Wagaung is observed as a festival of merit-making. The name of each member of the local *sangha* is written on a piece of paper, which is then rolled up and deposited into a large basket. A representative from each household of the community draws a slip of paper from the basket, and the next day, provides an elaborate feast for the monk named on the piece of paper. One layman will have drawn a paper containing the name of the Gautama Buddha and he has the honour of hosting the Buddha.

By mid-September the rainy season is at its height, and Burma's waterways, from the mighty Ayeyarwady to the smallest stream, are full. To celebrate this bounty, Tawthalin (boat-races) are held all over the country. The most impressive races are held in Shan State, at the Phaung Daw U Festival on Inle Lake. Heralding the end of Buddhist Lent and the approach of the cool season, the Thadingyut (Festival of Lights) celebrates the Buddha's return from heaven to earth, and means weddings and other secular celebrations can now take place. To symbolise the radiance of the Buddha on his return, mil-

NO EXPENSE SPARED

So popular are the Phaung Daw U and Thadingyut festivals held at Inle Lake each September that celebrants often spend all their savings on new clothing.

festivals, however, are held in other months over a period of several days, before, during and after the full moon. Among the most important are the Mount Popa Festival in Nayon (May/June), the Taungbyon Festival held in the town of Wagaung, about 30 km (19 miles) to the north of Mandalay, the Manao Festival in Myitkyina in Pyatho (December/January), and the traditional Shan Festival in Kyaukme in Tabaung (February/March). Pyatho (December/January), the month of temple festivals, was formerly a time

lions of candles and oil lamps illuminate monasteries, pagodas, houses and trees throughout the land. The festival of Tazaung-mone (the Weaving Festival) takes place between October and November. Under the full moon, unmarried women work at their looms all night to make new robes for the monks. These robes are then presented to the monks at the local temple early next morning.

Nat festivals

In Nadaw (November/December), when the full moon arrives, villages dedicate celebrations to the spirit world; this is the time most *nat* festivals take place. National or regional *nat*

when Burmese royalty displayed its strength with military parades. Today, this period is reserved mostly for local pagoda festivals. These local festivals are religious, with gifts presented to monks and offerings made for temple upkeep. But even more so, they are occasions for merrymaking, lasting three or more days. A few major temple festivals are held in Pyatho. The Ananda Temple festival in Bagan falls at this time, and the Shwedagon Pagoda festival in Yangon is held.

Other festivals

National holidays of a secular nature are dated according to the Western (international) calendar.

Independence Day, a secular holiday, is held on 4 January and celebrated with week-long festivities. Boat races are staged on the Royal Lake in Yangon and the palace moats in Mandalay. On 12 February, Union Day marks national unity with flag-bearing, feasting and celebrations. Peasant's Day is celebrated on 2 March, and on 27 March, fireworks and parades mark the annual Armed Forces Day, or Resistance Day, commemorating the World War II struggle against Japanese imperialism. The first day of May is

AWAY WITH ALL SINS

In Shan State each November sins are floated away in giant hot-air balloons. These spectacular two-storey-high leviathans are fired by coal braziers and drip with hundreds of candles.

past success or victory. The festival involves the sacrifice of cattle or buffalo to placate and honour the *nat*, with traditional Kachin music and dance centred around a *manao taing* (totem-pole). The festival may go on for 24 hours, and a lot of locally brewed alcohol is drunk. The most fixed of *manao* is held on 10 January at Myitkyina, the capital of Kachin State, to celebrate Kachin State Day. The Kayin New Year is based on the lunar calendar and held in December–January. Celebrated by

Worker's Day and 19 July is Martyr's Day which commemorates the assassination of Bogyoke Aung San and his comrades in 1947.

Minority festivals include the spectacular Kachin Manao – a celebration to placate Kachin *nat* and ensure peace, plenty and prosperity. It's difficult to predict with any accuracy the exact date on which a *manao* may be held. The decision to hold a *manao* is taken by the *duwa* (Kachin elders). The *sup manao* looks to the future, while the *padang manao* celebrates a

Kayin people throughout Burma, but especially in Kayin State and the Ayeyarwady Delta, it's a time of vibrant celebration.

Other widely celebrated festivals include Divali, the Hindu "Festival of Lights", as well as the Muslim celebrations of 'Id al-Fitr to celebrate the end of the fasting month of Ramadan, Maulid al-Nabi to commemorate the Prophet Muhammad's birthday, and 'Id al-Adha to celebrate the conclusion of the annual Haj Pilgrimage to Mecca. The Chinese community mark (discreetly) Chinese New Year, the Festival of Hungry Ghosts and the annual Moon Cake Festival, while Burma's Christians celebrate Christmas and Easter. ❑

LEFT: Phaung Daw U Festival, Lake Inle.
ABOVE: traditional festival dress.
RIGHT: Kachin Day, Myitkyina festival parade.

A FEAST OF FLAVOURS

Traditional Burmese dishes are influenced by Indian, Chinese and Southeast Asian cooking, but retain a distinctive character all their own

Sharing borders with two culinary giants, India and China, and with the Southeast Asian nations of Laos and Thailand, Burma has inevitably been influenced by the spices, seasonings, basic ingredients and cooking styles of its neighbours. Yet it is the way that these shared ingredients are combined

which makes the cuisine of Burma different. You'll find Chinese foodstuffs, particularly soybean products such as soy sauce, bean sprouts and bean curd, as well as a distinctive local variation of bean curd made from chickpeas which is popular among the Shan people.

Chinese noodles have become a staple, but appear in purely Burmese dishes such as *mohinga*, a noodle soup that starts with fish stock and simmered banana stem and finishes with a host of garnishes you'd never find in China. The Chinese wok is used for frying, along with traditional terracotta pots, modern metal saucepans and the ubiquitous banana leaf, used as a wrapper for steaming or grilling

everything from rice to meat to fish and cakes.

Indian influence is also noticeable, especially the use of chickpeas, not just whole, but toasted and ground to make a nutty powder which is sprinkled into soups, noodle dishes and over salads. The Burmese use only a few Indian spices, most notably turmeric, cumin and coriander, preferring to flavour their curry-style dishes with huge amounts of crushed onion, garlic and ginger, often slowly cooked to a rich brown. Indian curry leaves, very popular in the south of the subcontinent, are also used in parts of Burma, and a number of traditional Indian recipes have been adapted to local tastes.

The food of Burma is perhaps most similar to that of its Southeast Asian neighbours. Herbs, such as lemon grass and kaffir lime, pungent fish products and creamy coconut milk are frequently used, not forgetting chillies, fresh, dried and powdered.

In the central and southern parts of the country, fish sauce and *ngapi* (dried shrimp paste) are as common as salt in a Western kitchen. Fruity sour tamarind, various types of ginger, including common ginger and fresh turmeric, and buttterscotch-sweet palm sugar all add their particular magic to countless dishes.

Regional diversity

The land of Burma sprawls across the humid Ayeyarwady delta – fingered by rivers and irrigation canals and patchworked by rice paddies – and down south to the narrow Isthmus of Kra washed by the Andaman Sea. This region, traditionally known as "Lower Burma", is the nation's rice bowl. With rivers, estuaries, canals and coastal waters, it's not surprising that fish is the main source of protein in this part of the country.

Much of the huge array of seafood, especially from the far south of the country, is dried. The most important dried seafood consists of small prawns which are used in salads, soups, main dishes and spicy side dishes or condiments such as the indispensable Burmese *balachaung*, a combination of pounded dried prawns, deep-fried garlic and onions, vinegar and chilli powder. Sour, hot, salty and crisp, it can very quickly become addictive to lovers of emphatically flavoured food.

Burma's central plains around Mandalay are ringed by hills, which make it the driest part of the country. Being far from the coast, the people of this region rely on freshwater fish. Thanks to irrigation, crops including various beans and lentils are grown, and some of them fermented to make seasonings substituted for the fermented fish products of the south.

Pork and beef are greatly enjoyed in this area once called Middle Burma, for although the

grown and Lake Inle provides a variety of freshwater fish. As they lack the abundant fish and prawns of the southern regions of Burma, the Shan have developed fermented bean pastes that replace dried shrimp paste as a seasoning, and also make fermented soybean cakes similar to the Indonesian *tempeh*.

The staple diet

Allowing for some regional differences, what constitutes the average meal in Burma? A main meal – as opposed to breakfast or an between-meal snack – is based on rice, with the accompanying dishes chosen to provide a

majority of the population is Buddhist and not supposed to take life, there is no prohibition on eating food slaughtered by non-Buddhists.

The third geographic region known as Upper Burma encompasses the mountainous regions of the Shan area to the east, the western Chin Hills and the snowy mountains of the far north. Because many of these mountainous areas are poor, the local diet might well include items not found elsewhere, such as insect larvae, ants and grasshoppers. The Shan Plateau is a fertile exception, where hill rice, beans and lentils are

LEFT: fried snack seller at the market.
ABOVE: chatting at the dried fish stall.

PERFECT HOSPITALITY

If you're invited to a traditional home in Burma, don't expect your hostess to eat with you. Tradition dictates that women eat before their guests arrive, so they can give them their full attention. Courtesy demands that should anyone arrive unexpectedly at your home while you are eating, they must be invited to join you. They, in turn, are required by custom to refuse politely, saying that they have already eaten. On festive occasions, it is common for a neighbourhood to have a round robin of dining, with each household offering a dish. Even during Buddhist celebrations, Hindu households will offer traditional Indian sweetmeats to anyone dropping by.

contrast of flavours and textures. There will usually be a thin soup *(hingo)*, often slightly sour and with leafy greens floating in it, which is eaten throughout the meal to "help wash down the rice". Then there should be at least one curry of either meat, poultry, fish or even egg; you can tell by the colour roughly what the flavour will be like in advance, with red signifying lashings of chilli, white, a milder coconut gravy, and yellow, plenty of turmeric.

There will also be a cooked vegetable dish, maybe some lentils, a salad, a chilli-hot condiment and almost certainly *balachaung*. When it comes to vegetables, the Burmese living

outside the major cities or towns depend on a huge range of wild plants. These include aquatic plants gathered from rivers, canals and lakes, as well various leaves, tubers, shoots, buds, seeds, and fungi found in the forests or along the edges of the rice fields. The young leaves of many shrubs and fruit trees such as papaya and mango are also edible, as are the leaves of a number of root vegetables.

Salads and noodle dishes

The creativity of Burmese cooks is perhaps at its best when it comes to salads and noodle dishes. Salads – called *thoke*, which means "mixed by hand" – begin with raw vegetables, either a single vegetable or a wide range of leaves. For a salty flavour, fish sauce, salt or soy sauce are added, and for greater pungency, some dried shrimp paste or soybean powder.

Sourness comes in the form of tamarind, lime or vinegar, or perhaps some shredded sour fruit. To absorb the moisture of the sour juice, pounded dried shrimp, peanuts, roasted chickpea powder, sesame seeds or soybeans are added. To blend everything together, vegetable oil and sesame oil are added. The final garnishing comes in the form of crisp fried onion and garlic, roasted chilli and herbs such as mint, coriander, kaffir lime leaf or lemon grass.

Noodle dishes, too, can be dazzlingly complex in flavour and texture. Take, for example, the popular *mishee* from Mandalay, which begins with rice noodles. These are put into a bowl and topped with some deep-fried pork in batter, deep-fried beancurd puffs, a pickle made from fermented mustard greens and some crisp bean sprouts. A ladleful of shredded pork in rich stock is added, then a dollop or two of garlic sauce, chilli sauce and a salty sauce made from preserved chilli bean curd. The finishing touch comes in the form of a sprinkle of chopped spring onions. *Mishee* is usually eaten outside of homes, at food stalls or in restaurants which specialise in making it.

A more simple but equally tempting noodle dish – and one which has been "borrowed" by northern Thais – is *kyauk shwe*, which consists of chicken simmered in a spicy coconut milk gravy made with plenty of onion, garlic, ginger and chilli. This fragrant mixture is poured over egg noodles, with slices of boiled egg, crispfried onions, chilli flakes, fresh coriander and a wedge of lime adding up to total perfection.

BREAKFAST NOODLES

Burma's morning chorus is the sound of slurping as the "national dish" is devoured at food stalls throughout the country. Known as *mohinga*, this starts with pungent fish broth seasoned with lashings of dried shrimp paste, lemon grass, ginger, onion and garlic. This is added to a bowl of rice vermicelli, then topped off with the "small accompaniments" so beloved by the Burmese: crunchy wafers of dried soybean cake, chilli powder, fried garlic, coriander leaf, sliced fish cake, ground roasted chickpeas, egg and spring onions. Forget your breakfast rolls and coffee – *mohinga* is what real men (and women) eat for breakfast.

Snacks and stimulants

Burmese of all ages love to snack and along the streets and the markets, *longyi*-clad cooks stand or squat over a single burner holding a wok full of bubbling oil, into which fritters of spiced lentils, dried beans, prawns, and mixtures of pork or chicken and vegetable are plunged. Hawkers offer spiced nuts, salted broad beans, banana chips, pancakes with sweet fillings, brightly coloured squares of sweet jelly, preserved dried fruits coated in sugar and spiked with chilli powder... it is truly a snacker's paradise.

Only in Burma can you drink your tea and eat it, too. You will, of course, find the usual beverage (better known as Indian or Ceylon tea) as well as Chinese tea. If you're lucky, you might also get the chance to sample tea-leaf salad or *lepet*, made with young tea leaves packed into bamboo tubes and left to ferment. The leaves are mixed with salt and sesame oil, then served surrounded by lime juice, chilli and garnishes including fried garlic, dried shrimps, toasted sesame seeds, fried broad beans or dried peas. The secret is to take a pinch of two or three seasonings, together with some tea leaves, and discreetly pop it into your mouth.

The *lepet* is supposed to act as a stimulant, and eating it is traditionally accompanied by as much ritual as the preparation of betel. This old custom, now dying out, involves smearing betel leaf with lime paste, wrapping it around sliced areca nut and spicing it to taste with fennel seeds, cloves or some shredded dried liquorice.

Tropical fruits

Burma offers all the luscious fruits of the tropics, many of them available year round. You'll find juicy mangoes; sweet pineapples; papayas; bananas of different sizes, skin tones and flavours; pomelos (massive citrus fruits reminiscent of but far superior to grapefruit); giant jackfruit which can weigh up to 25 kilos (55 lbs), and the purple-skinned mangosteen, which has a translucent white flesh with a perfect balance of sweetness and acidity.

But the king of fruits in Burma is undoubtedly the durian, whose foul-smelling spiky exterior encloses large seeds covered with a buttery flesh that tastes, to the initiated at least,

LEFT: fruit stall selling jackfruit.
RIGHT: imaginative tea shop sign.

like heaven. Sir James George Scott, who wrote *The Burman, His Life and Notions*, said: "Some Englishmen will tell you that the flavour and the odour of the fruit may be realised by eating a "garlic custard" over a London sewer; others will be no less positive in their perception of blendings of sherry, delicious custards, and the nectar of the gods..."

Finding indigenous Burmese cuisine isn't as easy as you might expect. The migration of ethnic Chinese and Indians, particularly during British colonial rule, has resulted in many restaurants offering Chinese or Indian food, without a Burmese dish in sight. However, with

the recent increase in tourism, true Burmese cuisine is increasingly available in elegant restaurants in Yangon and in upmarket hotels elsewhere. If you want to sample the real food of Burma, try the simple, semi-open air restaurants and food stalls, especially those clustered around the markets.

If you are lucky enough to be invited to eat at someone's home, most families eat seated on mats around a low table. Food is usually eaten with the fingers or by using a fork and spoon, unless it is a noodle soup when a spoon and pair of chopsticks are used. If you have the opportunity, try some locally-brewed Mandalay Beer to wash down your food. ❑

ARTS AND CRAFTS

The time-honoured skills of lacquerware, metalwork, woodcarving
and embroidery are still much in evidence in modern-day Burma

From Yangon's Bogyoke Aung San Market to Mandalay's Zegyo Market, and at all local bazaars beyond and between, visitors to Burma will find a remarkable variety of native handicrafts. Stalls display lacquerware, metalwork, brass and marble sculpture, woodcarvings, embroidered textiles and more. The craftsmen of Burma may not have achieved the same international renown as artisans from other parts of Southeast Asia, but they are no less skilled.

Lacquerware

Lacquerware has developed into an art form of refined quality. Its history can be traced to China's Shang dynasty (18th to 11th century BC). The craft reached the area of present-day Burma in the 1st century AD by way of the Nan Chao Empire (modern Yunnan), and is believed to have been carried to Bagan during King Anawrahta's conquest of Thaton in 1057. Today, it thrives in northern Thailand and Laos, as well as in Burma.

Raw lacquer is tapped from the thitsi tree *(Melanorrhoea usitatissima)* in the same way as latex is taken from the rubber tree. As soon as the sticky-grey extract comes in contact with the air, it turns hard and black. In the past, extraordinarily fine lacquerware bowls were produced around inner cores made of a mixture of horsehair and bamboo, or even pure horsehair. This gave such flexibility that one could press opposite sides of the bowl's rim together without the bowl breaking or the lacquer peeling off. Today, two other techniques of manufacture prevail. Inferior products have a gilded lacquer relief on a wooden base. Better quality wares have a core of light bamboo wickerwork, which assures elasticity and durability.

This basic structure is coated with a layer of lacquer and clay, then put in a cool place to dry. After three or four days, the vessel is sealed with a paste of lacquer and ash, the fineness of

ash determining the quality of the work. It may come from sawdust, paddy husk or even cow dung. After this coating has dried, the object is polished until smooth. Over time, it is given several successive coats of lacquer to eliminate irregularities. At this stage, the ware is black. But the artist isn't finished yet: ornamental and

figurative designs must still be added. Cheaper articles are simply painted, while expensive ones are embellished by means of engraving, painting and polishing. A similar effect can be produced with coloured reliefs, which are painted and partially polished. Red, yellow, blue and gold are the most frequent colours used. The production of such multi-coloured lacquerware takes about six months, involving 12 or more stages of manufacture.

Generally, the designs represented in lacquerware are of Buddhist origin, derived from the *Jataka* Buddha life-cycle stories, images of the Buddha, and celestial animals from Hindu-Buddhist mythology. Among the most common

LEFT: painting in a handicraft workshop.
RIGHT: the art of making lacquerware.

icons are the *chinthe* or lion, the *hintha* or goose, the *naga* or serpent, the *galoun* or eagle, and – unlikely, perhaps, in such distinguished company – the unassuming *youn* or rabbit.

Metalwork

The most frequently seen evidence of Burmese metalwork is probably the gold leaf, pasted by Buddhist devotees on pagodas and Buddha images all over the country. The industry is especially prevalent in Mandalay.

The gold comes from the north of Burma in nuggets, which are flattened on a slab of marble until paper-thin. These sheets are then alter-nately cut and pounded between layers of leather and copper-plate until they are almost transparent. Then they are picked up with pin-cers, placed between sheets of oiled bamboo paper, and neatly packaged in 2cm-long (1 inch) stacks of 100 leaves, for sale at pagodas and bazaars. An ounce of gold can produce enough gold leaf for an area of 10 sq metres (12 sq yds).

Burmese silverwork dates back to the 13th century, when palace bowls, vases and betel-nut boxes, as well as daggers and sheaths, were made. Today, the work done at Ywataung vil-lage near Sagaing rivals the earlier silverwork. While silverwork is not as prominent as it once

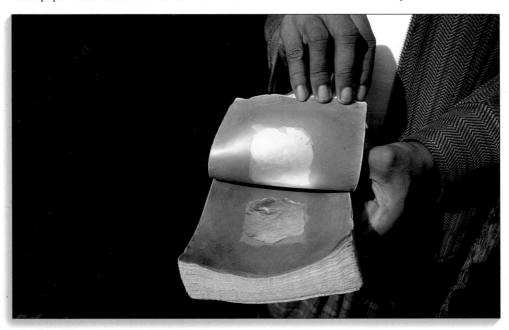

SILK

Before the influx of imported textiles that characterised the colonial period, silk was an important product of Henzada and Amarapura. Henzada silks were heavy, brocade-like materials, while Amarapura specialised in shot silks in red, green and yellow with the weft (the threads that lay across the cloth) colours generally lighter than those of the warp (the threads that run lengthways). Certain colour combinations such as two shades of green were considered unlucky, while rose-pink was deemed lucky and much sought-after. All textiles were traditionally made on simple frame looms found in just about every Burmese household.

was, work in copper and brass has never seri-ously declined in importance and it remains a major cottage industry in Mandalay for about 300 families. Bago (Pegu) is another important centre. Here, Buddha images, orchestral gongs, bells for pagodas and monasteries, and small cattle bells are in constant demand.

Bronze Buddha images

Buddhas made of bronze have been cast in Burma since at least the 10th century AD. Today, the main centre for this art – and well worth a visit – is the Mandalay quarter of Tampawaddy. The process is a complex one and requires real skill. The artisan begins by making a mould in three stages. First, a mix is made of dust, manure, ochre clay and rice husks; this is blended with water to make a fine clay-like mixture. The Buddha image-to-be is then moulded with consummate skill from the clay mixture. Next, the clay image is allowed to dry, then covered with layers of wax.

Finally, the wax is covered with two further layers of clay, and the whole is fired, allowing the wax to melt and run away – hence the technical term for the procedure: the "lost wax process".

MANDALAY MARBLE

Makers of marble religious works of art in southern Mandalay get their raw materials from a quarry at Sagyin (34 km/21 miles) north of Mandalay.

cooling, both the outer layers and inner core of clay are removed with a hammer and chisel. Then the Buddha image is filed, polished and generally made perfect. The resultant Buddha image, if produced by a master craftsman, is nearly always visually spectacular. It may also be improved by the addition of decoration – often a crown or flame-like halo. Buddha images may be the most obvious and the best-known products of Burmese bronze-making artisans, but they are far from being the only product. Other items

Cast Buddha images are generally made from a mixture of copper and zinc in a ratio of 5:4. Smelting takes place over a large pit filled with coal or charcoal; this is fanned to a great heat, permitting the metals to melt and blend in a huge clay crucible. The molten metal is then poured into the inverted mould through one of two small holes left there to permit egress of wax and ingress of molten bronze. The bronze is poured into one hole, taking the place of the lost wax, until it begins to emerge from the other hole. After a day or two solidifying and

cast or beaten in bronze include huge bells – the best example of which is the mighty bell cast on the orders of King Bodawpaya in 1790, and reputedly the second largest in the world after the cracked monster at the Kremlin. Burmese bells cast in this fashion have no hanging central clapper as in Europe, but instead are designed to be hit on the outside with a wooden club.

Also made of bronze, the small "opium weights" that were once used throughout Burma are now produced on a large scale for sale to visitors as souvenirs. Properly sold in sets of 10, these weights are kept with a set of scales in a specially carved wooden box,

LEFT: delicate gold leaf.
ABOVE: marble polishers at an image maker's workshop.

usually stained black. The earliest known weights date back to the 14th century, and today's reproductions have changed little. The weights are often in the form of mystical animals or birds from the Hindu-Buddhist pantheon, such as the *hintha* (celestial goose) and the *karaweik* (Indian cuckoo).

Woodcarving

Woodcarving is among the oldest of Burmese handicrafts, although evidence of the ancient artisans' skills have been destroyed. Significant 19th century works still remain in Mandalay, particularly in the ornamentation of monaster-

ies. Today, *nat* images are among the objects most commonly made. The artisans first sketch the figures they wish to carve on a solid block of wood, using charcoal and chalk, then shape an outline with chisel and saw. Details are completed with knives and other fine instruments.

Marionettes have traditionally been made for *yok thei pwe* or the marionette theatre. Often exquisitely carved and colourfully clad, these hinged, wooden figures make excellent gifts, and are now manufactured for sale at shops and bazaars all over the country, but especially in Yangon and Mandalay.

Up to a metre (3 ft) in height, the marionettes are controlled by as many as 60 strings, although 10 would be a more usual number. The function of the strings, together with skillful jointing, is to enable the puppets to portray basic human movements such as walking, dancing and stylised gesturing. Characters featured in traditional marionette theatre include Thagyamin, the King of the Nats, a human king, queen, prince and princess, a regent, two court pages, an elderly couple, a sage, a villain, four ministers and two clowns.

A typical troupe of marionettes includes 28 such traditional characters. Animals, real and mythological, also feature in the troupe – for example, horses, elephants, monkeys and *makara* or sea serpents.

Painting

Painting has long been an esteemed art throughout Burma, with the subject matter often derived from Buddha birth stories and related themes. The temples of Bagan were richly decorated with painted murals, many of which have survive to the present day, albeit in a faded and dilapidated state. In these early examples of temple decoration, Indian influence – and especially that of the Ajanta school – is apparent. Most murals were painted directly onto plaster made from a mix of clay, with sand and rice husks to provide a binding agent.

By the time of the Konbaung Dynasty (1752–1855), murals were more indigenous in style, with the faces, costumes and buildings all taking on a distinctly Burmese quality. Buddhist themes remain predominant, and are almost always drawn from the Theravada tradition, although Mahayana subject matter – for example representations of Avalokitesvara or Guan Yin – and some Hindu iconography

---

NATIONAL DRESS

The most common item of dress in Burma – indeed, it might almost be deemed the national dress – is the *longyi*. This is a piece of unstitched cloth about 4 metres (13 ft) long that is wrapped around the hips and folded over in front to make a simple cylindrical skirt. *Longyi* are worn by both men and women.

Men cover the upper part of their bodies with a slit-sleeved short jacket of sombre colours; women don an *eingyi*, or similar garment, which is double-breasted and usually white. *Longyi* may be of any shade or pattern, but the best ones are generally made of fine Mandalay silk in bright colours.

drawn from the *Ramayana* are also found. During the British colonial period, a school of Burmese watercolour painting developed, especially among artists in Yangon and Mandalay. The technique employed, which combines Western and Burmese artistic traditions and frequently features nationalistic subjects such as the exile of King Thibaw and the perceived uncouth mannerisms of the British, can be found today in a few galleries and art shops, especially in Yangon.

elaborate ornamentation of the Burmese court is mentioned as early as the 9th century AD in Chinese sources, while King Kyanzittha of Bagan felt able to boast in a 12th-century inscription that even his poor subjects were able to adorn themselves with precious gold and fine clothes.

Court dress in ancient periods often featured expensive silks and cloth embroidered with gold and silver threads, and adorned with fine lacework. Some court costumes from the days of King Mindon

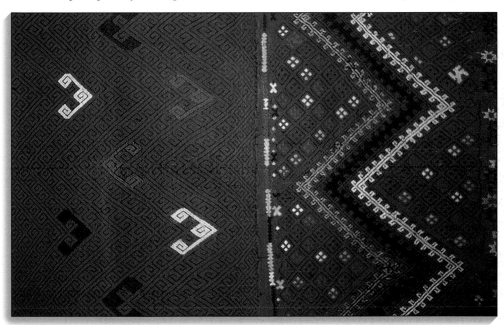

Embroidery

Embroidery remains a respected art form. Fine gold thread, silver sequins and coloured glass (to resemble imitation jewels) were traditionally stitched onto cotton or wool garments for royalty and other dignitaries. Today, expensive silk *longyi* often display peacock figures or broad belts of floral designs.

Dress and ornamentation have long been an important part of Burmese life, from the former royal court down to the simple *pwe*. The

LEFT: a traditional carving of a Burmese soldier on horseback.
ABOVE: Kachin textiles.

and King Thibaw were particularly elaborate.

Related to the art of embroidery and popular as souvenir items among visitors to the "Golden Land" are the hangings known as *kalaga* or "Indian curtains". These are elaborately sequined and padded wall hangings on black velvet, featuring scenes from the Buddha's life, Hindu-Buddhist mythology and – at least in recent years – more secular subjects such as elephant fights, warriors and princesses, flowers, trees and scenic views. The technique used for making *kalaga* is ancient but adaptable; today's artisans incorporate the art form into clothing, blankets and even gaily-coloured bags and caps. ❑

THE PERFORMING ARTS

*Most musical theatre and dance in Burma is inspired by ancient myths
and legends, and by Brahman-Buddhist beliefs*

"The description of the Burmese as a happy and smiling person is borne out on the stage more than one would think possible."
— James R Brandon, *Brandon's Guide to Theatre in Asia*, 1976

To the Burmese, a festival or fair of any kind means a *pwe*. It is a time to gather the entire family together and go along to watch a marvellous mixture of dance, music, comedy and the recreation of epic drama. Burmese theatre often has its audience shrieking, sobbing and rolling with laughter. Lively carefree dancers, as resplendent as tropical birds in their dazzling plumage, leap and whirl before the awed eyes of spectators of all ages. Clowns cavort across the stage, their antics and acrobatics inspiring fits of happy hysteria. An orchestra of drums and gongs beats out a strange melody, as the stage becomes "a fairyland peopled by ravishingly handsome princes and vivacious princesses", in the words of Asian theatre authority Brandon. Certainly, no one visiting Burma, especially between November and May, should miss an opportunity to take in at least one form of the Burmese performing arts.

Understanding pwe

There are several types of *pwe*. Most popular is the *zat pwe*, the ultimate mélange of music, dance and dramatics. *Anyein pwe* is a more "folksy" theatrical form presenting episodes from daily life, along with dancing and story telling. *Yein pwe* is pure dance, solos alternating with group numbers. *Yok thei pwe*, or marionette theatre, is a uniquely Burmese theatrical form not so often seen today. *Nat pwe* is ritual spirit-medium dance, only performed in public at animistic festivals, and rarely seen by visitors.

Among other forms of theatre, *pya zat* is often seen before *zat pwe* performances. A dance-play with mythical themes, it is generally set in a fan-

tasy world where a heroic prince must overcome the evil-doings of demons and sorcerers.

From the mid-18th to the mid-19th century, a masked dance-drama called *zat gyi* flourished in royal courts under the patronage of Burmese kings. Today, public performances are rare, although papier-mâché replicas of *zat gyi* dance

masks can be purchased at souvenir stalls along the stairs leading to the Shwedagon Pagoda.

Burma has a National Theatre, a company of 14 dancers and musicians who went on a highly acclaimed concert tour of the US in late 1975 but have since been, sadly, largely absent from the international scene. Other troupes are trained in the State Schools of Music and Drama in Yangon and Mandalay. Countless troupes travel around villages and during pagoda festivals, staging performances throughout the countryside during the dry season.

These troupes present their repertoire to throngs of villagers, performing on temporary bamboo stages, under a makeshift awning or

LEFT: *yok thei pwe* puppet master.
RIGHT: classical dancer re-enacts traditional *nat* stories.

(more often than not) in the open air. Large audiences sit on mats spread in front of the stage. Many bring their children, as well as picnics. Performances often last from sunset to sunrise; many spectators doze off for a couple of hours in the middle of the show, hoping to be nudged awake for their favourite dance sequence or story.

Dance-drama

The history of Burmese dance troupes dates back as far as 1767, when King Hsinbyushin

> **POPULAR MUSIC**
>
> Burmese pop music draws on a number of disparate traditions, but is strongly influenced by Western, Chinese, Indian and Thai imports.

Konbaung dynasty era in Mandalay. Although some stylistic leaps and turns of Western ballet were introduced and assimilated during the years of British colonial rule, enthusiasm for dance went into a period of decline. Only since independence has Burma's government made efforts to revive theatre arts, and while the programme has been quite successful, it's also been very inward-looking.

To visitors, Burmese dance may seem awkward, even double-jointed. Wrists, elbows, knees, ankles, fingers and toes are bent in

returned to Ava after his conquest of the Thai capital of Ayutthaya. Among his captives were the royal Siamese dancers. It was from these exquisitely trained performers that the Burmese developed the dance movements which prevail on stage today.

During the dominance of Bagan from the 11th to the 13th century, a form resembling Indian dance had been popular at pagoda festivals and royal audiences. This had disintegrated into popular drama after the fall of Bagan, and took a back seat to the highly refined Thai classical dance. But it still wielded some influence in shaping a uniquely Burmese dance form. Burmese dance reached its zenith in the late

stylised directions with seeming effortlessness.

Setting the mood is an orchestra, called the *saing*, akin to the Javanese *gamelan* and dominated by percussion instruments. Its centrepiece is a circle of 21 drums, the *patt-waing*. (Smaller orchestras have only nine drums.) Around this are a gong section (*kye-waing*), a single large drum (*patt-ma*), cymbals (*lingwin*), bamboo clappers (*wah let khok*), an oboe-like woodwind instrument (*hne*), a bamboo flute (*palwe*), and a bamboo xylophone (*pattala*).

Occasionally, an orchestra will employ the most delicate of all Burmese instruments, the 13-stringed harp. Shaped like a toy boat covered in buffalo hide, with silk strings attached to a curved wooden "prow", it is a solo instrument usually played by a woman, unlike other musical instruments, which are all played by men. When used in a *pwe*, it accompanies solo singing.

Legendary tales

Ancient legends permeate all aspects of theatre in Burma. Nearly all performances are based on the Hindu epics (the *Ramayana* in particular), or on the *Jataka* tales of the Buddha's 550 prior incarnations. The *Ramayana* is the best known saga in South and Southeast Asia; it

> **GEORGE ORWELL**
>
> "The girl began to dance... a rhythmic nodding, posturing and twisting of the elbows... like a jointed doll, and yet incredibly sinuous." *Burmese Days.*

bring them to life for audiences. The highlight of a *zat pwe* performance usually comes in the early hours of the morning at about 2am, when the stars of the show let go with a breathtaking exhibition of their skills. The more imaginative the actors are during a performance, the more the crowd will roar its appreciation.

Marionette theatre

An exception to all other forms of theatre is the *yok thei pwe*, or marionette theatre. A single

tells the story of the capture of the beautiful Princess Sita by the demon king Dasagir, and of her heroic rescue by her husband, Prince Rama. The *Jataka*, meanwhile, are familiar to every Burmese schoolchild or adult. The tales relate, in a quasi-historical moral fashion, how the Buddha overcame the various mortal sins to attain his final rebirth and enlightenment. The 10 tales of incarnations immediately preceding Buddhahood are seen as especially important. As the stories are well known beforehand, it is up to the troupe and its individual dancers to

master puppeteer manipulates 28 dolls, some with as many as 60 strings. He presents the dialogue simultaneously, while getting help from only two stage assistants.

Puppet theatre in Burma had its foundation not long after Hsinbyushin's return from Ayutthaya with the Siamese court dancers. The king's son and successor, Singu Min, created a Ministry for Fine Arts, and gave his minister, U Thaw, the task of developing a new art form.

In 18th century Burma, and to some extent even today, modesty and etiquette forbade the depiction of intimate scenes on the stage. Further, many actors refused to portray the future Buddha in the *Jataka* tales, considering

LEFT: *anyein pwe* dancers.
ABOVE: a *yein pwe* dancer takes the stage.

this to be sacrilegious. U Thaw saw a way around these obstacles. What human beings could not do in public, wooden figures could do without prohibition. And thus the *yok thei pwe* was born.

The *yok thei pwe* has been standardised more than any other Burmese dramatic form. The stage setting is always the same: a throne on the left for court scenes, a primeval forest of branches on the right, and a sofa in the centre, with the action taking place against a monochrome wall background. The order of the various scenes is likewise predetermined.

The orchestra opens with an overture to

According to traditional Buddhist doctrine, each organism consists of 28 physical parts. U Thaw, seeking to be consistent with this belief, directed that there should be precisely 28 marionettes. Each of these is almost a metre high, faultlessly carved and with costumes identical to the originals that U Thaw specified.

Each of the figures derives from a mythological being. In addition to those previously mentioned, the puppets include a king, two older princes, four ministers, an old woman, a Brahman priest, a hermit, two clowns and two heavenly beings. The two principal figures are a prince and princess – Mintha and Minthami –

create an auspicious mood. Then two ritual dancers appear, followed by a dance of various animals and mythological beings to depict the first stage in the creation of the universe. Next, making its appearance alone, is the figure of the horse, whose heavenly constellation brings order to the primeval chaos. Then (in order) a parakeet, two elephants, a tiger and a monkey come on stage.

The imagination of the audience is stirred with the entrance of two giants, a dragon as well as a *zawgyi* (sorcerer) who always flies on stage. These figures prepare onlookers for the magical world of Brahman-Buddhist belief, which provides the plot for almost all puppet plays.

around whom the romantic plot of the performance always revolves. The *yok thei pwe* is fast disappearing in modern Burma. Few puppeteers perpetuate the art, and there are no established texts to follow – only a prescribed order of events. It can be seen occasionally at temple festivals, including the Shwedagon Pagoda festival in Yangon, and regularly in Mandalay at a tourist-oriented marionnette theatre.

Musical performances

Burmese music lacks a chromatic scale, or even chords. But the melody pounded out on drums and gongs is mellowed by the other instruments, and love songs are as touching as they would be if they were played on violins. Traditionally, the Burmese compare their music to the rustling of the wind through the leaves of the rose-apple tree, and the splash of its fruit falling into a sacred river.

Legend has it that King Alaungsithu of Bagan, who reigned from 1112 to 1167, encountered Thagyamin, king of the *nat*, under the shade of a rose-apple tree "at the end of the world", where he was told the secret of the Burmese tonal system.

The structure of Burmese music is little known outside the country due to the political isolation which has been imposed since 1962. There has been little systematic study of it and writings by Burmese scholars are even today extremely rare. It is generally related to the music genres of Southeast Asia and often uses gong and chime instruments similar to those found in the neighbouring countries of Thailand, Laos and Cambodia. Although Burmese music draws upon the rich heritage of the Hindu-Buddhist cultural tradition, it is nonetheless strongly distinct from the music cultures of its neighbours.

Within the realm of traditional Burmese music, there are two distinct modes of performance, a chamber music ensemble which prominently uses the Burmese harp or *saung gauk*, and the outdoor gong and drum ensemble known as *hsaing*. Both ensembles share a single vast repertoire. This body of music is known as the *Maha Gita*, or great song, and was used during the reigns of the various Burmese dynasties.

Tonal scales

In essence, Burmese music consists of a series of seven tone scales referred to as *athan*. While there is a particular and unique name for each, there is no term in Burmese equivalent to the Javanese *patet*, or the Indian *raga*. A distinctive and clear performance practice, however, indicates a conscious awareness of a highly developed and clearly defined modal system among Burmese musicians. In theory, a series of seven tones are recognised as basic. Each of these seven pitches can be used as a starting tone for one or more "modes".

Fundamental to the technique of Burmese music is the use of two semi-independent

voices for the instrumental interpretation of all compositions in the classical repertoire. When performed on an instrument like the *saung*, the player executes the melody and at certain points, adds the secondary or harmonic tone. However, when using instruments such as the xylophone or piano, one hand plays the melodic line while the other plays the secondary notes, and periodically jumps up to aid in the articulation of the melody line. The melody is in the upper range while the lower voice supports the melody. In this form, each of the hundreds of poems in the *Maha Gita* (Royal Song) repertoire is memorised. ❑

LEFT: behind the scenes at a marionette show.
RIGHT: Shan drummer at a festival.

THE MANY IMAGES OF THE BUDDHA

Buddha images have been integral to Burmese fine arts for almost 1,500 years, reflecting the creative skill of artisans and their deep religious beliefs

Images of the Buddha in Burma come in many styles. Experts divide them into various groups, distinguished either by historical period or by region of origin. The earliest major group derives from Bagan and dates from the 11th to 13th century. Bagan-style Buddhas, whether of bronze, alabaster or wood, are usually heavy-set with broad shoulders and large faces. Often, the head, set on a short neck, tilts slightly forward. An equally distinguished but separate tradition developed across the Rakhaing Yoma in and around Mrauk U. This Rakhaing style, which favoured stout Buddhas with square faces, joined eyebrows and often elaborate crowns, was responsible for the famed Maha Muni image taken from Rakhaing in 1784 and now in the Maha Muni Paya in Mandalay. This image, the most revered in Burma, is coated in so much gold leaf that the lower part of the body is difficult to distinguish. Mon images, by contrast, are often slimmer and more etiolated in design, with fuller faces, downcast eyes and very long ears. Again quite distinct, Shan Buddha images tend to have semi-triangular shaped faces narrowing towards the chin. A broad forehead arches over narrowed eyes, partly open. Ear lobes are long, noses fairly pronounced, and necks shortened. Mandalay-style images are common in Burma. Earlier images dating from the Inwa (Ava) period are often carved from alabaster, while later images are made of bronze or gilded wood. Eyebrows are slightly raised, and nostrils flared.

△ **PA-O BUDDHA**
A Shan-style seated Buddha image, at a temple favoured by the Shan State's Kayin and Pa-O minority.

◁ **BAGAN-STYLE**
Large-faced, gilded Buddha image with right hand raised in *abhaya mudra* at the Ananda Temple, Bagan.

▷ **MANDALAY STYLE**
A Buddha image at a temple in Lashio in the *bhumisparsa mudra* or "calling the earth to witness" posture. Behind the image is an elaborate and characteristically Burmese halo.

△ SHAN STYLE
The famous Chao Phlalakhaeng image was brought to Mae Hong Son in northern Thailand during the 19th century.

▽ ALSO MANDALAY
Detail of a Buddha image with long ear lobes and slightly flared nose at Mandalay's Shwekyimyint Pagoda.

▽ BAGAN-STYLE IMAGE
A broad-shouldered, heavy-set Buddha image with a characteristic large visage in the Bagan style.

▽ BAGAN-STYLE BUDDHA
An alabaster figure in *bhumisparsa mudra* (calling the earth to witness) posture at Htilominlo Temple, Bagan.

▽ RAKHAING-STYLE
The greatly revered Maha Muni (Great Sage) image at the Maha Muni Paya in Mandalay. The image's body is covered by several centimetres of gold leaf, its face is ceremonially washed every morning.

ASANA AND MUDRA

The Buddha is invariably depicted in one of four traditional basic postures, or *asana*. These are standing, sitting cross-legged, walking or reclining. In the first three of these postures, the Buddha is perceived as teaching or meditating. In the fourth *asana*, by contrast, the Buddha's death and attainment of *parinirvana* (nirvana beyond death) is celebrated. Equally important and conventional are the various hand postures or *mudra* of the Buddha. In the *bhumisparsa mudra*, or "calling the earth to witness" posture, the right hand of the seated Buddha image touches the ground while the left rests on the lap. In the *dhammachakka mudra* or "turning the wheel of *dharma*" the thumb and forefinger of the image form a circle while the other fingers fan out to symbolise the preaching of the First Sermon. In the *abhaya mudra*, or "displaying no fear" posture, the palm of the right hand is raised and turned outwards to show the palm with straight fingers. In the *dhyana mudra* or "meditation" position, the hands rest flat on the lap, one on top of each other while in the *dana mudra* or "offering" position the right hand is palm up and parallel to the ground.

TEMPLE ARCHITECTURE

*The Burmese landscape is scattered with dazzling pagodas, shrines and stupas –
a legacy of the country's Buddhist merit-making traditions*

Burma possesses a singularly wide range of Buddhist architectural styles. One of the reasons for this is the eclectic nature of the Burmese Theravada Buddhist tradition, adopting that which pleases or appeals and rejecting that which does not.

Although the Bamar people are today the predominant ethnic group in Burma, dominating the great, temple-rich cities of the central plains, in times past they have borrowed seriatim from peoples they have eclipsed, absorbed or otherwise come to dominate, such as the Mon and the Rakhaing.

Burma's religious and cultural traditions have also been influenced by conquests abroad, most notably in the former Kingdom of Lan Na (now northern Thailand) and in Siam (Thailand). From the extinction of the Mon Kingdom of Thaton in the 10th century, through the long occupation of Lan Na (1564–1774), to the destruction of Ayutthaya in 1767, it was common practice for skilled artisans and religious scholars to be taken back to enrich and embellish the Burmese court of the time.

Buddhist builders

Another cogent explanation for the wide diversity of temple styles in Burma was the oft-repeated habit of new rulers to move the royal court to a new palace and capital on assuming power. Under these circumstances, it was often necessary to build new temples and religious edifices to compliment and serve the new palace and royal court. Yet the tradition of constructing *paya* (pagoda) of all kinds on top of almost every raised piece of ground has not been limited to royalty and nobility alone.

The sheer number of Buddhist structures scattered throughout Burma is testimony to the seemingly endless desire of all Burmese to build temples, shrines and, above all, stupas or *zedi*. In spiritual terms, this has everything to do with merit-making, the possibility of an improved rebirth and compensation for transgressions committed in the present life.

More cynically, raising funds to build *paya* of any sort also brings the sponsor respect and status in the current life, and leaves a fitting memorial for the family to be proud of after the builder has passed on to the next life.

Zedi styles

The most common *paya* seen throughout Burma is the *zedi*, more commonly known in Western literature as the stupa. There are numerous variations in *zedi* style, but the basic concept and structure remains the same.

The stupa in its present form evolved more than 2,500 years ago in India following the death of Gautama Buddha, when relics of the "Enlightened One" were taken by his disciples and enshrined within solid structures, usually of brick and stucco. In Southeast Asia, and especially in Burma, some stupas evolved to house Buddha images, and far from being solid structures, could be entered by devotees.

LEFT: early painting of Shwedagon Pagoda, Yangon.
RIGHT: the bell-shaped dome of a *zedi*.

Generally speaking, most Burmese *zedi* consist of square or octagonal terraces supporting a bell-shaped dome which is often likened to a *thabeiq* or monk's bowl, or sometimes to an *anda* or temple bell. Above the dome, the *zedi* narrows to a tall spire supported by concentric rings shaped like lotus petals and banana buds.

At the top of the spire rests the *hti* or decorated umbrellas (usually gilded and bejewelled) near the top of which is attached a metal, flag-like vane. The topmost part of the *hti* is surmounted by an orb, symbolising enlightenment, release from the cycle of rebirth

and the attainment of nirvana. Across Burma, *zedi* may be found almost everywhere, marking passes, raised mounds and hill tops, and sacred places of all kinds. Commonly, however, they form part of an extended *paya* complex comprising a *kyaung* or *pongyikyaun* – that is a Buddhist monastery.

Temple and monastery buildings

Typically, a Burmese monastery forms the spiritual centre of the village or district in which it may stand. Traditionally, it functions as a place of worship for monks and lay people alike, as well as a school, social centre and even a hospital.

Temples tend to be built around *zedi*, but include other buildings such as a *thein* or consecrated assembly hall for the ordination of novices, a *vihara* where the faithful assemble to pray and listen to sermons, living quarters for resident and itinerant monks, a library and a bell tower or gong.

The central *zedi* is often surrounded by several smaller shrines or *gyo-daing* which may house Buddha images, or equally may be dedicated to the local tutelary spirit or *bo bo gyi*. Sometimes there is also a *zayat*, a hall where lay people may rest by day or sleep overnight during pilgrimages and festivals.

Another common feature of Burmese temples is the *pahto*, a building which sometimes substitutes for but more usually compliments a *zedi*. *Pahto* tend to be square or oblong, often massively built with low passageways and small windows, sometimes with several floors and passages leading to outer terraces. The *Pahto* represents a symbolic Mount Meru, the home of the gods, which worshippers can climb and venerate.

There are certain constants in Burmese temple architecture which may well have characterised temples in ancient times. It is impossible to be certain, however, because temple buildings are by their very nature more fragile, and therefore more constantly in need of repair and even renewal by the local people than the more solidly built *zedi*.

Thus, most monastery buildings are usually crowned by elaborate multi-tiered roofs or *pyat-that*, while temple compounds are often surrounded by a thick wall distinguishing the realms of the sacred from the mundane and marking the limits of everyday life.

Pyu

The oldest surviving remains of religious buildings in Burma date from the pre-Bamar Pyu Kingdoms of Beikthano, Thayekhittaya (Sri Ksetra) and Halin (approximately 3rd to the 10th century). Brick-built structures at Beikthano, to the southeast of Bagan, that have been dated to between the 1st and the 5th century AD are clearly based on Indian prototypes.

The Beikthano Monastery complex is said by experts to be similar to that of Nagarajunakonda in South India and is believed to date from the 2nd century. Later structures at Thayekhittaya, also known as Sri Ksetra, near

Mon

Like the Pyu, the Mon were among the earliest known inhabitants of the region comprising modern Burma, being well established in and around Mon State and the Ayeyarwady Delta by the 6th to 9th centuries. The Mon were the first indigenous people on the east side of the Bay of Bengal to embrace Buddhism. The early Mon kingdom centred on Thaton, which according to legend was visited by Buddhist missionaries of the Indian Emperor Ashoka as early as 300 BC.

Today, little of ancient Thaton remains apart from sections of a ruined city wall. Even less remains at another former Mon capital, Bilin,

Pyay, have been dated to the 5th and the 9th century and include three bulbous stupas evincing clear Indian influence.

Also attributed to the Pyu, stupa-like brick structures at Halin, a short distance southeast of Shwebo, are thought to date from between the 9th to 11th centuries. Skeletons excavated here are aligned to the southeast, commonly considered the direction of the locality spirit or *ein-saung nat*, indicating that the religious beliefs of these early Burmese were probably as much animistic as Buddhist.

LEFT: 18th-century drawing of a Burmese pagoda.
ABOVE: elevation of the Ananda Temple at Bagan.

just south of the famous balancing boulder *zedi* of Kyaikto. Over the past millennium, the Mon have been substantially absorbed by the dominant Bamar, leaving little evidence of distinct Mon architectural styles.

It seems clear, however, that Mon traditions were not destroyed, but rather embraced with enthusiasm by Anawrahta when he conquered Thaton in 1057. The victorious Bamar monarch took back to his capital at Bagan not just the Mon king, but most of his court, including architects, painters and artisans. The style of temple which emerged at Bagan was therefore as much Mon as Bamar, and may be described as the first authentically "Burmese" tradition.

Bagan

Had Bagan been known to classical European antiquity, it would doubtless have been famous as one of the Wonders of the World. In its prime, the city would have looked very different from what it is today – it would have bustled with tens of thousands of people, and the greater part of the buildings would have been made of wood and bamboo. These structures have long since disappeared, leaving behind the immensity of Bagan's Buddhist architectural heritage. The Bagan plain is studded with a plethora of temples and stupas, constructed mainly of brick and decorated with stucco on the outside, and mural paintings within. Archaeologists often distinguish between the earlier, one-storey temples dating from the 10th to 12th century, which are sometimes ascribed to the Mon craftsmen of King Anawrahta. Many have Mon inscriptions, and they are distinguished by being smaller, darker and somewhat more numinous than the larger, later temples.

> ### HTI
>
> *Hti* refers to the umbrella-shaped pinnacle at the top of Buddhist stupas. The *hti* is often gilded and jewelled, and bears small bells.

Clear evidence exists that the building of *paya* was considered an act of merit-making during the Bagan era just as it is now, nor were such activities limited only to the great and the powerful. Bricks were donated by kilns in surrounding villages, and sometimes these were stamped with a village name. When finished, the temples at Bagan were decorated on the inside with elaborate murals, generally featuring *Jataka* Buddha life-cycle stories, while the exterior was decorated with ceramic tiles or stucco.

> ### REFINED INWA (AVA)
>
> Ava – officially named Inwa – functioned as the centre of the Shan Kingdom in the 14th to 16th century before becoming capital of Burma during the 17th and 18th century. As with Bagan, many religious and secular buildings were made of wood, but unlike Bagan, in Ava, a few wooden *paya* have survived, most notably the *Bagaya kyaung*, though in its present form this dates from the early 20th century. During its infancy, the religious architecture of Ava was distinguished by the use of stucco decoration, the refined elegance of its stupas – by now less bulbous and more tapering – as well as very elaborate *pyat-that* or multi-roofed pavilions.

Rakhaing

Isolated from the rest of the country by the coastal Rakhaing Yoma, and enjoying good seaway communications with neighbouring Bengal, Rakhaing – formerly known as Arakan, as well as by the panegyric "Land of the Great Image" in honour of the great Maha Muni Buddha – was an independent kingdom until its conquest by Burma's King Bodawpaya during the 18th century. For this reason, the architecture of Rakhaing is distinct from that of the rest of Burma.

Art historians recognise two distinct features of Rakhaing temple architecture: the combined use of brick and stone, and the enclosure of temples by massive walls, giving a fortress-like appearance.

It appears that Rakhaing temples often functioned as places of safe refuge during times of war. Within the massive walls, the narrow corridors and passages were often elaborately decorated with both painted murals and carvings. The inspiration for the Rakhaing temples, such as those found at Mrauk U, can be traced to distant Bihar, across the Bay of Bengal in India, rather than to the nearby but generally inaccessible Burmese heartlands.

Amarapura and Mingun

Amarapura, the "City of Immortality" was founded by King Bodawpaya in 1783 and remained the capital of Burma until 1857, with a hiatus between 1823 and 1841, when the city of Ava was briefly re-established.

The religious architecture of Amarapura is essentially a continuation of the Avan tradition. Marble was increasingly used in temple construction, and the period is also marked by the extravagant use of stucco in *paya* decoration, notably at the elaborate Nagayon shrine. Various Chinese and European architectural influences became apparent perhaps for the first

pleted. As a consequence, work stopped when the *zedi* was a "mere" 50 metres (160 ft) high, one-third of the height intended.

Mandalay

The last royal capital of Burma, Mandalay was established by King Mindon in 1857. The architectural style adopted by Mindon was in direct continuation with the Ava-Amarapura tradition, but if anything still more elaborate than the latter. Richly ornamented in stucco and marble, temples also benefited from a wealth of elaborate and highly-skilled woodcarving, much of which has survived. ❏

time. Murals surviving on the walls of the Kyauktawgyi Pagoda (completed in 1847) are particularly interesting, providing the visitor with some vivid examples of mid-19th century wooden monastic architecture.

Although never a Burmese royal capital, the city of Mingun, on the west bank of the Ayeyarwady River about 11 km (7 miles) upstream from Mandalay, was singled out by King Bodawpaya (1782–1819) as the site of the huge Mingun Paya. Work was started in 1816, but Bodawpaya died before the project was com-

LEFT: soldiers at a temple at Amarapura.
ABOVE: the exterior of the Royal Palace, Mandalay.

THE SPELL OF THE PAGODAS

The beauty of Burma's pagodas casts a spell over visitors that is hard to break. Ralph Fitch, the first Englishman to visit Burma (in 1586) and leave a record of his impressions, described the golden temple of Shwedagon as "the fairest place, as I suppose, that is in the world".

And Somerset Maugham on first seeing Bagan wrote: "A light rain was falling and the sky was dark with heavy clouds when I reached Bagan. In the distance I saw the pagodas for which it is renowned. They loomed, huge, remote and mysterious, out of the mist of the early morning like the vague recollections of a fantastic dream".
– *The Gentleman in the Parlour* (1930).

PLACES

A detailed guide to the entire country, with principal sites
clearly cross-referenced by number to the maps

A journey through Burma (Myanmar) is a journey through history. The visitor typically arrives in Yangon (Rangoon), where colonial and contemporary Burma continue to co-exist decades after the demise of the colonial administration. Travelling north to Mandalay, one encounters many reminders of the Konbaung dynasty, which dominated in the 18th and 19th century, here and in neighbouring Amarapura. In Inwa (Ava) and Sagaing, the Burma of the Shan sovereignty (14th–16th century) predominates. And in Bagan (Pagan), one can marvel at more than 2,200 stone buildings built during the First Burmese Empire (11th–13th centuries).

This route from Yangon to Bagan requires the visitor to call on his imagination to make the ruins come to life, and to adopt an advanced historical perspective. To "temple-hop" without an open mind is to end up exhausted or jaded. But, as is the case elsewhere, if you bring a sense of excitement, the imagination will flourish.

Bagan itself can be overwhelming, so focus on a choice selection of temples and you'll still be able to trace the history of an incredible era. At the same time, you can observe in the structures of Bagan the development of an architectural style born 1,000 years earlier in India, before maturing on the plains of Bagan.

Besides these places, the likes of Bago (Pegu), Tagaung and Mrauk U (Myohaung) are steeped in history. Burma's principal destinations lie along the Ayeyarwady (Irrawaddy) river like a string of pearls. Enjoying the sights of Bagan and Mandalay from the comfort of a modern river boat or a luxury cruise ship is one of Southeast Asia's great tourist pleasures. However, for the adventurous, wishing to capture the spirit of the past and the true flavour of river travel, you can still opt to join the locals on the regular slowboats.

Few people think of Burma as a beach destination but it has a lengthy, unspoilt coastline and there are a number of seaside resorts worth visiting.

Many trips that could not have been done 10 years ago are now possible. The north of the country is open now and places such as Mawlamyaing (Moulmein), the Myeik (Mergui) Archipelago, Kyaikto, Bhamo, Myitkyina, Indawgyi Lake and Lashio can be visited. For many regions, such as Putao, one will still need permission, a tour guide, and the ability to stay in places with little or no tourist infrastructure. But that, for some, is the challenge and the intrinsic beauty of travel. ❑

PRECEDING PAGES: Bagan at dusk; the Shwedagon Pagoda at Yangon; Mandalay Hill.
LEFT: walking along a tree-arched boulevard.

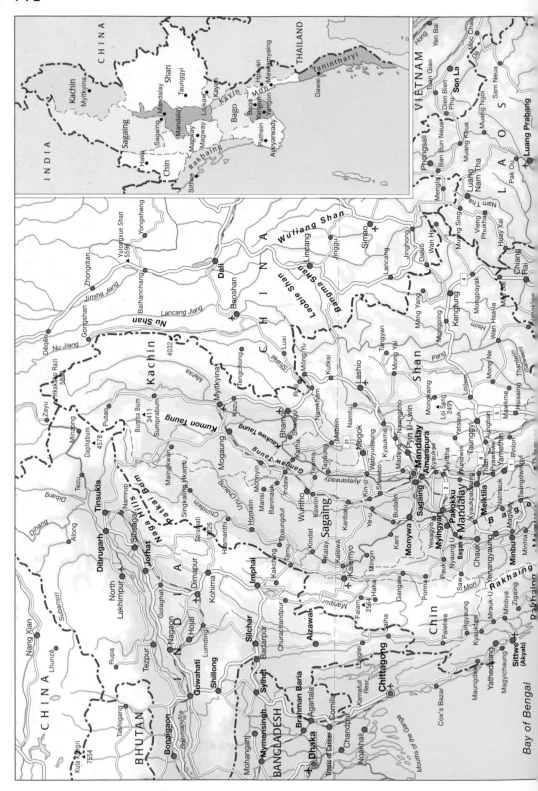

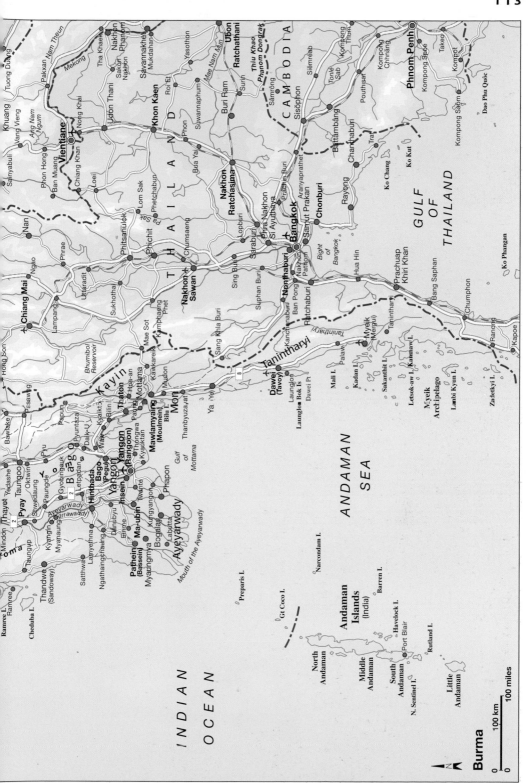

YANGON AND THE AYEYARWADY DELTA

Beyond old-world charms of the capital, Yangon, lie the vast Ayeyarwady Delta, a region dotted with lush rice fields

For a long time, Yangon was stuck in a time warp. Hot, noisy and dusty, it was an antiquated city like few others: there were no high-rises, only weathered buildings left by the British, and, on the roads, crowded buses, vintage Wolsleys and ageing trishaws.

Then, in the last years of the 20th century, and aided by investors from neighbouring countries, Yangon began to change. Vintage cars gave way to shiny Japanese models, and a more modern fleet of taxis (mainly Mazdas and Subarus) took over from the blue, toy-like utilitarian Trabant-type vehicles that had rattled through the streets. Old, decrepit buildings were demolished and international chain hotels and office towers were constructed in their place.

Yangon, meanwhile, has lost none of its magnetism for travellers. Indeed, while newer modes of transport have made travelling easier and the new high-rises tower over gracefully ageing monuments, the people have remained largely unaltered. For example, you can now take a 30-minute taxi ride to the former Portuguese settlement of Thanlyin instead of going by boat; but, despite this faster link, Thanlyin remains a sleepy hollow, its turbulent historic past still hidden behind the church ruins that punctuate the landscape.

Life in the Ayeyarwady Delta – and its green swathe of rice fields supported by the ample waters and rich alluvial silt of Burma's "mother of all rivers" – has not quickened much either. The transformation of Yangon has made little difference to the inhabitants of these plains who still travel by paddle boat through its canals. Pottery and umbrellas continue to be made in the towns and villages of the delta – which is best toured by slow river boat – evoking what must once have been the romantic days of water travel.

North of Yangon is Bago Division. The glory of ancient Bago is reflected in its timeless pagodas and Buddha images. Further north is Taungoo, once the hub of a powerful kingdom and now an important centre of the teak trade, thanks to the teak-forested Bago Yoma range of mountains that form a backdrop. Elephants still work in logging camps here. At the western end of Bago Division is Pyay, another ancient city. Its idyllic countryside is dotted with conical-shaped pagodas dating from the days of the ancient Pyu. Bullock carts trundle along the rural paths here – as if nothing has changed.

A visit to Yangon is thus not complete without venturing into its immediate environs. It is a chance to capture a bit of the timelessness that was once part of the capital's physical surroundings. ❑

LEFT: Yangon Buddha image in the *dhyani mudra* (sign of meditation) position.

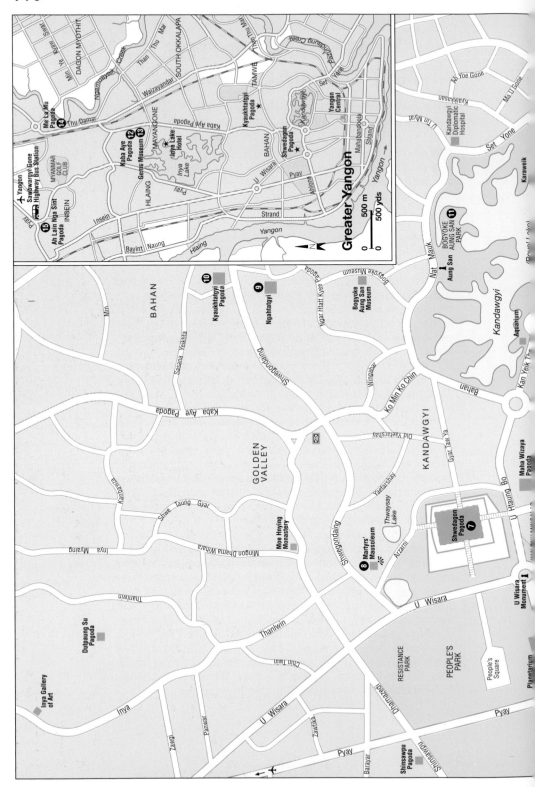

Greater Yangon

0 ___ 500 m
0 ___ 500 yds

DAGON MYOTHIT

Min Ye Kyaw Swar

Ngamoyeik Creek

Than Thu Mar

Waizayandar

SOUTH OKKALAPA

Thu Damar

Me La Mu Pagoda 14

Kaba Aye Pagoda

Kyaukhatgyi Pagoda ★

TAMWE

Yangon Central

MAYANGONE

Kaba Aye Pagoda

Gems Museum 12 13

Inya Lake Hotel

Inya Lake

BAHAN

Shwedagon Pagoda ★

Kandawgyi

Yangon

Yangon
Sawlwargyi Gone
Highway Bus Station

INSEIN

Ah Lain Nga Sint Pagoda 15

HLAING

MYANMAR GOLF CLUB

Insein

Pyay

U Wisara

Pyay

Ahlone

Strand

Bayint Naung

Hlaing

Yangon

Sef Yone

Padaung Creek

Ni Yoe Gone

Ma Li Gone

U Tin Myat

Kandawgyi Diplomatic Hospital

Kyaiktasan

Sef Yone

Karaweik

Karawik

BOGYOKE AUNG SAN PARK

Aung San 1 11

Nat Mauk

Kandawgyi

Aquarium

Bahan

BAHAN

Min

Kyaukhtatgyi Pagoda 10

Ngahtatyi 9

Sasana Yeikhta

Shwegondaing

Kaba Aye Pagoda

Ngar Hlatt Kyee

Bogyoke Museum

Bogyoke Aung San Museum

Wingabar

Ko Min Ko Chin

Old Yaetarshay

GOLDEN VALLEY

Yaganawza

Shwe Taung Gyar

Mingon Dhama Wihara

Moe Hnying Monastery

Inya Myaing

Thanlwin

Shwegondaing

Yaetarshay

Thwaysay Lake

Gyar Taw Ya

Arzami

KANDAWGYI

Martyrs' Mausoleum 8

Shwedagon Pagoda 7

U Haung Bo

Maha Wizaya Pagoda

Inya Gallery of Art

Dutpaung Su Pagoda

Thanlwin

Chin Twin

U Wisara

Inya

Panwat

Zawgi

Zawtika

U Wisara Monument 1

U Wisara

RESISTANCE PARK

PEOPLE'S PARK

People's Square

Planetarium

Pyay

Shinsawpu Pagoda

Shinsawpu

Barayar

Pyay

Dhammazedi

Kan Yeik Tha

Yangon

→ Pazundaung Creek

Pazundaung Mill Road Market

PAZUNDAUNG

THEIN BYU SPORTS GROUND

ZOOLOGICAL GARDENS

Natural History Museum

Aung San Stadium

Yangon Central

Shwe Bone Pwint Zedi

Nyaung-Gon Monastery

Sri Devi (Hindu Temple)

Botataung Pagoda

BOTATAUNG

Botataung Pagoda ❸

Central P.O.

Strand Hotel ❷

St Mary's Cathedral

Prime Minister's and Ministers Offices

KYAUKTADA

Central Telex Office

High Court

Immanuel Baptist Church

City Hall ❶

Sule Pagoda

MTT

Independence Monument

MAHABANDOOLA GARDEN

Yangon Duty-Free Shop ❺

FMI Centre ❹

Bogyoke Aung San Market

New Bogyoke Market

Sri Kali (Hindu Temple)

Moseah Yeshua

English Methodist Church

Defence Services Museum

Holy Trinity Cathedral

PABEDAN

Theingyi Zei (Indian Market)

Shwedagon Pagoda

CHINA TOWN

Kheng Hock Keong (Chinese Temple)

LATHA

Yangon General Hospital

MYOMA GROUND

National Theatre

DAGON

Shwedagon Pagoda

Ein Daw Yar Pagoda

Pyay Rd

New Yangon General Hospital

LANMADAW

National Museum ❻

N

500 m
500 yds

Yangon →

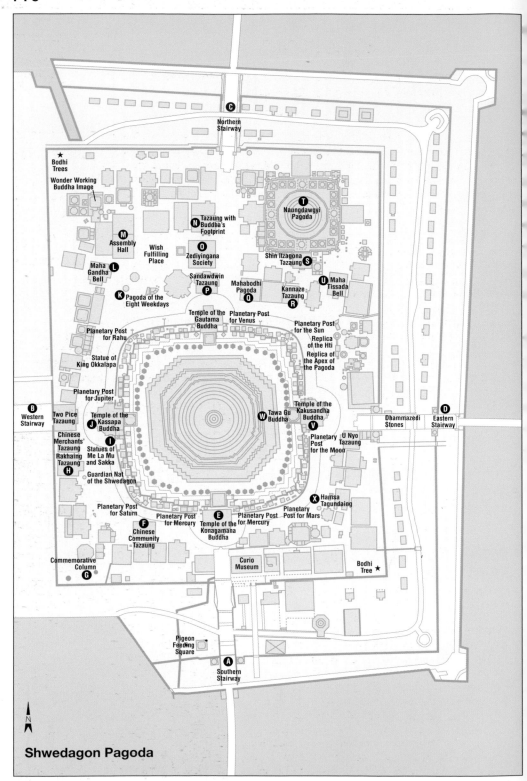

Shwedagon Pagoda

YANGON

*In Yangon, high-rises now tower over ageing monuments, yet
people and their lifestyles seem to have altered
little through the ages*

Map
on pages
116–7

I n *Letters From the East* (1889), Rudyard Kipling wrote: "Then, a golden mystery upheaved itself on the horizon – a beautiful, winking wonder that blazed in the sun, of a shape that was neither Muslim dome nor Hindu temple spire. It stood upon a green knoll... 'There's the old Shway Dagon,' said my companion... The golden dome said, 'This is Burma, and it will be quite unlike any land that one knows about'."

It's more than 100 years since Kipling sailed up the Rangoon (now called Yangon) River to the Burmese capital, but the glistening golden stupa of the Shwedagon continues to dominate Yangon's landscape as few other single structures do in any other major city in the world. The massive pagoda is not only a remarkable architectural achievement, it is also the perfect symbol of a country in which Buddhism pervades every aspect of life.

Indeed, it is hard to imagine a more stunning sight than that of the gilded pagoda basking in the golden-hued glory of a beautiful sunset. But while the Shwedagon Pagoda may dominate Yangon from its post on Singuttara Hill north of the city centre, it is far from the whole show. If you look beyond the ageing, British colonial architecture of most of Yangon's buildings you will find a cosmopolitan city that retains much of its 19th-century charm, with quiet, tree-lined avenues and a people known to be gracious and fun-loving.

BELOW:
standing in the
shadow of the
Shwedagon
Pagoda.

Admittedly, there have been changes evident in the high-rise buildings on all sides of the Sule Pagoda, a facelift that has been funded by both the public and private sectors. But these have changed only portions of the city's general appearance, preserving large chunks of the city centre in much the same state as when the British left in 1948.

Water on three sides

A burgeoning city of 4 million people – the population has more than quadrupled in three decades – Yangon is surrounded on three sides by water. The Hlaing or Yangon River flows from the Bago (formerly Pegu) Yoma (hills) down Yangon's western and southern flanks, then continues for another 30 km (20 miles) to the Gulf of Mottama (Martaban). To the east of the city, Pazundaung Creek is a tributary of the Hlaing. To the north are the foothills of the Bago Yoma; it is here that one finds the Shwedagon and the picturesque artificial lakes that were created by the British and that are now the centres of thriving residential districts.

Sri Lankan chronicles indicate that there was a settlement in the Yangon area 2,500 years ago. Probably a coastal fishing village or a minor Indian trading colony, Okkala, as the settlement was known, grew in fame after the building of the Shwedagon Pagoda.

A few city buses from the 1940s are still on the road. Old and new buses travel into town from the suburbs offering excellent value for money – if you can stand the crush.

BELOW:
Mogul Street in colonial days.

For centuries, its history was inextricably bound to that of the great golden pagoda. We first hear of "Dagon, the town with the Golden Pagoda" from European travellers of the 16th century. In 1586, the English merchant Ralph Fitch described Shwedagon as "the fairest place… in the world." The nearby town of Syriam, across the Bago and Hlaing rivers from Dagon, was the most important European trading colony and Burma's main port well into the 18th century.

King Alaungpaya essentially founded Yangon and set it on its modern path in 1755, when he captured the village of Dagon from the Mon. He called the settlement Yangon ("End of Strife"), which the British later changed to Rangoon. After the destruction of Syriam (Thanlyin) the following year, Yangon assumed its commercial functions. The British conquered the town during the First Anglo-Burmese War in 1824, and its port began to flourish. Unfortunately, a fire devastated the town in 1841 and, in 1852, it was again almost completely destroyed in the course of the Second Anglo-Burmese War.

Deltas and industrial suburbs

Yangon may well have been a coastal village when the Shwedagon was built. But after 2,500 years, a vast delta has been created in Lower Burma by the Ayeyarwady (Irrawaddy) and Hlaing rivers that carry silt to the sea. Yangon's river is easily navigable to the capital and beyond, and a vast majority of Burma's import and export trade is still handled on Yangon's docks.

Industrial suburbs have mushroomed in the eastern and northern sections of the city, providing work for many of the immigrants flocking to the Yangon area. There is a sizable Indian community in the city – a holdover from the time when Burma was still a part of Britain's colony in India – as well as a

large number of people of Chinese descent, and indigenous ethnic minorities. A stroll through Burma's capital is a unique experience. In what other modern city of 5 million people are one of the tallest structures golden pagodas? However, with business and tourism heralding a new economic age, traffic jams and an influx of foreign second-hand cars have further crowded streets crammed with old, jitney-type local buses, trishaws and bicycles. The nightlife has also undergone a makeover: where it was virtually non-existent, visitors can now visit pubs, karaoke lounges and discotheques.

Exploring Yangon

"Sule Pagoda Road, with its five theatres, was mobbed with people, dressed identically in skirt *(longyi)* and rubber sandals, men and women alike puffing thick green *cheroot*, and looking (as they waved away the smoke with slender dismissing fingers) like a royal breed, strikingly handsome in this collapsing city, a race of dispossessed princes." So wrote the contemporary travel author Paul Theroux in his book *The Great Railway Bazaar*.

To stroll the streets of Yangon is to know Theroux's "dispossessed princes". In the downtown area, amid the mildewing grey-brick government offices erected by the British colonialists, and the gleaming high-rise hotels built by Singaporean investors, thrives the city's commercial centre, markets and cinemas. And it is here that the true colours of Yangon's diverse population can be seen.

Walk through Yangon and you will see the pagodas' golden spires rise skyward among an assortment of latter-day Chinese and Hindu temples, mosques, Anglican and Catholic cathedrals, and even a synagogue. The cinemas feature Western, Burmese and Indian films. Enterprising vendors sell all manner of

Map on pages 116–7

TIP

Want to be reborn into a better life? For a pittance in kyats, you can buy a cageful of birds to be released on the spot for merit-making in the Buddhist tradition.

BELOW:
crumbling colonial architecture in downtown Yangon.

goods spread out on canvas sheets on the sidewalks of main roads and in the narrow alleys in between: out-of-print books enterprisingly photocopied and bound; cheap lint brushes made out of quality wood; calendars given away by airlines; combs, lighters and Chinese-made Swiss army knives.

The best places to meet and mingle with Yangon residents are the teahouses on the sidewalks of many downtown streets. Gathered at mini-tables and stools drinking cup after doll's cup of Chinese tea are Yangonian men and women in their *longyis.* The world of work is left behind while they chat, smoke hand-rolled cigarettes or *cheroot* and enjoy their favourite noodle snacks.

Heart of the city

If the Shwedagon is the soul of Yangon, the **Sule Pagoda ❶** (open daily) is its heart. For centuries, it has been the focus of much of the city's social and religious activity. The British established the pagoda as the centre of Yangon when they structured their Victorian grid-street system around it in the mid-19th century. Today, the regularly renovated 48-metre (157-ft) pagoda with its gilded spire remains one of the tallest buildings in the town area, and although the street names have been changed from English to Burmese, the thoroughfares in the centre of the city still intersect at right angles with geometrical symmetry.

The origins of Sule Pagoda are bound up in the mythical prehistory of Burma. Perhaps the most credible tale is that of the two monks, Sona and Uttara, who were sent from India as missionaries to Thaton after the Third Buddhist Synod around 230 BC. The King of Thaton gave them permission to build a shrine at the foot of Singuttara Hill. There the monks preserved a hair of the Buddha, which they had brought from India. For centuries, the pagoda was known as

BELOW: extracting juice for drinks at a street stall.

Kyaik Athok ("the pagoda containing the hair relic" in the Mon language) or Sura Zedi, after Maha Sura, minister to the King of Thaton who supervised the construction of the pagoda. The name Sule Pagoda comes from a later period and can be linked to the Sule Nat, guardian spirit of Singuttara Hill.

The octagonal structure of the Sule Pagoda, which is consistent up to the bell and inverted bowl, clearly indicates its Brahman-Buddhist heritage. During the first centuries of the Christian era, when the influence of Indian merchants and settlers was especially strong, astrology blended with *nat* worship and Buddhist doctrine to create the unique Burmese brand of Buddhism.

Around the outside of Sule Pagoda, which in the daytime acts as a tranquil traffic island in the middle of the city's busiest streets, are a number of small shops dealing in various trades. Inside, the pagoda's shrines and images include four colourful Buddhas with neon halos behind their heads. Temple festivals and feasts are frequently held in the evening, and visitors might be lucky enough to catch such a celebration after dark. As with all pagodas, visitors should stroll in a clockwise direction. The Sule Pagoda's eight sides, like those of the Shwedagon, are dedicated to the days, planets and animals of the eight cardinal points. Temple donations enable the gold coat to be re-applied from time to time.

Downtown

Sule Pagoda Road, a main artery in Yangon, leads to the bustling centre of downtown Yangon. It's a hazardous crossing from the pagoda because of the chaotic traffic at the intersection with Anawrahta Street, but once you manage to arrive at Sule Pagoda Road itself, you will be surprised at the relative calm, despite the presence of roadside vendors and their cages of pigeons.

On the northeast corner of Sule Pagoda Road and Mahabandoola Street, facing the pagoda, is the elegant **Yangon City Hall**. This massive stone structure, built by the British, is worth a glance for its colonial architecture with a Burmese touch. Note the traditional peacock seal high over the entrance. On the southeastern corner of the intersection is Mahabandoola Garden (open daily; entrance fee), named after a Burmese general of the First Anglo-Burmese War.

In the centre of the park, the 46-metre (150-ft) **Independence Monument** is an obelisk surrounded by five smaller, 9-metre (30-ft) pillars. The monument represents Burma's five former semi-autonomous states – Shan, Kachin, Kayin (Karen), Kayah and Chin – in harmonious union with their larger Bamar (Burman) brother. Facing the square on the east side stands the British-built Supreme Court and High Court building.

Southeast of the square, on Strand Road, stands the famous **Strand Hotel ❷**. Before its renovation in the 1990s, most of the mosquito-infested rooms were cooled by electric paddle fans. The Brits may have gone but the old-world charm of the hotel remains, with its colonial-style wicker furniture in the lobby lounge and the waiters' attentive service in the high-ceilinged restaurant. The hotel underwent a complete reconstruction in the early 1990s, and rooms are more expensive as a result. Still, it's worth stepping into

Map on pages 116–7

Relive the old colonial days at the Strand Hotel by propping up its bar. Happy hours are from 5pm to 8pm daily.

BELOW: a shrine at the Sule Pagoda.

The Legend of Shwedagon

The legend of the Shwedagon Pagoda goes back 2,500 years and centres on Okkalapa, King of Suvannabhumi, land of the Talaings. He lived in the region near Singuttara Hill in Lower Burma during the time when Siddharta Gautama was still a young man in northern India.

Singuttara Hill is still considered holy because of the relics of three Buddhas enshrined on top of the hill. It is said that a new Buddha comes into existence every 5,000 years. As it was nearly 5,000 years since the time of the last Buddha, it was thought that the hill would lose its blessedness unless a new Buddha offered a new gift to be enshrined as a relic for the next five millennia. To this end Okkalapa spent many hours on the hill meditating and praying.

In India, meanwhile, Gautama was close to achieving enlightenment under the Bodhi

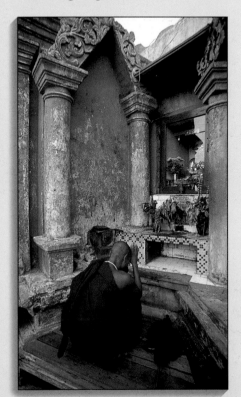

tree in Bodhgaya. Legend has it that he appeared before Okkalapa and promised that the king's wish would be granted.

Gautama Buddha meditated under the Bodhi tree for 49 days before he accepted his first gift from his disciples: a honey cake offered by Tapussa and Bhallika, two Burmese merchant brothers who had come from the village of Okkala. To express his gratitude, Gautama plucked eight hairs from his head and gave them to the brothers.

The brothers set off on a return journey that proved difficult. They were robbed of two of the Buddha's hairs by the King of Ajetta. Then, while crossing the Bay of Bengal, another two hairs were taken by the seabed-dwelling King of the Nagas. Despite the losses, the brothers were welcomed by Okkalapa who held a great feast attended by all the native gods and *nats* who decided a grand stupa should be built to house the relics of Gautama, the latest Buddha.

When Okkalapa opened the casket containing the Buddha's hairs, lo and behold, he saw eight hairs in place. As he looked on in astonishment, the hairs emitted a brilliant light that rose high above the trees, radiating to all corners of the world.

Suddenly, the blind everywhere could see, the deaf could hear, the dumb could speak and the lame could walk. As this miracle took place, the earth shook and bolts of lightning flashed. The trees blossomed and a shower of precious stones rained onto the ground.

As a result of the legend of the hairs, the site chosen to enshrine the Buddha's hairs – Singuttara Hill – is considered one of the country's most sacred places, and the golden Shwedagon Pagoda regarded as the holiest of the country's pagodas.

"*Shwe*" is the Burmese word for "gold", and "*dagon*", a derivative of "*trihakumba*", (contracted to "*trikumba*", "*tikun*" and then "*dagon*"), means "three hills".

The Shwedagon Pagoda was built over the shrine containing the Buddha's relics. Smaller pagodas, constructed with silver, tin, copper, lead, marble and iron brick were built, one on top of the other, in the golden pagoda to enshrine the relics. ❑

LEFT: Shwedagon Pagoda is one of the most sacred places in Burma.

the teak-furnished lounge, where you can take a cup of tea to the accompaniment of local harp music during the afternoon. In the bar, instead of the once mandatory Mandalay beer, you can now also imbibe the usual tipple of the colonial tropics – gin and tonic – which, just a decade ago, was unavailable in the country. All food and beverages are charged in US dollars at this upmarket hotel. Across the street from the Strand, on the other side of a small park, is the chocolate-brown Yangon River.

Several wharves jut into the river, which handles the country's maritime trade. Downstream, the Pathein, Pyay, and Mandalay jetties are for ships plying the slow route from these towns to Yangon.

Behold the Botataung

Heading east on Strand Road for several blocks, you'll come to the **Botataung Pagoda ❸**. It is said that, when eight Indian monks carried relics of the Buddha here more than 2,000 years ago, 1,000 military officers *(botataung)* formed a guard of honour at the place where the rebuilt pagoda stands today. The original Botataung pagoda was destroyed by an Allies' bomb in November 1943.

During the clean-up work, a golden casket in the shape of a stupa was found to contain a hair and two other relics of the Buddha. In addition, about 700 gold, silver and bronze statues were uncovered, as well as a number of terracotta tablets, one of which is inscribed both in Pali and in the south Indian *Brahmi* script, from which the modern Burmese script developed. Part of the discovery is displayed in the pagoda, but the relics and more valuable objects are locked away. Among these is the tooth of the Buddha, which Alaungsithu, a king of Bagan, tried unsuccessfully to acquire from Nan-chao (now China's Yunnan

Map on pages 116–7

Detail of the spectacular gold- and glass-encrusted pillars of the Botataung Pagoda.

BELOW: the interior of Botataung Pagoda.

TIP

To experience sailing
down the Yangon river,
go to the Pansodan
Street Jetty and board
one of the frequent
ferries for Dala. It's
about a 15-minute
ride costing US$1
(for tourists) one way.
Alternatively, hire a
rowboat.

BELOW:
Sri Kali Temple on
Anawrahta Street
in the Indian
Quarter of Yangon.

province) in 1115. China gave it to Burma in 1960. The 40-metre (130-ft), bell-shaped stupa is unusual in that it is hollow, and visitors can walk around the interior. Look out for the glass mosaic, and the many small alcoves for private meditation. The small lake outside is home to thousands of turtles; feed them, with food sold at nearby stalls, and acquire merit for a future existence.

Oriental bazaars

West and north of the Sule Pagoda are Yangon's main street markets. Before World War II, most of the inhabitants of Yangon were Indian or Chinese, and their influence is still reflected in the markets. Take a stroll through **Chinatown**, or rather, a shuffle through the dense crowds on sidewalks piled high with all manner of goods – bamboo baskets, religious images, calligraphy, peanut candy, melon seeds, flowers, dried mushrooms, handmade rice paper, caged songbirds, tropical fish for aquariums and live crabs. As with the Indian market, the earlier you arrive in the morning, the wider the selection. In the evening these streets turn into one large sidewalk restaurant with many stalls offering delicious soups, curries and other local dishes. Situated next to an iron bazaar, the **Chinese Market** starts at the corner of Lan Ma Daw Road, seven blocks west of Sule Pagoda Road. On the next block south is a colourful Chinese temple.

A few blocks away, the pungent aroma of curry powder and other ground spices emanates from the Indian Quarter. **Theingyi Zei** (Indian Market) offers mounds of red chillies and fragrant cinnamon bark, boxes of tropical fruits such as mangosteen and durian, dried fish and seafoods, medicinal herbs, bottled concoctions and local snacks. The market is at the side of a Hindu temple on Anawrahta Street. This quadrant of markets is best visited in the early evening

hustle and bustle. The racial diversity and air of industry for which Yangon was famous in colonial times can still be found. But betel-nut sellers are a thing of the past – the government has prohibited their sale on the street because betel-nut chewers have stained many kerbs with their red-hued spit.

Map on pages 116–7

The best market

The largest and most highly recommended of Yangon's markets, the **Bogyoke Aung San Market** ❹ (formerly the Scott Market) is to the north of the Indian and Chinese markets. At the corner of Sule Pagoda Road and Bogyoke Aung San Street, next to the red-brick Railway Administration Building with its Moorish arches, the market houses a wonderful range of Burmese handicrafts. Items sold here include jewellery, a wide variety of textiles and craft objects, woodcarvings, lacquerware, dolls, musical instruments, colourful *longyis*, Shan bags and wickerware. Opposite the Bogyoke Market, the New Bogyoke Market sells imported textiles, household appliances and medicines.

The days when it was difficult to buy a light bulb in Yangon are long gone. For Yangonians the problem has now become the affordability of the goods available. Since the government has introduced a market economy, those goods that once were smuggled in from Thailand are now imported legally. Some of the smaller streets off Merchant Street and around Anawrahta and Pansodan streets are full of TV sets, cameras, refrigerators, tape and video recorders piled case upon case. There are, however, no bargains, and prices are quite high.

On the streets around the markets, especially at the corner of Sule Pagoda Road and Bogyoke Aung San Street, you can sometimes find makeshift stalls selling cheap jeans, T-shirts and other clothes imported from Bangladesh,

The Railway Administration Building stands next to the Bogyoke Aung San Market.

BELOW: many people live in tenements built during the colonial period.

posters, maps and houseware. Walk along the west side of Sule Pagoda Road back towards Sule Pagoda, and you will find the **Yangon Duty-Free Shop ❺**. Tourists are encouraged to shop here, especially for precious stones, on which the Burmese government has a monopoly. The advantage of buying jewellery here is that quality is guaranteed. The shop sells a wide selection of other goods, including imported foodstuffs not readily available elsewhere, liquor and cigarettes; but all payment must be made in foreign currency or credit cards. A few doors away is the office of Myanmar Airways International.

Peek into the past

Travelling northwest of Sule Pagoda towards Pyay Road, you'll arrive at the **National Museum ❻** (open daily 10am–4pm; entrance fee) in a neighbourhood filled with foreign missions. The museum showpiece is the Lion's Throne, King Thibaw's throne in Mandalay Palace. Taken from Mandalay in 1886 after the Third Anglo-Burmese War, the throne and 52 other pieces of royal regalia were carried off by the British. Some items were left behind in the Indian Museum in Calcutta; others were kept in London's Victoria and Albert Museum. The artefacts were returned to Burma as a gesture of goodwill in 1964 after Ne Win's state visit to Britain. The wooden throne, 8-metres (27-ft) high and inlaid with gold and lacquer-work, is a particularly striking example of the Burmese art of woodcarving. Among the Mandalay Regalia, as the collection is known, are gem-studded arms, swords, jewellery and serving dishes. Artefacts from Burma's early history in Beikthano, Thayekhittaya and Bagan in the museum's archaeological section include an 18th-century bronze cannon and a crocodile-shaped harp. The area around the museum is full of street bazaars and lanes

BELOW: eating at one of Yangon's many food markets.

Map on pages 116–7

filled with popular teahouses and food stalls. From here, it's a short journey of 10 to 15 minutes by taxi to the **Shwedagon Pagoda** ❼ (open daily 4am–9pm; entrance fee, tickets are not sold to foreigners before 6am).

There are a number of entrances to the pagoda. Those unwilling to walk up the stairways can take the lift straight up to the pagoda where tickets to foreign visitors are sold. The southern and eastern stairways take the visitor past several stalls selling the typical Buddhist "*nibbana* goods". Buddha images in alabaster, ivory and marble, gilded *nat*-images, umbrellas and prayer flags, puppets and sandalwood prayer-beads are all found in a variety of stalls that offer fragrant jasmine, champak and magnolia flowers as well.

Shwedagon Pagoda

TIP

The best time to visit the Shwedagon Pagoda is at sunrise or sunset.

"The Shwe Dagon rose superb, glistening with its gold, like a sudden hope in the dark night of the soul of which the mystics write glistening against the fog and smoke of the thriving city."
– W. Somerset Maugham, *The Gentleman in the Parlour* (1930)

It has been said there is more gold on the Shwedagon Pagoda than in the vaults of the Bank of England. So even when not seen with mystical eyes, but rationally, Burma possesses a hidden kind of wealth. The massive bell-shaped stupa, which soars nearly 100 metres (330 ft) above its hilltop surroundings, is a treasure trove inside and out. Inside, according to legend, are eight enshrined hairs of the last Buddha, as well as relics of three previous Buddhas.

Outside, the stupa is plated with 8,688 solid gold slabs. The tip of the stupa is set with 5,448 diamonds and 2,317 rubies, sapphires and topaz. An enormous emerald sits in the middle to catch the first and last rays of the sun. All this is mounted on and above a 10-metre (33-ft) *hti* (umbrella), built upon seven gold-plated bars and decorated with 1,485 bells, 1,065 of them golden, 420 silver. The golden stupa is surrounded by more than 100 buildings – smaller stupas, pavilions and administrative halls.

BELOW: the stupa at Shwedagon Pagoda.

Although the origins of the pagoda are shrouded in legend, it is known for sure that the pagoda was well-established by the time Bagan dominated Burma in the 11th century. Anawrahta visited the Shwedagon during one of his southern campaigns and, in 1372, King Byinnya U of Bago (Pegu) had the pagoda renovated. Fifty years later, King Binnyagyan raised the stupa to a height of 90 metres (295 ft).

Binnyagyan's successor, Queen Shinsawpu (who ruled for 19 years from 1453 to 1472), is still revered for giving the pagoda its present shape and form. She not only established the terraces and walls around the stupa, but gave her weight in gold (40 kg/90 lbs) to be beaten into gold leaf and used to plate the stupa. Not to be outdone, her successor, Dhammazedi, donated four times his weight in gold.

In 1485, Dhammazedi erected three stones on the Shwedagon's eastern stairway. The stones recount the history of the pagoda, from the time of its legendary founding onwards, in the Burmese, Pali and Mon languages. The inscriptions can still be seen.

*Guard statues
outside a shrine at
Shwedagon Pagoda.*

BELOW:
the Maha Gandha
Bell at Shwedagon
Pagoda in 1825.

Much of the ensuing history of the Shwedagon revolves around its bells. A bell weighing approximately 30 tons, which Dhammazedi had donated, was plundered in 1608 by the Portuguese mercenary Philip de Brito y Nicote, who was based in Syriam, but unfortunately it fell into the Bago river.

King Hsinbyushin of the Konbaung dynasty raised the stupa to its current height after a devastating earthquake in 1768 brought down the top of the pagoda. His son, Singu, had a 23-ton bronze bell cast in 1779; known as the Maha Gandha bell, it can be found today on the northwest side of the main pagoda platform. The British pillaged the pagoda during their 1824–26 wartime occupation and tried to carry the bell to Calcutta, but once again, the ill-fated bell sank into the river. A third bell weighing more than 40 tons was donated by King Tharrawaddy in 1841 along with another 20 kg (45 lbs) of gold plating. Today, this Maha Tissada bell sits on the northeast side of the pagoda enclosure.

King Mindon's defiance

The Shwedagon was under British military control for 77 years between 1852 (the Second Anglo-Burmese War) and 1929. But despite the presence of the colonial rulers, the Burmese were not denied access to the pagoda. In 1871, King Mindon of Mandalay sent a new diamond-studded *hti* to the pagoda. The delighted Burmese celebrated with a festive procession involving more than 100,000 people at the Shwedagon. The British were none too pleased by the ruler's open statement of independence, but were powerless to stop the action.

In the 20th century, natural disasters took their toll. In 1930, the year before the Shwedagon was half-destroyed by fire, a small earthquake caused minor

damage. Another earthquake in 1970 led the government to initiate a special project to strengthen the pagoda's crown. For all the Shwedagon's roller-coaster history, the Burmese are convinced no lasting damage can befall it. Whenever the pagoda has been endangered, the unfailing generosity of the local people has facilitated work to restore it to even greater glories.

Fire on the stairway

The passageway most commonly used by visitors to the Shwedagon is the **Southern Stairway** *(zaungdan)*, which ascends from the direction of the city centre. Its 104 steps lead from Shwedagon Pagoda Road to the main platform. The entrance is closely guarded by a couple of statues representing two fearful mythological creatures – the *chinthe*, or leogryph, is a half-lion, half-griffin; the ogre, or giant, is a man-eating monster. There is a public lift next to the southern stairway.

The **Western Stairway** **Ⓑ**, which leads up from U Wisara Road, was closed for almost 80 years during the time of the British occupation. Originally erected by Ma May Gale, the wife of King Tharrawaddy, the stairway was damaged during the Second Anglo-Burmese War and kept closed by soldiers from the British garrison. In 1931, a stall at the foot of the stairs caught fire. The blaze raced up and around the northern flank of the Shwedagon, causing severe damage to the precincts before being halted on the eastern stairway; unfortunately not in time to save the many ancient monuments that were destroyed.

The Western Stairway is the longest *zaungdan* with 166 steps. The landing on the platform bears the name **Two Pice Tazaung** because of the contribution of two pice (a small copper coin) given daily by Buddhist businessmen and bazaar-stall holders for the stairway's reconstruction.

The **Northern Stairway** **Ⓒ** was built in 1460 by Queen Shinsawbu, and has 128 steps. The decorative borders to the steps are shaped like crocodiles. Two water tanks can be seen to the north of the stairway; the one on the right bears the name *thwezekan*, meaning "blood wash-tank". The name is derived from a popular legend, which recounts that during King Anawrahta's conquest of the Mon capital Thaton, his commander-in-chief, Kyanzittha, used the tank to clean his blood-stained weapons. The northern entrance also features a public lift.

The **Eastern Stairway** **Ⓓ** is much like an extension of the Bahan bazaar, which lies between the Royal Lake and the Shwedagon. Here there are souvenir and flower shops, and bookstalls. You might want to take a break at one of the teahouses on the stairway near the **Dhammazedi Stones**, placed there by the king in 1485. This stairway of 118 steps suffered heavy damage during the British attack on the pagoda in 1852.

"Fantastic richness"

Walk up the stairs and you'll be stunned by the sight of the upper terrace. In Maugham's words: "At last we reached the great terrace. All about, shrines and pagodas were jumbled pell-mell with the confusion with which trees grow in the jungle. They had been built without design or symmetry, but in the darkness,

Map on page 118

TIP

Visitors are required to take off their shoes and socks before climbing the steps of the Southern Stairway.

BELOW: one of the covered stairways leading to the Shwedagon Pagoda.

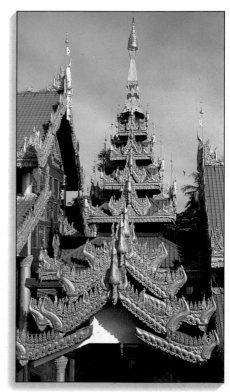

their gold and marble faintly gleaming, they had a fantastic richness. And then, emerging from among them like a great ship surrounded by lighters, rose dim, severe and splendid, the Shwe Dagon."

The terrace was created in the 15th century when the rulers of Bago levelled off the top of the 58-metre (190-ft) high Singuttara Hill. The terrace measures 275 metres (902 ft) from north to south and 215 metres (705 ft) from east to west. It is 5.6 hectares (14 acres) in area and is supported by a 15-metre (49-ft) high retaining wall. The main platform is inlaid with marble slabs, which can be very hot under unaccustomed bare feet, so a mat pathway is laid out around the platform. Walk around and discover various prayer pavilions *(tazaung)* and resting places *(zayat)* with traditional roofs of five, seven or nine tiers.

Eight sides, 64 stupas

At the centre of the platform is the famed gold-covered stupa. Its circumference at platform level is 433 metres (1,421 ft). Its base is octagonal and on each of the eight sides are eight smaller stupas, making 64 in all. The four stupas opposite the stairways are the largest. At each of the platform's four corners are *manokthiha* (sphinxes), each surrounded by several *chinthe*.

On top of the main platform are three rectangular terraces *(pichaya)* topped by octagonal terraces, which in turn support five circular bands. By means of this geometry, the vertical sides of the terraces merge with the swollen shape of the stupa's bell. The terraces account for 24 metres (79 ft) of the stupa's height. The next 22 metres (72 ft) comprise the bell *(khaung laung bon)*. This section is 105 metres (344 ft) in diameter and has a design of 16 petals on its shoulder. Above the bell is the 12.5-metre (42-ft) high vaulted turban *(baungyit)*, then an

BELOW:
pagodas dwarf
monks on the
Shwedagon terrace.

inverted bowl *(thabeik)* covered with lotus petals *(kyahlan)*, which together measure 9.5 metres (32 ft) in height. The slender, heavily bejewelled part of the stupa begins above this point with a 16-metre (52-ft) banana bud *(hnget pyaw bu)*. The whole edifice is crowned by the 10-metre (33-ft) vane capped by a golden orb *(seinbu)*, tipped with a single, exquisite 76-carat diamond.

Map on page 118

From the top of the southern stairway, begin walking left, or clockwise – the direction always to be taken at all Buddhist monuments. Straight ahead at the top of the stairs is the **Temple of the Konagamana Buddha Ⓔ**. Renovated in 1947, it is one of four *tazaung* dedicated to previous Buddhas. In this temple are a great number of Buddha figures, probably among the oldest to be seen at the pagoda. Notice how the style and finish of these figures differ quite markedly from those produced today.

Planetary posts

To the left and right of the Konagamana Temple you will see the **Planetary Post for Mercury**. There are eight of these planetary posts around the stupa, and a gilded alabaster Buddha figure is to be found beside each one. Locals give offerings of flowers and small flags here, and the figures are ritually washed. The planet Mercury is associated with a tusked elephant, and it has a special day, Bohddahu, which runs from midnight to noon on Wednesday according to the eight-day Burmese week.

On the southwestern side of the stupa is the **Planetary Post for Saturn**, which is allied to the *naga* (mythological serpent) and whose special day is Saturday. Opposite this post is the **Chinese Community's Tazaung Ⓕ**, a pavilion housing 28 small Buddha figures representing the 28 Buddhas who have so

People from all walks of life come to Shwedagon to make merit for the next life.

BELOW: lighting candles at a planetary post.

A Buddha image in the pavilion of the Maha Gandha Bell.

BELOW: devotee at Shwedagon.

far lived on earth. Not far from the southwest corner of the platform is a **Commemorative Column G** inscribed in Burmese, English, French and Russian. The column honours the 1920 student revolt which sparked Burma's drive for independence from Britain. A short distance north, the **Guardian Nat of the Shwedagon**, Bo Bo Gyi, is kept behind glass (on the right) with the figure of Thagyamin, king of the *nat*.

Entering Nibbana

Continuing down this side of the platform, the visitor encounters the **Rakhaing (Arakan) Tazaung H**. Next to this pavilion, built by two Rakhaing (Arakanese), is an 8.5-metre (28-ft) reclining Buddha. The Buddha's head is pointing north, indicating that he is in a state of transition into *nibbana* (nirvana). At his foot is a figure of Ananda, his favourite pupil, as well as figures of Shin Sariputta and Shin Moggalana, two of the Buddha's apostles who left this world before their teacher. Pictures on the rear wall of the Rakhaing Tazaung depict the legend of the founding of the Kyaik-tiyo Pagoda near Thaton. The pavilion is inlaid with beautiful, intricate woodcarvings, as is the neighbouring **Chinese Merchants' Tazaung**. There are many Buddha images here.

Opposite these two pavilions are **Statues of Me La Mu and Sakka I**. These two legendary figures are said to be the parents of King Okkalapa, the founder of the Shwedagon. They are situated under white umbrellas, the symbol of royalty, on the first terrace on the southwestern side of the stupa. The homeland of Sakka (or Thagyamin), king of the *nat*, is in the heavenly province of Mount Meru, the centre of the universe. Me La Mu, considered the founder of a pagoda bearing her name in northern Yangon, is said to have been born from the La Mu fruit. Directly across the platform from the Two Pice Tazaung is the **Temple of the Kassapa Buddha J**. Originally constructed by Ma May Gale in 1841, it was burnt down by the great fire of 1931 and later rebuilt. Flanking it is the **Planetary Post for Jupiter**. This planet is allied with the rat and associated with Thursday. Further to the north is a **Statue of King Okkalapa**, situated under a white umbrella on the northwestern side of the stupa. In the northwest corner is the **Planetary Post for Rahu**, the mythical planet allied with the tuskless elephant and associated with Wednesday afternoon.

In an open area to the northwest of the stupa is a small octagonal pagoda known as the **Pagoda of the Eight Weekdays K**. On each side of this pagoda is a niche containing a small Buddha image, with the image of an animal placed above it, corresponding to the eight Burmese weekdays.

Behind it is the **Maha Gandha Bell L**, the huge bronze bell King Singu had cast in 1779 and which was raised from the Yangon River in 1825 after the British attempted to steal it. The bell weighs 23 tons, is 2.2 metres (over 7 ft) high and has a diameter of two metres (6½ ft) at its mouth. A 12-line inscription requests that the donor *(singu)* reach *nibbana* for performing this good deed. Across from the bell pavilion is an **Assembly Hall M** in which there is a 9-metre (30-ft) high Buddha image. Lectures on Buddhist teachings are frequently held in this *tazaung*. The *sayadaws* (abbots), who often speak here in front of several hundred saffron-clad monks, are among the most respected men in Burmese society. The Buddha figure gives the impression that the Buddha is actually present and watching the proceedings.

Where wishes come true

There are a number of small stupas in the northwestern corner of the terrace. In one of these is the **Wonder Working Buddha Image**, which is nearly always decorated with flowers and surrounded closely by the faithful. The gilded Buddha in the stupa's niche has the reputation of being able to fulfil wishes and work miracles.

In the far northwest corner of the terrace are two **Bodhi Trees** decorated with flowers and small flags. The smaller of the two trees is a cutting from the holy Bodhi tree in Bodhgaya, India, under which the Gautama Buddha gained enlightenment. It was planted by U Nu, the first prime minister of Burma from 1948 to 1962. The second tree is slightly older, having been planted in 1903, and its roots have grown to surround several small altars.

Returning to the main part of the pavilion, you'll notice an especially busy area. This is known as the **Wish Fulfilling Place**, where devotees kneel, facing the great Shwedagon stupa, and earnestly pray that their wishes will come true. In a nearby cluster of pavilions not far from the north entrance is the **Tazaung with Buddha's Footprint** . Life-sized statues of Indian guards stand in front of this hall, and a dragon stands guard over a representation of the Buddha as prince. In front of the "prince" is a *chidawya,* or footprint of the Buddha. The footprint is divided into 108 sections, each of which has a special significance.

Buddhists show their devotion in many ways – chanting in unison, meditating, "reciting" beads, prostrating on the ground or bathing images with water.

LEFT AND BELOW: bathing Buddha images in lustral water is part of popular Buddhist practice.

Astrology plays an important role in deciding auspicious days for special occasions. Zodiacal planets are named after Hindu deities.

To the south is the library of the **Zediyingana Society** , which has more than 6,000 books, many of them rare texts on religion and Burmese culture. The Zediyingana Society is one of seven societies responsible for maintaining Burma's pagodas and making the necessary improvements.

Between the library and the stupa is the **Sandawdwin Tazaung** ⓟ, built in 1879 over the spring in which, according to legend, the Buddha's eight hairs were washed before they were enshrined. The spring is said to be fed by the Ayeyarwady (Irrawaddy) River. On the north side of the main stupa you will find the Temple of the **Gautama Buddha**. It is dedicated to the Buddha, whose world dominion, it is believed, will last until the 45th century. Beside it is the **Planetary Post for Venus**, which is especially popular among people born on a Friday. Across the platform is the **Mahabodhi Pagoda** ⓠ, a replica of the original pagoda of the same name in Bodhgaya. You will notice that it is very different from all the other pagodas in the Shwedagon precincts, which are built in distinct Bamar (Burman) or Mon styles.

A Burmese oracle

BELOW:
the Maha Tissada Bell at Shwedagon Pagoda.

Across from the northeast corner of the stupa is the **Kannaze Tazaung** ⓡ. According to legend, it was here that King Okkalapa prayed for relics of the Gautama Buddha. The Buddha figure in this shrine is thus called Sudaungbyi, meaning "Buddha grants the prayer of the king". In front of this is the "wish-granting stone", a sort of Delphic oracle. The etiquette is to bow before Sudaungbyi and lift the stone, saying, "May this stone seem light to me, if my wish is to be fulfilled." If the stone still feels heavy, the request has not been successful and the applicant's wish will presumably remain unfulfilled.

North of this pavilion is the **Shin Itzagona Tazaung** . Inside it is a Buddha statue with large eyes of different sizes. It is said to have been erected by or for Shin Itzagona, a *zawgyi* (alchemist) from Bagan's early period. According to legend, Itzagona's obsession with discovering the Philosopher's Stone, the mythical substance said to be able to change base metals to gold or silver, plunged the country into poverty. When his final experiment was about to end in failure, he poked out both his eyes to satisfy the king. But in his final casting, he did produce the Philosopher's Stone. He immediately sent his assistant to the slaughterhouse to obtain two eyes that would, with the stone's help, allow him to regain his sight. The assistant returned with one eye from a goat and another from a bull; from that time on, Shin Itzagona was known as "Monk Goat-Bull".

Just to the north is the **Naungdawgyi Pagoda** ❼, situated in the place where the eight hairs of the Buddha, carried by the merchants Tapussa and Bhallika, were originally kept. Nearby is the **Maha Tissada Bell** ❽, commissioned by King Tharrawaddy in 1841. It weighs almost 42 tons, is 2.55 metres (8 ft 4 in) high and has a diameter of 2.3 metres (7 ft 6 in) at its mouth.

The **Planetary Post for the Sun** is at the northeast corner of the great stupa. Its special day, of course, is Sunday and it is associated with the *galon*, the mythical bird (called *garuda* elsewhere in Southeast Asia) which guards one of the terraces of Mount Meru. Across the platform to the east are a **Replica of the Hti** originally donated by King Hsinbyushin in 1774, and a **Replica of the Apex of the Pagoda**, sent by King Mindon from Mandalay in 1871.

Keep your eye on the hand

Opposite the Eastern Stairway is the **Temple of the Kakusandha Buddha** ❾. This temple was built by Ma May Gale, the wife of King Tharrawaddy, as was the Western Stairway, and was destroyed by the fire of 1931. The temple was rebuilt in its original style in 1940. The Buddha figure in this *tazaung* is unusual in that the palm of its right hand is turned upwards, in contrast to that of other representations of the Buddha. In front of the niche are four sitting Buddhas, three of whom are also depicted in this unfamiliar posture.

Behind the temple, in a niche on the eastern side of the upper platform, is the **Tawa Gu Buddha** ❿. This statue is said to be able to work miracles. The upper platform of the pagoda is reserved for men, and only men are permitted to buy an admission ticket at the administration building on the west side of the pagoda. On the upper platform, the visitor will come across devout Buddhists, both monks and novices, deep in meditation. Beside the Kakusandha temple is the **Planetary Post for the Moon**, which is recognised as one of the eight planets in Burmese astrology. The tiger is its animal, Monday its day. From this point, the visitor can turn around and descend the Eastern Stairway just a short distance to arrive at the **Dhammazedi Stones**.

The *tazaung* which originally housed these stones was one of the last buildings destroyed by the 1931 fire before the blaze was finally brought under control. King Dhammazedi, himself a *zawgyi*, has gone down

BELOW:
taking a rest with the *chinthe*.

A constant stream of Buddhist devotees arrive at the Shwedagon to worship. These include people by themselves, families with toddlers, bearded hermits in leather hats and brown garb, and visiting hill-tribe groups dressed in traditional costumes.

in Burmese history as the "master of the runes". Next to the eastern entrance of the terrace is the **U Nyo Tazaung**, which has wood-carved panels that recount events in the life of the Gautama Buddha. Close to the southeast corner of the platform is a **Hamsa Tagundaing ✖** or prayer pillar. Such pillars are said to guarantee the health, prosperity and success of their founders. At the top of the pillars is a *hamsa* or *hintha,* sacred bird of the Bago dynasty. On the southeast side of the great stupa is the **Planetary Post for Mars**. This planet is associated with the lion and its corresponding day is Tuesday.

At the far southeastern corner of the terrace is a **Bodhi Tree** which, like its cousin in the northwest corner, is said to be a cutting of the original at Bodhgaya. On the octagonal base which surrounds it is a huge Buddha statue. A **Curio Museum** (open daily; entrance fee) is situated to the east of the pagoda's south entrance. It contains a collection of small pagodas, statues and other objects.

Part of the way down the Southern Stairway you will find a **Pigeon Feeding Square**. Pagoda pilgrims can buy food here to feed the dozens of pigeons, thereby earning merit for a future existence.

Modern martyrs

A short distance from the Shwedagon Pagoda is the **Maha Wizaya Pagoda**, a contemporary structure built in 1980 to commemorate the unification of all Theravada orders in Burma. On a hill on Arzarni Road (Transport Road), just to the north and past the Shwedagon Pagoda, is the **Martyrs' Mausoleum ❽**. This patriotic monument contains the tombs of Aung San, father of Aung San Suu Kyi and the leader of the Burmese independence movement, and six of his ministers who were assassinated during a cabinet meeting in 1947. Aung San

BELOW:
feeding the pigeons.

was only 32 at the time. The pre-World War II prime minister, U Saw, was subsequently found to be the instigator of the plot, and he was executed the following year, together with the hired assassins.

From the mausoleum, go north towards the intersection of Shwegondaing Road. Located here, on Campbell Road, is the **Ngahtatgyi** ❾ a huge sitting Buddha, sometimes called the "five-storey Buddha" because of its size. It is housed in the Ashay Tawya Kyaung monastery.

From here, turn east to the **Kyaukhtatgyi Pagoda** ❿. Not really a pagoda in the traditional sense, the Kyaukhtatgyi is actually a *tazaung* (pavilion) housing a 70-metre (230-ft) long reclining Buddha. The Buddha figure, which is only a few decades old, required donations amounting to approximately US$70,000 to construct. Before the Kyaukhtatgyi was built, an older Buddha figure dating from the turn of the 20th century was housed under the pagoda's roof. Although the newer sculpture is bigger than the reclining Shwethalyaung Buddha of Bago, it is not as well-known or as highly venerated.

Elsewhere in the pagoda enclosure is a centre devoted to the study of sacred Buddhist manuscripts. The 600 monks who live in the monastery annex spend their days meditating and studying the old Pali texts.

Picnics and playgrounds

There are more than a dozen public parks in the city of Yangon and locals take great pleasure in spending the hot hours of the day resting in them, preferably beside a lake, in the shade given by canopies of leaves atop enormous, old trees. The parks also provide pleasant breaks for visitors as they criss-cross the city from one sight to the other, wondering what to see and where to go next. On the

Maps:
City: 116
Site: 118

BELOW:
the reclining
Buddha at
Kyaukhtatgyi
Pagoda.

Visit Bogyoke Aung
San Park at night
when open-air
restaurants offer
barbecued food –
and in some cases,
folkloric
performances – in
cool surroundings.

BELOW:
the Karaweik
Restaurant on the
shores of the
Royal Lake.

north shore of **Kandawgyi** (Royal Lake), **Bogyoke Aung San Park** ⓫ features a statue of the country's most famous martyr. The park stretches beyond the **Aung San Statue** and into the lake like the fingers on a hand. The plants and trees have been labelled for easy identification, as though this were a botanical garden. The children's playgrounds and picnic areas have become very popular attractions among the people of Yangon, and families can be seen idling away their leisure hours beside the lake.

Other lake-side attractions

Another memorable view is from the **Karaweik Restaurant**, on the lake's eastern shore. This luxurious restaurant, constructed in the early 1970s, was designed after the distinctive *pyi-gyi-mun* barge that belonged to Burmese royalty. With its double bow depicting the mythological *karaweik*, a water bird from Indian pre-history, and a multi-tiered pagoda carried on top, the Karaweik Restaurant represents the style and workmanship of traditional Burmese architecture. The restaurant was constructed with brick and concrete (wood was not considered because it has a relatively short life span) and anchored to the lake bottom.

The interior contains some marvellous lacquerwork embellished with mosaics in glass, marble and mother-of-pearl. Although you have to pay a small admission charge just to take a look, once inside, you will probably appreciate the great food and the stunning view of the Shwedagon. Classical dance performances are normally held here in the evenings.

There are several attractions on the southern shore of the Royal Lake. The Natural History Museum that used to be here has been moved and the building's

structure has been remodelled into what is now the joint-venture Kandawgyi Hotel. In the museum's absence, local flora can be closely examined at the **Horticultural Garden** (open daily) off Lu Oh Yone Street.

Death of a white elephant

The **Yangon Zoological Gardens** (open daily 8am–6pm; entrance fee) on Bo Min Gaung Street (King Edward Avenue) has a good collection of birds, reptiles, apes and other animals. Elephant rides are available at the zoo at 4pm every day. A rare white elephant used to be the biggest attraction at the zoo. In the past, the possession of such a creature was enough to cause the outbreak of wars during the course of Burma's rocky history. Unfortunately, this particular white elephant died in 1979.

If you are travelling by train, get off at Kyemyindaing, the next station north-west of Yangon on the Circle Line. The **Koehtatgyi Pagoda** on Bargayar Road is just a short walk away from the station. There is a 20-metre (65-ft) high sitting Buddha inside the pagoda, and a small casket inside the statue is said to contain relics of the Buddha and some of his disciples. In the area surrounding the pagoda are a great many *kyaung* (monasteries). This is a good vantage point from which to watch the *pongyi* (monks) as they emerge onto the streets early in the morning carrying their alms bowls. Continuing northeast through the winding residential streets north of the Shwedagon, past the "Yangon modern" stucco houses built for Westerners in the colonial era, is the enormous artificial **Inya Lake**. The Yangon University is located on the southern shore, as is some of the city's most modern architecture. Also to be found here is the city's sailing club, which regularly organises races on the lake.

Motorcycles can be hired by visitors to get around the city – check your bike over before setting off.

There are several interesting handicraft and art galleries within the area of the lake, all of which sell décor items. There are also a number of artisan workshops. Those of weavers and woodcarvers are situated near University Avenue, Kaba Aye Pagoda Road and Thanlwin Road, whereas glass-blowers tend to congregate on Yogi Kyaung Street (off Insein Road) *(see Travel Tips section)*.

Probably the most famous structure on the lake is the **Inya Lake Hotel**, built by the Soviet Union in the early 1960s. In the decades after the Inya Lake opened, most visitors to Yangon had little choice but to stay there, in spite of its dismal reputation and bad food. But with growing competition from alternative sources of accommodation, the hotel underwent a major refurbishment – with a subsequent rise in room rates as well. Now that a Hong Kong-based company is one of its owners, the hotel has improved to 4-star standards and at last living up to its potential.

A little way north of Inya Lake is the **Kaba Aye Pagoda ⑫**. On the same road leading towards it is the fascinating **Gems Museum ⑬** (No. 66, Kaba Aya Pagoda Road; closed Mon; Tues–Sun 9am–5pm; entrance fee), which is well worth visiting. The jewellery shops are located on the first and second floors, while the museum is on the third floor. Twice a year, in March and October, the gems fair and auction held here attracts many jewel dealers from all over the

BELOW: a Buddhist saint image at Kaba Aye Pagoda.

world. Everywhere you go there are shining nuggets of star sapphires, luscious golden pearls, rare sparkling pigeon's blood rubies and slabs of precious jade that come in various sizes and shades.

The legend of Kaba Aye

U Nu, the first prime minister of independent Burma, ordered the Kaba Aye Pagoda to be built in the early 1950s. The story associated with its origins shows that, in Burma, legendary tales are not confined to its distant and mythical past but can also apply to contemporary people and buildings. An old man dressed in white is said to have appeared before the monk Saya Htay while the latter was meditating near the town of Pakokku on the Ayeyarwady River. The old man handed the monk a bamboo pole covered with writing. He asked Saya Htay to pass the pole on to U Nu, accompanied by a demand that the prime minister actively do more for Buddhism.

U Nu was as well-versed in religious affairs as in politics; he not only received the bamboo pole but amazingly complied with the old man's demand. The country's leader built the Kaba Aye Pagoda about 12 km (8 miles) north of downtown Yangon in preparation for the Sixth Buddhist Synod of 1954 to 1956, and dedicated it to the cause of world peace.

Although lacking some of the aesthetic appeal that distinguishes the other Yangon pagodas, the Kaba Aye is very interesting nonetheless. Architecturally, it is circular in shape, and its height and diameter are an identical 34 metres (112 ft). Theologically, it contains relics of the two most important disciples of the Buddha. These were discovered in 1851 by an English general serving in the Indian subcontinent, and were only returned to their rightful place in the Kaba

BELOW: a golden Buddha image at Kaba Aye Pagoda.

THE GEM FAIR AND AUCTION

Twice a year, usually in March and October, the week-long gems fair and auction at Yangon's *(see page 141)* Gems Museum attracts jewel merchants from around the world. The merchants first view the raw and cut gems on display before the bidding begins, normally during the last two days of the fair.

The main attraction is the variety and quality of raw jade; Burma is known to be the only country in the world still to have plentiful quality jade. The jade blocks can vary in size and value from a mere 2-kg (4½-lb) slab of the coveted deep-green Imperial jade (US$350,000 or more) to a 2-ton boulder of a lighter jade that might go for US$180,000. Rubies from the mines of Mogok in the north and pearls from the Myeik archipelago in the south are both highly prized and much sought-after.

Whether cut or in raw form, the gems are sold in lots, each of which has a stipulated reserve price. Although most of the lots exceed their reserve prices, gems can be withdrawn from sale if the reserve price is not met.

It's interesting to follow the merchants around as they assess the value of the raw materials. Armed with a magnifying glass and a torchlight, they look for cracks and other flaws that are not always visible to the naked eye.

Aye Pagoda after spending many years at the British Museum in London. You will see five 2.4-metre (8-ft) high Buddha statues standing opposite each of the five pagoda entrances. A platform holds another 28 small gold-plated statues that represent previous Buddhas. It took some 500 kg (1,100 lbs) of silver to cast the Buddha figure in the inner temple.

Map on pages 116–7

The great cave

On the grounds of the Kaba Aye Pagoda is the **Maha Pasana Guha**, or "great cave". U Nu had this artificial cave specially built for the Sixth Buddhist Synod. It is supposed to resemble India's Satta Panni Cave, where the First Buddhist Synod took place shortly after the death of Gautama Buddha.

Devout Buddhists worked voluntarily, without payment, on the construction of the cave. It was completed after 14 months' work in 1954, incredibly only three days before the start of the synod. The cave measures 139 metres by 113 metres (456 ft by 371 ft) and has an assembly hall that can accommodate up to 10,000 people. When the Sixth Buddhist Synod ended, the Institute for Advanced Buddhist Studies was founded with its headquarters in the Kaba Aye Pagoda compound. Funds from the Ford Foundation contributed to the construction of its handsome building, which successfully blends elements of modern architecture with traditional symbolism.

A striking Buddha image outside the Me La Mu Pagoda.

The **Me La Mu Pagoda** ⓮ is situated further north, near the Yangon Airport in the suburb of Okkalapa. This pagoda is named after the mother of King Okkalapa, founder of Dagon. According to legend, Me La Mu had this pagoda built to alleviate her grief after the untimely death of her young grandson. Her statue can still be seen on the southwestern flank of the Shwedagon Pagoda. This pagoda is of particular interest because it contains numerous illustrations and figures from the *Jataka* tales, depicting the Buddha in earlier lives and fashioned in a singularly Burmese style. The pagoda also features a reclining Buddha.

BELOW: a Buddha image at the Me La Mu Pagoda in the *abhaya mudra* attitude.

West of the international airport, in the township of Insein, you will find the fascinating **Ah Lain Nga Sint Pagoda** ⓯. This pagoda is a centre of worship for adherents of the branch of Burmese Buddhism that places great emphasis on the occult and supernatural phenomena. The grounds contain a five-storey tower, a hall with statues of all kinds of occult figures, and a *kyaung* which serves as a residence for monks and believers in the occult.

It is fitting that this pagoda is outside Yangon city itself. Generally speaking, the residents of Yangon are not as inclined to worship supernatural deities as are their counterparts in the countryside. But even though few houses in Yangon today have coconuts hanging in their corners in tribute to the house *nat*, few urbanites would totally deny the existence of such spirits.

Although much of what visitors would call "progress" has been stalled in Burma for nearly 30 years, Yangon is finally taking on a new coat of paint. Still, the streets of Yangon and much of the city's ambience lean towards the past, making it indeed, as Rudyard Kipling wrote, "quite unlike any land that one knows about". ❑

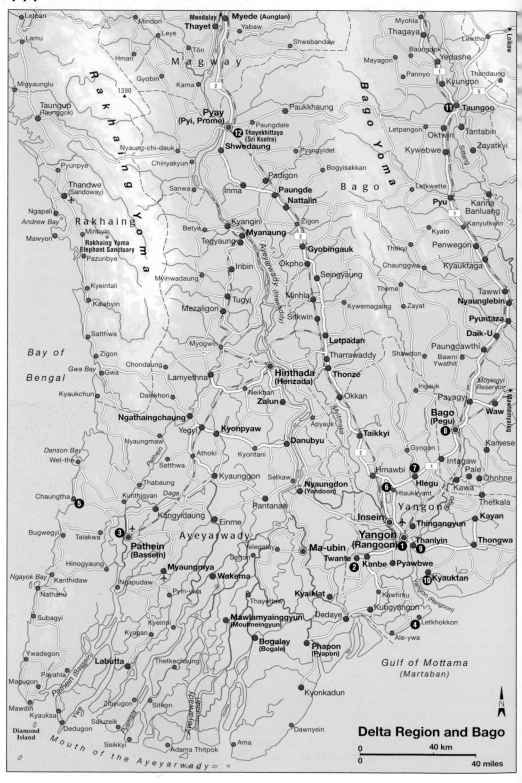

Delta Region and Bago

THE DELTA REGION

The fertile, green delta region – a patchwork of paddy fields stretching as far as the eye can see – offers one of the most beautiful journeys in Burma

Map on page 144

The **Delta Region** west of **Yangon** ❶ is the rice bowl of Burma where patchwork quilts of lime-green paddies dominate the landscape. It is one of the country's most fertile regions, due to the rich silt deposited by the Ayeyarwady as it courses the final stretch of its 1,200-km (750-mile) journey, from its source in Upper Burma to the Andaman Sea. The river threads, like so many fingers, into a number of narrow canals.

The delta is populated by the fairly large towns of Pathein, Myaungmya, Wakema, Ma-ubin and Twante, of which the most interesting are Pathein and Twante, which mark the beginning and end of the delta's navigable route. The delta also supports rice-cultivating villages and settlements, fish farms and the occasional pagoda. The fish farms, which grow carp, threadfin and giant sea perch, as well as shellfish such as crabs and freshwater lobsters, flourish on rich nutrients brought in by the Ayeyarwady. Most of the farm's produce is exported to Thailand, Singapore and the US. The rice paddies attract migratory wading birds such as the egret and heron.

The pottery town of **Twante** ❷ is easily reached by a combination of ferry and road from Yangon. The ferry leaves from the pier opposite the Myanmar Port Authority Building next to the Strand Hotel. The five-minute voyage across the Yangon River ends at Dalah where waiting jeeps can ferry you into the heart of the delta region at Twante. The drive to Twante takes about two hours. Five km (3 miles) before Twante, a turn-off leads to the **Snake Temple**, which comprises three red, Indian-style temples each crowned with a gilded stupa. Dedicated to the worship of the *naga*, the temple has a shrine where the former chief abbot of a nearby monastery lies embalmed.

BELOW: the town square in Pathein.

Twante Canal

Twante marks the start of the Twante Canal, dug by the British in the 19th century because the delta's slender rivers were too narrow for shipping. The canal allowed ships plying the Ayeyarwady to sail directly to Yangon from the north instead of tracing a convoluted journey through natural rivers that led first to the open sea and back to Yangon. It remains a vital waterway connecting Yangon with Pathein, the largest town and port in the delta. It is also the home stretch for ships sailing on the Ayeyarwady from the north. Twante has one significant pagoda, the **Shwe San Daw**, and its canal banks are lined with pottery in all shapes and sizes. Visitors can see potters working at kilns and completed pieces being fired.

Beyond Twante is **Pathein** ❸ with a population of about 350,000. Situated 112 km (70 miles) from the Bay of Bengal, it is a port that exports rice and jute (a

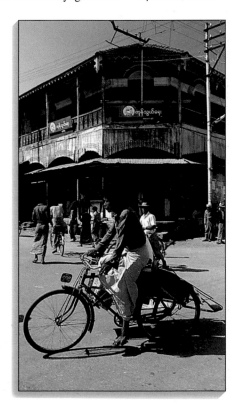

Pathein is famous for the production of pathin hti (parasols) – reflected in the name of the town.

natural fibre), and is well-known for its colourful umbrellas called *pathin hti*. Pathein can be reached from Yangon by train in a rather roundabout fashion (18 hours), but an inland-waterway voyage is still the best way to get there. It is not possible, however, to get to Pathein direct from Twante as the Yangon-Pathein ferry does not stop at Twante. The name "Bassein" was a European pronunciation of Pathein, which is said to derive from the Burmese word for Muslims: Pathi. In past centuries, the town was a settlement for Indian merchants, many of whom were Muslims. Today's inhabitants of Pathein include many Kayin and Rakhaing, some of whom are Christians. The town spreads out around the **Shwemokhtaw Pagoda Ⓐ**, on which pilgrims descend from the delta region during May's full moon.

According to legend, a Muslim princess was responsible for the construction of the pagoda. Princess Onmadandi ordered each of her three lovers to build a pagoda. The first built the Shwemokhtaw, the second the Tazaung Pagoda at the southern end of Pathein, and the third the Thayaunggyaung.

The Buddha's footprint

To the northeast, about a block away, is the rather quaint **Settayaw Pagoda Ⓑ**, which was built around a footprint said to have been left by the Buddha during his travels. A Mandalay-style Buddha image in bronze stands over the footprint. In contrast, at the northern end of town is the **Shwezigon Pagoda Ⓒ** with a sitting Buddha, while at the eastern end of town is the **Twenty-Eight Pagoda**, so named because of its 28 sitting and 28 standing images within.

There are also a number of interesting churches worth seeing. These include the red-and-white-brick **St Peter's Cathedral** (1872) Ⓓ in the southern part of

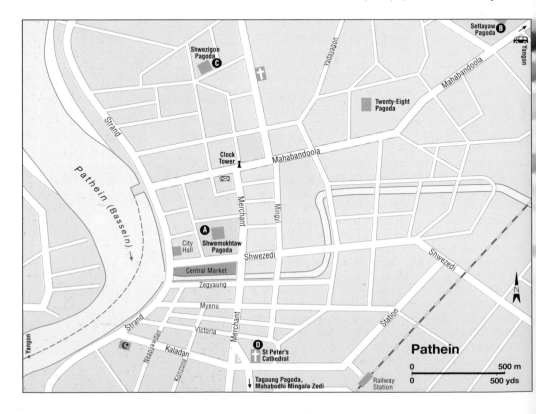

town, and the even older **St Joseph's Convent**, which was once a public school and now serves as an elegant, if rather dilapidated, house for the local clergy.

The main attractions in Pathein, however, are not ecclesiastical but commercial. There are some two dozen parasol workshops, most of them small, family-run affairs. Visitors can observe the various stages involved in making an umbrella – a painstaking process that can take as long as five days. The workshops produce burgundy-coloured umbrellas for monks, and hand-painted "summer" versions with flower motifs for lay people. If you're interested in visiting such a workshop, there are a multitude of them dotted around town in the neighbourhood near the Twenty-Eight Pagoda, for instance, and also on Taw Yakuang Road.

Turtle eggs, which are consumed by the Burmese, are another source of local income. The tiny wooded Diamond Island is located off the mouth of the Pathein (Ngawun) River, in the Andaman Sea some 110 km (70 miles) from Pathein. Hundreds of thousands of turtle eggs are laid on the islet's banks each year.

Beach resorts

Further to the south and to the east of the **Yangon River** estuary, a small seaside resort with a 30-room hotel has been developed at **Letkhokkon ❹** in the Delta region. Letkhokkon provides the nearest access to the sea from Yangon. If you would like to escape the hustle and bustle of city life and have a holiday by the sea without having to travel the long journey to Ngapali in Rakhaing or Chaungtha on the Bay of Bengal near Pathein, Letkhokkon is a good alternative. Do not expect a fancy resort, though. Facilities are rather basic at the Letkhokkon Beach Hotel, though it is popular with weekenders from Yangon. Its restaurant serves reasonably good seafood.

Maps:
Area: 144
City: 146

TIP

The best way to explore Pathein is by trishaw. Try to get one with a rider who speaks some English and who can take you to the main sights and umbrella workshops, which are tucked away along small lanes.

BELOW: sunrise at Letkhokkon.

TWANTE'S FIRED-EARTH

Plain, embellished, small or large – Twante's potteries are the source of virtually all kinds of pottery except the glazed variety. Among the articles made by potters here are vessels that can be used as cooking utensils, water containers, planters, or for holding the incense sticks.

There are about a dozen major pottery works in Twante. In addition to these commercial outlets, quite a number of small households churn out a few pottery pieces to supplement their agricultural income. Counting these, the figure is closer to a hundred potteries.

Ready-to-be-moulded clay is brought in from nearby villages and potters manipulate it into the required consistency. Labourers work in teams of two to fashion the clay by hand into various shapes. While one worker looks after the spinning on the wheel, his partner is responsible for the moulding. Once the moulding is finished, the completed piece of pottery is left to dry in the sun before it is fired, together with other pieces, for up to two days at extremely high temperatures. The complex process of firing and cooling takes about two weeks.

Although much of the pottery produced in Twante is sold locally in the town's market, it is also transported to other parts of the country for sale.

Map
on page
144

There is a village to explore at Letkhokkon and a handful of old wooden pagodas. Though the beach may not be of the same pristine quality as its counterpart at Ngapali, you can enjoy good sunsets, and vendors from the nearby fishing village sell cooked crabs and prawns here.

The beach resort of **Chaungtha ❺** is located at the edge of the Delta region, on the Bay of Bengal coast. It is less well known than Ngapali Beach in Rakhaing but it is quite unspoilt and has a better beach than Letkhokkon. Chaungtha is about 48 km (30 miles) northwest of Pathein. To get there, take a ferry across the Pathein River and continue by bus for another four hours. The ferry crossing is about 40 minutes by road from Pathein.

Chaungtha's facilities have improved considerably in recent years. Where not long ago there used to be just one hotel, there is now a choice of accommodation. And the resort now features windsurfing, sailing and other seasports. If you want to spend some time relaxing, swimming and sunbathing on the Bay of Bengal coast, this an ideal spot. But if you fancy partaking in the local culture, be sure to visit in November. That's when Chaungtha's pagoda is the object of a three-day festival that attracts pilgrims from all over the country.

A 17-hour river voyage

BELOW: river boat passengers.
RIGHT: water jars drying in Twante's sunshine.

If your itinerary doesn't allow you the time to travel the full length of the Ayeyarwady River, the 17-hour voyage from Yangon to Pathein provides a good, albeit quite long, sample of the journey. If you are sailing from Pyay, the boat will arrive at Henzada. From here you can take a train to Pathein, where you can catch the next boat that goes all the way to Yangon.

From Yangon, the river boats of the Inland Water Transport Company leave

once daily, at 5pm, docking overnight at Pathein. (Historically, this stretch of waterway was filled with ageing steamers, but nowadays the most frequent sight is that of more modern, and shallow, Chinese-made ships.) The river boat has two decks: on the open, lower one, floor space and deckchair space is sold for US$7 to foreigners. For greater comfort, there are 10 cabins on the upper deck. These cost US$21 (without air conditioning) or US$42 (with air conditioning) per cabin.

The vessel calls at Myaungmya and Ma-ubin – two typical delta towns – before reaching Pathein. These towns each feature crowded harbours fronted with *godowns* (warehouses) and stores filled with sacks and baskets of rice. The river journey offers some fascinating glimpses of life in the delta region. As your boat twists and turns through the meandering, sometimes narrow, sometimes wide, tributaries of the Ayeyarwady, you're bound to notice farmers hard at work in the rice fields beyond the modest houses on the canal's banks, children playing in the river, and fishermen casting their nets into the water.

Once sailing, you can get a meal from a small counter on the lower deck. Don't expect too much choice – the menu is usually limited to curries. Alternatively, you could buy vegetables from one of the vendors who regularly board the boat, and then get the cook to prepare a dish for a small fee. ❑

BAGO DIVISION

Map on page 144

The provincial capital of this rice-growing region was once a great seaport – its many monuments a sign of its glorious, legendary past

On leaving Yangon, you will find a very different Burma waiting to be explored and savoured. One of the best trips is the 80-km (50-mile) journey to Bago (Pegu), a popular one-day excursion from Yangon.

Early European travellers marvelled at the magnificence of Bago, which used to be the country's greatest seaport. Today, this bustling provincial capital to the northeast of Yangon on the Bago River is home to 50,000 people. Its centre is filled with open-air markets and a number of factories run on a cooperative basis. Most of the factories' goods, which include cigarette cases, wine goblets and other household objects carved from beautiful but hardy teak, are largely handmade. But it is the town's many religious monuments – which include the reclining Shwethalyaung Buddha and the massive Shwemawdaw Pagoda – that provide the main draw for visitors.

Bago is on the railway line between Yangon and Mandalay. There are six train departures every day and buses leave from the highway bus centre at Hledan Street in Kamayut Township every half hour. But, because the town and its sights are somewhat spread out, the best way to explore is in a taxi hired in Yangon. An advantage of choosing this mode of transport is that you will see the vista across the countryside between the Bago Yoma mountain range and the Sittoung River, which is one of the country's most intensive rice-cultivating regions.

LEFT: girlfriends near Kyauktan Pagoda.
BELOW: the Shwemawdaw Pagoda at Bago.

During the harvest months of January and February, it is especially rewarding to stop about halfway through the journey in **Hlegu**, where government stalls take deliveries from the newly harvested rice paddies. Observing the people at work one gets a clear sense of the easy-going cheerful spirit which, allied with a deep respect for the tenets of Buddhism, has determined the pattern of village life here for centuries.

British War Cemetery

The traveller from Yangon comes to a fork in the highway at **Htaukkyant** ❻ before reaching **Hlegu** ❼. The western road heads into Upper Burma via Pyay (once known as Prome and now also called Pyi) and the Ayeyarwady Valley. The eastern road follows the Sittoung (Sittang) Valley and leads to Mandalay via Bago and Taungoo. Taking the eastern fork, you'll discover the **British War Cemetery** shortly after leaving Htaukkyant on the right. Some 27,000 Allied soldiers who were killed during the World War II campaign in Burma are buried there. The Imperial War Graves Commission maintains the grounds.

Past the cemetery is **Hlawga Wildlife Park** (open daily; entrance fee), a 1,650-acre (670-hectare) wooded park that is home to 70 species of animals. Some of these animals, such as the barking deer, are

free to roam, while others – sun bears, tigers and leopards – are held in captivity. The park's 90 species of bird, including many migratory ones, make this a popular spot for ornithologists. The lake is also enjoyed at the weekends by Yangonians who come here for boating and fishing, and elephant rides.

TIP

Climb the tree tower in Hlawga Wildlife Park for a panoramic view of its surroundings.

Cult of the naga

A little further along the road, you are bound to notice a long Mandalay-style wall to the left. Behind it is a *kyaung* and the enormous Naga-Yone Enclosure, in which a Buddha figure sits entwined by a cobra. The enclosure, which is surrounded by a moat, houses the eight astrological guardian animals at its eight cardinal points. This combination of Buddhism, Brahman astrology and the *naga* cult provides a fascinating insight into the culture of the Burmese people.

Though the origins of the *naga* cult are still a mystery, its incorporation into Buddhist beliefs can be traced back to a typical mythical episode. According to the legend, during the fifth of the seven weeks that the Buddha spent meditating after he had achieved enlightenment, his life was placed in great danger by a storm which blew up over Lake Mucalinda. A nearby *naga*, (serpent), noticed the Buddha's predicament. The animal coiled its body beneath the Buddha to lift him above the flood waters, and covered the Enlightened One's head with its own hooded head, thereby shielding the Buddha from the storm.

This story, which symbolises the assimilation of the *naga* cult into Buddhist doctrine, forms the basis of all the country's *naga-yone* enclosures. Though the *naga*, a mythical creature that is half-snake, half-dragon, is itself no longer worshipped, it still plays a significant role in the customs of Upper Burma. For instance, a man who has been a monk will never, if he can avoid it, travel in the

BELOW: a *naga* on the road to Bago.

opposite direction to that in which the head of the *naga* is pointing – after every three months, the *naga* is said to change the direction of its gaze. It is believed that a journey into the jaws of the *naga* can only bring disaster.

The cult of the *naga* has left traces of its pure form in some regions in China and India, and the snake-dragon was worshipped in pre-Buddhist times in Tagaung. When Buddhist kings assumed power in those areas where the cult was dominant, it was assimilated into folk Buddhism.

A mythological duck

To fully appreciate a trip to **Bago ❽**, the visitor should first understand the history of the Talaing (Mon) people. Like the Pyu – predecessors of the Bamar – they originally came from the north. The Talaing, who arrived before the Pyu, ventured down the Thanlwin River rather than the Ayeyarwady. Theirs was the "Golden Land of Suvannabhumi", which stretched from what is today Malaysia to the Bay of Bengal. The Talaing built their capital, Thaton, on the east side of the Sittoung (Sittang) River.

According to legend, Bago was a tiny island just off the coast in the Gulf of Mottama (Martaban). The minute island was so small that there was room for only one *hamsa*, a mythological duck whose mate had to perch on his back. Even today, the women of Bago are teased about having a *hamsa*-like attachment to their men. The legend gave the town the name by which it was known during the years of its greatest power: Hamsawaddy (or Hinthawady).

Over the years, the mythological nesting place was joined to the Burma coastline by the accretion of silt deposited by the rivers. A seaport was founded there, allegedly in AD 825, by two brothers from Thaton. Much like numerous other

Map on page 144

The hamsa (*the mythological Brahminy*) *with its mate perching on its back.*

BELOW: temple wall mural in Bago town.

A monk at the Shwemawdaw Pagoda – Bago's most important Buddhist centre.

BELOW: giant *chinthe* at Shwemawdaw Pagoda with an image of Shin Upagot, a Buddhist saint, in its mouth.

inhabitants of this coastal stretch, the brothers were descendants of Talaing and Indian settlers. (Some historians believe that the name "Talaing", which until recently referred to the Mon people along the Gulf of Mottama coast, may be derived from descendants of immigrants from Telingana near Madras in India.)

In 1057, King Anawrahta of Bagan conquered Thaton, the Mon capital, and the whole of southern Burma fell under Bamar sovereignty, a situation that continued for the next 250 years. Indeed, some say that Thaton never recovered from the conquest. When Wareru established his own Talaing Empire in 1287 – after the downfall of the First Burmese Empire at the hands of Mongols led by Kublai Khan – he picked Mottama, near Mawlamyaing, as his capital.

Bago's golden era

His successor, Byinnya-U, transferred the capital to Bago (Hamsawaddy) in 1365. Thus began the city's golden era, a time of considerable prosperity that lasted until 1635. In that year, the capital was transferred by King Thalun's Second Burmese Empire to Inwa (Ava), not far from Mandalay. By that time, the harbour at Bago had become very shallow as a result of silt deposits, which meant that trading vessels could no longer dock there.

A feature of Bago's golden era, which endured for nearly three centuries, was the emergence of the Hamsawaddy dynasty's great rulers – such as King Razadarit (1385–1425), Queen Shinsawpu (1453–72) and King Dhammazedi (1472–92) – who are still revered by the people of Burma in the 21st century. Such respect is not surprising given the dynasty's legacy of sacred monuments, many of which can still be seen and admired today. Queen Shinsawpu, the daughter of King Razadarit, was born in 1394. Twice widowed, she was on her

third marriage – to the King of Inwa – when, in her thirties, she embarked on a study of ancient Buddhist texts. Two Mon *pongyi*, Dhammazedi and Dhamma-pala, who happened to be living in Inwa at the time, tried to help her understand the subject. By 1430, Shinsawpu had become unhappy with her life at the Inwa court, so she decided to return to her homeland, assisted by the two monks. Both men were familiar with the science of runes (a branch of alchemy) and, armed with this knowledge, they would change the colour of the boat in which they were sailed down the Ayeyarwady every day.

Map on page 144

A battle of runes

After Shinsawpu was installed as Queen of Hamsawaddy 23 years later, she wanted to nominate her successor to the throne. She concluded that the two monks were the best candidates. One morning she placed a robe, a model of a white (royal) umbrella, a yak's tail, a crown, a sword, and some sandals in one of the alms bowls used by the monks, and hoped the more worthy of the two would take up the bowl. Dhammazedi made the choice. Dhammapala, unhappy to find himself pushed into the background, immediately challenged his rival to a battle of runes. Unfortunately for Dhammapala, his runes were too weak to withstand the symbols of Dhammazedi, and he lost the contest.

Shinsawpu devoted the final years of her reign to a project close to her heart: enlarging the Shwedagon Pagoda. She settled in the village of Dagon, where she lived to the age of 78. The story goes that she cast a final glance at the famous golden stupa as she died. Dhammazedi ruled for 20 years after Shinsawpu's death, but was to be followed by a succession of weaker rulers.

In 1541, the Taungoo dynasty's King Tabinshweti, founder of the Second Burmese Empire, peacefully annexed Bago and made it the capital of his empire. His successor was the bellicose Bayinnaung, who extended the empire's boundaries but drained the treasury with his military campaigns. He twice conquered Ayutthaya, capital of Siam, but was unable to leave a stable government in the subjugated region. Thus while Bago was probably the most splendid city in the whole continent during this period, the country itself was reduced to poverty.

In 1599, the finishing touches to the country's decline were applied when Anaukhpetlun, ruler of Taungoo, conquered Lower Burma and razed both Bago and Thanlyin. Bayinnaung's magnificent Hamsawaddy, which had in no small measure been built up from the proceeds of his campaign booty, was reduced to ashes within 33 years of his monarchy.

In 1740, Bago became the capital of a short-lived Mon Empire. After only 17 years, however, the city again had to suffer the agony of total destruction. Alaungpaya, founder of the Konbaung dynasty, was ruthless in suppressing the upstart empire.

Bago's Mon inhabitants either fled to Thailand or intermarried with the victorious Bamar. Though King Bodawpaya (1782–1819) attempted to rebuild the city, partly due to the changing course of the Bago River, it never again approached its former greatness. Today, only Bago's many monuments serve as reminders of its glorious past.

BELOW: statue of King Tabinshweti.

A golden Buddha image at the Shwemawdaw Pagoda. After visiting the pagoda the trees around its base are a good place to sit and have a drink in the shade.

BELOW: the Shwemawdaw Pagoda.

Shwemawdaw Pagoda

The most outstanding of Bago's attractions is the **Shwemawdaw Pagoda Ⓐ** (open daily; entrance fee) which is to Bago what the Shwedagon is to Yangon. The stupa of Shwemawdaw Pagoda (Great Golden God Pagoda) can be seen from about 10 km (6 miles) outside the city. Located at the eastern end of Bago, the pagoda has many similarities to the Shwedagon, and, standing at a full 114 metres (374 ft) in height, is in fact even taller than its more famous cousin.

Legend has it that two merchant brothers, Mahasala and Kullasala, returned from India with two hairs personally given to them by Gautama Buddha. They built a small stupa over the relics, and in the following years, this shrine was enlarged several times, once by the historical founders of Bago, Thamala and Wimala. Sacred teeth were added to the collection of relics in 982 and 1385. King Dhammazedi installed a bell on the pagoda's main platform, which he had inscribed with runes that can still be seen, indecipherable though they are.

In the 16th century, King Bayinnaung gave the jewels from his crown to make a *hti* for the pagoda, and later, in 1796, King Bodawpaya donated a new umbrella and raised the height of the pagoda to 90 metres (295 ft). In the 20th century, the Shwemawdaw was hit by three serious earthquakes; it was almost completely destroyed by the last one in 1930. After World War II, however, it was rebuilt by unpaid volunteers with the proceeds of popular donations to stand higher than ever. In 1954, it got a new diamond-studded *hti*.

Like Yangon's Shwedagon, the Shwemawdaw's main terrace can be approached from four directions by covered stairways. There are not as many brightly coloured *tazaung* (pavilions) or *zayat* (resting places) as at the Shwedagon, but there is a small museum containing some ancient wooden and

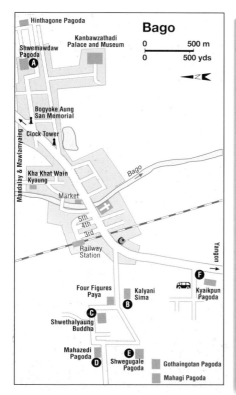

Map
on page
156

bronze Buddha figures salvaged from the ruins of the 1930 earthquake. The terrace also features the pagoda's eight planetary prayer posts, as well as a number of statues honouring certain *nat* – the heroes of Bago's history. The stairways leading to the pagoda are guarded by huge white *chinthe* (half-lion, half-griffin beast), each containing a sitting Buddha in its mouth. The stairways themselves are like bazaars, with everything from medicinal herbs to monastic offerings for sale. Faded murals along the main entrance steps recall the destruction of the pagoda by the 1930 quake and its later reconstruction.

Just behind the Shwemawdaw is **Hinthagone Hill**, on which the ruins of an ancient pagoda – the **Hinthagone Pagoda** – are located; in front of it is a statue of a pair of *hamsa*, one mythological duck on top of another. Geologists suspect that the hill was at one time an island in the Gulf of Mottama. A high-roofed platform atop the hill provides a good view of the region surrounding Bago. Unfortunately, the Shwemawdaw and other buildings of interest to visitors are situated at opposite ends of Bago. To see the town's other sacred structures, you have to retrace your steps in the direction of Yangon. Cross the Bago River bridge (behind which lies a market selling all sorts of interesting things) and the railroad tracks. About half a kilometre west of the station, a short distance to the north of the main road, the Kalyani Sima will come into view.

Ensuring the continuity of Burmese Buddhism

King Dhammazedi built the **Kalyani Sima** ❸, or ordination hall, in 1476, with the idea of rejuvenating the Burmese *sangha* (monkhood). When the unity of Buddhism in Burma was threatened by schisms following the downfall of the First Burmese Empire, Dhammazedi dispatched 22 monks to Ceylon (now Sri Lanka), which in those days was regarded as the stronghold of Theravada Buddhism. The monks were ordained at the island's Mahavihara Monastery, founded in 251BC on the banks of the Kalyani River. Upon their return to Burma after surviving a shipwreck, Dhammazedi built the Kalyani Sima, which he named after the Ceylonese river. The Mahavihara *pongyi* performed a unified ordination of Burmese monks here early in the 16th century, thereby assuring the continuity of Burmese Buddhism. To this day, novices are ordained into the *sangha* in this hall.

To the west of the Kalyani Sima, 10 tablets provide a detailed history of Buddhism in Burma, and of the country's 15th-century trade with Ceylon and south India. Three of the stones are inscribed in Pali, seven in Mon. Although some of the tables are shattered and others are illegible in places, the complete text has been preserved on palm-leaf copies.

The Kalyani Sima, which served as a model for nearly 400 other *sima* built by Dhammazedi, did not escape the ravages of the Mon's aggressive politics – or indeed the hostility of other ambitious imperialists. The Portuguese adventurer de Brito destroyed it in 1599; then Alaungpaya razed the reconstructed hall when he sacked Bago in 1757. And, as if the depredations of mankind were not enough to endure, the *sima* suffered the same fate as the Shwemawdaw during the terrible earthquake of 1930.

BELOW: a *thilashin* (10-precept Buddhist nun).

When the *sima* was reconstructed in 1954, it was rededicated to its original purpose at a ceremony attended by U Nu. Today, the monks live in lodgings around the *sima*. Indeed the park-like grounds radiate exactly the feeling of peacefulness that is associated with Buddhist *kyaung*.

The Shwethalyaung Buddha

To the northwest you will find the **Shwethalyaung Buddha** , which is revered throughout Burma as the country's most beautiful reclining Buddha. This statue is said to depict Gautama on the eve of his entering *nibbana* (nirvana). At 55 metres (180 ft) long and 16 metres (52 ft) high, the Shwethalyaung Buddha is not quite as large as Yangon's more recent Kyaukhtatgyi Buddha (built in the 1960s). But, as a result of its artistry and long history, it is much the better-known and loved of the two images. Bago's reclining Buddha was built in 994 by King Migadippa I, well before the Mon were overpowered by the Bamar.

It was left to decay for nearly 500 years until it was restored during Dhammazedi's reign. In the centuries that followed, Bago was destroyed twice. By the 18th century, the Shwethalyaung Buddha had become lost beneath countless layers of tropical vegetation, and it was only in 1881 that a group of contractors who were building a railway for the British administrative station stumbled across it. At the time it was viewed as no more than a "source of brick and stone" hidden in an earthen mound in the jungle. In 1906, after the undergrowth had been cleared away, an iron *tazaung* was erected over the Buddha. Although the *tazaung* detracts from the view of the statue inside, the pavilion does protect the Buddha from the elements. The statue was most recently renovated in 1948, when it was re-gilded and painted.

BELOW:
the great reclining
Shwethalyaung
Buddha.

The Mahazedi Pagoda

Also worth visiting is the exalted **Mahazedi Pagoda** Ⓓ, which comes into view after you pass a wall to the left of the road leading from Shwethalyaung and turn north. *Maha zedi* means "great stupa", and the appropriateness of this name is evident even when you observe this impressive structure from a distance. Unlike the other large stupas in Lower Burma, the Mahazedi has steep stairways that course two-thirds of the way up its exterior. It is reminiscent of some of the most beautiful buildings of Bagan.

The stairways leading almost to the top of Mahazedi Pagoda are unique in Lower Burma.

The Mahazedi was built in 1560 by King Bayinnaung to house a tooth of the Buddha. Bayinnaung, whose 11 white elephants (including seven taken from the King of Siam during the conquest of Ayutthia) confirmed the divine appointment of his reign, was intent on obtaining a tooth to assure his place in history as the greatest king of all time. As chance would have it, the latter half of the 16th century coincided with the apogee of Portugal's colonial power in the Indian subcontinent. Don Constantino de Braganca attacked the Buddhist kingdom of Jaffna in Ceylon and made off with a large booty that included a tooth, inlaid with gold and adorned with precious stones. He mistakenly thought it was the Tooth of Kandy, the most revered of all Buddhist relics, which had been taken to Jaffna for a religious festival shortly before the Portuguese raid.

The greedy Bayinnaung, upon hearing the news, offered the Portuguese a huge sum of money for the tooth. The governor of Portuguese Goa was willing to make what would have been a very lucrative deal, but the ever-menacing threat of the Inquisition made him think again. He ordered the tooth to be publicly pulverised in a mortar, then strewn into the open sea. The Portuguese Christians believed that they had rid themselves of one more heathen symbol.

BELOW:
Mahazedi Pagoda.

Bayinnaung's greatest day

The indestructible tooth, however, reappeared soon thereafter in the court of the King of Colombo. Bayinnaung dispatched a delegation to Ceylon to negotiate for both the tooth and the king's daughter. The delegation returned to Burma in 1576, its mission successfully completed, and Bayinnaung greeted them at Pathein. Contemporary documents tell of an enormous welcoming party on what was Bayinnaung's greatest day.

"The heavens have looked upon me with favour," said the vainglorious monarch. "Anawrahta could only get a replica of the tooth from Ceylon, Alaungsithu went in vain to China, but this tooth has been granted to me because of my piety and wisdom."

It wasn't long before Bayinnaung was informed that the Tooth of Kandy had never left Ceylon. The king chose to ignore the report, and locked the tooth away in the Mahazedi Pagoda with an alms bowl that supposedly had supernatural powers. As fate would have it, the tooth of the Buddha remained in the Mahazedi for only 33 years. In 1599, Anaukhpetlun conquered Bago, and he insisted on transferring the pagoda's cherished relics to his capital, Taungoo. The tooth was taken there in 1610. A short time later, King Thalun transferred the Burmese capital to Inwa and built the Kaunghmudaw Pagoda in nearby Sagaing as a venue in which to house the relics. The tooth and alms bowl

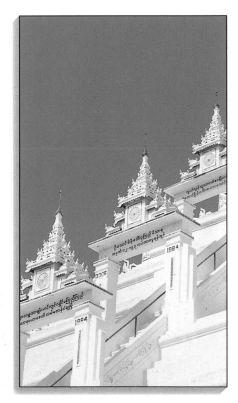

A stack of thanaka logs at the market at Thanlyin. The bark is ground up to produce a yellow paste that is then smeared on the face to give protection from the sun and beautify the skin.

BELOW:
Kyaikpun Pagoda.

were transferred again to the site where they can still be seen today. The Mahazedi Pagoda was destroyed during Alaungpaya's time, and was levelled again by the 1930 earthquake. With the reconstruction work recently completed, the uppermost walkway around the stupa affords a marvellous view of the surrounding plain, which is bejewelled with ancient monuments.

Sixty-four Buddhas in a circle

A short distance west of the Mahazedi stands the **Shwegugale Pagoda ❸**, in which 64 Buddha figures sit in a circle in a gloomy vault around the central stupa. About 1.5 km (1 mile) to the south of Bago and about 100 metres (330 ft) off the road to Yangon, you will find the **Kyaikpun Pagoda ❻**.

Built by Dhammazedi in 1476, it consists of four Buddha figures, each 30-metres (98-ft) high, seated back to back against a square pillar facing the four points of the compass. The figures represent Gautama Buddha (facing north) and his three Buddha predecessors, Konagamana (south), Kakusandha (east), and Kassapa (west). The latter was largely destroyed by the massive earthquake of 1930. Legend has it that four sisters took part in the building of the monument, and that if any of them were to marry, one of the statues would collapse. Believers in the legend feel the collapse of the Kassapa Buddha points a finger at one of the sister's marital status.

Another kilometre or so towards Yangon lies **Payathonzu**, where a number of buildings date to the time of Dhammazedi. The most important of these is the **Shwegugyi Pagoda**, modelled on India's Bodhgaya Temple. In a circle around the temple, buildings and figures represent the seven stages through which the Buddha passed while in his seven-week period of meditation following his attainment of enlightenment.

The serene atmosphere of **Thanlyin ❾** belies the turbulent history of wars fought here during the 16th and 17th centuries. Formerly the centre of foreign trade for all of Lower Burma, Thanlyin remains an important industrial town today, and is well worth a day trip from Yangon. Before the bridge linking the two cities was built, tourists tended to skip Thanlyin, thereby missing out on a pleasant – though slow – journey down the river.

The glory of this former Portuguese settlement, like that of so many other Burmese cities, lies in the distant past. At various times prior to Thanlyin's destruction at the hands of King Alaungpaya in 1756, it was home to trading posts set up by Portuguese, Dutch, French and British merchants. Its greatest moment (or folly, depending on your point of view) was in the early 17th century when the Portuguese adventurer de Brito established his own private kingdom here. If you look carefully, you can see the ruined walls of his Lusitanian, baroque-style buildings.

Handsome colonial buildings are evident in downtown Thanlyin, though many are in need of a new coat of paint. The town has an open-air market and is the centre of an important beer-brewing industry. A large number of Thanlyin's 20,000 inhabitants are employed by either the country's largest oil refinery, or the brewery, or else work in the rice trade –

Thanlyin is a centre for Burma's East Delta rice-cultivating region. When the British colonialists opened up the Ayeyarwady Delta for rice growing, they imported labourers from India to work in the paddy fields. At the height of the colonial period, there were an estimated one million Indians living in Burma, the majority in the delta region. Today, having survived both World War II and the dangers posed by Ne Win's 1960s nationalisation movement, the country's largest Indian community remains in the Thanlyin region.

Hindus then and now

Although Thanlyin's Indians have integrated into Burmese culture, the majority still observe the Hindu faith. In the third week of January, after the rice harvest has been gathered, the community observes the ritual of penitence known as *Thaipusam*. Devotees repenting past sins or asking future favours walk trance-like through the streets, heavy weights dangling from sharp hooks in their flesh; others walk barefoot over beds of burning coals.

The drive to Thanlyin takes a route past rice fields – rice cultivation here began in 1856 – punctuated with tiny hamlets dominated by either an old church or pagoda. Although, as is the case elsewhere in the country, Buddhism is the dominant religion, it was here that Christianity made its first inroads into the country. In the 19th century, Thanlyin was a cosmopolitan place and a magnet for foreign merchants and adventurers, many of whom never left but rather added to the population's ethnic mix. Thanlyin's multi-ethnic flavour and fusion of cultures makes it a fascinating place to visit.

The town's long history is believed to date back to 180 BC when Hindu colonists from the Andhra dynasty that reigned over all Middle India established

**Maps:
Area: 144
City: 156**

TIP

The most practical means of exploring the sights between Thanlyin and Yangon is to hire a taxi for the day (roughly US$15–20).

BELOW: women at Thanlyin market.

themselves along the Hanthawaddy coast, which included Thanlyin. These merchants had trade links with places as far afield as Rome and China.

The colonists became fervent Buddhists and were probably responsible for Hanthawaddy's laterite pagodas, remains of which are visible in Thanlyin. Detailed study of fragments have led historians to believe that the pagodas were built between 500 BC and AD 500. This was the time of the Orissa colonists, Buddhists of the "southern" school whose sacred Pali writings are the earliest form of Buddhist script found in Burma's pagodas.

Mongol invasion

In the 5th century AD, the colonists were driven out by the Talaing, also known as Mon, who formed part of a wave of Mongol migration from the north. This defeat coincided with the terminal decline of the Andhra dynasty and the end of its domination over Middle India. The Talaing were themselves kicked out in AD 1057 when Anawrahta of Bagan conquered Thanlyin on his way to Thaton. Anawrahta set up Bago as the capital of an empire that would later incorporate Mottama and Pathein. During the 14th to 16th centuries, in the course of several wars, assorted princes came and went. Remains in Thanlyin indicate that it was at one time a walled city. In 1541, Tabinshweti of Taungoo ascended the throne and Thanlyin assumed a new importance as a busy marketplace. Ships from Malacca, Sumatra and Mecca came to trade. From the mid-16th century, Thanlyin attracted merchants from many nations, although they rarely penetrated into the interior and left little mark on the local population.

BELOW: taking the ferry boat to the Kyauktan Pagoda.

Rival princes continued to fight wars often fomented by the Portuguese. The Portuguese first set foot in Thanlyin towards the end of the 16th century, when

the Bago empire began to flex its muscles. The pirate Philip de Brito established a colony here in 1581 and, by the time Portuguese Catholics had set up a mission in the town, de Brito, known to the Bamar as Nga Zin Ga, was ruler of the region. From his headquarters at Thanlyin, this tyrant controlled the lower provinces, largely by playing the kingdoms off, one against another. He sided with the Mon of Bago against the Bamar, although he had fought against the Mon in 1613. Eventually, the Bamar laid siege to Thanlyin, captured de Brito and, ensuring that he suffered a slow death, impaled him.

Map on page 144

The first Christian missionaries

Together, the Bamar and Mon drove out the Portuguese but the Europeans remained dangerous neighbours, thus prompting the move of the Second Burmese Empire from Bago to Inwa in 1635. Bago was still important though and Thanlyin became chief city of the province. In 1721, the arrival in Thanlyin of the Barnabite fathers marked the first recorded entry of Christian missionaries into the country; but it was only in 1750 that the Christians were able to build a large brick church. You can visit the ruins of the **Portuguese Church** which, to judge from the imposing walls that remain on the hill, must have been magnificent. The apse and tower can still be seen, and, in the middle of an interior now overgrown with shrubs, lies the tomb of an Armenian buried in 1750.

In 1756, Thanlyin was conquered by Alaung Paya of the Bamar who replaced it with Yangon as the country's main port. Dagon had just been wrested from the Talaing and renamed Yangon ("end of strife"). The Bamar suspected the Barnabites of calling on the French to assist the Mon. As revenge, they executed Father Nerini, and the mission came to an abrupt end. It was not until 1853

BELOW: elephants hauling logs.

ELEPHANTS AT WORK

Elephants are used in Burma to haul logs felled in the forest to the nearest main road to await transport by truck. The distances the beasts of burden have to cover can be lengthy if the log has been felled in a remote area.

An elephant can carry only one heavy log at a time, using its trunk to move it, guided by an *oozie* who rides on its back. *Pejeiks* are apprentices to the *oozies* and will eventually become *oozies* themselves.

The elephants are amply rewarded with lots of fodder, and at night after work, they are released into the forest, free to roam and to forage for their own food. Every morning, they are rounded up by their personal *oozie* who will make special calls, to which only their particular elephants will respond. They are then bathed and harnessed, ready for another day's work, which is usually limited to five hours.

Elephants start timber-working from the age of five, once they are independent of their mother. They are given transport duties until they are 16, followed by light extraction work, until they grow in strength at the age of 24. The elephants are in their prime in their thirties and generally work until they turn 53, at which age they are gradually retired. A trained elephant can cost US$4,000 or more.

Crowned Buddha image at the Kyaik-Khauk Pagoda.

when Bago was occupied by the British that missionary activity was revived. Thanlyin's subsequent decline matched Yangon's rise at the same time.

Thanlyin did retain some importance as a rice-distribution centre for the southern provinces. The former jungle area was turned into rice fields and coolie labour imported from India. The Mon, Kayin, Bamar, Shan and migrants from other parts of Burma were encouraged to work in the rice fields along with Europeans and Armenians who had settled earlier.

Christianity in Thanlyin is still practised, mainly by some Indians and Kayin. One of the main churches here is the **Church of the Sacred Heart of Jesus**, which was built in 1930 to replace a wooden church of 1908 that is now used as a parish hall.

The main monastery is the **Kyaik-Khauk Pagoda**. Like the Shwedagon and the Shwemawdaw, this pagoda is situated at the top of a hill, and its golden stupa is visible for miles across the delta. The Kyaik Khauk matches its famous cousins in architecture and atmosphere. In front of the pagoda are the graves of two venerated writers, Natshinnaung and Padethayaza.

The giant catfish of Kyauktan

In **Kyauktan ❿**, about 20 km (13 miles) south of Thanlyin on a tributary of the Yangon River, can be found the unusual **Kyauktan Pagoda**. The journey by jeep or bus takes about 45 minutes from Thanlyin. Also called the Ye Le Paya ("situated in the middle of the river") Pagoda, the Kyauktan is indeed on an island in the middle of the river. The island, which is covered by buildings, can be reached by rowboat from the riverbank. Within the pagoda complex are paintings of the most important pagodas in Burma, and some from other

BELOW:
Kyauktan Pagoda.

Theravada countries. At the boat landing, pilgrims can buy food for the huge catfish, some more than 1 metre (3 ft) long, whose dorsal fins can be seen piercing the waters on all sides of the island. A market stretches along the riverbank opposite the colourful pagoda buildings.

Map on page 144

Time in Taungoo

North of Bago is **Taungoo ⓫**, which, in the 15th and 16th centuries, was a powerful kingdom and the seat of seven kings spanning more than 150 years. These days Taungoo depends on the timber trade and the teak forests on the mountainous Bago Yoma backdrop to the east and west of the town.

TIP

As most of Taungoo's attractions are concentrated in the city centre, they can be visited easily by hiring a trishaw for a couple of hours.

For a long time Taungoo was off-limits to foreign visitors because of clashes in the area with insurgents from Kayin state, 35 km (21 miles) east of Taungoo, and Kayah state, further east. As a result of truces made with the rebels, the ban on visitors was lifted in the 1990s. Taungoo remains a pilgrimage site for Buddhist devotees who flock regularly to **Shwesandaw Pagoda**, the town's main temple. The object of their veneration is its gilded central bell-shaped stupa, built in 1597 on the spot of the original stupa, constructed centuries earlier and believed to have contained sacred hair relics of the Buddha.

In one of the shrine buildings *(tazaung)* surrounding the Shwesandaw Pagoda are sculptures of the seven kings who ruled Taungoo and, at the height of its power (1486–1636), nearly all Burma, until the capital moved north to Ava. Of these kings, the best-known is Bayinnaung, who ruled from 1550 till 1581. In unifying Burma he brought several kingdoms under his reign and defeated the Siamese so roundly that they did not venture into battle again for many years.

BELOW: a *sayadaw* leads a procession of monks.

Two Shwesandaw Pagoda pavilions stand out. One houses a reclining Buddha surrounded by various *devas*; the other features a sitting Buddha 3.6 metres (11 ft) high. This latter image was donated by a devotee in 1912 who gave the equivalent of his weight in bronze and silver to cast the statue, and whose ashes have been interred behind it.

Another of Taungoo's stupas, the **Myasigon Pagoda**, is also much visited. A shrine beneath the stupa houses a collection of paintings of Taungoo's kings and a silver-and-bronze sitting Buddha. Facing it are two Chinese images of goddesses, one seated on an elephant, the other on a Fu dog, which were gifts from a visiting German Buddhist in 1901. The adjacent museum features a three-headed bronze elephant, the Erawan, believed to have been Indra's mount and rubbed to a brilliant sheen by worshippers, a standing Buddha taken from the Siamese by King Bayinnaung, and two 19th-century British cannons. A moat, earth ramparts from a former palace, and the royal lake of **Lay Kyaung Kandawgyi**, on which a few islands are crowned by pavilions, are all reminders of Taungoo's past glory. You can stroll across the picturesque lake on wooden walkways that link the pavilions.

From Taungoo, it's a four-hour trip in a four-wheel drive over potholed roads to Bago Yoma (or "home of the best teak"), an area of beautiful streams, birds and flowers. Deep in the forest, the "eco-tourist" **Sein Ye Forest Camp** gives visitors a feel for the region's natural wonders and explains the workings of the timber

industry, of which Bago Yoma is a part. The camp, named after the nearby village and river of **Sein Ye**, comprises 16 rustic chalets and a dining hall. A map delineating areas reserved for logging and untouchable conservation zones is pinned on a camp wall. Some 1,500 acres (600 hectares) of teak plantation (established in the 1920s, near four Kayin villages) have been set aside for future logging.

From the camp, you can take a trip to **Kyetshar** village near the site of the first plantations, the Kabaung Reserve Forest, to see trained elephants in logging operations, or to the nearby **Kabuang** village where the traditional Kayin way of life centres around the production of rice. West of Taungoo, the main attraction of Pyay, the ancient capital, sits on a hill overlooking the town and the river – the serene **Shwesandaw Pagoda** and its huge standing Buddha. The pagoda is a landmark for river navigators and also one of the most beautiful spots in the country. The Tazaungdaing Festival is held here every November.

Thayekhittaya – the Pyu capital

A short trip south to **Shwedaung** brings you to the **Shwemyetmhan Pagoda** and its spectacled Buddha image. Some 8 km (5 miles) south of Pyay, near the railway station of **Hmawza**, lies **Thayekhittaya** (Sri Ksetra) ⑫, the Pyu capital. The Pyu were probably a Tibeto-Burman race who formed the second wave of migration from Central Asia into Upper Burma. Notice how the style of ancient stupas here is quite different from that of stupas elsewhere in the country. Little remains of Thayekhittaya, but eight brick pagodas and temples, some dating to the dawn of Christianity, testify to its greatness. The conical stupas at Thayekhittaya were based on Indian archetypes. The **Payagyi Stupa** and

TIP

Get off the beaten track and walk to the site of Thayekhittaya to examine at close range some surviving parts of the ancient city walls.

BELOW:
watering the crops at Thayekhittaya.

Map
on page
144

Payama Stupa north of the old city walls are conically styled, and were built about the same time as the **Bebe Temple**, between the 5th and 7th centuries. The Bebe is a cylindrical stupa lying on a hollow pedestal in which a statue of the Buddha, flanked by two of his followers, stands against a wall. The **East Zegu** and **Leimyethna temples** are similar in form, the latter having a central support pillar, which is atypical for a Burmese temple.

The dragon's tail

Archaeologists have maintained a presence in Thayekhittaya since 1907 (the only break was during World War II), and the artefacts they have uncovered prove that Theravada Buddhism was common in central Burma before Anawrahta's time. According to legend, Thayekhittaya was built by Sakka, king of the *nat*. Sakka delineated the city's boundaries by grabbing the tail of the dragon Naga and swinging him a full circle. Then he named the city "as beautiful as Sakka's home on Mount Meru", and appointed Duttabaung as king. Thayekhittaya endured until the 9th century AD, when it collapsed under the weight of the continuous conflict waged by the many tribes who had moved there. When King Anawrahta of Bagan passed by after his conquest of Thaton, he tore down the city's walls and requisitioned the temples' relics, claiming that the "true religion" could have no other home than Bagan.

Near the ruins of Thayekhittaya in the village of **Hmawza**, is the **Hmawza Archaeological Museum** (no set opening hours, just approach the caretaker of the museum who has the key), which houses artefacts dug up since 1907 from the old Pyu site. Displays include stone reliefs of Buddha. There are also Pyu terracotta votive tablets and a stone funeral urn thought to have contained King Sihavikrama's ashes. The king was part of the Vikrama dynasty that apparently ruled Thayekhittaya in the 7th and 8th centuries.

Students of ancient history should definitely visit **Beikthano**, about 135 km (85 miles) further north. The ruins of this large Pyu town, which predates Thayekhittaya by several centuries, can be found near the modern-day town of **Taungdwingyi** in Magway (Magwe) state.

The absence of Buddha images here suggests that the city existed before the 1st century. Little remains of the ruins, as many of the bricks and stones were used in recent centuries for constructing roads and railways. For all Beikthano's great age, it is far from being the country's oldest source of artefacts. Relics of even more ancient civilisations can be found north of Mandalay, in **Tagaung** and **Halin**.

Pyay is the last stop on the route from Mandalay. From Pyay, the journey to Yangon via the delta region takes another 2½ days. En route is **Tombo**, which is noted for its cliff of 1,000 images. These were placed there by sailors who had to wait at the windbreaker cliff for favourable winds before continuing their journey upriver.

The boat sails from Pyay via **Ma-ubin** and **Twante** back to Yangon. If you've seen and had enough of the river, there are regular air-con buses to Yangon that take less than four hours. ❑

The ruins of Thayekhittaya lie in idyllic countryside. As you travel to the Payama and Payagyi stupas, you will see a timeless landscape dotted with villages and rice fields with yoked water buffaloes ploughing the soil.

BELOW: Pyu ruins.

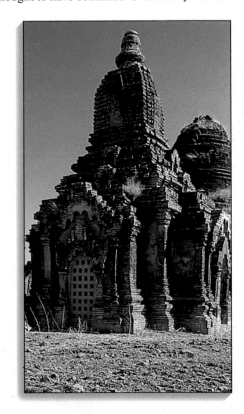

GETTING AROUND THE COUNTRY

Travel in Burma is seldom boring. The calendar may refer to the 21st century but some modes of transport are straight out of the 19th century

Visitors to Burma are often amazed at the outmoded and archaic forms of transport in the country. But they still work even though they may be frustratingly slow and even pollutive. One thing is sure however – they add to the fun and charm of travel around the country. When Burma was cut off from the outside world in the 1960s, practical solutions to getting around had to be found and people had to make do with whatever they had in hand – hence the reliance on animal power and farm equipment such as tractors. So bullock- or ox-carts and horse-drawn carriages – long abandoned in many countries – continue to be seen on the streets today.

RECYCLING CULTURE

The lack of replacement parts also means that where vehicles are available, owners have to be inventive to keep whatever they have on the road. No fuel tank? No problem. Just feed petrol off a plastic tube from a jerry can next to the driver's seat. Vintage cars and motorbikes are treasured by their owners and no vehicle is considered too old to be of use. With the country opening up to trade, newer forms of transport are now available in the cities but it will be some time yet before ox-carts, horse carriages and trishaws disappear completely.

△ **VINTAGE BUSES ON THE GO**
Pre-war, rickety, smoke-spewing buses chug along in the major cities replete with wooden gear-sticks and planks for floors.

▽ **DOOR-LESS CAR**
In Burma, anything that is capable of moving is used for transport, including car this without doors, still perfectly serviceable to its owners.

▷**TURNING TO TRACTORS**
Tractors don't die in the countryside, they are re-born as public transport.

◁ HANG LOOSE

A common form of transport is the modified pick-up truck with seats lining the sides. Passengers also sit on the rooftop or hang off the sides.

▽ MAMMOTH MOVEMENTS

Although elephants are not used to transport people, they are indispensable in Burma's logging industry, hauling huge teak logs like toothpicks.

THE EVOLUTION OF RIVER BOATS

The classic form of travel in Burma is by river. The ancient Burmese kings travelled in resplendent royal barges powered by 30 to 40 oarsmen. Ordinary folk sailed on steamers operated by the Irrawaddy Flotilla Company which started operations in 1865. In its heyday in the 1930s, 602 vessels were ferrying nine million passengers and tonnes of goods along the river from as far north as Bhamo to Yangon. The barges and steamers are long gone (many were scuttled into the Ayeyarwady during World War II to prevent them from falling into Japanese hands), replaced by double-decker diesel-powered riverboats. Until recently, tourists could only travel on these boats, sitting on bare floors, crammed in with other passengers and their goods. Despite the lack of comfort, this is still a great way to see the unfolding scenes on the banks of the river. Today, newer vessels and cruise ships are available to foreign visitors.

△ MUSCLE POWER

In places where the terrain is too harsh for vehicles, there is always the possibility of using muscle power: transport by majestic palanquin.

▽ TRAIN TRAVEL

Rail travel, introduced by the British, has deteriorated since colonial times but despite the lack of comfort, it is a great way to see the country.

▽ ROOM FOR ONE

Transportation problems are approached laterally: baskets for transporting vegetables to market have a double life as small people carriers.

▷ TRICYCLE TAXIS

From pedal power to motorised power, the *thoun bein* (three wheel) scooter cab is an improved and faster version of the trishaw, only with more pollution.

MANDALAY AND ENVIRONS

*This is not only Burma's cultural heartland, it is
also the spiritual hub of Buddhism in the country*

The next major destination after Yangon is Mandalay. The country's second city and a major commercial centre, Mandalay also represents the cultural heartland of Burma. The town was originally established by King Mindon as a new focal point for the teaching of Buddhism. He also made it his capital.

Mandalay did not survive long as the "Golden City" of Buddhist teachings, but it remains an important cultural hub, with numerous splendid pagodas. Today, despite the British choice of Yangon as capital, Mandalay has not lost its position among the Burmese as a religious centre. It is said that two-thirds of the country's monks still make their home in the Mandalay area.

As a result of its proximity to China, Mandalay has benefited from an influx of investment and development. The city is now home to a whole array of new hotels and commercial buildings. And the recently completed airport is taking it even further along the road of progress. Constructed with technical assistance from an Italian-Thai joint venture company, the airport has been designed to handle 45,000 aircraft movements a year.

In the environs of Mandalay, there are several places worth visiting – all reminders of the city's glorious past. The three ancient capitals of Amarapura, Inwa (Ava) and Sagaing, as well as the town of Mingun, all lie within a stone's throw of Mandalay. Among the ruins of palaces, pagodas and *kyaung*, the visitor can find abundant evidence of the political and religious power that belonged to Upper Burma between the 14th and 19th centuries, between the fall of Bagan and the British occupation.

Sagaing was the capital of the Shan-dominated Upper Burma for a brief period beginning in 1315. The seat of government was shifted to Inwa in 1364, and there it remained for almost 400 years.

Shwebo (Moksobo) was the royal capital from 1760 to 1764, but the government returned to Inwa, before King Bodawpaya moved the capital to his newly built Amarapura. Kings often moved their headquarters at this time; Ava was again the capital of Upper Burma from 1823 to 1841, then Amarapura regained the distinction for 20 more years until King Mindon moved his court to Mandalay.

To the east – in the foothills of the vast Shan Plateau – is the town of Pyin-U-Lwin (Maymyo), a former British hill station. A mild climate, pleasant gardens, quaint atmosphere and colonial trappings make the resort a popular tourist destination. Beyond lies the wild Shan state and the Kachin country of the north, parts of which have been off-limits to visitors due to the insurgency and opium trading.❑

PRECEDING PAGES: a monk in contemplation.
LEFT: crossing the U-Bein bridge near Mandalay.

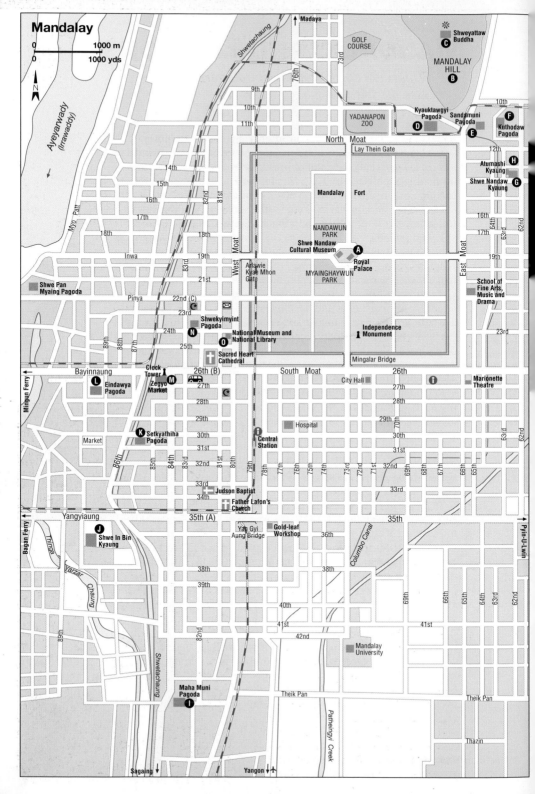

Mandalay

MANDALAY

*Romantic-sounding Mandalay reverberates
with a recent colonial past, still evident
in many of its buildings, railways and streets*

Maps:
City: 174
Area: 190

Th
here's no escaping echoes of *The Road to Mandalay,* Rudyard Kipling's
evocative 1887 poem: *"For the wind is in the palm-trees, and the temple-
bells they say: Come you back, you British soldier; come you back to
Mandalay!"* It is a triumph of romantic imagination rather than of observation,
however, since Kipling never set foot in the city. **Mandalay ❶**, the capital of
Upper Burma, is a young city, less than 150 years old. But its lyrical name – one
of the few in Burma that remain unchanged – evokes images as ancient as the
languid Ayeyarwady (Irrawaddy) River that flows past the city. Nostalgia for
Burma's last royal capital, enchantment with the myriad pagodas dotting all
corners of the region's landscape, and the warmth and vitality of the local people all weave a spell around the visitor that seems impossible to escape.

Sprawling across the dry plains of the upper Ayeyarwady rice-growing district,
Mandalay has a population of more than one million. This hot (except during the
December–February cool season), dusty city is 620 km (400 miles) into the
northern interior from Yangon, and 80 metres (260 ft) above sea level. Its streets,
full of trishaws, bicycles and horse-drawn carts, have none of the tree-lined
neatness and colonial character of Yangon, but to the Burmese, Mandalay, not
Yangon, epitomises Burma's past and present cultures, and Buddhist teachings.

In Mandalay, scenic beauty and historical tragedy
are inextricably meshed. There is the indestructible
Mandalay Hill with its kilometre-long covered stairways, fine pagodas and the restored Royal Palace. In
the middle of the city, Zegyo Market is the centre of
trade for most of the people of Upper Burma. Here,
skilled artisans and craftsmen work age-old wonders
with gold and silver, marble and chisel, thread and
loom. The sluggish Ayeyarwady is punctuated by
bustling wharves and flotillas of rice-laden boats.

BELOW: *chinthes* of
Mandalay Hill.

Fulfilling the Buddha's prophecy

Mandalay was founded in 1857 by King Mindon to
fulfil an ancient Buddhist prophecy. Legend has it that
Gautama Buddha visited the sacred mount of Mandalay
Hill with his disciple Ananda, proclaiming that, on
the 2,400th anniversary of his death, a metropolis of
Buddhist teaching would be founded at the foot of the
hill. The pious Mindon, who thought he had achieved
enlightenment, wanted to right the injustices wrought
during his reign by building magnificent temple
grounds. The prophecy became reality in 1861 when
Mindon deposed his half-brother Pagan Min as the
Konbaung king and moved his capital – with 150,000
people and most of the palace – from Amarapura, 20
km (12 miles) away, to Mandalay. He built the Royal
Palace at the foot of Mandalay Hill and established the
"Golden City" of Buddhist teachings.

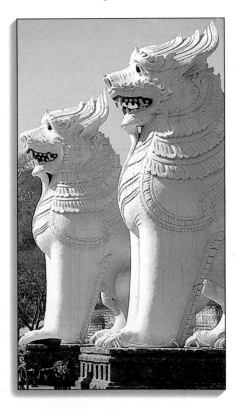

Mindon's vision was short-lived. On his death in 1878, he was succeeded by King Thibaw and his imperious wife, Supyalat. During a reign of terror, they had many of their friends and relatives killed to deter a royal rebellion. They also had subjects and foreigners murdered on the advice of astrologers to end a smallpox epidemic. Their excesses, along with the king's courting of the French, prompted an invasion by the British, who annexed Upper Burma in 1885. King Thibaw handed the town over to Britain's General Prendergast and went into exile with his queen. Mandalay soon became just another outpost of British colonialism, albeit one of richly furnished palace buildings, now renamed Fort Dufferin.

The palace structures were almost all built of teak, which did not prove to be very durable. In March 1945, British troops shelled the stronghold, at the time defended by a handful of Japanese and local soldiers. By the time the siege had ended, the Golden City's interior was in ashes. The walls and moat were all that remained. However, part of the palace has since been reconstructed.

Today, Mandalay is home to the country's finest dance and music traditions. Although Mindon's plan to make Mandalay a centre of Buddhist teaching was thwarted, his legacy is such that Mandalay's Buddhist monasteries are among the most important in the country.

The centre of the world

Mindon's **Royal Palace** Ⓐ (open daily; entrance fee) was constructed on the lines of Brahman-Buddhist cosmology to represent the centre of the world, the fabled Mount Meru. The palace formed a perfect square, with the outer walls facing the four cardinal directions, and the 12 gates, three on each side, marked with the signs of the zodiac. In the exact centre of the palace, above the throne

BELOW:
King Mindon's
Royal Palace.

room, or Lion's Room, rose a gold-plated, seven-storey, 78-metre (250-ft) high *pyathat* (tower). Through this **watchtower**, it was believed, the wisdom of the universe funnelled directly upon the king's throne to assist in his decision-making. In *The Golden Peninsula: Culture and Adaptation in Mainland Southeast Asia* (1977), anthropologist Charles Keyes described the palace thus: "The walls were a mile and one-eighth (almost 2 km) long and were, in turn, surrounded by a moat. The homes of the common people and of 'aliens', the markets, the workshops of the craftsmen and the shops, were located beyond the walls of the capital city. In contrast to Chinese and medieval European cities, the walls of a traditional Theravadin city were built not so much to serve as barriers against potential invaders as to demarcate a sacred space."

These days the renovated palace shares the grounds of **Mandalay Fort** with the army. The grounds and a museum on Mandalay's history are open to the public on payment of an entrance fee. Opening hours: Mon-Fri, 8am-6pm. Entry is by the east gate on East Moat Road. A little to the west, a scale model of the old palace shows the location of the interior buildings and gives an idea of the "centre of the world" concept. King Mindon's mausoleum is also in the palace grounds.

Mandalay Hill

You should perhaps start a visit to Mandalay by climbing **Mandalay Hill** Ⓑ (open daily 8am–5pm; entrance fee) which rises 240 metres (790 ft) above the surrounding countryside to the palace's northeast. British and Indian troops suffered heavy casualties here in 1945 when they stormed the Japanese strong-hold that controlled the plains. A British regimental insignia is the only visible remains of the battle.

The slopes of Mandalay Hill have covered stair-ways that lead to small temples, many of them the work of the monk U Khanti, at regular intervals. Two main stairways ascend from the south, under the glare of the ever-present white *chinthes*. Remember to take off your shoes before entering sacred grounds. There are 1,729 steps to the top, but the walk is not particu-larly difficult. The roof, which shades the stairways, keeps the stone steps cool and protects visitors from the sun while still allowing fresh air to circulate. Along the way, astrologers and souvenir peddlers ply their trades, while monks, nuns, children and women (often smoking huge *cheroot*) scale the steps. About halfway up the hill, you'll encounter the first large temple, which contains three bones of the Buddha.

When Gautama Buddha died at the age of 80 in Kusinara, India, he left no instructions regarding the disposal of his body. The Buddha's followers decided on cremation, but when only his bones remained, a downpour extinguished the flames. The Mallas of Kusinara took possession of the skeletal corpse, agree-ing to divide the bones equally among eight neigh-bouring monarchs, to be enshrined in stupas across Burma, only when the issue threatened to cause a war.

Three centuries later, while extending his reign over India, King Ashoka opened the relic chambers of the eight stupas and had their contents distributed among the 80,000 stupas of South and Southeast Asia.

Map on page 174

TIP

While away a hot afternoon in Mandalay with a few drinks at a beer-house at the corner of 25th and 80th streets, opposite the Post and Telegraph Office. This location has a good view of the Mandalay Fort walls.

BELOW: a pavilion above a fort gate, Mandalay Fort.

TIP

Mandalay Hill, the
Mandalay Palace
walls, the Pyigyimon
restaurant and the
moat can all be seen
in the same
perspective from the
corner of 67th Street
and South Moat Road.

King Kanishka, the second great Buddhist monarch of the Kushan dynasty, had several of the relics brought to Peshawar (in what is today Pakistan), where he built a 168-metre (550-ft) high stupa for them. The Chinese traveller Hiuen Tsang wrote a marvellous description of the stupa in AD 630. The stupa was apparently destroyed by Muslim conquerors following the Battle of Hund in the 11th century. It remained for the Peshawar Museum curator, who was conducting excavations at the Ganji Gate in 1908, to uncover the fabled Kanishka relic casket. Inside the casket he found a crystal vessel containing three of the Buddha's bones. The relics meant little to the Muslims of northwestern India, and the British government presented them to the Burmese Buddhist Society.

It was for these relics that the Burmese built a temple halfway up Mandalay Hill. So it's somewhat surprising that, although their authenticity was confirmed by the inscription of the Kanishka casket, the relics aren't held in particularly high esteem. By contrast, other relics, such as the seemingly countless teeth of the Buddha that are enshrined in so many stupas, are ardently venerated.

Redemption of an ogress

About two-thirds of the way up the hill stands the gold-plated statue of the **Shweyattaw Buddha** ©. His outstretched hand points to the spot where the Royal Palace was built. This stance is unique: in all other Buddha images across the world, Gautama is in a *mudra* position. The statue, erected before Mindon laid the first stone of his Golden City, symbolises Gautama Buddha's prophecy.

On the way up the steps, there is another unusual statue – that of a woman kneeling in front of the Buddha, offering to him her two severed breasts. According to legend, Sanda Moke Khit was an ogress, but she was so overwhelmed by

BELOW: the
southern access to
Mandalay Hill.

the Buddha's teachings that she decided to devote the rest of her life to following the Enlightened One. As a sign of humility, she cut off her breasts. The ogress's brother asked the Buddha why he smiled as he accepted the gift. He replied that Sanda Moke Khit had collected so many merits that in a future life she would be reborn Min Done (Mindon), the king of Mandalay.

Map on page 174

A view of the plains

The view from the summit of Mandalay Hill is phenomenal. To the west lies the Ayeyarwady and beyond that, crowned with pagodas and temples, the Sagaing and Mingun hills. To the north, the Ayeyarwady rice country extends into the distance. The purple Shan Plateau can be seen in the east. To the south, in the midst of this vast plain, lies the city of Mandalay and its huge palace fortress. In all directions, the Ayeyarwady plain – from which the hill juts like a huge boulder – is studded with pagodas, erected over the centuries by devout Buddhists seeking to obtain merit for future lives.

Not far from the **South Stairway** is the **Kyauktawgyi Pagoda ❹** (entrance fee). Work on this pagoda began in 1853, to a plan that sought to model it after the Ananda Temple at Bagan. After delays caused by a popular revolt in 1866, the building was eventually completed in 1878. The main point of interest here is a huge Buddha figure, carved from a single block of marble from the Sagyin quarry. This undertaking was of Herculean proportions: 10,000 men took 13 days to transport the rock from the Ayeyarwady to the pagoda site. The statue was dedicated in 1865, with 20 figures on each side of the image representing the Buddha's 80 disciples. A painting of King Mindon hangs inside the pagoda.

To the east of the Kyauktawgyi Pagoda, the **Sandamuni Pagoda ❺** (open

Monks at Mandalay Hill.

BELOW: the view from the top of Mandalay Hill.

daily 8am–5pm; entrance fee) was built on the site of King Mindon's provisional palace, where he resided while the Mandalay Palace was under construction. The Sandamuni Pagoda was erected over the burial place of Mindon's younger brother, Crown Prince Kanaung, who was assassinated in an unsuccessful palace revolution in 1866. Commentaries on the *Tipitaka* (Buddhist scripture) have been chiselled into 1,774 stone tablets housed in the pagoda, a work credited to the monk U Khanti.

The makers of oiled bamboo paper are found at Mandalay's 37th Road. This kind of paper, which is placed between layers of gold leaf, is produced by a remarkable 3-year process of soaking, beating flat and drying of bamboo.

The world's largest book

Further to the east, at the base of Mandalay Hill's southeast stairway and surrounded by a high wall is Mindon's **Kuthodaw Pagoda** 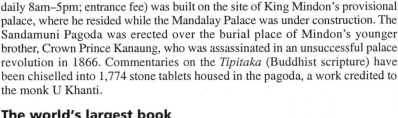 (open daily 8am–5pm; entrance fee). Its central structure, the 30-metre (100-ft) high Maha Lawka Marazein Pagoda, built in 1857, was modelled on the Shwezigon Pagoda in Nyaung U, near Bagan. The 729 *pitaka* pagodas that surround it were built in 1872 during the Fifth Buddhist Synod to individually house the marble tablets upon which, for the first time, the entire *Tipitaka* was recorded in Pali script. Sometimes called "the world's largest book", this version of the *Tipitaka* was created by a team of 2,400 monks who required almost six months to record the text. The words were inscribed on the marble slabs by devoted Buddhist scholars, and the letters were originally veneered with gold leaf. A number of other important pagodas and monasteries can be found in the proximity of the Kuthodaw.

There are two monasteries south of the Kuthodaw Pagoda, not far east of the palace moat. The **Shwe Nandaw Kyaung** (open daily 8am–5pm; entrance fee), at one time part of the royal palace, is the only building from Mindon's Golden City that has survived. It was in this building that Mindon died. After his father's death, Thibaw moved the Shwe Nandaw Kyaung to its present site, which is just as well given that the palace was destroyed in World War II. Thibaw used the building for a time as a private meditation centre, but he later gave it to the monks as a monastery. In 1979, the monastery celebrated its 100th anniversary. Today, the Shwe Nandaw is most famous for its intricate woodcarvings. Every square metre of the entire Golden City must have been covered with ornamental figures or flowers. Although the monastery was once gold-plated and adorned with glass mosaic, both inside and out, all that's left of the gold is layered on the imposing ceiling. Thibaw's couch and a replica of the royal throne are inside.

BELOW: detail of a wood-carving depicting a scene from the Jataka tales at Shwe Nandaw Kyaung.

Beside the Shwe Nandaw stands the renovated **Atumashi Kyaung** (open daily 8am–5pm; entrance fee) or the Incomparable Monastery. Before it burnt down in 1890, taking with it four sets of *Tipitaka* in teak boxes, this was a building of extraordinary splendour. Today, the Atumashi Kyaung has been restored, and closely resembles its former glory. A famous Buddha image clothed in silk, coated with lacquer and with an enormous diamond set in its forehead, was once the pride of the Atumashi Kyanung, but unfortunately it was stolen during the British seizure of Mandalay in 1885. The *kyaung*, which is currently being rebuilt, was described by European visitors as one of the most beautiful buildings in all of Mandalay.

The legend of the Maha Muni

Mandalay's most important religious structure is the **Maha Muni Pagoda**
(entrance fee) translated as the Great Sage Pagoda but also known as the
Rakhaing (Arakan) Pagoda or Payagyi ("Great Pagoda"). Located about 3 km
(2 miles) south of the city centre on the road to Amarapura, this pagoda was built
in 1784 by King Bodawpaya and was reconstructed following a fire a century
later. The shrine's Maha Muni Buddha image, taken as booty by Bodawpaya's
troops during a Rakhaing campaign, is an object of intense devotion to pilgrims
from all over the world.

It is said that Gautama Buddha himself went to teach for a week among
the people of Dhannavati (now northern Rakhaing), stressing the five precepts and the Eightfold Path and showing the way to salvation. King Chandra
Surya (Candra-suriya) asked Gautama to "leave us the shape of yourself", to
which the Buddha agreed. He spent an additional week meditating under a
Bodhi tree while Sakka, king of the gods, produced a likeness of the Buddha
that was so lifelike it could only have been created by a heavenly being. The
Buddha was pleased. He breathed upon the image and said, "I shall pass into
nibbana (nirvana) in my 80th year, but this, with my essence, will live the
5,000 years I have prescribed for the duration of the religion." Gautama then
departed, but the Maha Muni took its place on a diamond-studded throne atop
Rakhaing's Sirigutta Hill. It was one of only five likenesses of the Buddha said
to have been made during his lifetime; according to tradition, two are in India
and two in Paradise.

So much for the legend. In fact, archaeologists claim the city of Dhannavati
was built in the first century AD, about 600 years after the Buddha's lifetime. The

Map
on page
174

BELOW: the
fabled Maha Muni
Buddha image.

A golden Buddha image at Maha Muni Pagoda.

BELOW: detail of a woodcarving at Shwe In Bin Kyaung.

Maha Muni Buddha was probably cast after Chandra Surya became king in AD 146. It was during his reign that Buddhism spread to Rakhaing. King Anawrahta of Bagan conquered the northern part of Rakhaing in the 11th century. During his reign, all non-Buddhist buildings and statues were destroyed. He was unable to carry the Maha Muni to Bagan and his grandson, Alaung-sithu, raided Rakhaing again in 1118. Alaung-sithu's soldiers destroyed all the temples, removed the gold from the Maha Muni, and took one of its legs as booty. However, the ship transporting the treasure home sank in the Bay of Bengal.

Over to Bodawpaya

By the late 12th century, when another foray from Bagan intimidated Rakhaing, jungle had enveloped Sirigutta Hill and the legendary Maha Muni could not be found. The people of Rakhaing later succeeded in restoring the Buddha image, only to have it carried off by Bodawpaya's forces in 1784. The king sent his crown prince with a force of 30,000 men to take Rakhaing, and the troops returned with the Maha Muni in three separate pieces. It was reassembled at Amarapura, and Bodawpaya had a beautiful seven-story pagoda built about 8 km (5 miles) north of Amarapura to house it. In 1884, the original pagoda was destroyed by fire – today's structure is a copy of its predecessor, although its terraced roof of gilded stucco is unmistakably late 19th-century in origin. The Maha Muni Buddha figure is 3.8 metres (12 ft 7 in) high and is coated with layers of gold leaf several centimetres thick. Except during the rainy season, when the Buddha's body is cloaked with robes, one can watch Buddhists pasting on the thin gold leaf, while devotees kneel at the feet of the Buddha to pray. The statue was cast in metal but, due to the thick gold leaf, it now has an irregular outline.

Map on page 174

Six bronze statues

Six bronze Khmer sculptures were carried back from Rakhaing with the Maha Muni. Their story provides a vivid glimpse of Southeast Asia's speckled history. The statues, which originally stood as guardians of Cambodia's immense Angkor Wat, were among 30 such items taken during a Thai raid in 1431. In 1564, the Mon king Bayinnaung looted Ayutthaya (Siam) and took the statues to Bago. Then in 1600, King Razagyi of Rakhaing razed Bago and carried the statues to his capital of Mrauk-U (Myohaung). Bodawpaya's forces took them in 1784. The six Khmer bronzes that have survived – two *dvarapalas* (warriors or temple guardians), three lions and a three-headed elephant – are kept in a small building in the Maha Muni Pagoda courtyard. The warriors are a special attraction for pilgrims because their healing powers are said to be activated when the corresponding place on their bodies is touched. If the polish on the warriors' stomachs is any sign, intestinal ailments must be widespread in Burma.

Not far from the bronzes, the courtyard has a shed with a five-ton gong, and hundreds of stone slabs with religious inscriptions that Bodawpaya collected during his military campaigns. A statue of Bodawpaya is on the southwestern side of the pagoda, in front of a curio museum that displays life-sized statues of Mindon, Thibaw and Supyalat. Streets with covered stalls lead up to the Maha Muni Pagoda, providing a bazaar atmosphere. Along with simple artefacts, one can find precious stones and antiques – whose export is strictly forbidden. On one side of the pagoda is a small pond containing "holy" fish and turtles; feeding them is said to improve one's merit standing on the path to nirvana.

Gold-leaf workshops

Four other Buddhist buildings in the vicinity of downtown Mandalay are definitely worth visiting, and the city's grid street plan makes them easy to find. Heading north from the Maha Muni Pagoda, one first encounters the **Shwe In Bin Kyaung** ❶. This beautiful monastery, situated to the south of 35th Road, contains very fine 13th-century woodcarvings depicting the Buddha's life. At 31st Road and 85th Street stands the **Setkyathiha Pagoda** ❷, which was rebuilt after being badly damaged in World War II. The pagoda contains a 5-metre (16-ft) high bronze Buddha, cast at Inwa (Ava) by King Bagyidaw in 1823. A Bodhi tree in front of the entrance was planted by U Nu, the country's first prime minister. In the streets in between are the gold-leaf workshops where gold sheets are beaten and cut into paper-thin leaves for plastering Buddha images. Proceeding in a northerly direction, you will arrive at the **Eindawya Pagoda** ❸, at 27th Road and 89th Street. The pagoda houses a chalcedony Buddha figure that was carried to Burma in 1839 from Bodhgaya in India, where Gautama achieved Buddhahood. The pagoda, today covered in gold leaf, was built in 1847 by King Pagan Min.

Zegyo Market

Mandalay is the economic centre of Upper Burma. For the Chin, the Kachin and the Shan, **Zegyo Market** ❹, on the west side of the city centre, on

BELOW: a bronze *dvarapala*.

84th Street between 26th and 28th Roads, is Mandalay's most important market for goods. The Italian Count Caldrari, first secretary of the Mandalay municipal government, had the market built around the **Diamond Jubilee Clock**, erected in honour of Queen Victoria. Zegyo Market, which used to be known for its lively night market and as the one place to get foreign-made goods (smuggled over the Thai border), has been rebuilt into a new concrete structure. The market economy has removed most of the incentives from the once-profitable smuggling business. These days, Mandalay's markets sell goods imported from China, and Chinese currency is surging through the Mandalay economy. The city is now a trading post on the crossroads between India and China.

A lesson in history

The oldest pagoda in the city is the **Shwekyimyint Pagoda **, on 24th Road between 82nd and 83rd streets. Erected in 1167 by Prince Minshinsaw, the exiled son of King Alaungsithu of Bagan, it houses a Buddha image consecrated by the prince himself. It also contains a collection of gold and silver Buddha figures adorned with precious stones. The images, which were removed from the Royal Palace during the British occupation and previously worshipped by Burmese kings, are brought out for public veneration on religious occasions.

A couple of blocks from the Shwekyimyint, at 24th Road and West Moat Road, are the **National Museum and National Library** (open Wed–Sun 10am–4pm; entrance fee). The museum collection, which extends across many eras of Burmese history includes a picture of King Thibaw and Queen Supyalat on the eve of their exile and a collection of Mandalay regalia. The library is widely noted for its assemblage of important Buddhist documents.

BELOW: a vegetable seller near Zegyo Market.

Part of Mandalay's enchantment comes from its location by the Ayeyarwady River. At the western end of A Road, which follows the railway tracks north of the Shwe In Bin Kyaung, you can see the jetties where the ships that ply the so-called "Road to Mandalay" are docked. The activity on the wharves is fascinating, and it is worth spending some time here. Perhaps even more enthralling is the marvellous view across the river to the Sagaing and Mingun hills, on the Ayeyarwady River's west bank, which is studded with pagodas and *kyaung*. At the end of C Road is **Buffalo Point**. Here you can see how these powerful animals pull out of the river heavy logs that have been floating down the Shweli and the Ayeyarwady rivers from the north. The whole scene serves as a potent reminder that, whatever happens elsewhere, some ways of life remain exactly as they used to be centuries ago.

Craftsmen's quarters

In the southern part of Mandalay, especially in the precincts around the Maha Muni Pagoda, travellers can easily find the neighbourhoods of Mandalay's artists and craftsmen. The evocative sight of craftsmen using the same skills and methods as were employed by their forefathers, is fascinating. The main focus of their work is of course religious sculptures – Buddha images in all positions, Buddha footprints, lotus-blossom pedestals and, as a throwback to colonial days and the early missionaries, even an occasional statue of the Virgin Mary. You can observe Buddha figures being hewn from alabaster and marble by stonemasons on a street near the Maha Muni Pagoda.

West of the Maha Muni are the makers of pagoda crafts, a booming trade given the Burmese propensity to seek merit through the building and renovation

Map on page 174

A woman works on a carving of an image of the Buddha's hand made from alabaster.

BELOW: life on the banks of the Ayeyardwady River.

BELOW: a bamboo
raft sails on the
Ayeyarwady.

of pagodas. Not far away, woodcarvers create more Buddhas, as well as altars for worship at home and in pagodas. Foundry workers cast replicas of ancient Buddha images and musical instruments. The makers of oiled bamboo paper can be found on 37th Road, between 80th and 81st streets. This is a craft worth seeing in action: oiled bamboo paper, which is placed between layers of gold leaf, is produced by means of a remarkable three-year process during which the bamboo is soaked, beaten flat and finally dried.

Gold leaf is produced in a large number of workshops in the southeastern section of Mandalay. This venerable craft is extremely old, and even in the 21st century, the manufacturing process is carried out according to a time-honoured tradition. When travelling in the neighbourhoods in and around Mandalay, you should make a point of visiting other artisans, among the most interesting of which are the skilled silk and cotton weavers of Amarapura.

By boat from Mandalay to Bagan

This stretch of the Ayeyarwady provides most visitors with their only experience of the mighty waterway that the Burmese call the "mother of all rivers". A river-boat journey on the Ayeyarwady makes for a pleasant and more interesting alternative to travelling by road to Bagan. Since 1995, a variety of modern boats have catered for visitors travelling between Bagan and Mandalay *(see also page 243)*. These include the luxury cruise ship, *The Road to Mandalay*, operated by Orient-Express, the company that runs the Eastern & Oriental Express train between Bangkok and Singapore. The vessel is a refitted Rhine steamer that offers 72 passengers air-conditioned cabins, a swimming pool, bar and restaurant.

More charming (and affordable) is a cruise on the *Pandaw III*. Built by the London-based Irrawaddy Flotilla Company to recall the experience of river travel during colonial times, but minus the hardships, the new *Pandaw III* has 39 cosy staterooms and makes a pleasant trip from Mandalay to Bagan and vice versa. Both overnight and two-night trips with leisurely stops along the way are available *(see page 333)*.

If taking the cheaper local slowboat, the trip takes 18 hours or more, while the faster express boat takes nine hours. These local boats from Mandalay leave early, at around 5am and 6am respectively. A typical river journey will chart the following course along the Ayeyarwady.

Passing the only bridge that spans the Ayeyarwady with the Sagaing hills in the distance, the traveller can begin to understand why the capitals of Burma's kingdoms since the 14th century were built here, for this is a place where the earth seems to radiate an air saturated with Buddhism's inherent serenity.

After leaving the environs of Mandalay, this 36-km (20-mile) stretch of river passes through one of the most cultured places in the world. Modern civilisation has largely bypassed this region, where the spiritual wealth is felt in the *kyaungs* of the Sagaing valleys, which have been preserved over centuries.

Between Inwa and Sagaing, the river flows for a short while towards the west but soon turns south again. The **Ava** (Inwa) bridge, across which runs the road and railway line to Myitkyina, was destroyed during World War II and rebuilt in 1954. At present, this bridge and one at Pyay are the only bridges to cross the Ayeyarwady along its entire 2,170-km (1,350-mile) length. Shortly after navigating this part of the river's treacherous shoals, the boat passes the confluence with the Mu river that drains from Sagaing province.

The boat the passes **Yandabo** where, in 1825, the treaty that ceded Assam, Rakhaing and Tanintharyi to the British was signed. Yandabo, which can only be accessed by river, is well known for its terracotta pottery made with the yellow mud collected from the river bank. The boat then carries on for many miles along the confluence with the Chindwin and its many shifting sandbanks. If travelling on a local slowboat and the water is low, this is where the boat has the most chance of running aground. When this happens, it can take hours before the boat is ready to be refloated.

Once the boat has turned south again, the heartland of the Bamar people lies to the left. This land south of Mandalay, which has benefited from the irrigation of more than 2,000 years, was the breadbasket that fed the various Burmese kingdoms. Its surplus permitted the development of the advanced civilisation that started with the First Burmese Empire in the 11th century.

Passing **Myingyan** during the dry season, one can feel the dust and heat that bakes this part of the country where rain is scarce. Eventually, the boat reaches **Pakokku** – the gateway to western Burma. Pakokku is worth visiting for its bustling market and workshops producing hand-woven cloths and local cigars. From here you can reach **Mount Victoria** which, at more than 3,000 metres (10,000 ft), is the highest peak of the Rakhaing Yoma. Once past Pakokku, the jetty at **Nyaung-U**, the jump-off point for Bagan, is but a few miles away. ❑

Map on page 174

BELOW: a gold leaf workshop.

GOLD LEAF MAKING

The making of gold leaves is one of the country's typical cottage industries. To the devout, the application of gold leaves on to Buddhist statues is a sign of reverence. Indeed, when a Burmese family makes a pilgrimage to a pagoda, its members usually make sure they buy a packet of gold leaves at one of the pagoda bazaars and paste their offerings to a stupa or Buddhist image at the pagoda. Mandalay has several workshops engaged solely in the production of these gold leaves.

Typically, a worker begins with a 2.5 cm x 1 cm gold leaf. To get an idea of the thinness, 200 of these leaves weigh 12 grams. The leaf is pounded with a wooden mallet for half an hour, resized, then pounded again for about one hour, resized and then again pounded for another five hours.

Workers then take the ultra thin pieces with which they manufacture individual 2.5 sq cm gold leaves before packaging them in multiples of 10. The original piece is enough to make about one packet of leaves, which normally sells for 400 kyats.

Visitors are welcome to drop in at Shwe Hninsi Gold Leaf at 108, 36th Street between 77th and 78th streets to witness the leaf-making process.

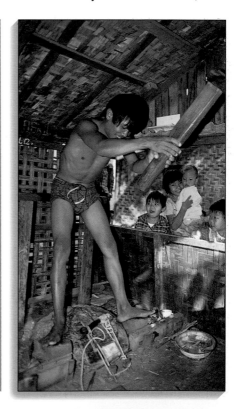

AROUND MANDALAY

From the ancient city of Amarapura to the
sacred shrines of Sagaing, the environs of Mandalay
have much to interest the traveller

Once known as the "city of immortality", **Amarapura ❷** is now called Taungmyo, "the southern city", by those in the northern city of Mandalay. It is only 12 km (7½ miles) south of Burma's second city, and as the metropolitan area burgeons, the two are slowly becoming joined. Centuries ago, King Bodawpaya had a colonnade-flanked road built from his palace in Amarapura to the Maha Muni Pagoda near today's Mandalay.

Amarapura – built by Bodawpaya in 1782 – is the youngest of the royal cities near Mandalay. It was moved there from Inwa (Ava) on the advice of court astrologers, the Manipurian Brahmans, who were concerned about the circumstances surrounding Bodawpaya's ascendancy to the throne. The power struggle had begun with a massacre and was followed by the horrifying destruction of Paungga village near Sagaing, where the entire population was ordered to be burned. The Brahmans felt the only way to prevent further mishaps was to transfer the capital. In May 1783, all of the inhabitants of Ava, together with the court, packed up their belongings and moved on to the land allocated to them around the new Amarapura palace.

The Barnabite priest Sangermano witnessed the mass migration and described in some detail the new city of 200,000 people. Foreigners inhabited their own separate quarters – Chinese, Indians, Muslims and Manipuris alike – and the smattering of Christians (primarily Portuguese and Armenians) lived in the Chinese quarter. At the centre of the city stood Bodawpaya's palace, surrounded by a wall 1.6 km (1 mile) in circumference, with a pagoda standing at each of its four corners. Within the wall were the secular buildings made of wood. Seventy-five years later, they were partly torn down and rebuilt in Mandalay by the Konbaung King Mindon.

Bodawpaya was finished with Inwa. He had the final remains of the city pulled down, the ancient trees felled and the river diverted to flood the city. His actions did not, however, prevent his successor, King Bagyidaw, from rebuilding the city of Inwa and moving the capital back there in 1823. In 1841, King Tharrawaddy resettled in Amarapura, and the capital remained there until Mindon moved the seat of the Konbaung dynasty to Mandalay.

Weavers and bronze casters

Amarapura is a city of 10,000 inhabitants whose main livelihood is weaving cotton and silk into Burma's loveliest festive clothing. The *acheik htamein* (ceremonial *longyi*) which can be knotted over the chest or worn as a train on all special occasions, is the most famous product of this city, in which every second house is said to have a loom.

LEFT:
earthquake damage
at Mingun Pagoda.
BELOW:
ancient murals at
Kyauktawgyi
Pagoda, Amarapura.

A second noted industry of Amarapura is bronze casting. Cymbals, gongs and images of the Buddha are made here out of a special alloy of bronze and lead. The famous statue of Bogyoke Aung San which stands at the entrance to Aung San Park in Yangon was cast here. Today, nothing remains of the **Royal Palace**. Some of the wooden buildings were reconstructed in Mandalay by Mindon, and the walls that were still standing were used by the British as a source of cheap material for roads and railways. The four pagodas which once marked the corners of the city wall, however, can still be seen. So can two stone buildings – the treasury and the old watchtower. The graves of Bodawpaya and Bagyidaw are also here. In the southern part of the city sits the well-preserved **Patodawgyi Pagoda**, built by King Bagyidaw in 1820. A bell-shaped stupa, it stands on five terraces which are covered with Jataka reliefs. There is an inscription stone nearby which tells the story of the construction of the pagoda.

One of the largest monasteries in Burma is in Amarapura. The presence of up to 1,200 monks (during the Buddhist lent) in the Mahagandhayon Monastery contributes to the religious atmosphere of the city. Visitors are welcome and it is a spectacular sight to witness the hundreds of monks lining up for their one daily meal every morning at 11am. This meal is donated each day by someone (at a considerable cost). There are always plenty of donors waiting for their chance to earn merit for the next life. To experience the distribution of the food (often by the family of the donor themselves) and the way in which the *pongyi* accept it without a word of thanks, is a real insight into the Buddhist concept of merit-making.

To the south of Amarapura lies **Lake Taungthaman**, an intermittent body of water which dries up in the winter and leaves fertile, arable land in its stead. It

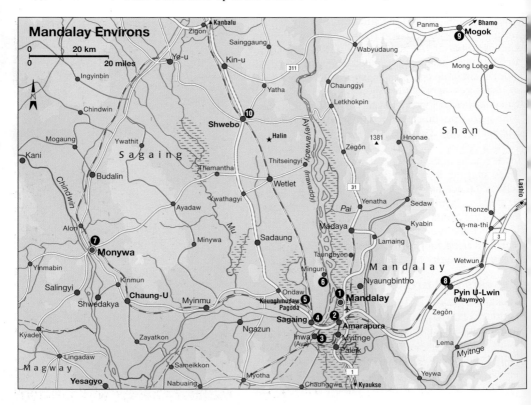

is spanned by the 1.2-km (0.7-mile) long **U Bein Bridge**, constructed from the teak planks of Inwa by King Bodawpaya's mayor (U Bein) following the move to Amarapura. This rickety teak bridge stands today just as it has for over two centuries. It takes about 15 minutes to cross the bridge, and during the hot season one is thankful for the resthouses which line it, providing much-needed shelter from the merciless sun.

Map on page 190

Kyauktawgyi Pagoda

In the middle of a widely scattered village on the east side of the bridge is the **Kyauktawgyi Pagoda**, built by King Pagan in 1847. Like the Kyauktawgyi in Mandalay, this pagoda was intended to be a replica of the Ananda Temple in Bagan. The exterior is a successful imitation, but the interior arches do not do justice to the original. Instead of the four standing Buddhas in the Ananda Temple, this pagoda contains an enormous Buddha made of Sagyin marble. The colour resembles that of jade and its height reaches the ceiling of the inner chamber.

Within the shrine stand 88 statues of the Buddha's disciples, as well as 12 *manusiha*, mythical half-man/half-beast beings. The temple's east and west entrances are decorated with murals depicting the daily life of the Burmese at the time of the pagoda's construction. Under careful scrutiny, European faces can be seen among the Burmese in the paintings. A repeated theme of the murals is the goodwill of King Pagan toward his people; this is ironic because Pagan was one of the cruelest kings of Burma's Konbaung dynasty. It is said that as many as 3,000 death sentences a year were carried out during his reign.

The area surrounding the Kyauktawgyi Pagoda is full of smaller pagodas in various stages of decay. These temples have been systematically plundered ever since the prices of ancient Burmese artifacts reached astronomical levels in the antique shops of Bangkok. On Amarapura's Ayeyarwady bank, two white pagodas – the **Shwe-kyet-yet Pagoda** and the **Shwe-kyet-kya Pagoda,** fronted by a pair of carved lions – remain from the Era of the Temple Builders. They were built by a 12th-century king of Bagan, and can be found about 30 minutes' walk away from Amarapura's main street. A short distance downriver lies the **Thanbyedan Fort**, which King Mindon had French and Italian advisors erect in the European style. The fort was intended to stop any hostile armies from striking with warships from the Ayeyarwady. Yet when the British invaded Mandalay in 1886 in exactly this way, not a shot was fired – the Burmese, lacking strong armed forces, had already given up.

Ancient Inwa (Ava): the city of gems

It is a short bus journey from Amarapura to **Inwa** ❸ (entrance fee). Alternatively, near the famed Inwa Bridge over the Ayeyarwady, a dusty, pot-holed road leads to the Myitnge River ferry; on the river's far bank, horse-drawn carriages wait to take travellers to the ancient capital. During the rainy season, this entire region is flooded, and Inwa can be reached only by boat. The city's name means "entrance to the lake", a variant of the Shan phrase *in-va*. It is appropriate, as the entire rice trade of the Kyaukse Plain was once

TIP

You can travel across Lake Taungthaman one way by oar-powered gondola to the Kyauktawgyi Pagoda, then return by walking over the U Bein Bridge to get a perspective of the lake's size. Sunset is a good time to cross the bridge for the breathtaking views.

BELOW: crossing the U Bein Bridge.

controlled from this capital at the junction of the Ayeyarwady and Mytinge rivers. Such economic control was necessary for the foundation of a sound state and strong dynasty, and it was in this region, around the 11 hamlets of the Kyaukse district, that the nucleus of a new Burmese empire took shape after the fall of Bagan in 1287 to the Mongol army of Kublai Khan.

The city of Inwa was founded in 1364 by King Thadominbya, who built it in the northeast corner of an artificial island created by the Myittha Chaung, a channel dug from the Myitnge to the Ayeyarwady. Even during the 19th century, the entire Burmese Empire was generally known as "Ava" and when the seat of government moved to Amarapura and later to Mandalay, the government was still referred to as the "Court of Ava". The classical name by which Inwa is known in Burma, however, is Ratnapura – "the city of gems".

Unlike most other royal cities of Burma, Inwa's city wall is not square, but is shaped like a sitting lion, such as those found in front of large pagodas. Only a part of the wall still stands; the most complete section is at the north gate, known as **Gaung Say Daga**, the gate of the hair-washing ceremony. Every April during the Thingyan Festival, this ritual hair-washing takes place as a purification rite to welcome the king of the *nat*. Today, it exists only in homes, but in imperial times, even the king washed his hair at this gate.

Near the north gate are the ruins of the **Nanmyin Watchtower**, the so-called "leaning tower of Inwa". All that remains of Bagyidaw's palace, this erstwhile 27-metre (89-ft) lookout was damaged so heavily by an 1838 earthquake that its upper portion collapsed. Shortly afterwards, the construction began to lean to one side due to the earth sinking beneath it. Not far from the "leaning tower" is the best preserved of all buildings in Inwa, the **Maha Aungmye Bonzan**

BELOW:
Kyauktawgyi
Pagoda.
RIGHT: Inwa's Maha
Aungmye Bonzan
Monastery.

Monastery. Also known as the Ok Kyaung, the brick structure was built in 1818 by Nanmadaw Me Nu, wife of King Bagyidaw, for the abbot Sayadaw Nyaunggan, who was rumoured to have been her lover. A tall, stucco-decorated building, it was built in the same style as that of more common teak *kyaung*; yet its masonry guaranteed that it would survive longer than its wooden cousins. In the middle of the monastery is a statue of the Buddha, placed on a pedestal trimmed with glass mosaic. Beside the entrance archway stands an old marble plaque which tells, in English, the story of an American missionary's Burmese wife who was a staunch convert to Christianity until her death during the First Anglo-Burmese War. Next door to the *kyaung* is a seven-tiered prayer hall, which suffered heavy damage in the 1838 earthquake, but was repaired in 1873 by Hsinbyumashin, the daughter of Nanmadaw Me Nu.

In the vicinity of the monastery is the **Adoniram Judson Memorial**. Judson, an American missionary who compiled the first Anglo-Burmese dictionary, was jailed during the First Anglo-Burmese War and endured severe torture during his imprisonment. He had mistakenly assumed that the Burmese would distinguish between the British colonialists and the American missionaries. The white stone memorial stands on the site of the notorious Let Ma Yoon prison.

Inwa's pagoda's

There are many pagodas to be seen in the Inwa region. Among the most interesting is the **Htilaingshin Pagoda**, built by King Kyanzittha during the Bagan era. Other important shrines include the four-story **Le-Htat-Gyi Pagoda** and the **Lawkatharaphy Pagoda**, both in the southern part of the city. Some 1.5 km (1 mile) south of the city stands **Inwa Fort**, once considered part of the

Map on page 190

BELOW: the British-built Inwa Bridge.

Detail of a door-carving at Bagaya Kyaung. The ground floor of the monastery library contains works of art and over 400 Buddha statues.

"unconquerable triangle", which include the Thanbyedan and Sagaing forts. Also worth a visit is the **Bagaya Kyaung**, a teak monastery from old Ava that survived the weather, although it was built much later than its masonry counterpart. The wooden *kyaung* is a masterpiece of intricate carving, best exemplified by the details on the portals, doors and roofs. A total of 267 massive pillars hold the building together. Next door stands a working monastery that was built more recently.

South of the existing city of Inwa is an old brick causeway leading across the canal to the village of **Tada-U**. Within the old city walls are other small villages and paddy fields where the centre of the Burmese Empire once stood.

North of Inwa is the famous **Inwa Bridge**, built by the British in 1934 and one of the two bridges that span the Ayeyarwady River. It has 16 steel spans and carries a railway line. It connects Inwa with Sagaing (the crossing can also be made by ferry) some 20 km (12½ miles) south of Mandalay. There are military posts at each end of the bridge, and a small toll is collected there. Because of its strategic importance, the British blew the bridge up in the face of the Japanese advance in 1942, and it was not reopened until 1954.

Sagaing – the living centre of the faith

Whereas Amarapura and Inwa are ancient capitals left largely at the mercy of the elements, **Sagaing** ❹ remains very much alive. In fact, most Burmese consider Sagaing to be the living centre of the Buddhist faith in Burma today. The city reverberates with the echoes of cymbals, gongs and pagoda bells. Refugees from the hectic pace of urban life retreat here – for a day or a lifetime – to meditate. Devout families bring their young sons to undergo the *shin pyu*

Map on page 190

ceremony and thereby join the community of the faithful. In the hills and in the many-fingered valleys of the west bank of the Ayeyarwady are some 600 monasteries, as well as numerous temples, stupas and caves dedicated to the memory of the Gautama Buddha. About 5,000 monks live in this arcadian landscape laced with endless stairways and colonnades. From Sagaing, north to Mingun, the slopes are covered with frangipani, bougainvillea, tamarind and mango trees, in whose shadows earthen water bowls await thirsty pilgrims. The monasteries and private houses are hidden in the hills and valleys, but the big temples and pagodas ride the crests of the verdant heights and glitter across the land.

Of all the four deserted cities (including Inwa, Amarapura and Mingun), Sagaing is perhaps the most picturesque. Sunset is the best time to view the city when the white-washed pagodas on the Sagaing Hills glow faintly pink in the amber rays of a setting sun – contrasting sharply with the muddy waters of the Ayeyarwady river flowing alongside.

Indeed, Sagaing is different at each hour of the day – in the morning, when the *pongyi* and their students stream out of the *kyaung* with their alms bowls; in the midday heat, when the ringing of the stupa bells and the droning of the monks' prayers rise over all other sounds; in the evening, when the lights of Mandalay illuminate the banks of the Ayeyarwady. The Burmese view Sagaing as a "foothill" of the mystical Mount Meru, and certainly it is easy to rise above everyday banalities here. However, if you've come here on a day tour, there will be no time for contemplation.

The jeep stops briefly at the **Sun U Ponya Shin Pagoda**, the snapshot enthusiast's favourite viewpoint, then rushes on to other sights which can be crammed into a single day's sightseeing. The independent traveller can best savour the inimitable atmosphere of Sagaing by staying overnight. From Mandalay, Sagaing is reached by bus from the corner of 29th Road and 83rd Street. In Sagaing, horse carriages will take the visitor to the foot of the monastery-studded hills behind the town.

BELOW:
Kaunghmudaw
Pagoda.

Ancient Shan capital

The city of Sagaing was the capital of an independent Shan kingdom beginning about 1315, after the fall of Bagan. The capital was moved to Ava in 1364, and most of the buildings in the vicinity were constructed during the Inwa period.

Probably the most famous temple in Sagaing is the **Kaunghmudaw Pagoda ❺**. It actually lies 10 km (6 miles) behind the city on the far side of the Sagaing Hills. Built by King Thalun in 1636 to house relics formerly kept in the Mahazedi Pagoda in Bago (Pegu), it is said to contain the Buddha's "Tooth of Kandy" and King Dhammapala's miracle-working alms bowl.

Built in Ceylonese style, this pagoda's rounded shape – a perfect hemisphere – is, according to legend, a copy of the perfect breasts of Thalun's favourite wife. The huge egg-shaped dome, 46 metres (151 ft) high and 274 metres (900 ft) in circumference, rises above three rounded terraces. The lowest terrace is decorated with 120 *nat* and *deva*, each of which can be found in a separate niche. A ring of 812 moulded

stone pillars, each 1.5 metres (5 ft) high, surround the dome; each of these posts has a hollowed-out head in which an oil lamp is placed during the Thadingyut Light Festival on the occasion of the October full moon. Burmese Buddhists come to the Kaunghmudaw Pagoda from far and wide to celebrate the end of Buddhist Lent at this annual festival. The history of the pagoda, which is also called the Rajamanicula, is written in Burmese script on a white marble pillar that stands 2.5 metres (8½ ft) high in one corner of the pagoda's grounds.

Two lakes lie behind the Kaunghmudaw Pagoda. One of them was formed when bricks used in the construction of the pagoda were stacked; it is now used for breeding fish. The other, called Lake Myitta Kan, has a legend attached to it: it is said that no leaf from surrounding trees has ever touched its surface.

There are two interesting attractions on the road between the Kaunghmudaw Pagoda and Sagaing. One is the village of **Ywataung**, home of silversmiths who still work the precious metal in much the same way as their ancestors did. The other is the **Hsinmyashin Pagoda**, also called the Pagoda of Many Elephants. Built in 1429 by King Monhyin, it was destroyed in 1482 by an earthquake. It was restored, but a 1955 quake nearly levelled it, and it has recently been rebuilt again. Two large, colourful elephants have also been reconstructed at the long entrance to the pagoda.

Sagaing's pagodas

The **Htupayon Pagoda** in Sagaing town, built by King Barapati in 1444, is also unfinished. It was destroyed by the 1838 earthquake, and King Pagan – who wanted to have it rebuilt – was dethroned before repairs were completed. The 30-metre (98-ft) high base is still standing, however, and it represents a rare

BELOW: *htis* for Sagaing's pagodas.

Map on page 190

style of temple architecture in Burma. In a nearby hut is a collection of stone engravings which include the history of the Shan Prince Thonganbwa. The prince wanted to re-establish the ancient Nan-Chao Empire in present-day Yunnan (China), but he was pursued by the Chinese and took refuge in Inwa. King Narapati provided him with sanctuary and defeated the Chinese in a battle on the prince's behalf in 1445. A year later, the Chinese returned with a stronger army – and rather than allow himself to be handed over to the Chinese, Prince Thonhanbwa committed suicide. His body was found, and Inwa was committed to paying allegiance to the Chinese.

Like the Htupayon, the **Ngadatgyi Pagoda** rests on the western side of Sagaing. There is an enormous seated Buddha image in this temple. The Ngadatgyi was erected in 1657 by King Pindale, the ill-fated successor to King Thalun. Pindale was dethroned by his brother in 1661, and a few weeks later was drowned, together with his entire family (this was a common means of putting royalty to death as no blood was spilled on the soil).

King Bodawpaya's pagoda

The **Aungmyelawka Pagoda**, built by King Bodawpaya in 1783 on the Ayeyarwady riverfront near the Htupayon Pagoda, is a cylindrical sandstone replica of the Shwezigon Pagoda in Nyaung U. Bodawpaya had it built on the site of the house where he spent the years prior to his coronation. According to the will of Bodawpaya's father, King Alaungpaya, he should have become king upon the death of his brother, Hsinbyushin. However, when the latter proclaimed his son Singu to be his successor, Bodawpaya had to stand aside until a short-lived coup by another aspiring ruler in 1782 gave him the opening he needed to claim the throne that was rightfully his. In the interim, Bodawpaya lived in Sagaing. Construction of the Aungmyelawka Pagoda was intended to balance the "necessary cruelties" of his reign and improve his merit for future incarnations. This pagoda is also known as the Eindawya Pagoda.

The **Datpaungzu Pagoda** is of rather recent vintage, having been built only upon completion of the Myitkyina Railway. It is a repository for the relics of a number of stupas which had to be demolished or relocated in clearing the way for the railway to cross the Inwa Bridge. The relics are much venerated by the people of the region.

On the most easterly point of the two ridges rising above Sagaing stands the **U Min Kyaukse Pagoda**, the architectural style of which is immediately reminiscent of a mosque. Its roof affords a fine view over Mandalay and the Ayeyarwady. The **Shwe Ume Kyaung**, a monastery attached to this pagoda, is a popular *shin pyu* site. On the western hill stands the **Sun U Ponya Shin Pagoda**, easily reached by car from Sagaing market.

Farther back in the western hill-chain lies the **U Min Thonze Pagoda**, where 45 Buddha images bask in a soft light, arranged in a semi-circle. Mural paintings dating back hundreds of years can be found in the **Tilawkaguru Cave** as well as in the **Myipaukgyi Pagoda**. The **Pa Ba Kyaung** is one of the best-known

BELOW: a yethi or shaman of north Burma.

TIP

Mingun has some
interesting shops
where you can pick up
inexpensive antique
baskets and other
handicrafts. There are
also some artists'
studios that are worth
browsing around.

monasteries in Burma. Situated in a valley between the two ridges, it is enveloped in silence and ideal for the quiet meditation demanded by *pongyi*.

Mingun – home to the world's biggest working bell

At the northern end of the chain of hills flanking Sagaing, resting on the banks of the Ayeyarwady, is the village of **Mingun** ➏, home of the largest intact bell in the world – as well as an unfinished pagoda sometimes described as the biggest pile of bricks on earth. Sharp eyes can spot it from Mandalay Hill, although it lies more than 10 km (6½ miles) to the northwest.

Unlike Inwa and Amarapura, Mingun was not a royal city but it is significant in its own right and has many interesting sights. The village is accessible only by river. Boats leave Mandalay daily and it takes only about an hour to make the trip. Visitors who do not intend to take the Ayeyarwady steamer from Mandalay to Bagan (Pagan) should not miss out on this short trip, as there is no better way to observe life on Burma's throbbing artery. Ferries, teak and bamboo rafts, diesel-powered riverboats, and numerous small boats which always appear to be on the brink of sinking, ply the Ayeyarwady between Myitkyina in the far north and Pathein (Bassein) in the delta all the way to Yangon. Women can often be seen travelling north from Mandalay, walking along the river bank and towing their boats behind them, as their husbands sit at the tillers to make sure the boats do not strike any hidden obstacles. Parallel rows of well-trodden paths are evidence of widely varying water levels on the Ayeyarwady: the banks can sometimes be 12 metres (40 ft) above the river during the dry season.

Mingun is a favourite destination for Mandalay residents on day outings. To cater to their tastes, a series of tea shops line the road from the jetty. Where the

BELOW: the *tazaung* (shrine building) of the Mingun Bell.
RIGHT: the massive Mingun Bell.

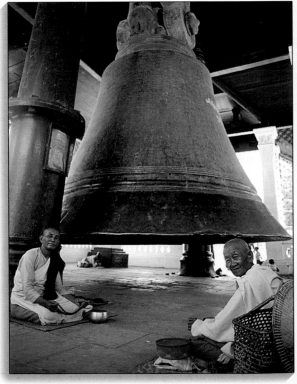

row of tea shops ends, there is a convalescent home for homeless Burmese behind the embankment. Behind and to the left of the home is the famous **Mingun Bell**. It weighs 87 tons, stands 3.7 metres (more than 12 ft) high, and is 5 metres (16½ ft) wide at its mouth. What's more, it still works. The world's only larger bell is in the Kremlin in Moscow, but that one is cracked and can no longer be used. King Bodawpaya had this bell cast in 1790 to be dedicated to his huge Mingun Pagoda which was intended to be the world's largest. By imagining how painstaking the moulding and casting procedures must have been in the 18th century, one can appreciate what a fine work of art this bell really is. Bodawpaya recognised this fact, and to prevent the feat from being repeated elsewhere, he ordered the creator of the bell to be executed.

During the terrible earthquake of 1838, the Mingun Bell and its supports collapsed. Fortunately, there was no damage. Today, the bell is held up by heavy iron rods beneath a shelter. Small Burmese boys who frequent the site are only too willing to show visitors where to strike the bell with a wooden mallet in order to produce the best sound.

Map
on page
190

Bodawpaya's pagoda

The **Mingun (Mantara Gyi) Pagoda** stands some 100 metres (330 ft) south of the Mingun bell. From a distance, its appearance is that of a large mound, nothing more. Yet it has played an extremely important role in Burmese history during the last century. The pagoda was built between 1790 and 1797 by Bodaw-paya, fourth son of Alaungpaya, founder of the Konbaung dynasty. Bodawpaya was lord of Tanintharyi (Tenasserim), the Mon lands, and Rakhaing, as well as central Burma. He had underscored his invincibility by carrying the Maha Muni

BELOW:
the historically
important Mingun
Pagoda.

Nuns waiting for alms at the stairs of Hsinbyume Pagoda.

from Rakhaing to Amarapura, and he had just become the proud owner of a white elephant. He was at the peak of his power and wanted the world to see it.

In 1790, a Chinese delegation visited Bodawpaya's court, carrying as gifts, a tooth of the Buddha and three of the Chinese emperor's daughters as wives. Bodawpaya had the pagoda built to house the tooth – the same one that both Anawrahta and Alaungpaya coveted but had failed to obtain.

Bodawpaya then moved his residence to an island in the Ayeyarwady for the next seven years while he supervised the construction work on the pagoda. Bodawpaya intended to make his Mantara Gyi Pagoda reach a full 152 metres (500 ft) in height. In order to achieve this, he imported thousands of slaves from his newly conquered southern territories to work on the pagoda.

Ambitions of a king

The pagoda, however, was not Bodawpaya's only project. At the same time as the pagoda's construction was commencing, the king had renewed work on the enormous Meiktila Dam project, for which he had also "recruited" thousands of workers from outside. In addition, large armies were deployed to help keep his empire under tight control.

Under great oppression, 50,000 Rakhaing (Arakanese) fled to neighbouring Bengal, which was then under British rule, and began a guerrilla war against the Burmese. This later exploded into the First Anglo-Burmese War.

The lack of available labour in central Burma was irritating to Bodawpaya. Worrying rumours, which had circulated some 500 years earlier during the construction of the Minglazedi Pagoda, had resurfaced, and concerned voices were saying, "When the pagoda is finished, the great country will be ruined."

BELOW: the Hsinbyume Pagoda was built in 1816.

But Bodawpaya, convinced of his destiny as a future Buddha, was not to be dissuaded. He had the pagoda's shrine rooms lined with lead and filled with 1,500 gold figurines, 2,434 silver images, and nearly 37,000 other objects and materials, including a soda-water machine, just invented in England, according to Hiram Cox, the British envoy to Bodawpaya's court. Only then were the shrine rooms sealed.

However, the economic ruin which raged at the turn of the 19th century persuaded Bodawpaya to halt construction work on the pagoda. The king died in 1813, aged 75, having ruled for 38 years. He left 122 children and 208 grandchildren – but none of them continued his work on the great pagoda.

Even though it was never completed, the ruins of the Mingun Pagoda are impressive. The upper sections of the pagoda collapsed into the hollow shrine rooms during the 1838 earthquake, but the base of the structure still towers nearly 50 metres (162 ft) over the Ayeyarwady. An enormous pair of griffins, also damaged in the quake, guard the riverfront view. The lowest terrace of the pagoda measures 137 sq metres (450 sq ft) in size, and arches project from each of its four sides.

Map on page 190

Miniature monstrosity

In the immediate vicinity is the smaller **Pondawpaya**, a small replica of the original Mantara Gyi. Compare it to its large neighbour, and you'll see that King Bodawpaya's monstrosity on the Ayeyarwady reached only one-third of its planned height. After making the comparison, take off your shoes and climb to the platform on the north side of the Mingun Pagoda for the view.

A short distance downstream of the Ayeyarwady is the **Settawya Pagoda**. This building is entirely white, and has a stairway leading to its hollow vault from the water's edge. Built by Bodawpaya in 1811, it holds a marble footprint of the Buddha.

At the north end of Mingun, beyond the village, stands one of the prettiest pagodas in Burma. This is the **Hsinbyume** or **Myatheindan Pagoda**, built by Bodawpaya's grandson Bagyidaw in 1816, three years before he ascended the throne, as a memorial to his favourite wife, Princess Hsinbyume. The temple's architecture is founded in Buddhist cosmology, according to which the Sulamani Pagoda stands atop Mount Meru in the centre of the universe. The king of the gods (known as Indra Sakka, or Thagyamin) lives here on the mountain top, surrounded by seven additional mountain chains.

The Myatheindan Pagoda is based on this model: seven concentric terraces with wave-like railings lead to the central stupa, which is guarded by five kinds of mythical monsters placed in niches around the terraces. (Temple robbers have unfortunately decapitated most of the monsters.) In the highest part of the stupa, reachable only by a steep stairway, is the *cella* containing a single Buddha figure. This pagoda suffered severe damage in the 1838 earthquake, but was rebuilt by King Mindon in 1874. Most visitors to Mingun remain only half a day, depriving themselves of the magical scenery at the foot of the

BELOW: the Hsinbyume Pagoda, modelled on Mount Meru with its seven hills.

Mingun hills. As in Sagaing, the mountainside is covered with *kyaung* and small pagodas woven together by a network of shadowy paths. Those wishing to explore the enchanting hinterland of Mingun must spend the night at one of the monasteries, as the return boat to Mandalay leaves Mingun at 3pm.

Beyond Sagaing, 160 km (100 miles) west of Mandalay is the little visited town of **Monywa** ❼, famous for its **Thanboddhay** shrine. Monywa lies in the heart of the Chindwin Valley and serves as a major trading centre for the area. The Chindwin, a large placid river, is a tributary of the Ayeyarwady which it joins 110 km (73 miles) downstream from Mandalay. The Chindwin gives access to many parts of the Sagaing Division.

Little is known about Monywa except that it was founded in the Bagan Period and that it took its present name in 1888. Sixteen km (10 miles) from Monywa is the lacquer-making centre of **Kyaukka**.

Also in Monywa is the crater lake of **Twinn Hills**, located in the Budalin township. By geological accounts, the lake was formed in the crater of an extinct volcano some 5 to 7 million years ago. It measures 5.3 km (3½ miles) in circumference and reaches a depth of nearly 50 metres (66 ft).

Pyin U-Lwin – British hill station

Those who have a weak spot for the atmosphere of British colonial times, and others just seeking to escape the dusty misery of Mandalay's hot season, must visit **Pyin U-Lwin (Maymyo)** ❽, in the foothills of the Shan Plateau. A two-and-a-half-hour drive by jeep from Mandalay takes the traveller to 1,070 metres (3,510 ft) elevation, where there are breathtaking views of the Mandalay plain.

Pyin U-Lwin was named in the colonial era after Colonel May, a British

BELOW: Monywa's Thanboddhay shrine.

THANBODDHAY TEMPLE

Near Monywa lies the stunning Thanboddhay Temple, which has been likened to the Borobodur temple complex near Jogjakarta, Indonesia, because of the similarities in architectural design. It was built in 1939 by Moe-hnyin Sayadaw. The magnificent temple, guarded by a pair of white elephants, is a sprawling complex comprising a central stupa that is surrounded by a forest of smaller stupas rising from a series of multi-level terraces said to represent the multi-layered realm of the mythical Mount Meru. Ringing the complex is a colonnade of pillars resembling the Indian-influenced Mahabodhi Pagoda in Bagan. Every one of the pyramidal pillars is made up of tiers, each housing a row of seated Buddha images. Even the terraces and stupas contain seated Buddha images in niches. It is claimed that a total of 582,357 images are enshrined in the temple.

More Buddha images – this time in caves – can be found in another temple complex on Pho-win Hill on the west bank of the Chindwin river, 25 km (15 miles) after the ferry crossing. Crowning the hill are three temples – Shweba-taung, Panga-taung and Nwatho-taung – impressively carved out of extinct volcanoes with 446,444 Buddha images placed in sandstone niches.

officer in the Bengal Infantry who was posted to this hill station in 1887 in order to suppress a rebellion which flared up after the annexation of Upper Burma to India. The city, called Pyin U-Lwin by its native inhabitants, lies at a strategically important point on the road from Mandalay to Hsipaw, a major Shan principality in north Burma.

Pleasant temperatures predominate in Pyin U-Lwin even during the hot season, and in the cold season there is no frost. It's no wonder the British felt at home here. A number of Indian and Nepalese gurkhas, whose forebears entered the country with the Indian army, have settled here, retaining many of the old colonial traditions in their work as hoteliers, carriage drivers and gardeners. They also run many of the tea shops in the hill resort.

Pyin U-Lwin offers a line of stylish former British country houses, rebuilt into small 6- to 8-room hotels. They are jewels of European comfort in Burma's up country and yet quite inexpensive. The best known is the former Candacraig, now called Thiri Myaing. This hotel, once a relaxation centre for the Bombay Burma Trading Company, was built in 1905 in the style of an English country home. It still offers many of the traditional niceties which once made the lives of the company's clerks so pleasurable – freshly cooked English food, early-morning tea and a great big fireplace.

Pyin U-Lwin also has a 175-hectare (430-acre) **Botanical Garden** (open daily 7am–5.30pm; entrance fee) where you can take a relaxing stroll or picnic by a lake. There is an 18-hole golf course, and there are three waterfalls in the vicinity for swimming and picnics. Horse-drawn carriages that resemble Wells-Fargo stage coaches are the chief mode of transportation; these closed vehicles with their high doors appear to have been left behind from the 19th century.

Map on page 190

The exterior of the Jamah Mosque in Pyin U-Lwin, serving the spiritual needs of the Muslim community.

BELOW: Candacraig Hotel, Pyin U-Lwin.

TIP

For a panoramic view
of Pyin U-Lwin, climb
to the hill-top Naung
Kan Gyi Pagoda, north
of the railway station.

The resort's cool weather has allowed many flowers and fruits commonly found in temperate climes to thrive here. There are magnolias, chrysanthemums, cherry blossoms, peaches, strawberries and plums. It is a plum, locally known as *danson,* that a rather sweetish-sour local wine is made from.

Pyin U-Lwin has two rather interesting markets – the main market in the town centre which has stalls selling handicrafts in addition to the usual fruit and vegetables, and an early-morning market frequented by the turbanned Shans who live in the surrounding villages.

Twenty-seven km (15 miles) east of Pyin U-Lwin are the **Maha Nandamu caves** depicting scenes of Buddha's life in a fairy-tale surrounding. Most of the images have been donated by the leaders and family members of the present government to atone for sins previously committed.

Beyond Pyin U-Lwin, Burma's northern and eastern frontiers are now easily accessible to foreigners. The rail line which passes through Pyin U-Lwin from Mandalay continues as far as the northern Shan administrative centre of Lashio. The road from Singu along the Ayeyarwady, opposite Kyaukmyaung, leads to the town of **Mogok ❾**, famous for its ruby mines. Independent tourists are barred from visiting Mogok, although accompanied tours to the city are readily available through local travel agencies in Yangon and Mandalay.

Alaungpaya's capital

The northern rail line from Mandalay has its terminus in Myitkyina. En route, the traveller passes through **Shwebo ❿**, about 100 km (60 miles) north of Upper Burma's metropolis. Shwebo was an 18th-century capital for Alaungpaya, and it was from here that the reconquest of Burma began after the Mon had

BELOW: early
morning bathing.

seized Inwa in 1752. Alaungpaya's grave lies in Shwebo, and his headstone is inscribed in very fractured English. Any other trappings of royalty have long since disappeared. Eighteen km (11 miles) southeast of Shwebo are the ruins of the old Pyu city of **Halin** (Halingyi).

Legend takes Halin's origins back into pre-history – an Indian dynasty is said to have produced a continuous line of 799 kings until the city one day disappeared under a cloud of ash. Archaeologists, however, place the city's establishment between the 2nd and 6th century AD, based upon radiocarbon analyses of the city wall's burnt remains. Remnants of 12 gates in the 3 by 1.5-km (2 by 9-mile) wall can still be seen today. In all likelihood, Halin was the northern Pyu capital overrun by the Nan-chao kingdom of the Tai in AD 832.

To the west, beyond the Chindwin, connected by air with Mandalay and Yangon, is **Kalemyo**, the gateway to the "skyline road" into the southern Chin hills. As it lies on the border to Chin State, the authorities have closed this area to foreign travellers.

Spirit Festival

Each year in August, for eight days before the last full moon, the village of **Taungbyon,** 20 km (13 miles) north of Mandalay, becomes the focus of the Taungbyon Spirit Festival.

Tens of thousands of Burmese attend this annual celebration, held in honour of the Taungbyon Brother Lords. The rites for these two brothers, honoured as *nat*, originated during Anawrahta's 11th-century reign. Wooden figures representing the brothers are ceremonially washed and paraded through the crowds as everyone present strains to touch each of the effigies at least once. The

Map on page 190

A young man dressed as a female spirit medium to take part in the summer Taungbyon Spirit Festival.

BELOW: *nat* altar at the Taungbyon Spirit Festival.

Map on page 190

brothers are in fact historical figures. They were sons of Byatta, a Muslim warrior from India who used supernatural means to recover the Mon's Buddhist scriptures during Anawrahta's conquest of Thaton.

According to legend, Byatta was appointed Anawrahta's flower officer, but he fell in love with Me Wunna, an ogress who lived on the wooded slopes of Mount Popa. She bore Byatta two sons, Shwepyingyi and Shwepyinnge. Byatta spent so much time at home with his beloved family on Mount Popa that he failed for the third time to provide the king with his daily flowers, and was subsequently executed.

After Byatta's death, his sons were coerced into accompanying Anawrahta on a campaign in Yunnan. Upon their return, the king's forces paused at the present site of Taungbyon village, where Anawrahta ordered the construction of a pagoda. The two brothers, unused to such hard work, shirked their assignment of laying bricks in the new Taungbyon pagoda and were consequently condemned to death.

The Burmese mourned the deaths of these two young men. Their new spirits quickly became so powerful that Anawrahta proclaimed them *nat*, had a shrine built for them in Taungbyon, and ordered that an annual summer festival be held in their honour.

Perhaps nowhere else is there such an open display of Burmese Buddhism's animistic essence as at the brothers' festival in this small village. There are ritual offerings, ceremonial dances, dozens of *pwe*, consultations with shamans, an enormous bazaar, and lots of eating, gambling, and general carousing. In the words of anthropologist Melford Spiro, it is a "combination, Burmese-style, of an American state fair and a medieval miracle play". ❑

BELOW: a local bus in Mandalay.

The train ride from Pyin U-Lwin to Lashio

The rail journey from Pyin U-Lwin to Lashio is a picturesque one. Although it starts from Mandalay, many travellers prefer to board the train at Pyin U-Lwin, combining it with a visit there. This saves precious time as the train journey from Mandalay to Pyi U-Lwin is about four hours compared to 45 minutes by road. Departures are also later in Pyin U-Lwin (in Mandalay, it starts at 4.45am); and besides, the most interesting part of the journey is from Pyin U-Lwin to Lashio.

Although the rail journey originates from Mandalay Division, most of the towns it passes through are in northern Shan State.

Until 1995, these towns were unexplored, as the route from Mandalay to Lashio was considered a haven for bandits. When this problem was eliminated, restrictions on train travel by foreigners were also lifted. Although it is possible to go by road, the train provides a more comfortable ride, albeit in carriages that have seen better days. The journey covering the 220 km (146 miles) between Pyin U-Lwin and Lashio takes about 11 hours and is a great way to glimpse northern Shan State.

After Pyin U-Lwin, the train passes gardens full of cabbages and strawberries which soon open out into broad valleys dotted with hamlets. Mist-covered mountains loom in the distance as **Wetwun**, the first stop 90 minutes later, approaches. As soon as the train stops, vendors hop on board to sell snacks.

The highlight of the journey is the **Gokteik Viaduct**, which is a magnificent steel bridge spanning a 300-metre- (990-ft)-deep river gorge which the train passes after Wetwun. The approach is stunning – the giant steel girders stand out from the dense jungle like silver latticework, set against a craggy, ochre mountain face. The steel viaduct was something of an engineering marvel when it was completed in 1903. In his book, *The Great Railway Bazaar*, Paul Theroux, who travelled this way in 1973, described it as "a monster of silver geometry in all the ragged rock and jungle... Its presence there was bizarre, this man-made thing in so remote a place, competing with the grandeur of the enormous gorge and yet seemingly more grand than its surroundings, which were hardly negligible – the water rushing through the girder legs and falling on the tops of trees, the flight of birds through the swirling clouds and the blackness of the tunnels beyond the viaduct."

After crossing the viaduct, the train passes through lush valleys surrounded by green mountains. The following stop, **Kyaukme**, is deep in Shan territory and dotted with Shan hill tribe villages. Green valleys soon give way to rice fields, banana plantations, bamboo groves and orange orchards on the approach to the next station, **Hsipaw**. Then the train snakes through jungle-clad valleys that are cut through by the rapid-strewn, emerald-coloured Namby river which flows all the way to **Lashio**. By twilight, the panorama fades and darkness envelopes the rest of the ride until Lashio is reached at about 8pm. ❑

RIGHT: early morning on a train journey.

THE PLAINS OF BAGAN

Bagan's glory days are over, but what remains are fantastic temple ruins that are the most beautiful in Burma

Bagan is one of those truly marvellous places which demand superlatives and yet remains almost impossible to describe in a satisfactory manner. It may not have been listed as one of the classical marvels of antiquity – after all, it wasn't built until around half a millennium after the fall of the Roman Empire – but today it must certainly rank as the most amazing sight in Burma and a genuine wonder of the world.

The remains of Buddhist Bagan stretch across almost 40 sq km (15 sq miles) of the flat, dry east bank of the Ayeyarwady River. All that remains of this once mighty capital of the first Bamar Kingdom (11th to 14th centuries AD) are the religious structures which were made of brick, sandstone and stucco. Secular buildings, whether the palaces of the rulers or the simple dwellings of ordinary folk, have long since disappeared, being made of easily degradable wood, bamboo and thatch. It requires some effort, then, to imagine the extent and richness of Bagan in its prime. Even today, after conquest by the Mongols and subsequent centuries of abandonment to the whims of harsh climate and earthquakes, Bagan is an impressive sight indeed.

Fortunately we have a description of Bagan in the late 13th century, just before Bagan succumbed to its Mongol conquerors. The great Venetian traveller Marco Polo visited and penned the following evocative description: "The towers are built of fine stone, and one has been covered with gold a finger thick, so that the tower appears to be of solid gold. Another is covered with silver in a similar manner and appears to be made of solid silver. The King [of Burma which, interestingly, Polo styles Mien Guo after the Chinese usage] caused these towers to be built as a monument to his magnificence and for the benefit of his soul. They make one of the finest sights in the world, being exquisitely finished, splendid and costly. When illuminated by the sun they are especially brilliant and can be seen from a great distance".

Today the gold and silver have long since disappeared, but much of the glory that was Bagan still remains, and that which survives is more than enough to make the passing traveller stop and wonder. It's no good rushing here, and the visitor should plan to spend at least three days taking in the sights. In a single day, however, it is possible to visit several of the most important temples before relaxing over a cool drink by the banks of the great Ayeyarwady River to watch the sun, usually a ball of fiery, dust-clad red, descend behind the Chin Hills to the west. ❑

PRECEDING PAGES: magnificent Bagan at dawn.
LEFT: bull cart at Bagan.

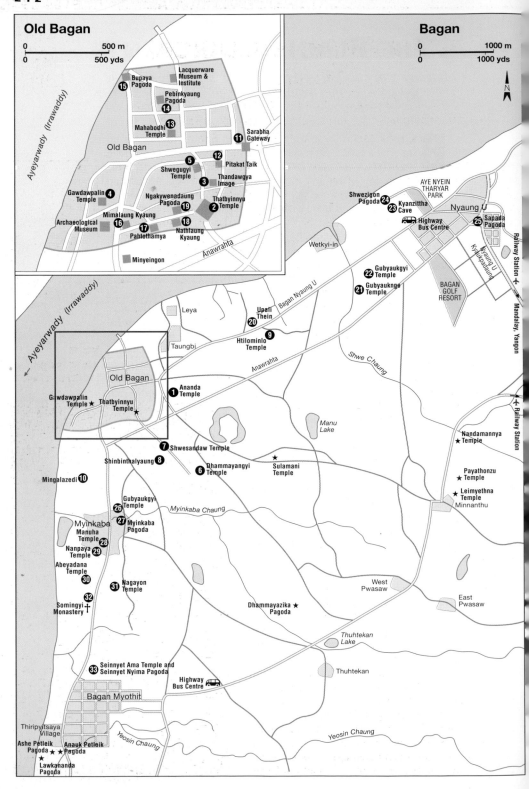

Old Bagan

0 — 500 m
0 — 500 yds

Ayeyarwady (Irrawaddy)

Lacquerware Museum & Institute

Bupaya Pagoda **15**

Pebinkyaung Pagoda **14**

Mahabodhi Temple **13**

Old Bagan

Sarabha Gateway

11

12 Pitakat Taik

Shwegugyi Temple **5**

3 Thandawgya Image

Gawdawpalin Temple **4**

Ngakywenadaung Pagoda **19**

2 Thatbyinnyu Temple

Mimalaung Kyaung **16**

17 Pahtothamya

18 Nathlaung Kyaung

Archaeological Museum

Minyeingon

Anawrahta

Bagan

0 — 1000 m
0 — 1000 yds

N

AYE NYEIN THARYAR PARK

Shwezigon Pagoda **24**

Kyanzittha Cave

23 Kyanzittha Cave

Nyaung U

Highway Bus Centre

25 Sapada Pagoda

Railway Station

Mandalay, Yangon

Nyaung U Kyaukpadaung

BAGAN GOLF RESORT

Gubyaukgyi Temple **22**

21 Gubyauknge Temple

Wetkyi-in

Ayeyarwady (Irrawaddy)

Leya

Taungbi

Upali Thein **20**

Htilominlo Temple **9**

Bagan Nyaung U

Anawrahta

Shwe Chaung

Railway Station

Manu Lake

Old Bagan

Gawdawpalin Temple ★

Thatbyinnyu Temple ★

1 Ananda Temple

Nandamannya ★ Temple

Shwesandaw Temple **7**

Shinbinthalyaung **8**

6 Dhammayangyi Temple

Sulamani ★ Temple

Payathonzu ★ Temple

Leimyethna ★ Temple

Minnanthu

Mingalazedi **10**

Gubyaukgyi Temple **26**

27 Myinkaba Pagoda

Myinkaba Chaung

Myinkaba

Manuha Temple **28**

Nanpaya Temple **29**

Abeyadana Temple

30

31 Nagayon Temple

West Pwasaw

East Pwasaw

Somingyi Monastery **32**

Dhammayazika ★ Pagoda

Thuhtekan Lake

Thuhtekan

Seinnyet Ama Temple and Seinnyet Nyima Pagoda **33**

Highway Bus Centre

Bagan Myothit

Thiripyitsaya Village

Ashe Petleik Pagoda ★

Anauk Petleik Pagoda ★

Lawkananda Pagoda ★

Yeosin Chaung

Yeosin Chaung

BAGAN ARCHAEOLOGICAL ZONE

Map on page 212

The great plain of Bagan is the site of several thousand ancient Buddhist monuments, including the temple of omniscience and a multitude of magnificent pagodas

I t has been calculated that, between Anawrahta's conquest of Thaton in 1057 and Kublai Khan's forces overrunning Bagan in 1287, some 13,000 temples, pagodas, *kyaung* and other religious structures were built on this vast plain. After seven long centuries just over 2,000 of these remain standing. Many of the others have been reduced to piles of rubble, while the Ayeyarwady (Irrawaddy) River has washed away about one-third of the original city. The legacy of Burma's Era of the Temple Builders is here for all to see, however. If Bagan were situated on a main Asian tourist route rather than on a hot dusty plain in central Burma, every child in the West would know Bagan as well as the Great Wall of China or the Taj Mahal of India.

There has been a settlement in the region of Bagan since early in the 2nd century AD, when Thamuddarit, a Pyu king, led his followers here. The walls of the city were erected by King Pyinbya in 849, but it was left to King Anawrahta, 42nd ruler of the Bagan dynasty, to usher in the city's age of glory, and to his successor, King Kyanzittha, to perpetuate that glory.

Anawrahta ascended to the Bagan throne in 1044 after killing his predecessor, Sokkate, in a duel. His victory over the Mon through the conquest of their capital of Thaton in 1057 marked the turning point in Bagan's history.

BELOW:
mother and child at a Bagan stupa.

The spread of Buddhism

Theravada Buddhism had not yet permeated Upper Burma at the time of Anawrahta's ascent to the throne. Instead, there was a mix of animistic beliefs blended with Shaivism, Mahayana Buddhism and Tantrism. But a young monk from Thaton, a Brahman priest's son named Shin Arahan, was so successful in converting Anawrahta to the Theravada school that the king became consumed with spreading the doctrine.

There are several stories about how this occurred. The most generally accepted is that Shin Arahan, as a young man of about 20, travelled north from his home in Thaton to live as a hermit in the woods near Bagan. Anawrahta heard of his presence and sent for him, curious about what this saffron-clad monk might have to offer. Upon arriving at the palace, Shin Arahan promptly sat himself down on the king's throne – an act that was punishable by death – to illustrate his belief that the only truth was that of the Buddha.

Rather than punishing this dauntless monk, Anawrahta took him in as an ally. At the time of his meeting with Shin Arahan, the king was engaged in a cultural and religious campaign against *nat* worship and the Tantric debauchery of the Ari monks of Upper

Burma. But in Shin Arahan's teachings, he founded a belief based upon rationalism rather than mysticism. Now committed to exposing his empire to Theravada doctrines, Anawrahta sent to King Manuha of Thaton a messenger requesting several copies of the *Tipitaka* (scriptures). But Manuha hesitated, repulsed by the thought of sharing sacred writings with "barbarians" – and that was his demise. Anawrahta wasted no time in responding to this affront: he massed his armies and invaded Lower Burma, sacking Thaton and bringing back to Bagan everything his elephants and men could carry – 30 sets of the *Tipitaka*, architects, Buddhist monks, even King Manuha himself and the royal family. Almost immediately upon returning to his capital, Anawrahta embarked on his programme of embellishing the countryside with Buddhist monuments. The Shwesandaw Pagoda was the first of these, and many others followed.

A king is born

As king, Anawrahta was entitled to several wives. He had received glowing reports of an Indian princess named Panchakalyani, and sent an envoy to woo her. The princess' father consented to the match, but on the return journey, the envoy had an affair with the princess. To keep this a secret and avoid the King's wrath, the envoy ordered Panchakalyani's escorts to return to her father's court, then informed Anawrahta that the princess' claim to royal descent was highly doubtful because she did not have any escorts.

Anawrahta could not return Panchakalyani to her home because he was by law already married to her, so he banished her to Payeinma on the Chindwin River, and it was here that her son Kyanzittha, later to become Bagan's greatest king, was born. The boy was by law the king's son, but was more probably the

BELOW: a European artist's impression of Bagan in 1825.

Map on page 212

envoy's. Like his biological father, perhaps, young Kyanzittha was easily enthralled by a pretty face. After the conquest of Thaton, he was ordered to accompany the daughter of the King of Bago (Pegu) to the court of Bagan, where she was to become Anawrahta's wife. But Kyanzittha fell in love with her, and when Anawrahta caught wind of the affair, he ordered Kyanzittha bound. Anawrahta planned to kill the youth himself.

However, according to legend, on this one occasion Anawrahta's mythical spear "Areindama" failed him; instead of piercing Kyanzittha's flesh, the blade cut his bonds, and the youth fled and hid near Sagaing with a sympathetic monk.

Anawrahta was killed in 1077 by a wild buffalo. His son Sawlu succeeded to the throne only to be faced with major rebellions among the Mon to the south. He asked Kyanzittha – a master warrior – for his military assistance.

There was no love lost between the half-brothers. In one important battle in 1084, Sawlu ignored Kyanzittha's tactical advice and attacked the Mon forces. His army was soon defeated and Sawlu was taken prisoner. Kyanzittha stole into the enemy camp one night to attempt to free his king, but Sawlu thought Kyanzittha had come to kill him. Kyanzittha managed to escape, but Sawlu was killed to prevent any further rescue attempts.

These events put the popular Kyanzittha on the Bagan throne. Shin Arahan, who had been Buddhist primate since Anawrahta's time, crowned him, and Hkin U, the Bago princess whose love had almost cost Kyanzittha his life, became his wife. Under Kyanzittha, Bagan became known as "city of the four million pagodas". Hundreds of monuments were erected during his 28-year reign. A deeply religious man, Kyanzittha established the Mon Buddhist culture as paramount. It was not difficult to do so; the 30,000 Mon captives who had

A terracotta detail at the Mingalazedi Pagoda.

BELOW: a view of Bagan's pagodas with balloons overhead.

The lack of primogeniture in traditional Burmese kinship made for trouble between siblings, an insecure succession, and eventually contributed substantially to the loss of Burmese independence.

been brought north after the conquest of Thaton had already significantly altered the lifestyle of the Pyu and Bamar (Burman).

Kyanzittha's grandson Alaungsithu succeeded him as ruler of Bagan, and held the throne for another 45 years after Kyanzittha's death in 1112. A highly developed irrigation system supported the production of rice by 17 surrounding communities and provided the economic backbone of the empire. But the empire began to weaken in the 13th century under the threat of growing Shan power and the menacing Mongol army of Kublai Khan, which had already overwhelmed China. When King Narathihapate refused to pay a tribute to the Khan, his armies were defeated on the battlefield, and the Mongols took Bagan.

Bagan was not, as some say, laid waste by the Mongols. Kublai Khan was a Buddhist himself and never would have permitted his armies to wantonly damage Buddhist shrines. Some of the temples may have been torn down by the Burmese themselves in a last-ditch attempt to build fortifications to slow the Mongol advance. Others became victims of the ages, of the neglect that followed the transfer of power. Only religious monuments were built of brick; royal buildings and other structures were of wood and bamboo, and they could not have survived unmaintained in Upper Burma for more than 100 years.

Contemporary Bagan

BELOW:
the Ananda Temple
dates back to 1091.

The economic centre of the Bagan plain today is at **Nyaung U**, about 5 km (3 miles) to the north of the walled village of Bagan. There are a few important monuments in the vicinity of Nyaung U, notably the Shwezigon Pagoda, and there are others a few kilometres to the south of Bagan village near Myinkaba. This picturesque Bagan village, once situated around the main temples, was

relocated in a controversial military operation in 1990, to clear the principal temple quarter of local housing. New Bagan, as it is called, has now been reconstructed some 8 km (5 miles) south of its original site, close to the village of Thiripyitsaya.

Before that, a massive earthquake jolted the plain of Bagan in 1975, raising fears throughout the nation and world that the ancient bricks had crumbled and the city had been left flattened. Thankfully, that was not the case. There was, indeed, serious damage to many of the important temples, but Burma's Directorate of Archaeology, led by the late U Bokay, immediately began repair work. The reconstruction was finally completed in 1981.

Many of Bagan's temples – especially those containing wall paintings or glazed *Jataka* panels – are closed to protect them from vandalism. Each of the temples has wardens, however, who are pleased to admit visitors for a small fee.

The best way to get around the ancient city is by horse-drawn cab. Drivers waiting outside the Myanmar Travels and Tours office usually speak passable English and are happy to work as a guide/driver for a small fee.

Admission to the **Bagan Archaeological Zone** is US$10 per head plus an additional US$2 per day. The **Bagan Archaeological Museum** is open daily Tues–Sun 9.30am to 3pm. Admission US$5.

Map on page 212

Women doing temple restoration work at Bagan.

Ten great monuments

Many visitors begin their exploration of the ruins at the **Ananda Temple ❶** just to the east of the old city wall. This impressive whitewashed edifice dominates the view as one enters the village from the north. Considered by most to be the surviving masterpiece of Mon architecture, it was completed in 1091.

BELOW:
Ananda temple's hovering Buddha.

According to *The Glass Palace Chronicle*, the Ananda Temple was inspired by a visit to Kyanzittha's palace of eight Indian monks, who arrived one day begging for alms. They told the king they had once lived in the legendary Nandamula cave temple in the Himalayas. Kyanzittha, always fascinated by Buddhist tales, invited the monks to return to his palace daily during the rainy season to tell him more about this imaginary province.

Using meditative powers, the monks made the mythical landscape appear before Kyanzittha's eyes – the king, overwhelmed, immediately opted to build a replica of this snow-covered cave on the hot, dry plain of central Burma. When the great temple was completed, Kyanzittha is said to have been so awe-struck by its unique style that he personally executed the architect by Brahman ritual to assure that the temple could not be duplicated.

The structure of the Ananda Temple is that of a simple corridor temple. Four large vestibules, each opening out symmetrically into entrance halls at the temple's axes, surround the central superstructure, which itself is inlaid with four huge niches. The entire enclosure, 53 metres (174 ft) on each side, is in the shape of a perfect Greek cross.

In the niches facing the four cardinal points are four 9.5-metre-tall (31-ft) teak Buddha images that represent the four Buddhas of this world-cycle. Each is

Carriage drivers can be hired to see the sights. Always settle a fare before you set off to avoid any disputes later on.

dimly lit from the slits in the sanctuary roof, giving visitors the impression that not only are they hovering, but are striving upward. Gautama, the most recent Buddha, faces west, Kakusandha faces north, Konagamana east, and Kassapa south. The north- and south-facing statues are originals, but those facing east and west are later copies. The originals were destroyed by temple thieves.

Temple robbers

The desecration of temples has been, in fact, a serious problem in Bagan. That the Ananda and other temples could have been vandalised as they have been, and that the robbers have escaped without sanction, indicate that Buddhist rules have not always been followed with the same intensity found during the Era of the Temple Builders. Perhaps it is a reflection of the long periods of neglect and anarchy that Burma has gone through in its troubled past.

The true extent of desecration in Bagan is particularly evident at some of the less well-known ruins, at those piles of brick not being renovated by Burma's Directorate of Archaeology. Many Buddha figures have gaping holes in their stomach areas, and many smaller stupas have at least one side broken open – the legacy of thieves searching for valuable relics. Thoganbwa, a mid-16th century Shan King of Inwa (Ava), gave impetus to robberies when he said, "Burma pagodas have nothing to do with religion. They are simply treasure chambers" and he ordered many of the Bagan pagodas to be plundered to fill his own treasure chambers. The damage at the Ananda temple, thankfully, has been restored or replaced. Precautions are still taken, however. Access to Ananda's upper terraces, for example, is restricted. Temple authorities will provide a key to keen visitors, who will then be able to climb onto the roof via a narrow staircase.

BELOW:
roof detail at the
Ananda Temple.

Map on page 212

Terracotta tiles

The roof above the central superstructure consists of five successively diminishing terraces. There are 389 terracotta-glazed tiles here illustrating the last 10 *Jataka* tales. Together with those inside the temple and at its base, these tiles represent the largest collection of terracotta tiles at any Bagan temple.

The temple's beehive-like crown (*sikhara*), capped by a golden stupa that reaches 51 metres (168 ft) above the ground, rises from the tiered roof. Smaller pagodas, copies of the central spire, stand at each of the roof's four corners, bearing witness to a measured Buddhist harmony and supposedly creating the impression of a mountainous Himalayan landscape.

Proof of this temple's purpose as a place of meditation and learning can be found within Ananda's labyrinthine corridors. Each of the four main halls contains the same 16 Buddha images as the other three, enabling four groups of Buddhist students to undergo their instruction simultaneously.

From these halls, facing the vestibules containing the large Buddhas, one can continue into the central corridor where 80 reliefs depict the life of the Buddha from birth through to enlightenment. On the west-facing porch are two Buddha footprints, each one divided into 108 parts as dictated by ancient texts.

Nearby are two statues of particular interest. One represents Kyanzittha, the Ananda Temple's founding father, and the other, Shin Arahan. By the time the Buddhist primate died in 1115 at the age of 81, he had served four kings.

The most important period of the year at the Ananda Temple is January, when the exuberant temple festival is held to raise money for the upkeep of the temple. This is a joyous spectacle, the corridors and vestibules of the temple, while normally lined with small stalls, being especially lively.

Due to the magnificent view that the Gawdawpalin Temple affords over the Bagan plain, the Directorate of Archaeology became especially intent on its renovation. It has now become the best-loved "sunset-view" pagoda in Bagan.

BELOW: a young novice monk.

Temple of Omniscience

The centre of Bagan is dominated by the **Thatbyinnyu Temple ❷**, about 500 metres (1,500 ft) to the southwest of the Ananda. Known as the "temple of omniscience", it is the tallest building in Bagan at 61 metres (201 ft). It stands just within the city walls, and is the archetype of the Bamar architectural style.

Built by Alaungsithu in the mid-12th century, the Thatbyinnyu is similar in shape to the Ananda, although it does not form a symmetrical cross – the eastern vestibule projects out of the main structure. The construction of thsis temple introduced the idea of placing a smaller "hollow" cube on top of a larger Bamar-style structure, whereas the previous Mon-style temples were of one storey. The centre of the lower cube is solid, serving as a foundation for the upper temple, which houses an eastward-looking Buddha figure.

There are two tiers of windows in each storey of the Thatbyinnyu, as well as huge arches inlaid with flamboyant pediments, making the interior bright and allowing a breeze to flow through. The first two storeys of this great temple were once the residence of monks. The third level housed images, and the fourth, a library. At the top was a stupa containing holy relics. The upper storey can be reached by climbing interior stairs to the intermediate terraces, then taking an exterior staircase to the *cella*. From here, a narrow internal

stairway leads to the three upper-most terraces, which are crowned by a *sikhara* and a stupa. The view from this platform is marvellous. A half-kilometre away is the Ananda Temple which lies before a huge plain.

A short distance north of the Thatbyinnyu is the **Thandawgya Image ❸** – a great seated Buddha figure. Six metres (19½ ft) tall, it was erected by Narathihapate in 1284. The Buddha's hands are in the *bhumisparsa* mudra, signifying the moment of enlightenment. The plaster has crumbled away over the centuries, leaving only greenish sandstone blocks, which give the statue an entrancing, mystical appearance.

Earthquake's epicentre

Back on the road through Bagan village, close to the bank of the Ayeyarwady River, is the 12th-century **Gawdawpalin Temple ❹**. It was built by King Narapatisithu in Bamar style to resemble the Thatbyinnyu Temple. This impressive building suffered more damage than any other monument in the 1975 earthquake. The *sikhara* and stupa, which previously reached a height of 60 metres (200 ft), collapsed during the quake, and a wide crack opened through the middle of the two-storey cube of the central structure.

Just south of this temple, not far from the Thiripyitsaya Hotel, is a museum containing displays of Bagan's varied architecture, iconography and religious history. Along the verandas are stones collected from the region, bearing inscriptions in Burmese, Mon, Pyu, Pali, Tamil, Thai and Chinese.

The oldest of the Bamar-style temples, **Shwegugyi Temple ❺** is only a short distance up the road toward Nyaung U. The hall and inner corridor are well lit by large windows and doorways, one of the main features distinguishing Bamar

Nearby to Thatbyinnyu temple is a small monument known as the "Tally Pagoda". For every 10,000 bricks used in the construction of Thatbyinnyu, one brick was set aside to build this pagoda.

BELOW: Children participating in an ordination ceremony at the Gawdawpalin Temple.

architectural style from the older Mon style. The temple was built by King Alaungsithu in 1131 and took just seven months to raise, according to the inscription within. Unlike most Buddhist monuments, which face east, the Shwegugyi stands on a high platform facing north, where the royal palace was.

Alaungsithu died in the Shwegugyi Temple at the age of 81. When the king lay on his deathbed in his palace, his son, Narathu, second in line after his older brother, Minshinsaw, brought Alaungsithu to the temple and smothered him in his bedclothes. Minshinsaw at that time was away from Bagan, so Narathu immediately proclaimed himself ruler. His short reign (1167–70) was, however, characterised by brutality.

Atonement for patricide

Despite his brief tenure as king, Narathu is remembered as the founder of Bagan's largest shrine, the **Dhammayangyi Temple ❻**. Deeply concerned about his karma for future lives after having murdered his father, Narathu built the Dhammayangyi intending to atone for his misdeeds.

It is today the best preserved temple in Bagan, with a layout similar to that of the Ananda Temple but lacking the delicate, harmonious touch of its prototype. The masonry, however, is without equal at Bagan.

It is said that Narathu oversaw the construction himself and that masons were executed if a needle could be pushed between the bricks they had laid. The building, however, was never completed as Narathu himself was assassinated. Narathu had by law taken his father's wives as his own, but, especially displeased with the Hindu rituals of one of them – the daughter of the Indian prince of Pateikkaya – he had her executed.

Map on page 212

Temple window detail at Bagan.

BELOW: Novice monks outside the Dhammayangyi Temple in Bagan.

Her vengeful father sent eight officers, disguised as Brahmans, to Bagan, and when Narathu received them, they drew swords and killed him. The officers then slew one another, as agreed beforehand, to avoid any additional bloodshed.

The Dhammayangyi Temple is over a kilometre to the southeast of the city walls in the direction of Minnanthu. About halfway between the temple and the walled Bagan centre are **Shwesandaw Pagoda ❼** and **Shinbinthalyaung ❽**, which houses a reclining Buddha. One of only three religious structures Anawrahta built in Bagan, the Shwesandaw was erected in 1057 upon his victorious return from Thaton. Its stupa enshrines some hairs of the Buddha sent to Anawrahta by the king of Bago.

The Shwesandaw is sometimes called the Ganesh (or Mahapeine) Temple after the elephant-headed Hindu god whose image once stood at the corners of its five successively diminishing rectangular terraces. The cylindrical stupa stands on an octagonal platform atop these terraces, which originally was adorned with terracotta plaques depicting scenes from the Jataka. The chief curiosities on the terraces today, however, are the "antiques" being peddled to tourists by local boys. The pagoda spire collapsed in the 1975 quake, and although it has been replaced, the original *hti* can still be seen lying near the pagoda.

The long flat building within the walls of the Shwesandaw enclosure contains the **Shinbinthalyaung Reclining Buddha**, over 18 metres (60 ft) in length. This 11th century Buddha lies with its head facing south and therefore depicts the sleeping Buddha; only the dying Buddha faces north. The walls of the brick building are erected very close around the reclining Buddha, thus making it virtually impossible for the visitor to photograph the statue. The last Bamar-style temple built in Bagan – the **Htilominlo Temple ❾** – is about 1.5 km (1 mile)

BELOW:
Shwesandaw
Pagoda.

Map on page 212

northeast of Bagan proper on the road to Nyaung U. The building was constructed in 1211 under the orders of King Nantaungmya. According to *The Glass Palace Chronicle*, Nantaungmya was the son of one of King Narapatisithu's concubines and was selected as heir when, as was the custom, the white umbrella of the future ruler tilted in his direction. He and his four brothers created the Council of Ministers to determine state policy; the council called itself the *Hluttaw*, the name since given to Burma's parliament.

The Htilominlo Temple is 46 metres (150 ft) high and 43 metres (140 ft) long on each side at its base. Four Buddha figures placed on the ground and four more figures on the first floor face the cardinal points. Some of the old murals can still be discerned, as can a number of the friezes. Several old horoscopes, painted to protect the building from damage, can be found on the walls.

The last of the great stupas

A short distance south of walled Bagan is the **Mingalazedi Pagoda ⑩**, the last of the great stupas erected during the Era of the Temple Builders. Narathihapate – the last of the Bagan kings to reign over the entire Burmese Empire – had it constructed in 1284. Six years in construction, it represents the pinnacle of Bamar pagoda architecture. The Mingalazedi's stupa rises high above three terraces mounted on a square superstructure. Flights of stairs lead up to the main platform from the middle of each side. Small stupas in the shape of Indian *kalasa* pots stand at the corners of each of the terraces, and at the corners of the uppermost terrace four larger stupas reinforce the heavenward-striving form of the pagoda. The terraces are adorned with large terracotta tiles depicting scenes from the *Jataka*.

However, because many of the Mingalazedi's tiles have been broken over the years, the door leading to the pagoda grounds is kept locked. Visitors should contact the pagoda warden in Myinkaba village ahead of time if they wish to enter the enclosure.

In addition to those already mentioned, there are a number of other structures within Bagan proper that are worthy of note. Entering the city from Nyaung U, the road passes through the **Sarabha Gateway ⑪**, the only section of King Pyinbya's 9th-century city wall that is still standing and that has recently been reconstructed. Although the rest of the wall consists of overgrown hillocks strewn with rubble, Bagan's guardian spirits – the Mahagiri *nat* – have their prayer niches in this eastern gateway. The two *nat*, Nga Tin De ("Mr Handsome") and his sister Shwemyethna ("Golden Face") are called "Lords of the Great Mountain" because it is believed they made their home on sacred Mount Popa. After Thagyamin, king of the *nat*, they are the most important spirit beings in Burma.

One of the few secular buildings in Bagan that has been preserved over the centuries is **Pitakat Taik ⑫**, King Anawrahta's library. Anawrahta had it built not far within the city's east gate to house the 30 elephant loads of scriptures he brought back to Bagan after his conquest of Thaton. From this structure, it is possible to get an idea of what the wooden secular buildings might have looked like during Bagan's golden age.

In times past, members of Burma's royalty who fell from grace were generally wrapped in a crimson sack and bludgeoned to death with a sandalwood club to avoid the spilling of royal blood.

BELOW: astrological birth charts, inscribed on palm leaves, for sale at Nanpaya Temple.

The Mahabodhi Temple showing its unusual pyramid-shaped temple tower.

Its original appearance, however, was altered in 1783, when King Bodawpaya had finials added to the corners of the five multiple roofs.

The library is situated near the Shwegugyi Temple. Across the main road is the **Mahabodhi Temple** ⓭. This temple is a replica of a structure of the same name in India's Bihar State, built in AD 500 at the site where the Buddha achieved enlightenment. The pyramid-like shape of the temple tower is a kind that was favoured during India's Gupta Period, and it is quite different from the bell-shaped monuments common elsewhere in Burma.

Constructed in Bagan during the reign of Nantaungmya (1210–34), it followed a tradition of fascination with Indian architecture. Kyanzittha more than a century earlier had sent men and materials to India to carry out some renovation work on the Bodhgaya Temple, and Alaungsithu in the mid-12th century made the king of Rakhaing (Arakan) do the same.

The lower section of Bagan's Mahabodhi is a quadrangular block supporting the pyramidal structure, which in turn is crowned by a small stupa. The pyramid is completely covered with niches containing seated Buddha figures. Apart from a copy that was erected on the terrace of the Shwedagon in Yangon, the Mahabodhi is the only temple of its kind in Burma. It was severely damaged by the 1975 earthquake, but renovation work has been successful.

Of warships and monks

BELOW: Mahagiri Nat's "Golden Face".
RIGHT: "Mr Handsome".

A short distance north stands the **Pebinkyaung Pagoda** ⓮, notable for its conical Sinhalese-style stupa. The stupa contains relics mounted on top of the bell-shaped main structure in a square-based relic chamber. The construction of this pagoda in the 12th century confirms that close ties existed between Burma

and Ceylon (now Sri Lanka), a result of the concern shown by King Anawrahta for the propagation of Theravada Buddhism. Although the Theravada school of thought had been introduced to Thaton by the Sinhalese monk Buddhaghosa in AD 403, it was not until 1076, when Anawrahta was in power at Bagan, that the bond between Burma and Ceylon was strengthened.

The Hindu Cholas had invaded Ceylon, and the island's ruler, Vijaya Bahu I, asked his fellow believer Anawrahta for assistance in driving them out. Bagan's king sent his ships laden with war materials, and the added support gave the Ceylonese the boost they needed to re-establish their hold on the island.

But after 50 years of occupation by "non-believers," the Buddhist infrastructure had badly deteriorated. So Anawrahta sent a group of monks to help in the regeneration of Theravada Buddhism in Ceylon. A century later, Narapatisithu sent another group for the same reason. Among them was Sapada, who built a pagoda bearing his name in Nyaung U. Many scholars feel the *Tipitaka* texts which Anawrahta reputedly seized in Thaton actually came from Ceylon.

Map on page 212

The model pagoda

A few steps from the Pebinkyaung, on the banks of the Ayeyarwady, is the **Bupaya Pagoda ⑮**. According to tradition, the pagoda was built by the third king of Bagan, Pyusawti (AD 162–243), who found a way to get rid of a gourd-like climbing plant *(bu)* that infested the riverbanks. He was rewarded by his predecessor, Thamuddarit, the founder of Bagan (AD 108) with the hand of his daughter and the inheritance of the throne. In commemoration of his good luck, Pyusawti had the Bupaya Pagoda built. As the original Bagan Pagoda, this edifice became the basic model for all pagodas built after it. It has a bulbous shape,

BELOW: view of the Bagan Moat.

The Burmese have long had a love-hate relationship with India, being anxious to preserve their independence and separate identity, but at the same time deeply conscious of their cultural and spiritual debt to the subcontinent.

similar in some ways to the Tibetan *chorte*, and is built on rows of crenellated walls overlooking the river. Because of the way it stands out on the banks, it is used as a navigation aid by boats. On the pagoda grounds, beneath a pavilion with a nine-gabled roof, is an altar to Mondaing, *nat* of storms.

The **Mimalaung Kyaung 16**, near the old city's south gate, was erected in 1174 by Narapatisithu. The small, square temple is characterised by multiple roofs and a tall spiral pagoda standing on a 4-metre (13-ft) high plinth, intended to protect it from destruction by fire and floods.

The temple's creator, Narapathisithu, is noted in Bagan's history for the way in which he acceded to the throne in 1173: his brother, King Naratheinka, had stolen his wife and made her queen while Narapatisithu was on a foreign campaign. The wronged sibling returned to Bagan with 80 trusted men, murdered his brother and ensconced himself on the throne. His wife, Veluvati, remained queen.

To the east of this temple is the **Pahtothamya 17**, which according to tradition dates from before Anawrahta's reign. King Taungthugyi (931–964), also known as Nyaung U Sawrahan, is said to have built the temple to look like those at Thaton. No temple ruins have been unearthed at Thaton, however, and the style of this temple has been proven to be that of the 11th century.

Hindu temple

To the east is the **Nathlaung Kyaung 18**, a perfect example of the religious tolerance that prevailed in Bagan during the Era of the Temple Builders. It is thought to have been constructed by Taungthugyi in 931 – more than a century before Theravada Buddhism was introduced from Thaton – and was dedicated to the Hindu god Vishnu. The Nathlaung Kyaung remained Bagan's greatest

BELOW: a horse-cart waits for visitors at Pahtothamya Temple.

Hindu temple throughout its golden age, a time when Theravada and Mahayana Buddhism, and *nat* and *naga* worship were followed, and the Tantric practices of the Ari monks were tolerated.

The main hall and superstructure of the Nathlaung Kyaung still stand today, although the entrance hall and outer structures have crumbled and disappeared. The 10 *avatar* (past and future incarnations) of Vishnu were once housed in niches on the outer walls of the main hall. Seven can still be seen today.

Remains of the Nathlaung Kyaung's central relic sanctuary indicate that it once contained a large Vishnu figure, which sat on the mythical *garuda* with spread wings. It is now in the Dahlem Museum in Berlin.

Immediately to the north, the **Ngakywenadaung Pagoda** ⓳ is much like the Pahtothamya Temple, attributed to King Taungthugyi in the 10th century. A bulbous-shaped structure on a circular base, it stands 13 metres (43 ft) high. Examples of the cylindrical form of this stupa are found in ancient Thayekhittaya.

Map on page 212

Buddha mural at the Wetkyi-in Gubyaukgyi Temple.

To Nyaung U and beyond

About 1.5 km (1 mile) down the road from Bagan proper to the regional centre of Nyaung U, and opposite the Htilominlo Temple, lies the **Upali Thein** ⓴, or hall of ordination. Named after the monk Upali, it was erected in the first half of the 13th century. Although of brick construction, it is said to resemble many of the wooden buildings of the Bagan Era which have long since disappeared. The span roof has two rows of battlements and a pagoda at its centre.

The Upali Thein was renovated during the reign of the Konbaung dynasty in 1794 and 1795; its walls and ceilings were decorated with beautiful frescoes representing the 28 previous Buddhas, as well as scenes from the life of

BELOW: woman smoking a *cheroot.*

Gautama. Sadly, the plaster came off the walls during the 1975 earthquake, and most of the fresco work was irreparably destroyed.

Near the village of Wetkyi-in are the **Gubyauknge Temple** ㉑, notable for the fine stucco work on its exterior walls, and the **Wetkyi-in Gubyaukgyi Temple** ㉒, a short distance east. The Gubyaukgyi dates from the early 13th century and has a pyramidal spire similar to that of the Mahabodhi. Inside are some of Bagan's finest frescoes of the *Jataka* tales. Unfortunately, many of these paintings were "collected" in 1899 by a German and apparently spirited out of the country.

A short distance west of Nyaung U village is the **Kyanzittha Cave** ㉓, a cave temple that served as a place of lodging for monks. Although its name would seem to indicate Kyanzittha as its creator, in all probability it dates from Anawrahta's reign. The long, dark corridors are embellished with frescoes from the 11th, 12th and 13th centuries; some of the later paintings even depict the Mongols who occupied Bagan after 1287. Visitors are advised to carry their own flashlights when visiting the temple, as the attendant family has only candles.

Bagan's greatest reliquary

The **Shwezigon Pagoda** ㉔, a short walk north of the cave temple, is the prototype for all Burmese stupas built after the rule of Anawrahta. It was built as the most important reliquary shrine in Bagan, a centre of prayer and reflection for the new Theravada faith Anawrahta was establishing in Bagan.

King Anawrahta, convinced that he was a "universal monarch", set about obtaining all possible relics of the Buddha. From Pyay (Prome) he acquired the Buddha's collarbone and frontal bone; he also obtained a copy of the Tooth of Kandy from Ceylon and an emerald Buddha figure from Yunnan. To deter-

BELOW:
walkway to the
Shwezigon Pagoda.

mine a location for the pagoda that would be built to house these relics, he set loose a white elephant – the animal which had borne the tooth from Ceylon – and where it rested, the Shwezigon Pagoda was built. Ironically, only three terraces of the pagoda had been finished when Anawrahta was killed in 1077. King Kyanzittha supervised completion of the structure in 1089.

The bell of the Shwezigon stands upon the three terraces, reached by stairways from the cardinal directions. The pagoda spire, crowned by a *hti*, rises above the bell in a series of concentric moldings. Smaller stupas can be seen at the corners of the terraces, each one decorated with glazed plaques illustrating the *Jataka* tales. Small square temples on each side of the central stupa contain standing Buddhas of the Gupta style. To the left and right of the eastern entrance are two stone pillars, each inscribed on all four sides, recording the establishment of the pagoda during Kyanzittha's reign.

Buddhist pilgrims from throughout Burma converge on the Shwezigon every year when the Shwezigon Pagoda festival is held during the second week of the Burmese month of *Nadaw* (November and December). The festival is one of the nation's most popular, largely because *nat* worship was combined with Buddhism in the pagoda's construction. Anawrahta had the images of the traditional 37 *nat* carved in wood and erected on the lower terraces, believing that "men will not come for the sake of the new faith. Let them come for their old gods and gradually they will be won over." The *nat* are no longer on the terraces, but they are housed in a small hall to the southeast of the pagoda, where they are still worshipped today.

An example of a stricter adherence to orthodox Theravada Buddhism can be seen at the **Sapada Pagoda** ㉕, at the southern end of Nyaung U on the airport

Map on page 212

Notable collections of Burmese art and architectural artefacts may also be found outside Burma at the Victoria & Albert and British museums in London, as well as at the Musée Guimet in Paris.

BELOW: Kyanzittha Cave.

ARCHITECTURAL STRUCTURES

The spread of Theravada Buddhism in Burma has been responsible for the great number of wondrous pagodas and temples that we still see today in Bagan. While the wooden structures have disappeared and most of the sandstone ones too, the great majority of the remaining ones are made of brick. The stupa structure is a solid mass, almost pyramidal in silhouette, finely detailed and usually taking the form of a bell-shaped dome atop receding terraces with a finial crowning the dome. The temple type is the more usual kind of religious architecture in Bagan, its forms depicting space without light and light within space, its components clearly articulated, the main entrance and windows plainly indicating their purpose, the corners properly defined. The entrance arch-pediment protruding from the vestibule gives an impression of space and extends a welcome to the spiritual world within.

In the temple type of structure, there are two sub-types, one of which has a single entrance, with a main hall or vestibule and a central inner sanctum for the Buddha image. The other sub-type has four identical entrances although in some rarer temples there is a main entrance – usually on the eastern side – with a bigger vestibule than the other three entrances.

Fake antiques for sale at Bagan. For details of export restrictions, see page 324 Travel Tips.

BELOW:
nuns and lay women attending a lecture at the Shwezigon Pagoda.

road. Built in the 12th century by the monk Sapada, it is similar to the Pebinkyaung Pagoda, but bears witness to a great schism in the Theravada school.

Sapada was one of the monks sent to Ceylon in the latter part of the 12th century. He returned to Burma in 1190, after 10 years in Ceylon, expounding a very orthodox version of Buddhism. It differed markedly from the Theravada Buddhism, absorbed from the Mon who predominated in Bagan at the time. And it was distinctly different from the courtly religion of Mahayana Buddhism, as well as the Vishnu and Shiva cults of Hinduism. But Sapada's interpretation was accepted by King Narapatisithu and embraced by Bagan's people.

Cave temples

There are several cave temples to the east of Nyaung U. Just 1 km to the southeast of the town are the **Thamiwhet** and **Hmyathat caves**, formed by the excavation of hillsides during the 12th and 13th centuries. Their purpose was to give monks a cool refuge from the scorching heat of central Burma.

About 3 km (2 miles) upstream from Nyaung U, on the ledge of a cliff overlooking the Ayeyarwady, stands the **Kyaukgu Temple**. The structure could be described as an ideal cave temple – the manner in which it is built into the hillside gives the impression that a small stupa stands on top of the temple, when it actually rests on a pillar. A maze of passages leads from the pillar into the caves behind: the stone-and-brick-built temple is in fact an enlargement of the natural cave structure. A large Buddha sits opposite the entrance, and the walls are embellished with stone reliefs.

The Kyaukgu's ground storey dates from the 11th century; the upper two storeys have been ascribed to the reign of Narapatisithu (1174–1211).

About a kilometre down the Ayeyarwady toward Nyaung U are a number of stupas and temples, among them the **Thatkyamuni Temple** and the **Kondawgyi Temple**. In the former are panels of paintings that depict Ashoka, the great Buddhist king who ruled in India during the 3rd century BC, as well as scenes recording the introduction of Buddhism to Sri Lanka. In the Kondawgyi are wall paintings of *Jataka* scenes as well as floral patterns.

Map
on page
212

Myinkaba and Thiripyitsaya

When King Anawrahta returned to Bagan in 1057 with the Mon royalty in tow, he exiled King Manuha and his family to Myinkaba (Myinpagan), 2 km (1 mile) south of the Bagan city walls. With Manuha present, Myinkaba became the site of the most splendid Mon-style architecture on the Bagan plain. Many of those monuments still stand.

In addition, the village has a fine lacquerware industry that has become its economic backbone. A lacquer school and museum in Bagan give visitors an opportunity to observe the various stages of lacquer production and to view some outstanding antique pieces of work.

Approaching Myinkaba from the north, a short distance after passing the Mingalazedi Pagoda, one encounters the **Gubyaukgyi Temple ㉖**. Of great importance for its inscriptions, Rajakumar built it in 1113 upon the death of his father, Kyanzittha. A very religious man, Rajakumar – whose mother was the niece of the monk with whom Kyanzittha found refuge on his flight from Anawrahta – was the rightful heir to the throne. But Kyanzittha had designated his grandson, Alaungsithu, as heir, and Rajakumar relinquished his right. Rajakumar's one storey temple was built in wholly Mon style. In the dark main

BELOW: statue of King Manuha and his queen.

hall (lit only by perforated stone windows) are nine rows of contemporaneous murals depicting the 547 *Jataka* tales. The east-facing vestibule contains a representation of a 10-armed Bodhisattva typical of Mahayana Buddhism.

The most notable feature of the Gubyaukgyi is the **Myazedi Stone**. It is sometimes called "Burma's Rosetta Stone," and was inscribed by Rajakumar in four languages of the time – Burmese, Mon, Pali and Pyu. It was discovered in 1887 and provided the key to understanding the previously indecipherable Pyu language. The inscription also provided the final word on the dates of the reigns of Bagan's kings beginning with Anawrahta.

On the banks of the Myinkaba River in Myinkaba village is the **Myinkaba Pagoda ㉗**, marking the spot where Anawrahta slew his predecessor and half-brother, Sokkate, in a duel for the kingship in 1044. Sokkate and his elder brother Kyiso had wrested the Bagan throne from Anawrahta's father, Kunhsaw Kyaunghpyu, himself a usurper, in 986; but Anawrahta's victory over Sokkate with his mythical spear "Areindama" put an end to over a century of court intrigues. This shrine's bulbous form and round terraces mark it clearly as pre-dating the establishment of Mon Buddhist influence in the Bagan region.

The **Manuha Temple ㉘** was built by the captive king of Thaton just south of Myinkaba village in 1059. Because he feared he would be made a temple slave, Manuha sought to improve his *karma* for future incarnations – and so sold some of his jewels in order to have this temple built with the proceeds. One reclining and three seated Buddha images cramped within the narrow confines of the pagoda are said to symbolise the distressed soul of the defeated king.

In contrast to most other Mon-style temples, the Manuha Temple has an upper storey. This collapsed during the 1975 earthquake and buried the Buddhas

BELOW: the reclining Buddha at Manuha Temple.

beneath it, but renovation work on the temple was completed in 1981. A corner of the temple compound is dedicated to the *nat* of Mount Popa.

Map
on page
212

A short path leads past two recent statues of King Manuha and his wife, Queen Ningaladevi, to the **Nanpaya Temple** ㉙. Said to have once been Manuha's residence, it was converted into a temple. The Nanpaya is square in plan, with a porch. Its interior is evidence of the Brahman influence affecting the Theravadin Mon kings. Four pillars are decorated with friezes and bas-reliefs, the relief of the god Brahma being particularly striking. On the outside of the temple are friezes of the mythological *hamsa* bird, which, besides being the heraldic crest of Mon royalty, was also the vehicle on which Brahma was usually depicted riding. The temple is kept locked most of the time but it is possible to go inside by arrangement – ask for details at Manuha Temple.

A short distance south lies the **Abeyadana Temple** ㉚. It bears the name of Kyanzittha's first wife, whom he married as a young warrior, and is situated at the place where she waited for him during his flight from Anawrahta. Abeyadana was probably a follower of Mahayana Buddhism: the frescoes on the outer walls of the corridor represent *bodhisattva*, or future Buddhas, and on the inner walls are images of Brahma, Vishnu, Shiva and Indra, gods of the Hindu pantheon.

Selling religious screen prints outside a temple in Bagan.

The **Nagayon Temple** ㉛, where Kyanzittha is said to have hidden during his flight from Anawrahta, is a few steps away. Legend has it that a *naga* offered him protection here, much as the Naga Muchalinda shielded the meditating Buddha from a storm. Like all temples built by Kyanzittha, this one has a characteristic Mon style. It is similar to temples in India's Orissa region; the main difference is that the Nagayon has some receding roofs which are topped by *sikhara* and stupa, whereas the Orissa temples' *sikhara* tower directly from the central structures.

BELOW:
exterior of the
Nanpaya Temple.

In the interior of the Nagayon are stone reliefs depicting scenes from the life of the Buddha. A standing Buddha, flanked by two smaller seated Buddhas, is housed within the shrine.

Rare brick monastery

Almost halfway between Myinkaba and the village of Thiripyitsaya is the **Somingyi Monastery** ㉜, one of the few brick *kyaung* on the Bagan plain. It is an example of the myriad monasteries that once dotted this plain; most of them, then as now, were built of wood and over the intervening centuries have left no trace of their existence. A lobby surrounds the raised platform of the *kyaung* to the east, monks' cells to the north and south, and a two-storey chapel, which houses an image of the Buddha, to the west. It is thought to have been built around 1204 and is named after the woman who built it.

The **Seinnyet Ama Temple** and **Seinnyet Nyima Pagoda** ㉝ are a short distance down the road. Tradition attributes these sanctuaries to Queen Seinnyet, who lived during the 11th century, although the style is more typical of the 13th century. The pagoda in particular is notable for its design, incorporating Buddhas in niches at each of the cardinal points on the bell-shaped dome, and lions guarding miniature stupas in the corners of the second terrace. ❏

AROUND BAGAN

*Overshadowed by the magnificent Mount Popa, the environs
of the Bagan architectural zone are scattered with
ancient temples and bustling market towns*

Map
on page
236

A bout 5 km (3 miles) south of the walls of majestic **Bagan** ❶ is tiny **Thiripyitsaya Village**, where King Thinlikyaung's 4th century palace was situated. During Bagan's Golden Era, there was a mooring place here where foreign ships – plying the Ayeyarwady from lands as far away as Sri Lanka – dropped anchor. Today, the chief attractions are a trio of well-preserved pagodas. Two of them, known as the **Anauk** or **Eastern Petleik** and **Ashe** or **Western Petleik** were built in the 11th century, but collapsed in 1905. The unglazed terracotta plaques originally housed in the vaulted corridors are now preserved under replicas of the original roofs. Of the two *paya* the Anauk is the better preserved. The numbered plaques depict 550 *Jataka* tales; they include the only known representations of three Buddha life-cycle stories, as only 547 *Jataka* are officially recognised by the Theravada Buddhist *sangha*.

At the south end of Thiripyitsaya is the **Lawkananda Pagoda**, raised in 1059 as one of only three pagodas known to have been built by Anawrahta in the Bagan area. (The other two are the Shwesandaw and the Myinkaba.) The Lawkananda has a cylindrical bell, and is reminiscent of a Pyu stupa. It stands on three octagonal terraces, the lower two having stairways on each side. This *paya* still functions as an everyday place of worship and houses what is believed to be a replica of the Buddha's tooth. The views across the Ayeyarwady from Thiripyitsaya are particularly spectacular at sunset – during the hot and dusty months between March and May the heavy dust-haze transforms the sun into an iridescent disk of fire.

LEFT: Shin Upagot image at a shrine at Mount Popa. **BELOW:** young boy at Bagan.

New Bagan

Just to the east of Thiripyitsaya – and rapidly outgrowing the latter – is the recent settlement of **Bagan Myothit** or **New Bagan**. This is where most hotels, guest houses and restaurants are located, and it is here that most visitors to Bagan will stay. As recently as 1990 the inhabitants of Old Bagan were issued with a military diktat ordering them to move to Bagan Myothit within 15 days. Old traveller's standbys dating from the 1970s like the Moe Moe Inn and the (aptly but accidentally named) Soe Soe Restaurant disappeared overnight as the residents were forced to up sticks and move. The new town is laid out on a north-south grid system and for several years after its establishment it was both dusty and unappealing. In recent years, however, prosperity has increased through the growth of tourism, trees and shrubs planted by the villagers have begun to give shade, and Bagan Myothit is no longer the unreservedly barren place it once seemed to be.

Finally – for the immediate vicinity of Bagan, at least – **Pwasaw**, located midway between Myinkaba and Minnanthu, is the site of a circular stupa called

Dhammayazika Pagoda. Built in 1196 by King Narapatisithu, this unusual *zedi* rises from three five-sided terraces. Five small temples, each containing a Buddha image, ring the terraces; some contain Konbaung Dynasty murals. The outer wall also has five gateways, leading to speculation that the figure five was of special significance to the temple builder. It has been suggested that this fifth aspect (added to the more usual four) represents the Maitreya Buddha or the Buddha to come.

Bamar temple style

The village of **Minnanthu** is located about 5 km (3 miles) southeast of Bagan proper. There are a large number of temple ruins in the vicinity, but few of major significance. One of the largest Minnanthu temples is the **Sulamani Temple**, not actually in Minnanthu itself but about halfway between the village and Bagan. Considered one of Bagan's great two-storied monuments, it resembles the Thatbyinnyu in plan, and was built by Narapatisithu in 1183. The Sulamani is named after the legendary palace of the god Indra, crowning the peak of Mount Meru high above the plane on which ordinary mortals live. A paragon of the fully-developed Bamar architectural style, the Sulamani Temple's upper storey rests on a huge central pillar that occupies the middle of the ground floor. The lower floor has seated Buddha images on all four sides. There are porches facing the four cardinal points on each storey, with those facing east being larger than the others. The remains of some 18th century murals can be seen inside the temple. To the north of the Minnanthu village is the **Leimyethna Temple**. It was built by Ananthasuriya, Naratheinhka's minister-in-chief, commemorating a poem written by his predecessor and close namesake,

BELOW:
woman road
worker at Bagan.

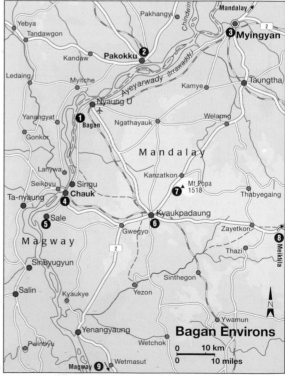

Bagan Environs

Ananthathurya. Sentenced to death by King Narapatisithu, this man penned a poem that is still regarded as a Burmese literary treasure. "If... I were to be released and freed from execution I would not escape Death," he wrote. "Inseparable am I from Karma." The king was reportedly so moved he reconsidered and decided to pardon the poet, but the king was too late – the unfortunate minister had already been executed. The temple, which faces east, is topped by a spire in the same style as that of the Ananda Temple.

Map on page 236

The **Payathonzu Temple**, a short distance north, actually consists of three interconnected buildings – the name means "Three Shrines". Joined by narrow vaulted passages, each building is crowned with a *sikhara*. Three empty pedestals stand inside, their Buddha images having long since disappeared. This temple is of particular interest because of its Mahayanist and Tantric frescoes: as the Payathonzu was erected in the late 13th century, it can be deduced that some form of Mahayana Buddhism, albeit as a minority faith, was practised in Bagan throughout the Era of the Temple Builders. It has also been suggested that the triple nature of this *paya* harks back to the *trimurti* of Indian religion, the Hindu pantheon of Vishnu, Shiva and Brahma – though Buddhists might argue that the triple nature of Buddha, *sangha* and *dhamma* would provide an equally valid interpretation. This temple is often locked (except for group tours), so make enquiries beforehand at the nearby museum in Bagan.

Sugar plantations in the Bagan area provide a much needed source of local income.

Mahayana frescoes

Also known for its supposedly Mahayana Buddhist frescoes is the much smaller **Nandamannya Temple** nearby. The erotic murals contained within might not normally be expected to appear in a Theravada Buddhist temple; but there they

BELOW: villagers on the outskirts of Bagan.

are, the nubile daughters of Mara attempting to seduce the Buddha painted on the temple's southern wall. Originally called Ananta Panna ("endless wisdom"), the temple's name was changed to Nandamannya to avoid confusion with the Ananda Temple. The temple, which dates from the 13th century, shelters a seated Buddha image in a state of advanced decay.

Market towns and river ports

Further afield, but still within the general Bagan area, the town of **Pakokku** ❷, on the right bank of the Ayeyarwady, is open to foreign visitors but remains mostly unvisited. There's little to see in this busy market town which makes a living from agriculture – especially the thriving tobacco business – but just 20 km (12 miles) to the northeast, the 19th century ruins of **Pakhangyi** are worth visiting for the old city walls, an archaeological museum and a great wooden temple – one of the oldest in Burma – supported by a forest of more than 250 teak pillars.

About equidistant between Mandalay and Bagan, on the left bank of the Ayeyarwady, the market town of **Myingyan** ❸ is both a river port and an important cotton-trading centre, forming a junction between a branch railway to Thazi and the main line between Yangon and Mandalay. Myingyan is a cotton spinning centre which is strongly Bamar in character. There isn't much of historical interest to see, but the Central Market is busy and thriving, while the are people amiable and relatively unused to visitors. Adequate food and accommodation are readily available, making Myingyan a convenient overnight stop for travellers by road between Mandalay and Pagan. Myingyan is located just downstream from the mighty **Chindwin River**, the main tributary of the Ayeyarwady River

BELOW:
a Mon family
home near Bago.

Map on page 236

and one of the great rivers of Southeast Asia. The Chindwin is formed in the Patkai and Kumon ranges of the Indo-Burma border by a network of head-streams including the Tanai, Tawan, and Taron. It drains northwest through the Hukawng valley and then begins its 840-km (520-mile) main course. The Chindwin flows south through the Naga Hills and past the towns of Singkaling Hkamti, Homalin, Thaungdut, Mawlaik, Kalewa, and Monywa. Below the jade-rich Hukawng valley, falls and reefs interrupt it at several places. At Haka, goods must be transferred from large boats to canoes.

The Uyu and the Myittha are the main tributaries of the system, which drains around 114,000 square km (44,000 square miles) of northwestern Burma. During part of the rainy season (June–November), the Chindwin is navigable by river steamer for more than 640 km (400 miles) upstream to Singkaling Hkamti. The Chindwin's outlets into the Ayeyarwady are interrupted by a succession of long, low, partially populated islands. According to tradition, the most southerly of these outlets is an artificial channel cut by one of the kings of Pagan. Choked up for many centuries, it was reopened by an exceptional flood in 1824.

About 30 km (19 miles) south of Bagan, **Chauk** ❹ is a small town and petroleum port for the Singu-Chauk oil fields. Traditionally, people of the Mon group gathered asphalt in the area to weatherproof houses. In 1902, the British discovered the Chauk-Lanywa oil field. Later, crude oil from Chauk was sent by a 563-km (350-mile) pipeline to Thanlyin for refining. Insurgent sabotage of the pipeline after World War II confined marketing of Chauk's oil to northern Burma. Tankers began operation on the Ayeyarwady as an alternative means of transport to the damaged pipeline. The Chauk refinery was renovated in 1954, and the pipeline was repaired between Chauk, Tagaing, and Yenenma and between Pyay and Thanlyin. Abundant natural-gas reserves are found in the Chauk oil fields, but the area has nothing of archaeological interest.

Just 8 km (5 miles) south of Chauk, the small riverside settlement of **Sale** ❺ (also spelt Salay) developed as an adjunct of Bagan during the 12th and 13th centuries. It's well off the beaten track, and a more active Buddhist centre than Bagan, with fascinating colonial architecture, a strong Bamar flavour, and little-visited ruins. **Kyaukpadaung** ❻, a small junction town about 40 km (25 miles) south-east of Bagan, is the railhead and bus station for nearby Mount Popa, about 10 km (6 miles) to the south. There's nothing of historical interest to see, but basic accommodation and food are available *in extremis*.

Flower mountain

In 442 BC, as legend has it, a great earthquake roared through central Burma – and from out of the barren Myingyan plains arose **Mount Popa** ❼. Volcanic ash gradually became fertile soil, and the peak blossomed with flowers of many colours. (*Popa* is the Sanskrit word for "flower".) For the inhabitants of the surrounding regions, the peak became known as the home of the gods, the "Mount Olympus" of Burma. Alchemists and occultists made their home on the slopes, and people generally became convinced that mythical beings lived in its woods and flowers.

BELOW: view of Mount Popa, home of the *nat*.

TIP

The climb up Mount
Popa is steep and
trying, especially in
the heat of the day.
Wear a hat or carry
an umbrella, drink lots
of fluids and
stop to rest often.

The mountain, 1,518 metres (4,981 ft) high, is located about 50 km (30 miles) southeast of Bagan. Part of it has recently become a national park. One can go by car from Bagan village, or take a bus trip requiring transfers in Nyaung U and Kyaukpadaung. Overnight visitors can stay at the ancient Popa monastery at the foot of the peak. During the month of Nayon (May/June), the annual Festival of the Spirits is held here. While the volcanic cone can be climbed by means of a path beginning at the monastery, it should be attempted only if you are fairly fit. On clear days, the view from the top across the vast dry plain is perhaps the most beautiful panorama to be seen anywhere in central Burma.

Mount Popa is the highest peak in the **Bago Yoma** mountain range which extends 435 km (270 miles) north-south between the Ayeyarwady and Sittoung rivers, ending in a ridge just north of Yangon. The range averages about 600 metres (2,000 ft) in height. Teak and other tropical hardwoods are extracted in the eastern Bago Yoma. Ethnic minority tribes of hill people practice shifting cultivation in these mountains, growing upland rice, corn (maize), and millet. During the 1960s, the Pegu Yoma mountain range was an important refuge for communist insurgents. During the 1970s, the disintegration of the Communist Party of Burma (CPB) began here with a series of vicious internal purges.

The legend of the Mahagiri Nat

The goal of a trip to Mount Popa should be to see the shrine of the **Mahagiri Nat**, situated about halfway up the mountain. For seven centuries preceding the reign of Anawrahta, all kings of central Burma were required to make a pilgrimage here to consult with the two powerful *nat* about their reign.

The legend begins with a young blacksmith and his beautiful sister who lived

BELOW: shrines
and monasteries
on the summit of
Mount Popa.

outside the northern city of Tagaung in the mid-4th century, when King Thinlikyaung of Thiripyitsaya ruled in the Bagan area. Nga Tin De was both popular and good-looking and he posed a threat to the king. He was hounded by the king's henchmen until he fled into the woods. The king then became enchanted with the blacksmith's sister, Shwemyethna ("Golden Face") and married her. Now that they were related through marriage, the king convinced his wife that Nga Tin De was no longer his rival and he asked her to call her brother back from the forest. But when Nga Tin De emerged, he was seized by the king's guards, tied to a tree and set alight.

As the fire lapped at her brother's body, Shwemyethna broke free from her escorts and threw herself into the blaze. Their physical bodies gone, the siblings became mischievous *nat* living in the *saga* tree. To stop them from causing him harm, the king had the tree chopped down and thrown into the Ayeyarwady. The story of their deaths spread rapidly throughout Burma. Thinlikyaung, who had wanted to unite the country in *nat* worship, learned that the tree was floating downstream through his kingdom. He ordered the tree fished out of the river and had two figures carved from it. The *nat* images were then carried to the top of Mount Popa and given a shrine where they reside to this day. Every king crowned in Bagan between the 4th and 11th century would make a pilgrimage to the brother and sister *nat*, who would supposedly appear before the ruler to counsel him.

Nat worship

In Burmese folk religion, *nat* are a group of spirits that are the objects of an extensive, pre-Buddhist cult. The most important of the *nat* are a group known as the "thirty-seven", made up of spirits of human beings who have died violent

Map
on page
236

Coconut palms are cultivated in the Bagan region. The milk is used to flavour curries.

BELOW: inscription on a monastery wall, Mount Popa.

deaths. They are capable of protecting the believer when properly propitiated and of causing harm when offended or ignored. Other lesser types of *nat* are nature or tutelary spirits; hereditary *nat*, whose annual offering is considered an inherited obligation; and village *nat*, who protect a community from wild animals, bandits, and illness and whose shrine is attached to a tree or pole near the entrance to the village. All over Burma, people also hang a coconut from the southeast pillar of their homes in honour of Min Mahagir, the house *nat*.

Nat are appeased by offerings of food or flowers, given on all important occasions. Among the special *nat* festivals are those honouring the Taungbyon brothers – a prominent, rather rowdy pair of *nat* said to have been executed in the 11th century – and the king of the "thirty-seven", Thagya Min, associated by scholars with the Indian god, Indra, known in Burma as Sakka.

Located on Meiktila Lake, **Meiktila ❽** is a major road and rail centre on the Thazi-Myingyan railway. Apart from having an airfield, the town is also a Buddhist centre, the site of a teacher-training college and a diesel electric plant, as well as a centre for wood and bamboo products and textile manufacturing. Meiktila Lake is an ancient irrigation reservoir, which legend says was begun by the grandfather of Gautama Buddha, the founder of Buddhism. It covers an area of 9 sq km (3½ sq miles) and, with connected lakes, irrigates a large region and supplies drinking water. The surrounding area is primarily a dry, undulating plain with stretches of dark cotton soil, very much a part of Burma's central Dry Zone. For the visitor, Meiktila is chiefly significant as the place where the Yangon-Mandalay and Bagan-Taunggyi roads intersect.

There is little of historical interest here – much of the town was burned down by a major fire in 1991 – but there's a vibrant atmosphere due to Meiktila's success

BELOW: illustrations from Sir Richard's Temples famous book, *The Thirty-seven Nats.*

MOUNT POPA AND THE LORD OF ZINME

In 1558 the Burmese King Bayinnaung conquered and annexed the ancient Lan Na Kingdom, with its capital at Chiang Mai, known to the Burmese as Zinme. Lan Na would remain a Burmese tributary for more than two centuries, during which time elements of Burmese art, architecture, language, cuisine and religion were permanently introduced to northern Thailand. Yet the traffic wasn't all one way; the Burmese may have brought their *nat* with them to Zinme, but they took one more home with them when they left.

The Burmese pantheon of 37 *nat* are exclusively Burmese with only two exceptions – the chief of the order, Thagya Nat, who originates from India, and the 22nd *nat*, Yun Bayin Nat, who is a former ruler of Zinme. In 1558, Yun Bayin was taken prisoner by King Syinbyumyashin of Pegu and carried away to Burma, where he died and became a *nat*. Although all but forgotten in his native Thailand, Yun Bayin Nat is still revered in Burma, being generally represented as seated on a lotus throne, holding a sheathed sword. In this way a former Lord of Zinme came to Mount Popa, where he still resides today, emphasising the close cultural links that once existed between Chiang Mai and the ancient Burmese kingdoms of Inwa and Bago.

as a burgeoning market centre, with adequate accommodation and restaurants. The capital of Magway Division, **Magway ❾** is situated on the Ayeyarwady 850 km (530 miles) north of Yangon and 150 km (90 miles) south of Bagan. It is the site of Magway College, affiliated to the Arts and Science University at Mandalay, and has an airfield. The population is almost exclusively Bamar, and the town is still little visited by foreigners. There's not a lot to see, but should you be travelling to Bagan by road from Pyay, Magway makes a convenient place to stop for the night.

Journey to Bagan

The easiest way to reach Bagan is by plane. Daily flights connect both Yangon and Mandalay with the airport, located a short distance south of Nyaung U. Travelling to Bagan by a combination of train and road is not recommended, as the journey requires a full day. Coming from either Yangon or Mandalay, you must disembark in the town of Thazi and catch a bus for the rest of the trip. There is also a "whistle-stop" line to Kyaukpadaung, branching off the main north-south route at Pyinmana, but it is even slower and less comfortable than travelling via bus from Thazi. Since mid-1995 a comfortable bus line connects Yangon with Bagan. The bus leaves Yangon at 4pm and arrives in Bagan at 5am, via Pyay and Kyaukpadaung. An alternative is to travel to Bagan by boat. The southbound Pyay (Prome) ferry, which docks in Mandalay at the end of "A" Road, heads down the Ayeyarwady several times a week, leaving at 5am. It's an all-day voyage – more if the river is low and the boat gets stuck on a sandbank – but those not overly concerned with comfort will find it a fascinating experience. For the wealthier traveller, two vessels, *The Road to Mandalay* and the *Pandaw III* make the trip with all the splendour of a bygone era *(see also pages 186–7 and 333)*. ❏

Map
on page
236

TIP

Always remember that Buddha images are sacred and venerable objects. Don't climb on them, sit on them, or pose ostentatiously in front of them for photographs.

BELOW: *The Road to Mandalay* travels between Bagan and Mandalay.

THANAKA AND LONGYI: BURMESE TRADITIONS

Longyi, the national costume, is worn every day by both men and women, while thanaka is the cosmetic of choice for Burmese women

A Burmese, it is said, never feels comfortable in anything but a *longyi* (a panel of cloth or sarong wrapped around the waist). And still fewer Burmese women will step out of their homes without a protective daub of *thanaka* bark paste on their cheeks (*see side bar opposite*).

Since time immemorial, the *longyi* has been the mode of dress for all Burmese – from the commoner to members of the royal court. It is a practical outfit; and one size fits all – whether weight is lost or gained, the *longyi* easily accommodates it.

The traditional *longyi* is a panel of unsewn cloth. These days, it comes in 2-metre (6½-ft) lengths sewn into a tube shape. *Longyi* is a general term. When it is worn by men, it is called a *pasoe* and when it is worn by women, it is called a *htamein*. Though they may look similar, the way the *longyi* is worn is not the same for both sexes.

Men tie the *longyi* with a knot in front, while women tie it to the side, with the knot tucked into a black waistband sewn to the top of the *longyi*. Simple, checked or sometimes striped patterns in subdued colours are used for men's *longyi*, while women's *longyi* sport flowery designs and bright colours. The *longyi* is worn with a shirt for men, while women wear a short blouse or matching top. Both will team their outfits with, for everyday wear, a pair of rubber-thong slippers. For special occasions, more elegant *longyi* are worn. Men will wear a jacket with their *longyi* and occasionally a turban, and women a more elaborate top; for footwear, velvet-thong slippers are preferred.

△ THANAKA LOGS
Thanaka comes from the bark of a small tree grown in Upper Burma and is sold in small sawn-up logs.

◁ GRINDING STONE
The bark is ground on a *thanaka kyauk pyin* (grinding stone) with a few drops of water to make a paste.

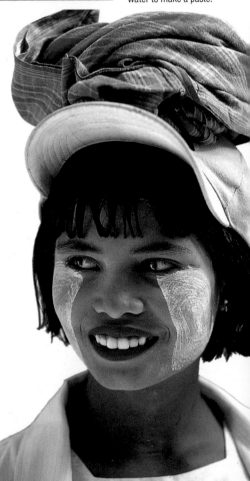

▷ KEEPING COOL WITH THANAKA
A woman working outdoors keeps cool by painting her face with *thanaka*, which is also an effective sun block.

△ TAILORED LONGYI
Many young Burmese women favour a tailored *longyi* with a coordinated top, like a trouser suit, for a more modern look.

▽ YARNS FOR LONGYI
Cotton is first hand-spun into threads, dyed in various colours and dried in the sun before it is ready for the loom.

▽ WRAP IT AROUND
Spread out the *longyi* panel and wrap the excess cloth around the waist from the front to one side.

▽ THEN TUCK IT IN
The excess cloth is tucked into a band with a safety pin to keep it in place.

▽ LONGYI OFF THE LOOM
A weaver and a hand-woven men's *longyi*. One weaver can complete three to four *longyi* in a day.

▷ ENTERTAINER'S LONGYI
Entertainers individualise their *longyi*, setting their own styles as in this comedian's use of bold and flamboyant colours.

THANAKA – THE FACE OF BURMA

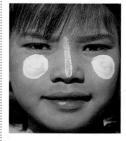

The most striking feature of Burmese girls, women and even young boys, is the yellow daubs of *thanaka* powder on their cheeks, noses and sometimes foreheads. Thanaka is traditionally used by women as it tightens the pores and controls oiliness, giving a smooth, unblemished skin. It also cools the skin – a boon in tropical Burma – and acts as an effective sun block. It's not uncommon for women who work in the fields to layer not only their faces with *thanaka*, but also their arms and exposed parts of their legs. Men working outdoors sometimes apply the substance to their arms and legs to "cool off" and prevent sunburn. The powdered substance has a light fragrance, no chemical additives, and some women believe that it lightens the skin. Traditionally obtained by grinding tree bark into a paste, for the woman in a hurry, pre-mixed *thanaka* is available.

NORTHEASTERN BURMA

The diverse Shan State stretches north to China and the Kachin State, east to Thailand and Laos and south to the Kayah State

The idyllic picture of an Intha fisherman standing at the stern of a slender boat, rowing with one leg past a backdrop of mist-shrouded mountains sets the azure Inle Lake in Shan State apart as one of Burma's most picturesque spots. Mystical and magical are other words used to describe the fairy-tale land of Inle Lake and the amazing Intha who populate its surface and shores.

This minority tribe has adapted so perfectly to its lake environment that its homes are built over the water on stilts, its vegetable fields float on the lake's surface, and its fishermen paddle their long, narrow boats with a unique leg-rowing motion that has gained them much fame.

An oasis surrounded by the southern Shan Plateau, Inle Lake may be the area's main attraction for visitors, but it is not the only one. About 550 metres (1,800 ft) in elevation and 27 km (17 miles) by road uphill from the lake is Taunggyi, a former British hill station. Taunggyi is today the administrative capital of Shan State, a centre of Shan culture (its museum is worth visiting) and a major marketplace. In the vicinity are pine forests, colourful bazaars and, some 110 km (70 miles) to the northwest, the fabulous Pindaya Cave with its thousands of carved Buddha images inside. There is also Kalaw, another former hill station of the British, now a magnet for those keen on trekking to Pa-O and Palaung villages.

Shan State is by far Burma's largest, extending west as well as east from Taunggyi for 350 km (220 miles) to Laos and the notorious "Golden Triangle" of the opium trade; nearly as far north to the Burma Road and the Chinese border; and south a lesser distance to the tribal states of the Kayah and Kayin (Karen). This is largely a region of high, roadless peaks, of rugged river gorges, of fiercely independent tribespeople, and of endless anti-government rebel activity. However, as long as the Wa Army controls the region along the Thai border, nearly all of the Shan Plateau beyond Taunggyi remains off-limits to tourists.

North of Shan and Kayah states is Kachin State which has slowly opened to foreigners. It remains a region of unsullied beauty. Home to colourful tribal groups, Kachin State's Indawgyi Lake, the largest in Burma, is breathtaking, as are its snow-capped mountain ranges in the far north, near to the border with India.

The state is also an important source of Burmese jade, which has long enthralled gems merchants far and wide. ❏

PRECEDING PAGES: fishing on Inle Lake at dawn.
LEFT: the mountainous region of northern Burma.

SHAN AND KAYAH STATES

The former lands of the Shan princes are home to gilded Buddhas and hot sulphur springs, while in Kayah you will encounter the "giraffe women" of the Padaung

Map on page 252

The quickest way to arrive in the **Inle Lake ❶** region in the south of the **Shan State** is by plane, although visitors still come by road from Thazi after getting off the train from Yangon or Mandalay. The flight is about 40 minutes and the 35-km (22-mile) journey from Heho airport can be made by bus or taxi. Visitors will either head for **Nyaungshwe**, where Inle Lake begins, or Taunggyi, the highland capital, both via the junction of **Shwenyaung**.

A snarl of silt and water hyacinths

At **Nyaungshwe ❷**, the surprising elements of the Intha first come to life. The town – the oldest of about 200 Intha settlements around the shallow, 158-sq-km (61-sq-mile) lake – stands on the fringe of the 5-km (3-mile) wide belt of silt and tangled water hyacinths that girds the lake and conceals its true dimensions.

This snarl of silt and weed, left to its own devices, takes about 50 years for a metre-thick humus-like layer to form. Most Intha make their own floating gardens by collecting the omnipresent, hollow-stemmed floating weeds and lashing and weaving them together to form a light, deep trough. Others do the same with dried reeds and grasses matted into strips. The garden is then anchored to the bed of the lake with bamboo poles and filled with mud scooped from the lake bottom with ladles. These gardens, called *kyunpaw*, are cultivated from boats, usually by women, who use both sides of the fertile strip to plant and harvest crops year-round. Cauliflower, tomatoes, cucumbers, cabbage, peas, beans and eggplant flourish in the moist conditions. The vegetables are a good source of income for the Intha who export them country-wide by truck.

The Intha people like to say they live off the lake. That cliché refers not only to their gardens, but to their remarkable fishermen, whose fame is due to their technique of propelling their slender craft through the water. Perching precariously on the boat's stern with one foot, the fisherman adroitly twists his other leg around a single long oar and thus manoeuvres through the lake water, keeping his eyes open to avert clumps of the tangled weeds floating just beneath the surface.

The fishermen's trick

Nearly as curious is the unique method of fishing. Carrying a tall conical trap containing a gill net, the fisherman looks for indications of movement on the water's surface. He then thrusts the trap to the lake bottom (it is 3 metres/10 ft at its deepest point), releasing a ring that holds the net up. As the meshwork drops, any fish within its limited range – a metre-long Inle carp, a catfish, or perhaps an eel – becomes a meal for the fisherman's entire family.

LEFT: a leg-rowing fisherman on Inle Lake.
BELOW: selling produce.

A Shan man gets his arm tattooed. The most popular motifs represent animal deities.

There are an estimated 70,000 Intha living on the lake or near its shores. An immigrant tribe from Dawei (Tavoy) and Tanintharyi (Tenasserim), they left their former homeland in the 18th century to escape the perpetual conflicts between the Burmese and Thais. They settled on Inle Lake and adopted their name, which means "sons of the lake".

Here on the Shan Plateau, they have developed an amazing culture, as their farming and fishing skills attest. Their additional talents as metalworkers, carpenters and weavers have helped to make them one of the wealthiest tribes in Burma. The famous Shan shoulder bags and *longyi*, sold throughout the country, are manufactured here on the Intha looms.

Until a short time ago, Nyaungshwe was the only place where a more upmarket hotel could be found but now there is also the Inlay Kaung Daing Hotel in **Kaungdaing** or Kaungdine. The hotel is right on the lake shore with bungalows built out over the water. It has **hot sulphur springs** close by and is a popular destination for day-tripping tourists wishing to see the "long-necked"

Northeastern Burma

Padaung tribeswomen who wear brass coils around their necks. The small community, who live on a reserve near the hotel, are originally from Loikaw in Kayah State.

There is no shortage of budget accommodation, however, as many small inns and lodges have sprung up during the past few years. Nyaungshwe is thus a convenient base for travelling in the Inle Lake area. The primary destination for Inle's visitors, however, is the village of **Ywama ❸**, about 12 km (7½ miles) away on the lake's southwestern shore. Motorised narrow boats ply the route between the two communities, carrying 10 passengers each way across the lake.

A floating market and five balls of gold

Ywama is the site of a daily "floating market" which, unlike its distant cousin in Bangkok, has so far managed to retain its authentic flavour. A boat ride across Inle Lake is the best way to appreciate the lake's vastness and its attractions which are not too evident away from the water.

The early part of the journey is an uneventful one as the boat chugs along the narrowest part of the lake. It passes a small pavilion named Inlai Bo Te before the first floating gardens and stilt houses come into view as the lake widens. It narrows again as it approaches Ywama where the slim boats filled with Shan handicrafts – tapestries, betel-nut boxes, brass weights and conical hats – await to entice buyers. After that come a series of pagodas before the boat berths at Ywama's main jetty, which is surrounded by weaving workshops offering Shan textiles, shirts and shoulder bags for sale. There are restaurants here, and also the imposing **Phaung Daw U Pagoda**, the venue of one of Burma's most important festivals celebrated in October as part of the Festival of Lights (Thadingyut), which marks the beginning of the Buddhist Lent.

The festival revolves around the procession of four sacred images which are enshrined with a fifth image in the Phaung Daw U Pagoda. The five Buddha images were carried back to Burma by the widely travelled 12th-century King Alaungsithu upon his return from the Malay Peninsula. The images were deposited in a cave near the lake, and were not rediscovered until centuries later. They were then placed in the Phaung Daw U Pagoda where they have been venerated by devotees who have covered them with so many layers of gold leaf that they look more like balls of gold than Buddha figures.

During the Phaung Daw U Festival, the golden images are paraded for two weeks. They are transported to Inle's 10 largest settlements aboard a recreated royal barge with a huge gilded *karaweik* bird at its prow. The procession is a reminder of the pomp that once marked the Buddhist courts. Only four of the five sacred images are used in the parade. Legend has it that all five were at first employed in the procession, but that in 1965, a storm capsized the barge carrying the images, and it sunk to the bottom of the lake. Only four images were recovered and these were taken back to the Phaung Daw U Pagoda, where lo and behold, the fifth one was also found, still covered with weeds. Since then, this fifth image has never left the pagoda. Today, the spot on the lake where the

Map on page 252

TIP

The Phaung Daw U Festival is celebrated at 18 villages around Inle Lake. Find out the name of the village where it will take place on the day you wish to see it and hire a boat the night before. Start out early (before 5am preferably) as festivities kick off before dawn.

BELOW: a guesthouse on Inle Lake.

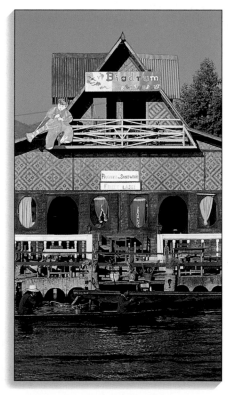

TIP

For an account of life in Burma during the time of the Shan princes, read *Twilight over Burma: My life as a Shan Princess* by Inge Sargent.

barge capsized is marked by a pole crowned by the sacred mythological *hintha* bird. The Phaung Daw U Festival draws crowds from all over Burma, arriving in boatloads carrying elaborate offerings. They come not only for the "royal" procession, but also for the famed leg-rowing competitions, where crews of Inle Lake oarsmen race each other in sprints around the lake.

The "big mountain"

Inle Lake lies at an altitude of 878 metres (2,880 ft) above sea level. Overlooking the watery basin in which it lies are numerous lofty peaks – among them **Taunggyi**, or "big mountain". The wooded height offers a lovely view of Inle Lake from its summit elevation of about 1,800 metres (nearly 6,000 ft). Two paths lead to the top.

At the mountain's foot is the Shan capital of **Taunggyi ❹**, the seat of the Shan Parliament during the British colonial period, where three dozen *sawbwa* – hereditary Shan princes – met regularly to make decisions for their subjects.

Taunggyi was founded by Sir James George Scott, one of the most respected colonial officers in the history of British Burma. A devoted student of Burmese history and culture, Scott, under the pseudonym Shway Yoe, wrote the book *The Burman, His Life and Notions* – generally regarded as the 19th century's finest work on Burma and one which remains a frequently consulted source.

Despite its altitude, Taunggyi no longer enjoys as mild a climate as it did in the past; modernisation has also robbed the town of its hill-station atmosphere. Still, the area where the old Taunggyi Hotel is located is quite pleasant, but instead of British colonials who came here to escape from the lowland heat, it now houses a Burmese government tourist office. Once called the Taunggyi

BELOW: Ywama's floating market.

Strand, the hotel is situated a short distance east of the town centre in a pine and eucalyptus grove, while nearby, on the mountain's lower slopes, is a villa where the British superintendent of the Shan State once lived, and which today is strictly reserved for state guests.

A major attraction of Taunggyi is its market. Every fifth day, markets are held alternately in Taunggyi and the towns of Nyaungshwe, Shwenyaung, Heho and Kalaw. The market in Taunggyi is perhaps the best known and a good place to observe colourfully dressed members of the region's hill tribes who flock here to buy and sell homegrown fruit and vegetables.

In the city centre, close to a monument to Bogyoke Aung San, stands the **Taunggyi Museum** (also known as Shan State Museum: open: Mon–Fri, 9am–4pm; entrance fee). It is small, but highly recommended to those interested in regional ethnology. The indigenous costumes of the 30-plus tribes of the Shan Plateau region are displayed within, and a large map indicates their locations.

On a hill 3 km (2 miles) south of Taunggyi is a temple known as the **Wish Granting Pagoda**. It is a popular pilgrimage destination for Shan and other Buddhists of the region who believe a visit to the shrine will do as the name implies. The temple's architectural style is distinctly different from the Mon and Bamar-style stupas of Bagan and other lowland locales. From its base there is a wonderful view of the Shan countryside and the Inle Lake.

The road leading east from Taunggyi is controlled by Shan rebel troops, so visitors trying to reach even **Hopong**, 20 km (12 miles) away, will be stopped by the military authorities. The drive, however, from Hopong to **Kengtung ❺** or Kyaingtong is said to be a picturesque stretch of green-clad hills. Kengtung, capital of the "Golden Triangle" and gateway to northwestern Thailand, may be

Map on page 252

A Shan woman in colourful traditional dress at Taunggyi market.

BELOW: cultivated land in the Shan highlands.

Water buffalo are used to plough fields for rice cultivation.

visited only by air or overland from the Thai border at **Mae Sai**. **Tachileik**
(at the time of writing) is the town on the Burmese border across from Mae Sai. Visas (fee payable) are issued on the spot. To cross the border into Tachileik for the day, pay US$5 at the Burmese immigration post, located at the Burmese end of an international bridge crossing the Ruak River. Like most border towns, the main activity in Tachileik is shopping, although there are a couple of nearby monasteries that may be visited.

If you would like to continue north to Kengtung or Mengla, a two-week travel permit is available at the Tachileik border crossing upon paying a US$10 fee. Sleepy Kengtung is known for its striking Tai Khün temples and local village trekking. while Mengla farther north is a wild-west town controlled by the Wa army and patronised mainly by Chinese tourists visiting from neighbouring Yunnan. Your two-week tourist visa may be extended for another two weeks in Kengtung if you wish to stay longer. Travel westward to Heho or Mandalay is permitted by air only, from Kengtung or from Tachileik.

The road to Kengtung is rough but scenic as it passes through bamboo-forested valleys inhabited by tribal groups comprising the Akha, Palaung, Kachin, Lahu, Pa-O, Shan and Wa. The Mong Tai Army for Shan liberation, led by Khun Sa, was in control of opium production in the Shan State for two decades. Khun Sa resigned in 1996 and this resulted in new economic ties between Burma, Thailand and China, and led to the lifting of the ban on travel across the Thai-Burmese border.

Between the 14th and mid-20th centuries, the Tachileik-Kengtung road was a conduit for trade from China. Mule trains were used as transport; today, trucks have taken over but the link remains as vital as ever. The wares have changed over the centuries, however, so now instead of carrying tea, silk, camphor and walnuts from China and, on the return journey, lacquerware, silver and cotton, the trade today consists of mainly electronic goods and gemstones.

BELOW: Inle Lake *cheroot* maker.

Kengtung, the "Walled City of Tung", was so named by the Siamese King Mangrai, who founded Chiang Mai. It was he who encircled the city with a 12-km (8-mile) wall. Only one arch remains from the seven gates originally built.

South of Taunggyi lies **Kekku** (also spelt as Katku), a previously off-limits area now open to foreigners. It's a three-hour drive criss-crossing the railway line to Loikaw. The road passes through Pa-O country of mainly undulating hills before it reaches the archaeological site of Kekku.

The site of a forest of stupas on the mound rising from the flat Shan plains is astonishing. Reminiscent of Monywa's Thanboddhay Temple, Kekku is a complex of stupas, large and small. It is said to comprise 5,257 individual stupas, some of which are said to date from the Bagan period (11th to 13th centuries). Little else is known about them but closer examination reveals a remarkable wealth of detail. Rising high on the plain are some 20-metre (66-ft) stupas surrounded by hundreds of smaller stupas enshrined with a Buddha image (either seated or standing) and measuring about 8 metres (26 ft) high. Other details include carvings of lotus flowers and buds, and various dancing figures.

Kalaw – the cool hill station

About 70 km (44 miles) west of Taunggyi, well beyond the Heho airport, is the town of **Kalaw** . Perched on the western rim of the Shan Plateau, it was once a favourite hill-station retreat for British officials and their families during the hot season. Little wonder, considering its beautiful rustic setting amid the bamboo groves, orange orchards and pine trees. The British left behind some colonial buildings which enhance the hill station's character – such as the half-timbered Tudor-style Kalaw Hotel – and gardens.

Now a peaceful town, Kalaw provides an ideal starting point for visits to Palaung villages and the Pindaya Cave. About 60,000 Palaung inhabit the plateau near Kalaw. This tribe, which belongs to the Mon-Khmer language family, can be easily recognised by the striking costumes worn by the women. Their characteristic dress is a blue jacket with a red collar, and a skirt with a crinoline effect achieved with a bamboo frame.

Palaung villages such as **Ta Yew** and **Shwe Min Pone** welcome visitors. Indeed, there are several hiking trails to some of the villages, ranging from one-day to multi-day trips as far as the Pindaya Cave and Inle Lake. Without too much strain, you can hike to most of the villages inhabited by the Pa-O, Palaung, Taungyo and Danu – the four main tribes living in the area.

Your trek takes you over ridges into lush valleys that are a patchwork quilt of tea plantations, *tanaq-hpeq* bushes, orange groves and rice paddies. The *tanaq-hpeq* is a leaf used to wrap tobacco to produce the Burmese *cheroot* or cigar.

If there is no time for a day's excursion, the alternative is to observe the tribespeople at the highland market held in Kalaw every fifth day. Several kilo-metres east of Kalaw, a short distance before the main road passes through the

Map on page 252

TIP

You can hire a minibus through your hotel or guesthouse for the trip from Nyaungshwe to Kekku. The round trip fare costs about US$60 and the vehicle can comfortably seat six people.

BELOW: *cheroot* smoking.

TIP

Trekkers are welcome to drop by at any of the Pa-O houses to see how they prepare the *tanaq-hpeq* leaves, which are first dried in the sun and then roasted in a kind of kiln. The leaves are then packed into huge baskets and sent to Yangon, Mandalay and other cities to roll with tobacco to make *cheroots*.

BELOW: the morning market at Lashio.

village of **Aungban**, there is a turn-off to the north. This route leads to the village of Pindaya, 41 km (26 miles) from the junction. The road takes you through a region of such great scenic beauty that it has become known as "Burma's Switzerland". Villages of the Pa-O and Danu minorities dot the hillsides to the left and right. In Pindaya village itself is the Taungyo tribe, whose homes sit in the hills above a small lake. From this lake, a covered stairway leads to the **Pindaya Cave**  (open daily; entrance fee). No one seems to know why the countless Buddha images within the cave were kept here. Thousands of them are many hundreds of years old, but it is certain that new statues have been erected there over the years (as a form of merit-making) as several different sculptural periods are represented in the work.

Nearly 9,000 images have been counted so far and they are found in almost every nook and cranny of the cave's stalagmite and stalactite formations. The most famous of these is the Antique Pagoda built by King Sridama Sawka more than 2,000 years ago, comprising tiny golden Buddha images sitting in niches, one above the another.

Not far from the lake is the gilded Shwe Ohn Hmin Pagoda where the hillside is dotted with yet more white pagodas. Situated near the village of Ye-ngan, northwest of Pindaya, are the **Padah-Lin Caves** ❾ (open daily). These caverns form Burma's most important neolithic excavation site. Countless chips created by the hacking away of stone axes have been found here, leading archaeologists to believe the caves were a site of tool- and weapon-making in prehistoric times. In one of the caves, traces of early wall paintings can still be seen. Images of a human hand, a bison, part of an elephant, a huge fish, and a sunset are clearly visible.

Northern Shan State

While Inle Lake and its surroundings in the south are the main lure for travellers to Shan State, its northern region has attractions, too. The most frequent route is by rail from Pyin U-Lwin to Lashio *(see page 207)* via the **Gokteik Viaduct** but you can also go by road. **Kyaukme** ❿ is the first town of some significance on the Pyin U-Lwin-Lashio road. Located 85 km (56 miles) from the ruby, sapphire and jade mines of restricted **Mogok** in the northwest and the silver mines of **Namtu** in the northeast, Kyaukme, consequently, is an active trading town for gemstones and jewellery and is a good place to shop for gems.

The next town, **Hsipaw** ⓫, was once the administrative centre for the state of Hsipaw, one of nine states formerly ruled by Shan princes. Hsipaw is noted for its *haw*, or palace, where the last *sawbwa* (Shan prince) and his Austrian-born wife lived until 1964. Their 1924 European-style palace is now occupied by the *sawbwa*'s nephew; although it is not officially open, visitors can drop in if he is in residence.

A good time to come to Hsipaw is around the full moon in March when the Bawgyo Pagoda Festival takes place. The 700-year-old **Bawgyo Pagoda** is the focus of festives for a week when pilgrims from all over Shan State arrive to worship the four holy images of the Buddha. A festival atmosphere pervades the grounds of the pagoda. Ox-carts trundle in with pottery, lacquerware, baskets and other handicrafts to sell, while vendors set up stalls offering games of chance and food. Lively *pwe* (shows) are held in the evening. The end of the rail line is **Lashio ⑫**, 100 km (66 miles) away from the Chinese border. Yet, despite the distance, Lashio possesses something of a frontier town atmosphere; it is the last large town before the start of the historic **Burma Road** leading to China. "Downtown" Lashio, with its strong Shan-Chinese population, is bustling. It receives a large inflow of visitors from China and the town's shops are well-stocked with a wide array of Chinese-made goods. Only Chinese nationals are allowed entry into Burma from China and vice versa. Travel beyond Lashio to **Muse** and **Namkham** – two other border towns lying to the north – is also strictly prohibited.

Map on page 252

State of Kayah

Southwest of Shan State is the small, diamond-shaped state of **Kayah**, which is off-limits to foreigners. Its capital is **Loikaw**, now linked by a new railway line to Aungban, which supplements the old road. Eight ethnic groups are said to comprise the state's inhabitants, among which, the Padaung are the best known. Padaung women wear brass coils (often mistaken for rings) to make their necks appear elongated. In reality the heavy coils depress their collarbones, creating the illusion of a longer neck.

Padaung woman traditionally wear brass coils around their necks.

The best place to see the Padaung and other tribal groups such as the Bre, Yinbaw, Taungthu and Kayah, is at Loikaw's Thirimingala market. Outside town, on the twin-peak summit of Taungkwe, is the **Taungkwe Zedi**, which offers views of Loikaw. You can also visit the **Lawpita Falls**, which drive a large hydro-electric power plant. ❑

BELOW:
a wooden bridge
in Kayah state.

LEGEND OF THE BAWGYO PAGODA IMAGES

According to local legend, a celestial being gave the 11th-century King Narapathisithu of the Bagan Dynasty a piece of wood out of which four Buddha images were carved. The king built the Bawgyo Pagoda to house the images for his people to worship. The rest of the wood was planted in the courtyard and it miraculously took root. The tree is still thriving and is considered sacred.

The four Buddha images are enshrined in the inner sanctum of the Bawgyo Pagoda and brought out only once a year during the March pagoda festival to allow devotees to venerate them and gild them with gold leaves.

For many years in the past, due to fears of robbery, the images were kept in the *haw* in Hsipaw for safe-keeping. When it was time to take out the images for display, there would be a grand ceremonial procession, including a parade of elephants, to accompany the images back to the Bawgyo Pagoda.

During the reign of the *sawbwa*, the festival was the only time when gambling was allowed; it was also an important social event that brought together the Shan, as well as ethnic minorities from all over Burma, to display and sell their goods.

KACHIN STATE

Map on page 262

Here in the far north of the country, gold mines spread out along the banks of the Ayeyarwady, while Burma's largest lake, the Indawgyi, rests among high hills and teak forests

Kachin is the northernmost state in Burma and the second largest of the country's seven states. It contains rich deposits of gold, jade, ruby and other precious gems. Previously off-limits, Kachin State is gradually opening up to tourism although access to some places is restricted to guided tours. The independent traveller can visit Myitkyina, Hopin, Mohnyin, Mogaung, Bhamo and Indawgyi. The state comprises three districts: Myitkyina, Bhamo and Putao. The Kachin of Kachin State make up 2 percent or just under one million of Burma's 46 million people. The Kachin are not homogeneous; they consists of seven sub-groups: Rawang, Lisu, Jingpaw, Maru, Azi (Zaiwa), Khamti Shan and Lashi.

Myitkyina ❶, the state capital, is located 144 metres (476 ft) above sea level and lying below the foothills of the Himalayas. Following the completion of the Yangon–Mandalay–Myitkyina rail link in 1898, Myitkyina became the commercial hub of the north and today it is the largest town in the region.

The city was levelled during World War II in fierce fighting between the Allies and the Japanese, and it changed hands several times. Today, an overgrown Allied landing strip is still recognisable at the city limits – a place of pilgrimage for the few surviving British "Marauders" and "Chindits".

LEFT: sunset on the Ayeyarwady at Bhamo.
BELOW: sharpening knives at Katha.

Since the 1993 ccasc-fire agreement between the SLORC and the KIO, ending more than half a century of civil war, Kachin, Shan, Bamar and Chinese live peacefully together again in a city where Christian churches, Buddhist *kyaung* and Chinese joss-stick houses cater for the different religious needs. Due to the proximity of the jade mines, there has been an influx of Chinese money which has helped to modernise the city. A sign of this change is that several hotels are now allowed to accept foreign visitors. There is a laid-back, provincial fccl to Myitkyina. You can hire a bicycle to explore the uncrowded town with its interesting street market that sells mandarin oranges, apples, grapefruit and kumquats, all of which grow abundantly in the north.

In the cradle of the Ayeyarwady

At the edge of the town, by the banks of the **Ayeyarwady**, gold-panning and mining goes on relentlessly day and night. Near the shoreline are gold-prospecting camps set up by young men trying their luck. About 45 km (25 miles) north of here is some of Burma's most beautiful and important natural beauty spots, in the cradle of the Ayeyarwady, where the **Malihka** and **Mehka** rivers meet. Surrounded by high hills, their confluence, **Myit-son** ❷, meets in a series of spectacular rapids through which hardy northern tribesman navigate ramshackle rafts.

TIP

Try to find a place to stay in town as Myitkyina is rather spread out and you may have to travel by taxi to get around. If your hotel is out of town, enquire about bike hire. It is a good way of getting about economically and efficiently.

BELOW:
a northern shaman.

The road leading to the junction of the Mehka and Malihka was only opened to foreigners in the '90s. The confluence of rivers is a place of exceptional natural beauty, the Mehka being quiet and peaceful, while the Malihka rushes and foams. For some distance you can observe how the differently coloured waters mix. Beyond the basin, the newly-born Ayeyarwady meanders peacefully through the jungle, past sand banks and huge rocks towards Myitkyina.

Besides its scenic beauty, this place also has an emotional quality for the locals. It is here where, with the birth of the river, the birth of the nation also took place, and like the merging of waters from different geographical regions, so the different peoples that make up the Burmese nation are unified in this dramatic natural setting. Many of them have come along these Himalaya-born rivers from far-off China to settle in the hills beyond. Since this area will be permanently open to outsiders, the government plans to construct a hotel on the hillock overlooking the junction. At present, there are only a couple of pagodas in the vicinity and a small café with a good view of the river. The jungle and surrounding hills here are ideal for trekking. Halfway between the confluence and Myitkyina is a scenic point with a small restaurant which is popular with Myitkyinites.

Festivals and feasts

One of the best times to be in Myitkyina is on 10 January, when the Manao Festival is celebrated in the town stadium. It brings together all seven tribal groups in dance, fun and games. The date is also Kachin State Day, marking the anniversary of the entry of the state into the Union of Burma. It's one of the most colourful gatherings you'll ever attend, showcasing the unique costumes of each of the seven groups in tribal dances around four totem poles, complete

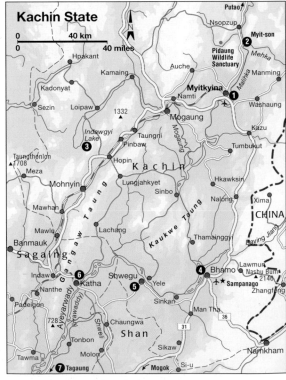

with ceremonial regalia, including swords. Some of the astonishing headgear on display includes tassels, beads, horns, feathers and even stuffed birds. The rhythms of the drums and chants, the file-dances and stomping resemble the gatherings of Native American Indians. Apart from the dancing, there are tug-of-war matches, bean-bag slugging and swing contests. Since most Kachin have converted to Christianity, this originally animist festival has now become a mixture of religion and culture. Because of the civil war, the festival was, for several decades, toned down to a village affair. With peace restored, thousands of Kachin from all tribes now meet to celebrate their cultural identity.

A *manao* is one of many dances at a thanksgiving feast hosted by the tribal chieftains honouring various *nat* (spirits) to ensure good weather for a bumper harvest or to celebrate good fortune and success. Meaning "centre" or "summit", the *manao* was referred to by the ancient Kachin as a "meeting of gods" as it was a festival offered to the Madai god or noble king of gods. For this reason, it could only be hosted by rich and noble chieftains.

Today, it has become a traditional dance performed as part of a festival of offerings to the Kachin *nat*. *Manao* are generally held among the Kachin to celebrate an occasion (the Ninghtan Manao is a wedding feast, for instance, and the Hting Hkring Manao is performed when moving to a new house). The whole neighbourhood is often invited and the celebrations may last for days.

Northern cities

Only two cities of mentionable size are found north of Myitkyina, both in the vicinity of the Malihka: Putao and Sumprabum. **Putao** (population: 10,000) was formerly known as Hkamti Long and renamed Fort Hertz by the British. It

Map on page 262

A pagoda in Myitkyina, the capital of Kachin State.

BELOW: view of the Kachin Hills.

HATAPRU HKALUP HPUI
NAWKU HTINGNU

The majority of people in Kachin are Christian or Buddhist, but many festivals have animist elements.

BELOW: travelling on a river boat.

is at the northern end of the Hukawng valley and is the centre of the far north. As the northernmost town in Burma, Putao has earned itself the sobriquet, "the Switzerland of Burma", due to its backdrop of snow-capped mountains. Only tourists on guided tours are allowed to enter Putao and only by air. Putao is near the Assam border, at the centre of the Rawang and Lisu settlement areas. North of Putao is the country's highest peak, **Hkakabo Razi**. At 5,889 metres (19,320 ft), it is also the highest in Southeast Asia. This region, at the triangle where India, China and Burma meet, is so rugged and impenetrable that few have ever explored it.

There has been talk of developing skiing facilities and promoting mountaineering here, but so far, nothing appears to have been done. Putao's **Myoma market** – closed on Sundays as its population comprises mostly Kachin and Lisu Christians – stocks unusual produce, such as wild Eland meat and smoked freshwater fish. Fresh fruit stalls are plentiful, particularly apricots, cherries and grapefruit.

Sixteen kilometres (10 miles) from Putao, at Machembo, some government-owned bungalows form a hilltop resort with flair while the nearby **Muladashi suspension bridge** over the Mula River, surrounded by bamboo groves and hills, makes an excellent picnic spot. Another noteworthy suspension bridge is the rope bridge connecting Putao and Machanbaw. Measuring 213 metres (705 ft), it is the longest in the country but only 1.8 metres (6 ft) wide. Farther south is **Suprabum**, the trading centre of the northernmost tribes. To the west live the Nagas and to the east a variety of Kachin tribes, their settlements spilling over into India and China.

Indawgyi Lake

One of the more worthwhile attractions of Kachin State is **Indawgyi Lake ❸**, the largest lake in Burma. The jump-off point is **Hopin**, a sleepy town with a large ethnic Chinese population. It's a five-hour train ride from Myitkyina via **Mogaung** (the centre of jade mining) to Hopin where cargo and passenger trucks are available to ferry travellers up and down snaking mountain roads to Indawgyi. The sight of the lake is something to behold at a pass just before the truck makes its way downhill. One family-run guesthouse (with no name) provides accommodation; otherwise it's possible to stay in a local monastery near the lake. The Indawygyi region (population: 20,000) is rich in gold deposits and a Canadian technical team is currently assisting the Burmese government in prospecting the ore. It is also home to extensive teak forests and there are three logging camps.

Several picturesque villages dot the lake shore, comprising clusters of wooden houses built on stilts. The lake measures 24 km (16 miles) between its farthest points and is 12 km (8 miles) across. Indawgyi means "large royal lake" and was created by a dozen streams feeding into a depression surrounded by hills.

In the middle of the lake is the dazzling white **Shwe Myitzu Pagoda** where relics of the Buddha are said to be enshrined. It sits on a two-tier platform consisting of a central golden stupa surrounded by scores of smaller white stupas. Panels depicting scenes from the Buddha's life decorate the ceilings covering the lower tier of the platform, which is also adorned by statues of *nat,* said to still roam the Indawgyi area. Visitors can take in the various villages, wooden monasteries, Kachin churches and *manaotaing* (decorative totem poles used for festive occasions), or drop in at one of the three logging camps to see elephants at work. To the north of Indawgyi Lake are the jade mines of **Hpakant** which are strictly off-limits to tourists.

Map on page 262

An ancient trading post

South of Myitkyina is **Bhamo ❹**, a trading town since time immemorial. Being the closest and most accessible point to China, it was one of the main reasons for the British occupation of the country and has inspired western colonialists since the 16th century. The ancient trading city of Sampanago was mentioned as early as the 15th century. Not far from the city, remnants, including ruined pagodas and an overgrown city wall, testify to its former greatness. The **Eikkhawtaw** and the **Shwekyaynar** stupas are ancient structures that tell of the legend of a Shan boy who solved a riddle during a Chinese invasion, thus becoming the king's son-in-law. Chinese intrusions in internal politics, from Kublai Khan to the aid that the Communist Party of Burma (BCP) received from Beijing, have made the Burmese cautious in their dealings with China. Not long ago, the city was destroyed by a huge fire, but its centre has now been rebuilt with a spacious marketplace that caters to the people who live in the surrounding hills. The **Thein Maha Chedi**, which contains a tooth relic and is supposed to have been built by King Ashoka in the 3rd century BC, recently received a new invaluable ruby-encrusted *scinbu* (golden orb).

TIP

Train tickets to Hopin should be booked on the eve of departure. Arrive at the Myitkina railway station early as there is almost always a long queue.

BELOW: the Ayeyarwady River near Bhamo.

THE LEGEND OF INDAWGYI LAKE

According to local legend, Indawgyi was once the capital of the Htamanthy tribe. Two dragon brothers were looking for a place to call home and chanced upon Indawgyi. They found the people there living wicked lives and as punishment flooded the city and turned it into a lake for themselves.

Until about 240 years ago, Indawgyi Lake remained uninhabited as it was believed to be guarded by fierce spirits. It was only when the Shwe Myitzu Pagoda was built by a monk, U Thawbita, during the reign of King Mindon, that people's fears were sufficiently allayed and they started to settle in the area.

The pagoda has since been built over three times until it gained its current height of 15 metres (50 ft). Shwe Myitzu is the most important pagoda in Kachin State and is the focus of a 10-day festival held each year in March.

Apparently, just before the start of the festival each year, two sandbanks emerge. One of these stretches all the way from the shore to the Shwe Myitzu Pagoda, allowing pilgrims to walk the entire distance. The other is broken in parts and is believed to be a passage for the gods. Strangely, both sandbanks disappear into the water after the festival is over.

Cruising the Ayeyarwady – Bhamo to Mandalay

The aforementioned rivers that form the Ayeyarwady – the Malihka and the Mehka – at the Myit-son confluence in Myitkyina, both have have their source on the slopes of the Hkakabo Razi. Further on, the two rivers gather strength while flowing south through deep valleys, while rivulets, brooks and creeks join from both sides.

After Myit-son, the Ayeyarwady flows through a fertile plain at the confluence with the Mogaung river that turns into a huge lake after the snow has melted in the mountains. Then, 54 km (36 miles) before reaching Bhamo, comes the **First Defile** and narrowest defile of the river.

Here, the Ayeyarwady is very shallow and cannot be reached by the big boats that ply between Mandalay and Bhamo. To embark on any of the river trips, travellers have to take one of the twice-weekly flights from Myitkyina to Bhamo where the vessels begin to ply. The water level in the First Defile can rise to 12 metres (40 ft) and there is an untold number of rocks either submerged or prominently protruding at mid-river, producing dangerous whirlpools.

The Ayeyarwady cruises start from Bhamo near where the **Second Defile** begins. There are four express boats a week that connect Bhamo with Mandalay. The express boat stops six times at Shwegu, Katha, Tigyaing, Tagaung, Thabeikkyin and Kyaukmyaung. The cheaper slowboats – the original riverboats of the Irrawady Flotilla Company – still service the Bhamo-Mandalay route and they stop at any of the 47 mooring places along the river where there is cargo and where passengers want to embark or disembark. Due to the rising and falling water levels, the boat has to be moored at different elevations along the steep – up to 20-metre (60-ft high) – embankments.

Along with the hundred-plus passengers on board the slowboats, there are usually Chinese goods and produce like molasses, salted fish, rattan, beans and peanuts being shipped to Mandalay. Upriver, cooking oil, rice, chillies, salt and building materials are the main cargo. The morning express boat takes two days to reach Mandalay, while the slowboat takes twice as long.

After leaving Bhamo the boat crosses a fertile plain and reaches the second defile some 50 km (33 miles) later at **Sinkan**, a small town which is home to several ramshackle monasteries. The 13.5-km (7½-mile) long defile is the most scenic along the entire length of the river. During the rainy season, the water's depth can reach an amazing 61 metres (180 ft), while when the water is low, elephants haul huge teak logs from the jungle to the river's shore.

At the narrowest point of the defile, stands a 300-metre (985-ft) cliff, the **Nat-Myet-Hna-Taung** (Face of the Nat Mountain). Also called the Welatha cliff, it adds significantly to the grandeur of the area. Not far away is the famous **Parrot's Beak**, a painted rock that acts as a marker.

If the water reaches the parrot's red beak, the force of the river has become too strong for boats to pass through the defile. As the river is so narrow at this point, most boats have steel-plated lounges and a military escort. This is also the place where the Kachin rebels fired their shots during the civil war.

It was the Tibetans who gave the mountain Hkakabo Razi its name. It is derived from the original Tibetan "Ka Karpo Ri", which means "peak of white snow".

BELOW: the Parrot's Beak marker.

Leaving the defile, the boat docks at **Shwegu** ❺, a gateway to the Shan hills. Elephants still roam the jungle in the mountains behind the town. Opposite Shwegu lies the island of **Kyundaw**. It is covered with more than 2,700 ancient pagodas; although they are smaller, the stupas here outnumber those in Bagan. This island is also the venue for one of the Shan's most important annual festivals, and every March, Shan from the hills to the east gather here to celebrate.

Before it turns south again, the river turns west and crosses a wide and fertile plain. At **Katha** ❻, it reaches a side track of the Mandalay–Myitkyina railway. It is on this line that the goods destined for Bhamo are transhipped.

The charms of Katha are its raintrees, probably planted a hundred years ago. Today, the trees have converted the town into a shady place; their huge branches stretching across the roofs of the houses, protecting them against rain and sun in a charming style that harks back to the colonial past.

In this beautiful and peaceful place, people live simple lives. It is the great river, and the link the railway offers to the outside world that makes this place different from those to the north in Kachin State. The atmosphere in Katha is bucolic; there are shady riverside tea houses to pass the time in while watching the boat traffic, and a lively market to visit.

Sailing into the past

As Bhamo is not readily accessible, some tourists find it easier to begin their Ayeyarwady cruise downriver from Katha. Express boats and slowboats leave thrice weekly for Mandalay. On a cool, sunny day, this trip is very pleasant: the landscape of Upper Burma moves through your field of vision to the hum of a barely audible engine. On the slowboats, wherever they dock during the

Map on page 262

TIP

The Ayeyarwady boats usually have tiny cabins more suited to single than double occupancy. If you are travelling with a companion, you may prefer separate cabins as the fare is per person, not per cabin.

BELOW: a guesthouse at Bhamo.

One of the traditional dwellings to be seen on a cruise of the Ayeyarwady.

harvesting season, huge drums of molasses and sacks filled with sesame seeds are brought on board. While cargo is being loaded, vendors line up on the deck to sell fruits, cookies, *shashlik* meats and a variety of other local snacks. This boat is the lifeline to the outside world for the people of the Upper Ayeyarwady, since land routes are much too cumbersome and, in many areas, non-existent.

Walking across the deck one finds the whole spectrum of commodities that the country produces: fruit, beans, tomatoes and onions reflect the basic diet of this secluded people. Flowers, *cheroot*, candles, tobacco leaves, sweets, Mandalay beer, rum and soft drinks are their luxuries.

The vendors line their space with wares – towers of woven cane hats, baskets, handwoven blankets and live chickens in cane cages. Some of the men bring their *carrom* boards along, and hour after hour, with a snap of their fingers, they shoot the discs into the appropriate holes. The players are always surrounded by a crowd of other men who offer zealous advice.

There is even a stall for cheap second-hand romance books, sold for a small fee whenever the boat docks at a remote village. Monks have their own platform on which they reside in their common lotus position, puffing one *cheroot* after another while running their prayer beads through their fingers. In the rear of the upper deck is the kitchen where, on an open fire, tea, coffee and a variety of foods are prepared.

Some of the vendors rent up to three of the narrow deck spaces to set up their stores. Their customers are the passengers on board and the villagers who rush onto the boat at every stop. The traders sell commodities that are not usually available so far upriver – all the small items for daily use that make life easier,

BELOW: passengers on the upper deck of a slowboat.

but at little cost. This form of trade has a long tradition; during the days of the Irrawaddy Flotilla Company, this was the way supplies were distributed to the most remote villages.

On the express boats, the atmosphere may be less bustling but it's no less congenial. There are also vendors on board selling food, drinks and second-hand books. Most of the patrons are the passengers themselves and many of the locals while away their time playing cards and dominoes.

Map on page 262

Old-world atmosphere

The sunsets on the Ayeyarwady are glorious, and are best seen from the bridge. Often, during the night, the boat docks somewhere along the high, sandy embankment and the air is filled with the shouting of villagers carrying barrel after barrel of heavy goods on board.

South of Katha the boat passes the estuary of the **Shweli**, a main tributary of the Ayeyarwady. The Shweli enters Burma from China and while crossing the jungles of the Northern Shan State, it turns into Burma's main logging river. It also brings along a lot of silt which has built up into a sandbar at the confluence at **Inywa** and prohibits the entry of larger boats from the main river. Due to this heavy silting, slowboats have to anchor in mid-river abeam of Inywa, since even the local pilot, who knows every metre of the river's contours, cannot steer the boat safely through the shifting sandbars by night.

Express boats are also subject to the vagaries of shifting sandbanks, which may hinder their progress. Otherwise, they continue travelling throughout the night as they are equipped with radar and have a shallower draft.

BELOW: communal cooking in Myadaung.

Enchanted landscapes

Leaving the Shweli sandbars, the boat calls next at **Myadaung**, a city opposite the southern end of the **Mangain Taung**, the densely forested ridge that stretches south from Myitkyina. It has a mystical quality when the white pagodas on the hilltop above Myadaung appear slowly through the dawn fog.

Wide landscapes and high river banks form the typical setting of the fertile Upper Burma plain. Each of the docking stations is fairly similar to the one just passed, with locals embarking and disembarking while balancing huge sacks, cartons and baskets on their heads.

From Myadaung the boat crosses the river to dock at **Tigyaing**, an equally enchanting town with an old pagoda on its hilltop. Both the pagodas at Myadaung and Tigyaing are said to have been built by King Alaungsithu back in the 12th century – more outposts of the Bagan kingdom.

Strolling through this little community of Tigyaing is a true encounter with the life of Upper Burma. Small stalls and tea shops line the narrow lanes. Life is calm and peaceful. Only when the Ayeyarwady boat arrives does the whole town seem to turn into a frenzy of activity. Regardless of the time of day, the town's entire population assembles on the steep shore, joined by those from far-off regions for whom Tigyaing is the vital gateway to the rest of the world.

Remnants of a Sakya kingdom

The boat later reaches **Tagaung** ❼, one of the highlights of the trip, though at first sight it seems rather uninspiring. However, here lies the origin of the Burmese nation. The first kingdom on Burmese soil was founded in pre-Christian times by immigrants from India. According to the chronicles, it was a prince from the Sakya tribe at Kapilavastu, Gautama's home town, who founded this first kingdom, which most probably was a city state. Until the last century, all the kings of Burma had traced their ancestry from this dynasty.

In actual fact, the ruins of two lost cities are found here: Tagaung and **Old Bagan**; but most of them have been buried underneath the shifting riverbed or lie beneath the huts, shacks and houses of today's settlements. At the centre of the village, after passing the market, stands the shrine of the **Tagaung Nat**, a huge golden *nat*-head said to represent the founder of the ancient city.

On leaving Tagaung, the calmness of the river at night produces a most mesmerising, peaceful atmosphere. Occasionally, a village drifts by that still has a fire burning; but otherwise, there are only the distant moonlit mountains, the silhouette of the raintrees and palm trees, interspersed by the *hti* of pagodas which seem to perch on every prominent outcrop. Although the boat reaches a region settled predominantly by Bamar, the passengers are still a good mix of Kachin, Shan, Chinese and Bamar.

In former times, there were three ferry crossings between here and Mandalay: at **Mali**, **Thabeikkyin** and **Kyaukmyaung**. There are also roads, coming from the Shan hills, leading to the Mu valley in the west and across the jungles of Upper Burma to the Chindwin. At present, only the one crossing at Kyaukmyaung ferries cars across the river.

BELOW: the main road in Tagaung.

Map on page 262

River of gold

Here, the river runs in a straight north-south direction and enters the **Third Defile** 45 km (26 miles) before it reaches Kyaukmyaung. During the low-water season, hundreds of boats can be seen panning gold from the river's sand at **Kabwet**, in the middle of the defile. This is the gold that colours the stupas across the country, giving Burma its name of the "Golden Land".

About 29 km (18 miles) west of Kyaukmyaung lies **Shwebo**, the city from which Alaungpaya, the founder of the Third Burmese Kingdom, came. Today, it is seen as the cradle of Burmese nationhood. Not far away are the ruins of **Halin**, the last capital of the Pyu people that was destroyed in AD 832. Across the river in **Singu** is the road that leads to **Mogok**, Burma's main ruby mine. A little further downriver, also on the eastern side, lies **Sagyin**, the marble mountain that provides the raw material for the typical Burmese Buddha images.

Arriving in Mandalay by boat from the north is a memorable moment. When you pass **Mingun** and its broken stupa, Mandalay Hill becomes visible in the distance, and though this trip is something special, the prospect of spending a night in a comfortable hotel bed adds to the feeling of well-being.

If the boat is carrying too much cargo, it cannot dock at the usual Inland Waterways' dock at **Gawwein**. Instead, it will continue to a muddy anchoring place a quarter of a mile further on where everyone disembarks, as usual in the north, by walking across narrow planks onto the steep shore. Jeeps and horse-drawn *tongas* will bring you downtown from this point on. Here, the journey from the north ends, and you'll have to take another boat down to Pyay. As the boat changes, so does the landscape, the hilly, fertile regions giving way to the dry central belt that divides the monsoon-swept delta from the northern plains and jungles. ❑

BELOW: gold-panning camp at the Third Defile.

NORTHWESTERN BURMA

*Isolated from the Bamar heartland, northwest Burma
has a distinctly South Asian feel to it*

Only open to visitors since the 1990s, Northwestern Burma is still very much off the beaten track. It's a vast region of placid, sandy beaches, slow-moving broad rivers and jungled, all-but-impenetrable hills. From the beaches of Rakhaing in the south, to the border with India's Manipur state in the north, it is isolated from central Burma by a series of hardy mountain ranges – the Rakhaing Yoma, the Chin Hills and the Letha Taung. To the southwest, the region is washed by the Indian Ocean, then the land frontier marches north by Bangladesh's Chittagong Hill Tracts and the Indian states of Mizoram and Manipur.

In historical terms, Northwestern Burma is a peripheral land, neither Burmese nor Indian, though it becomes more Burmese by the year as Yangon asserts itself militarily and culturally throughout the region. Rakhaing is where the historically independent Kingdom of Arakan once flourished, a Buddhist state where the kings traditionally also carried a Muslim title, and where Southeast Asian Buddhism met and intermingled with Bengali Islam. Even today the area holds a distinctively South Asian feel in its cuisine, dress, and the facial characteristics of its people.

North of Rakhaing the unexplored hill tracts of Chin State remain one of the least-known parts of Burma – not just unvisited by foreigners, but unfamiliar to all but a handful of Bamar, most of them military men or frontier police. The most traditional part of Chin State is in the south, where unmarried Chin women still wear traditional dress. Further north, around the more accessible capital, Falam – which is linked to central Burma by a single, tenuous, surfaced road – the Chin have been Christianised and have, in large part, adopted Western dress.

For the traveller, Northwest Burma is not the easiest part of the country to visit. While access by sea or by road is certainly possible, these are slow and unreliable options. Most people will choose to fly in from Yangon or Mandalay, the great majority landing at the Rakhaing capital of Sittwe. Once in Rakhaing – Chin State remains, for the moment, off the tourist itinerary unless by special invitation or arrangement – the best way of getting about is by boat, often an old, overcrowded river steamer. Despite these discomforts, it is well worth making the trip. Rakhaing offers some of the finest beaches in Southeast Asia, and while the facilities are still rudimentary, the waters are clear, the sand pristine, and there are almost no other visitors – for the present, that is. Moreover, beyond the beaches, up the rolling Kaladan River, lies the mystic and all-but-forgotten city of Mrauk U, the temple-studded capital of Old Arakan. ❑

PRECEDING PAGES: mountain stupa and shelter in Mrauk U.
LEFT: Mrauk U market.

MRAUK U AND CHIN STATE

Map on page 296

On an isolated plateau in western Burma an ancient royal city is now open to foreign travellers, while further north, the secluded hills of the Chin people remain off-limits

High on a rocky plateau in western Burma are the remains of what was once among the most spectacular royal cities of Asia. Today, jungle vines creep over its stupas, and priceless Buddha images peer out from the undergrowth. Mrauk U (also known as Myohaung) is the youngest of eight ancient capitals, its bricks crumbling under the dense vegetation of inland Rakhaing (Arakan). Rivers like the Kaladan and Lomro have carved deep indentations in the Rakhaing littoral. Jungle river boats that ply these waters are the only dependable means of transportation along this isolated coast. The starting point for many of these launches is Sittwe (Akyab), the Muslim-flavoured capital of this most unusual Burmese state. Further down the seaboard, 240 km (150 miles) or so toward the Ayeyarwady (Irrawaddy) Delta, is the beach resort of Ngapali, where a beautiful stretch of tranquil sand stretches 11 km (7 miles) along a palm-fringed coastline.

The fabled name of Rakhaing has meant mystery and surprise to all who have stumbled upon the state from time immemorial; even today, it is one of Burma's best-guarded secrets. Only for a few years have foreigners been granted government permission to travel to Sittwe and Mrauk U, and Sandoway's beaches are still seldom visited.

LEFT: pagodas at Mrauk U.
BELOW: woman at a market in Mrauk U.

"Wild, uncivilised people"

Rakhaing is the land where the Mongol and Aryan races, the Brahman and Buddhist traditions, had their closest encounters in Burma. Called *Argyre*, "the silver land", by Ptolemy in the 2nd century AD, its modern appellation came from the name given to it by the early inhabitants – *Rakhaing-pyi*. It may be that the Aryan invaders of northern India used the term *Rakhaing* in pre-Buddhist times, referring alike to the Mongoloid peoples of the east and the Dravidians of the south as "wild, uncivilised people".

It is generally agreed that Buddhism did not become established in Rakhaing until the reign of King Chandra Surya, which began in AD 146. It was during his time that the famous Maha Muni Buddha is thought to have been cast. The Maha Muni and the Yattara Bell, with its astrological ciphers, became the symbols of an independent Rakhaing. From their home atop Rakhaing's Sirigutta Hill, they were revered as the protectors – the palladia of this small nation. When the Maha Muni was removed by King Bodawpaya in 1784 and taken to Amarapura, Rakhaing's fate appeared sealed. Even today, the Rakhaing (Arakanese) associate the loss of their independence with that of the Maha Muni.

Until AD 957, when Rakhaing was overrun by the Pyu, the land was dominated by Indian culture. Ten

TIP

Rakhaing, especially in its northern reaches, has a substantial Muslim population. If visiting mosques remember to dress modestly – and behave respectfully. Remember, too, to remove your shoes.

centuries of blending the Pyu and Indian races have produced the people now known as the Rakhaing. When their cultures clashed in the 10th century, the indigenous Indian inhabitants of Rakhaing, who had already accepted a fusion of Brahmanism with Buddhism, further adapted their spiritual beliefs by embracing the animism of the Pyu to form a uniquely Rakhaing mystical union.

External threats

At the time of the dominance of the First Burmese Empire, Rakhaing was required to pay tribute to the rulers of Bagan. Due to its geographical isolation, however, the land was able to retain its autonomy. King Anawrahta attacked Rakhaing and intended to take the Maha Muni for his capital, but the project was abandoned due to the transportation problems it would have entailed.

A more immediate threat to Rakhaing was perhaps Muslim Bengal, which borders the state to the northwest. Islam had been pushing its frontiers east from Arabia for centuries – yet could make few inroads upon the bulwark of Buddhism and Brahmanism put up by the Rakhaing. By the late 13th century, Islam had by-and-large bypassed mainland Southeast Asia entirely, instead establishing a foothold on the Indonesian island of Sumatra. Islam didn't entirely fail in Rakhaing – many of the state's people today are, in fact, Muslims. In medieval times, Bengal was a strong supporter of Rakhaing independence: when Rakhaing was incorporated into the Shan kingdom of Inwa for a short time in the 15th century, it was only with Bengal's assistance that it was able to break away. After this time, all of Rakhaing's kings, even Buddhist monarchs, bore an honourific Islamic title as well.

Mrauk U was founded in 1433 by King Minsawmun, and until the decline of

BELOW:
a mosque in Sittwe.

the Rakhaing empire three and a half centuries later, remained the region's capital and cultural centre. The city had thrived for nearly a century by the time the first Europeans – Portuguese slavers – appeared in the Bay of Bengal in 1517. These seafarers based themselves on the Rakhaing coast at Dianga, 20 km (12½ miles) south of Chittagong in present-day Bangladesh. Their coastal raids were far more successful than a miscalculated siege on the impregnable citadel of Mrauk U; it wasn't long after this failure that the Portuguese, recognising that discretion was the better part of valour, put their ships and cannons at the disposal of the Rakhaing kings. The early 17th century was Rakhaing's Golden Age. In 1599, King Razagyi returned from a campaign in Bago (Pegu) – then Burma's most powerful kingdom – with a white elephant, regarded as one of the seven symbols of the "universal monarch". It remained with his successors.

Map on page 296

Elixir of immortality

Razagyi's grandson, Thiri-thu-dhamma, who ruled from 1622–38, was the most respected king in Rakhaing's history. He saw himself as a future "universal monarch" and sought immortality. According to accounts by the Augustinian Father Friar Manrique – who came to Mrauk U in 1629 as the ambassador from Portuguese Goa – Thiri-thu-dhamma had a famed Muslim doctor brew him an "immortality elixir" containing the essence of the hearts of 2,000 white doves, 4,000 white cows and 6,000 humans. It didn't work, of course, and he was eventually poisoned by another elixir concocted by enemies in his court.

Sap harvested from Burma's toddy palms provide most of the sugar consumed by the Burmese.

After Thiri-thu-dhamma's death, the situation in Rakhaing deteriorated. The Portuguese slave traders in Dianga switched allegiance, supported the Mogul Emperor Aurangzeb, and broke Rakhaing's power at sea. In the court at Mrauk U,

BELOW: a 1920s map of Mrauk U (Myohaung).

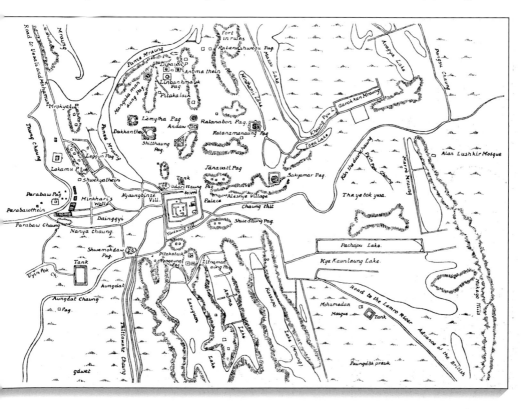

Afghan and Turkish archers, who had been serving as mercenaries, assumed power. In the first half of the 18th century, there was turmoil in the government, chiefly because no ruler held power for longer than two and a half years.

Portentous events

In 1761 and 1762, Rakhaing was struck by a pair of exceptionally strong earthquakes. The epicentres of both were near Mrauk U. The city survived, but along the coast, sections of land rose by as much as 7 metres (23 ft). The superstitious among the inhabitants, of course, saw the quakes as an indication of major changes to come.

And come they did. In 1784, King Bodawpaya, on a campaign from central Burma, used Rakhaing's confused political situation to annex the territory to his empire. It wasn't a military conquest; he took Mrauk U by betrayal, with tacit support from a Rakhaing populace who were tired of perpetual civil war. Not satisfied with the popular acclaim, however, Bodawpaya strove to assure his success by making off with the Maha Muni – thus making its fabled magic powers his own.

Even today, more than two centuries after the conquests of Bodawpaya, Rakhaing remains a part of greater Burma. But many of its people still see themselves as a separate entity. In particular, the Muslim minority, the Rohingya, along the border of Bangladesh, feel estranged from and hostile to the current Bamar-Buddhist regime dominated by the Burmese military. More than 200,000 Rakhaing of Bengali or part-Bengali descent recently fled to Bangladesh by crossing the Naaf River and are now slowly returning, often under pressure to do so from the Bangladeshi government.

BELOW:
a 17th-century depiction of Mrauk U.

A 17TH-CENTURY METROPOLIS

Father Sebastiao Manrique, writing in the 17th century, left a vivid description of Mrauk U's formidable appearance. Surrounded on all sides by high rocky mountains, its thoroughfares were waterways navigable by large and small vessels alike. "The greater number of houses in the city are made of bamboo... much ingenuity and labour are spent on making the houses' mats of the finest material and of many colours, which are very neat and handsome."

His description of Mrauk U's market at the time of the king's coronation is a portrait of a true metropolis: "So numerous were the different classes of dress and language, such the varied customs at that capital, that the eye was kept busy trying to distinguish the different nationalities by their apparel."

The town also had a vibrant and rich trading community: "In the shops were being sold in abundance, diamonds, rubies, sapphires, emeralds, topazes, gold and silver in plates and bars, tin and zinc. Besides these articles, there was much copper, fine brass ambergris, musk, civet scent, fragrant resin, essence of almonds, incense, camphor, red lead, indigo, borax, quicksilver, saltpeter, opium, tobacco..."

It is this continuing conflict that is the major reason for Burma's reluctance to allow tourists into northern Rakhaing, though visits to Mrauk U are now both possible and encouraged.

Sittwe (Akyab) is the capital of Rakhaing. In its present form it was founded in 1826 by the English general Morrisson, who moved his troops from Mrauk U to the Kaladan River mouth to escape the inland humidity during the First Anglo-Burmese War. Of far greater interest than Sittwe, and indeed the unmissable destination in Rakhaing, is Mrauk U. (The name Myohaung, which is still sometimes used, means "old city", a label that was given when the British relocated Rakhaing's administrative headquarters from Mrauk U to the coast.)

Faded grandeur

Rakhaing's medieval capital of **Mrauk U** ❶ lies 80 km (50 miles) inland from the Kaladan's mouth, occupying a rocky plateau between the Kaladan and the Lomro river. It's a five- or six-hour voyage from Sittwe, aboard a boat reminiscent of Bogart's in the film *The African Queen*. The craft travels first up the Kaladan, then along several small creeks until the settlement of Aungdet is reached. From there, it's a short walk to contemporary Mrauk U, built atop and amid the ruins of the ancient city of the same name.

King Minsawmun constructed Mrauk U to replace the "unlucky" royal city of Launggyet, and thereby placate his citizenry. The king's Brahman astrologers warned him, however, that he would die within a year if he moved his capital from Launggyet; and it wasn't long after the move was made that this prophecy was fulfilled. Mrauk U was an ideal capital though; natural barriers, walls and artificial lakes – the dams of which could be opened to repulse the enemy – helped make the town virtually impregnable. Bengali, Manipuri, Portuguese and Bamar (Burman) all tried in vain at one time or another to capture the city.

In its heyday, Mrauk U was a major cosmopolitan city. The remnants of a 30-km (19-mile) long fortification which surrounded the settlement can still be found today. In the centre of the city was the Royal Palace, looming high over the surrounding area like an Asian Acropolis. Three layers of square-shaped stonework are all that remains of the palace. Where the king of Rakhaing once had his reception rooms and private chambers, now there is only an exposed platform from which to view the hilly landscape that surrounds the city.

North of the palace site, hidden behind low hills, are the most important religious shrines of medieval Mrauk U. But within Mrauk U's city wall – in every field, and upon each and every hill – stand Buddha images, temples or pagodas. Some of these structures are in use even today, whitewashed by their devotees to keep them sparkling. Others are in various stages of decay, shrouded in the jungle's dense vegetation and crumbling at the mercy of the strangling green vines.

Temple of 80,000 Buddhas

Visitors must walk for at least 8 km (5 miles) over the hills and through overgrown fields to reach some of the more important edifices. Unlike most buildings

Map on page 296

TIP

En route to or returning from Mrauk U, especially near dusk, watch out for mosquitoes – wear long-sleeved tops and trousers and always carry and apply liberally a spray repellent.

BELOW: houses on the bank-side of the Kaladan River.

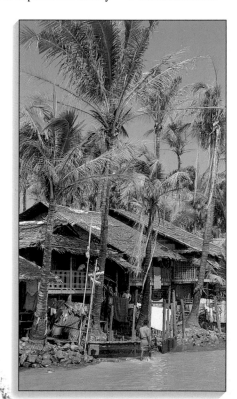

elsewhere in Burma, these sacred structures were intended to be fortifications as well as shrines. Among the most beautiful is the **Shittaung Temple Ⓐ**, located atop a small hill. Erected in the 16th century after the unsuccessful Portuguese attack on the city, it is known as "the temple of 80,000 Buddhas". This may be an allusion to the number of statements found in the Buddha's speeches to his followers. But one is left wondering if it isn't the actual number of Buddha images and reliefs enshrined here, many of them gracing the temple's courtyard and outside wall. Other figures out of Buddhist and Brahman mythology are also represented here. Not far distant is the **Dukkanthein**, an ordination hall. It has a bell-shaped stupa, and the entire structure is built upon a series of high terraces. In its courtyard are several images which exhibit styles of clothing that were popular in the 16th century.

Buddha images and temple murals

Numerous sitting Buddha figures are also found in the **Andaw Pagoda Ⓑ**. One of the Buddha's teeth, reported to have come from Ceylon, is in the Andaw sanctuary. King Minbin, who built this shrine, is also believed to have founded the **Leimyethna Temple** and the **Shwetaung Pagoda**; both contain frescoes which give visitors a detailed pictorial account of daily life in the Mrauk U court during Minbin's reign.

Virtually all of Mrauk U temples have carved reliefs. There are several thousand in all, depicting Hindu and Mahayana Buddhist religious scenes as well as glimpses of 17th-century royal life. Armed with a strong torch, the visitor can stroll for hours through the dimly lit corridors and be surprised by unfamiliar stories, gods and mythological animals.

BELOW:
Shittaung Temple.

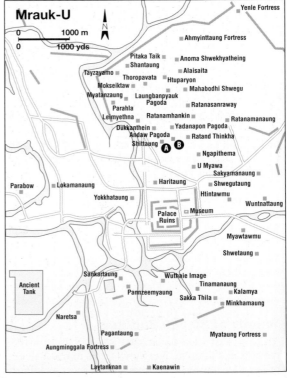

Between these temple corridors, standing back-to-back in the light arches, are hundreds of Buddha figures. Buddha images, in fact, are to Mrauk U as trees are to a forest. They are everywhere; in all sizes, shapes and materials. Very often they are broken, a legacy of times when Rakhaing had no stable government and the citizen's morale was low. Strewn about as if worthless, these Buddhas could doubtlessly fetch hundreds of dollars apiece in the antique markets of the world. But here at Mrauk U, they seem too commonplace to arouse curiosity.

South of the old royal palace, still within the old city walls, are the three large artificial reservoirs once used to flush out approaching enemies. Today, they are an inviting place for the tired, dust-covered visitor to take a swim.

Stepping back in time

Despite its former cosmopolitan nature and its great historical importance, Mrauk U today is a quiet destination. The visitor will find himself flanked only by his guide, maybe the chairman of the township council and a half-dozen curious locals for whom visitors are still a rarity.

At the time of writing the isolation of, and lack of services in Mrauk U militate against a long stay in this isolated region. Still, facilities do exist and are improving all the time. There are at present two hotels which accept foreign visitors overnight – neither very good, but then nobody is likely to travel to Mrauk U in search of comfort. There are also a handful of restaurants, and if you don't mind roughing it, then Mrauk U definitely merits two or even three days of your time. It is a remarkable site, which promises to become more so as archaeological excavations are mounted and restoration takes place.

Another factor to consider is the sheer isolation of the site. It takes considerable

Map on page 282

Visitors can get around Mrauk U by foot or by trishaw.

BELOW: stupas at Mrauk U.

time, planning and effort to get here, so it makes little sense to rush around and try to see everything in a single day. Both government and privately-owned ferries make the journey between Sittwe and Mrauk U on a daily basis. The boats are old double-decker steamers which are invariably overloaded and probably quite dangerous. Travellers sailing up or down river in this way should try to arrive early and head for the upper deck. Ferries leave daily from the Mrauk U Jetty on Sakoya Canal in northern Sittwe. Alternatively, it is possible to charter a boat privately to make the same journey; at around US$54, it's six times the price of a US$9 ferry ticket, but it's more comfortable, more convenient, and it's possible to break the journey en route. Once in Mrauk U you will be expected to purchase a US$5 "zone fee" ticket which permits access to the major monuments in the vicinity. The fit may choose to walk from temple to temple, but those in a hurry or wanting to see everything with a modicum of comfort may choose to rent a battered old jeep on a daily or half-daily basis.

Other ancient capitals

Although it is nearly six centuries old, Mrauk U is the youngest of all the cities between the Lomro and Kaladan rivers. Near the "old city", situated slightly to the northeast of the main ruins at Mrauk U is **Launggyet** – the capital before Mrauk U – and **Vasali ❷**, which dates to the 4th century AD. These cities have fewer visible remains than those of Mrauk U, but their hills, too, are studded with pagodas and Buddha images.

At Vasali, wherever topsoil is removed, the ground reveals a layer of red tiles. The peasants who reside here have innumerable ancient images of all kinds in their bamboo huts. These images once adorned the walls and walkways

BELOW:
waiting for the
ferry, Ponnagyun
Jetty, Mrauk U.

of a palace which today is buried beneath the huts; the figures are now regarded as the guardians of trees and springs. The government's archaeological department cannot take them away because of the local peoples' strong religious attachment to them.

Several other former royal cities – Hkrit, Parein, Pyinsa and Thabeiktaung among them – await excavation. The same is true of **Dhannavati** ❸, some 30 km (19 miles) north of Mrauk U near present-day Kyauktaw. The capital of Rakhaing between the 6th century BC and AD 350, it was here that the famed Maha Muni image is believed to have been cast in the 2nd century AD.

To reach this site, one must return to Sittwe and take another boat, this time travelling up the Kaladan as far as Kyauktaw, about 5 km (3 miles) from Dhannavati and Sirigutta Hill. If one climbs **Sirigutta Hill** with the knowledge that it was once the centre of Buddhist devotion for all of Rakhaing, there is a certain sadness in finding it as it is today. While still the most venerated site in the entire Mrauk U area, it is but a shadow of its former self. The pagoda on the hill was rebuilt in the Bagan style after being destroyed by the Pyu in 957. Three walls enclose a series of courtyards around the structure. In the outer courtyard are a library and a well; in the middle one are statues of 12 Hindu gods who served as guardian spirits of the Maha Muni, therefore symbolising the Brahman deities' association with Buddhist thought. The pagoda itself stands in the inner courtyard, flanked by the legendary Yattara Bell.

Stone-carved statue at a temple in Mrauk U.

Signs of superstition

The bell – a duplicate of the original – is covered by astrological signs and runes of great importance to the superstitious Rakhaing of medieval times. Their alchemists wove a magic spell that is difficult to understand even to this day: "And let the Yattara Bell be hung and struck at the eastern archway, and the enemies of the east will be panic stricken and quit by flight... Let also the Yattara *bidauk* drum be struck at the relic chambers of Buddha. By these means foreign invaders will be seized by fear and take to flight." Modern observers might be sceptical of the claim that these methods could single-handedly, as it were, fend off enemy attacks. But the fact remains that as long as the Maha Muni stood beside the Yattara Bell on Sirigutta Hill, Rakhaing remained independent.

BELOW: bath time for a buffalo.

Tattoos and traditional dress

Sturdy travellers with special permission can go by boat further north along the Kaladan into the southern Chin Hills to Paletwa and Kaletwa, a region of exceptional natural beauty and a people that still live far from modern amenities. The Chin people living in this remote and isolated region are reportedly more traditional than their compatriots further to the north, being isolated from the more developed areas of northern Chin State, and enjoying better (though still very primitive) communications with Aizawal, the capital of India's Mizoram State, than they do with central Burma, let alone distant Yangon.

Should you succeed in penetrating this remote place, you will find that people still dress in the traditional

Map on page 296

way. Tattooing the face remains a living practice, at least for the present, in the southern Chin Hills. However, the use of *thanaka* – and no doubt, before long, Western-style make-up – will usurp the practice of face tattoos, especially among the young women.

Paletwa **❹**, the most important settlement in all of southern Chin State, is best reached by river boat up the Kaladan River from Sittwe or Kyauktaw. A new road under construction from Mrauk U to Paletwa, when completed, will make travel to southern Chin State a much more simple affair, as well as tying the Paletwa area into the economy of northern Rakhaing State and increasing the area's isolation from the Chin capital at Falam. If you do make it into this backwater, look out for the heavy and attractively striped Chin cotton blankets, various copper and bronze jewellery, and the Khamui traditional dress.

Undiscovered riches

Chin State is still pretty much off-limits to outsiders, though the situation might change at any time. It is interesting to speculate why this should be the case – there was no insurgency in Chin State until fairly recently, and it remains a low-key affair. The Burmese authorities would doubtless claim that, in keeping Chin State virtually off-limits, they are protecting an indigenous minority people from exploitation and exposure to corrupting external influences. The truth is certainly very different. To begin with, the frontiers of Chin State merge with those of Bangladesh's Chittagong Hill Tracts as well as India's Mizoram and Manipur states – troubled areas whose indigenous peoples are very closely related to (and sometimes identical with) the Chin. The last thing the Burmese authorities (or, for that matter, their Bangladeshi or Indian counterparts) would

BELOW: eating saffron rice.

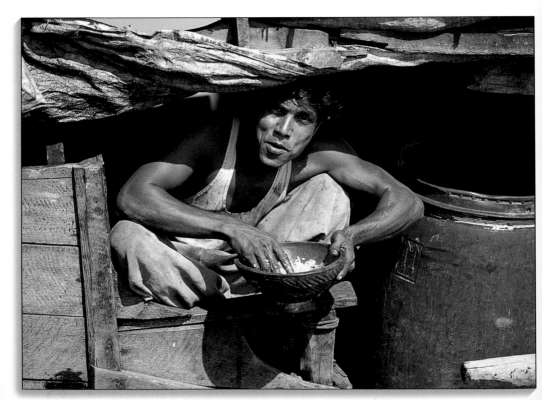

wish to see is a full-fledged Chin insurgency seeking independence for a putative Chin State – uncomfortable shades of Nagaland to the north (*see box story on the Naga Hills on page 293*).

Nor is that all: The isolated and remote hills of Chin State have become a major drug trafficking route in the illicit export of Burmese opiate derivatives, most notably heroin, from Burma's Shan State to South Asian consumers in Bangladesh, India and Nepal. The international community is well aware of this, and it is no coincidence that some of the first foreigners permitted to visit Chin State in recent decades were drug enforcement officers from Australia, cooperating with their Burmese and Indian counterparts. Chin State may well be isolated and undeveloped, but it's no longer ignored, especially in the corridors of power in New Delhi.

Map on page 296

Rivers and mountains

Chin State is a mountainous region of northwestern Burma extending along the Indian border and forming the central and widest part of a mountain arc that stretches northward from the Arakan Mountains to the **Patkai Range**. These mountains vary from 2,100 to 3,000 metres (7,000 to 10,000 ft) in height and reach their tallest point in Mount Victoria (3,053 metres/10,016 ft). Along the Burma-India frontier, the Chin Hills adjoin the Mizo Hills and the Manipur Hills of the Purvachal, or Eastern Highlands, of India.

Demarcated by the Myittha River on the east and the headstreams of the Kaladan River on the west, the Chin Hills comprise a tangle of forested hill ranges that are broken by deep, narrow gorges, with humid valley bottoms and cooler ridges. Above 900 metres (3,000 ft), the tropical forest gives way to oak

BELOW:
a working elephant.

MAURICE COLLIS ON THE MAHA MUNI IMAGE

The Yattara bell was not sounded as a warning, but as an occult offensive. The notes, provided the particularities of the tables were complied with, would operate to put the invaders to flight by deranging their astrological chart and so placing them in jeopardy. In the exact centre of the top of this enclosure was the shrine (of the Maha Muni image). The original had been destroyed at the time of the Mongolian or Arakanese invasion of 957 and… rebuilt during the period when the country was a feudatory of the Pagan kings of Burma. In Manrique's time it must have resembled a small pagoda of the Pagan Dynasty type, a structure with massive brick or stone walls enclosing a chamber and surmounted by a spire. In the chamber was the famous image, a bronze over 10-feet high representing the Buddha…seated on a throne, his legs folded under him, his left hand opened on his lap, the right touching the earth with the tips of his fingers, a symbolic gesture denoting active compassion for mankind. The image was removed in 1784 to Mandalay… it has been plastered so thickly with gold leaf that its antique beauty has been smothered… you would never guess that it belonged to the first centuries of Indian colonisation eastwards, a classical bronze perhaps 1,800 years old.

A young woman selling onions at a local market.

and pine and, above 2,100 metres (7,000 ft), to rhododendron. Slash-and-burn, or shifting, agriculture is practiced in the hillside woods where the population is concentrated. Clearings are abandoned after two or three years of cultivation to become covered with a useless and infertile tangle of bamboo. Jowar millet is the main crop. Corn (maize) is grown in the north, and in the south dry rice is grown on lower slopes that are terraced with felled timber.

The Chin people

The arc of the Arakan Mountains, the Chin Hills and the Patkai Range exemplify the north-south trend line of Indochina, which has hindered east-west movement and facilitated the populating of the region by Mongoloid peoples from the north. The various Chin peoples belong to the southern Mongoloid racial group and are linguistically related to the Tibeto-Burmans. The Chin Hills constitute a frontier zone between Burmese and Indian cultures, and the local tribes remained independent of the British until the end of the 19th century, when the area was annexed to the Raj to prevent raids on the plains of central Burma. A Chin special division was created by the Burmese constitution of 1947 and Chin state – within its present confines – by the constitution of 1974.

The various Chin peoples are a group of tribes of Mongol origin, occupying the southernmost part of the mountain ranges separating Burma from India – to the north are the Naga Hills. Their history from the 17th to the late 19th century was a long and obscure sequence of tribal wars and feuds. An initial British expedition into the Chin Hills in 1889 was soon followed by annexation. British administration brought some peace to the area, ending raids by the Chin on the plains of Burma and the carrying off of unfortunate Bamar, Rakhaing and

BELOW: enjoying a companionable *cheroot.*

Rohingya farmers to serve as slaves. Chin villages, often of several hundred houses, were traditionally self-contained units, some ruled by councils of elders, others by headmen. There were also hereditary chiefs who exercised political control over large areas and received tribute from cultivators of the soil.

Map on page 296

People of the mountain

Agriculture remains the basis of the Chin economy; the land is cultivated in rotation, consecutive cultivation for several years followed by reversion to forest. Rice, millet and corn (maize) are the main crops. Domestic animals, kept mainly for meat, are not milked or used for traction. Chief among them is the *mithan*, a domesticated breed of the Indian wild ox. Prowess in hunting has religious significance for the Chin; the slayer of much game is believed to enjoy high rank in afterlife. Status in life, and presumably in afterlife, is achieved by providing feasts for village and clan. The Chin have much in common with the neighbouring Kuki, Lushai and Lakher peoples, and speak related Tibeto-Burman languages. They practice polygyny and trace their descent through the paternal line. Young people are expected to marry outside the paternal clan. Traditional religion comprises a belief in numerous deities and spirits, which may be propitiated by offerings and sacrifices. Christian missions have made many converts in this part of Burma. The tribes have retained their identity, however, and outside influence has remained limited.

The Chin call themselves Zo-mi or Lai-mi, meaning "mountain people", a term which is often shortened to Zo. Indeed, they share close linguistic and cultural links with the Zo of neighbouring Mizoram – a fact noted and disapproved of by the authorities in Yangon, who seek to weaken the cultural and historic

BELOW:
a Naga woman.

links of northern Rakhaing, Chin State and the Naga Hills with neighbouring India while at the same time promoting Bamar culture and "Burmese-ness" in the region. At present, Chin belief systems still remain predominantly animistic, though both Buddhism and Christianity are making increasing inroads, especially among the more sophisticated and less isolated urban population. The Chin of northern Chin State have been most influenced by these religions, and are now predominantly Christian.

A movement exists which seeks to fully Christianise Chin State and which operates under the slogan, "Chin Christianity in One Century" – though the process is unlikely to be a long and tedious one. Meanwhile, the Bamar authorities, suspicious that Christianity will increase ties to the Zo in neighbouring Mizoram and thereby promote separatism, are encouraging Buddhist missionary work throughout the region. In short, under the present conditions it seems probable that Chin traditional culture has a limited and very insecure future.

Warriors of the "Chin nation"

Strangely, despite their isolation, warrior tradition and sense of separate and distinct identity – not to mention their apparent disdain for the lowland rice farmers like the Rakhaing and the Bamar – the Chin have remained perhaps the least restive of all the major minority groups in Burma. While other ethnic minorities, notably the Kayin (Karen) who rebelled against central Bamar rule almost immediately after independence in 1948, have long rejected the authority of Yangon and sought autonomy or outright independence, the warlike Chin have remained passive. Across the frontier in Bangladesh, where their cousins felt threatened by Bengali migration into the Chittagong Hill Tracts, it was another story – the

BELOW: on the way to the rice mill in Mrauk U.

indigenous people have waged a low-scale but intractable guerrilla struggle against Dhaka for decades. This notwithstanding, it was not until 1985 that the Chin National Front (CNF) was set up to contest the authority of Yangon and seek to bring autonomy or independence to Chin State. Its founder and chairman, John Kaw Kim Thang, established close links with the leadership of the Kachin Independence Organisation (KIO) in distant Kachin State, and sent some Chin volunteers to receive military training from the experienced Kachin Independence Army (KIA) at Pajau and elsewhere in Kachin State.

The military wing of the CNF, the Chin National Army (CAN), also answers to John Kaw Kim Thang, but is believed to number no more than a few hundred fighters, fairly poorly armed and motivated, who offer no real threat to Yangon's hold on the region. The CNF joined the National Democratic Front (NDF), Burma's main opposition alliance in 1989, but has so far achieved little apart from publicity.

Recent reports suggest that the Chin rebel leadership has eschewed violence, but seeks to establish an independent "Chin Nation" encompassing Burma's Chin State, the Chin-inhabited regions of Bangladesh's Chittagong Hill Tracts, together with the Indian states of Manipur and Tripura. Needless to add, these aims hardly endear the CNF to the authorities in Yangon, Dhaka or New Delhi. The CAN, albeit weak, remains a potential embarrassment to the Burmese military authorities, and their presence in the hills along the India-Burma frontier has not helped in the opening of Chin State to outside visitors.

In future, as Chin State gradually opens, the easiest access is likely to be by road from Mandalay to Shwebo, due west across Sagaing Division along the surfaced road to Kalewa and Kalemyo – areas still well off the beaten track.

Map on page 296

BELOW: the United Liberation Front of Assam receiving training by the National Council of Nagaland.

Map
on page
296

Leopards can still be found in heavily forested areas of Burma.

BELOW: sailing boat.

Beyond Kalemyo the road rises briefly to cross the intervening Ponya Daung before descending to the important northern Chin junction town of Thaingngin. Here, the road branches north to the frontier with India's Manipur State – a smugglers' route absolutely closed to travellers, and likely to remain so for the foreseeable future.

Southwards is a better bet, the road leading first to Falam, the capital of Chin State, and then on to the small settlement of Haka set amid the Chin Hills.

The state capital of Falam

Little enough is known of **Falam** ❺ at present. It remains closed to non-Burmese travellers with the exception of certain United Nations officers chiefly concerned with the suppression or limitation of the flourishing cross-border trade in heroin and other opiates with India. The town rises in several levels against the surrounding hills and is reportedly green and pleasant.

Chin people claim that Falam is perhaps the most open and friendly place in Chin State, with its people less clannish and more open to outside influence than in more remote settlements. There's also a strong Christian presence. Falam lacks an airport, and the nearest internal air strip is at Kalemyo. Still, Chin entrepreneurs in the travel business in Yangon are keen to see their capital and indeed their state open to outside visitors – a development which can be only a matter of time in coming.

That said, Chin State remains one of the most isolated regions in modern Burma, and like the Naga Hills of Sagaing Division, the Triangle in northern Kachin State, and the Kokang region of Shan State remains, for the present, very much "off limits". ❑

The Naga Hills

The Naga Hills of northern Division are as isolated and remote from the 21st century as anywhere in Southeast Asia. Centred on the mountainous Angpawng Bum, Burmese Nagaland is really just the eastern third of the Naga-inhabited hill tracts spanning the Burma-Assam frontier. The state of Nagaland in India, albeit isolated and still in a state of partial rebellion, is a hundred years more advanced than the Naga Hills of Burma. Remote, without a decent road or any airstrip, the Naga Hills are completely off-limits and inaccessible The only Westerners known to have visited the Naga Hills in the past three decades are the travel writer Gavin Young – who made an illicit exploratory visit in 1961 – and Swedish foreign correspondent Bertil Lintner, who entered Burma clandestinely from India in 1985 and spent three months in the area. Both writers found the Burmese Nagas poor, backward and all but untouched by Yangon's authority.

The term Naga is loosely applied to a group of more than 20 tribes inhabiting the Naga Hills of the Burma-India frontier. The many Naga languages (sometimes classified as dialects) belong to the Tibeto-Burman group of the Sino-Tibetan language family. Almost every village has its own dialect; different groups of Naga communicate in broken Burmese, Assamese, or sometimes in English and Hindi. The largest tribes are the Konyak, Ao, Tangkhul, Sema and Angami.

Most Naga live in villages strategically placed on hillsides near to water. Shifting cultivation (jhum) is commonly practised, although some tribes practice terracing. Rice and millet are staples. Manufactures and arts include weaving and wood carving. Naga fishermen are noted for the use of intoxicants to kill or incapacitate fish.

Tribal organisation ranges from autocracy to democracy, and power may reside in a council of elders or tribal council. Descent is through the paternal line; clan and kindred are fundamental to social organisation. Due to missionary efforts in 19th-century British occupation of Indian Nagaland, a sizeable majority of Indian Naga became Christians. while in Burma, animism remains predominant.

In the 1970s, Burmese Nagaland became a base for Naga rebels fighting for independence in neighbouring Indian Nagaland. When Lintner visited Burmese Nagaland he found a bizarre situation had developed, with the National Socialist Council of Nagaland (NSCN) led by Indian Naga Isak Chishi Swu and Thuingaleng Muivah, together with the Burmese-born Naga S.S. Khaplang, ruling the Burmese Naga Hills. They preached a strange blend of nationalism and born-again Christianity under the slogan "Nagaland for Christ".

In 1988, Burmese Naga under Khaplang rebelled against the Indian leadership of the NSCN and took over the rebel movement in the Burmese Naga Hills. Khaplang maintains a force of perhaps 500 fighters in a remote area north of the town of Singkaling Hkamti and east of the small Indian Nagaland settlement of Mon. Even when peace returns to the area, it will be years before the Naga Hills become accessible to foreign travellers. ❑

RIGHT: a group of animistic Naga pose in ceremonial dress.

THE NORTHWEST COAST

*Access may be difficult, but the jungle-clad hills of Burma's
Northwest Coast lead down to unspoilt beaches,
natural harbours and offshore islands*

Map
on page
296

Shut off from the central plains by an all-but-impassable mountain range,
the Northwest Coast, comprising the greater part of Rakhaing State, lies
at the foot of the Rakhaing Yoma. These thickly-jungled hills catch the
bulk of the heavy Southwest Monsoon. In the north, **Mount Victoria ❻**, the
highest peak, rises to 3,053 metres (10,016 ft), while further south the massif
around Pauksa Taung reaches 1,708 metres (5,550 ft), sundering the Rakhaing
littoral from the Ayeyarwady plains and making overland communications all
but impossible. Since 1960, a single paved road of indifferent quality has pierced
the Rakhaing Yoma near its southern extremity, linking Pyay (Prome) with the
small coastal town of Taungup via the Taungup Pass. It's a seven-hour bus journey from Pyay, however – nearer 18 hours from Yangon – and it is hardly surprising, therefore, that virtually all visitors to the Northwest Coast arrive by air.

Access to the Northwest Coast is limited, too, by political factors. Although
it is now routine for visitors to fly into Sittwe in the north of Rakhaing en route
to the temples of Mrauk U, they are unlikely to be permitted to travel along
the coast north of Sittwe. Here, a low range of hills, the Mayu Taungdan,
separate the bulk of Burma from the muddy estuary of the Teknaf River and the
southern frontier of Bangladesh. This is yet another of Burma's troubled borders.
Over the past two decades, around 200,000 local
Muslims (mainly Rakhaing Rohingya from the area
around Buthidaung and Maungdaw) and impover-
ished, land-hungry illegal migrants from Bangladesh
have been driven out of Rakhaing by the Burmese
military, or pushed back into Rakhaing by the
Bangladeshi authorities. The area is a tinderbox, still
contested by armed *mujahids* of the Rohingya
National Alliance and until recently haunted by remnants of both the Burmese Communist Party and the
Red Flag Communists. It is hardly surprisingly, then,
that it remains strictly off-limits to tourists.

LEFT:
Ngapali Beach.
BELOW:
palms surround
a Buddhist shrine
in Sittwe.

The state capital

Sittwe ❼ is the largest city in Rakhaing and also the
state capital. Until Burmese nationalism's recent
reassertion of Bamar place names, it was known inter-
nationally by its Bengali name, Akyab. The city,
which is also a sizeable port, is located near the mouth
of the wide Kaladan River. Because the waterfront is
protected by offshore islands, making the area a
natural safe harbour, Sittwe has been an important
settlement for more than a thousand years. In its
present incarnation, however, it owes much to its
colonial past. Together with the rest of the Rakhaing
coast, the area came under British rule at the end of
the first Anglo-Burmese war in 1826, substantially
increasing Sittwe's already significant links with

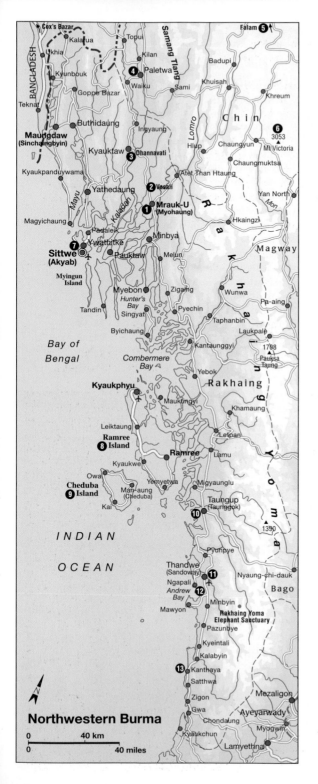

Northwestern Burma

0	40 km
0	40 miles

South Asia, and bequeathing the town a distinct Anglo-Indian feel in terms of its architecture, people and cuisine. In times past, steamers linked Sittwe with Calcutta on a daily basis, but today the old port is remarkably isolated from the outside world. Direct air links with Yangon have been supplemented by a direct road link with Meiktila in central Burma. Still, Sittwe remains rooted in its past, and the city is noted chiefly for its spicy cuisine and excellent seafood, and its mixed Burmese-Muslim population.

There isn't a great deal to see in Sittwe, but the town makes a good stopping over point for visitors to Mrauk U. There are three main streets, running parallel to each other a short distance apart on the right bank of the Kaladan River. The jetty for Mrauk U is situated at the northernmost point of the town, where the Sakoya Chaung flows east into the much larger Kaladan. From here the town meanders south all the way to Sittwe Airport. It's worth visiting the strangely named **Buddhistic Museum** (Main Road No. 1; Mon–Sat 10am–4pm; entrance fee) just south of the jetty. Here there's a fine collection of Rakhaing-style Buddha images, some resting on pedestals borne by elephants, as well as Buddhas of various materials – bronze, quartz, alabaster – from India, Thailand and even Japan. Further south along the same road is the **Rakhaing State Cultural Museum** (open Mon–Sat 10am–4pm; entrance fee) that features noteworthy displays of Wethali and Mrauk U period artefacts, such as stone inscriptions, carvings and images.

To the north and east of the state museum stands an old cast-iron Dutch clock tower, said to date from the 18th century when Sittwe was more open to international shipping than it is today. The area around the clock tower is the town's main market area, centred on Zegyo Lan (Market Street) and Ye Dwin Lan (Merchant Street). Immediately to the east, beside the muddy Kaladan River, lie Strand Road and the

Map on page 296

Five Star Jetty. The latter is the centre of Sittwe's waterfront, and the departure and arrival point for long-distance boat services to Thandwe and Yangon – the ticket office, belonging to Myanmar Five Star Line, is located on Strand Road just south of the Jetty Market.

South of Five Star Jetty, between Strand Road and Main Road No. 1, is the South Asian style **Jama' Masjid** which marks the centre of Sittwe's predominantly Muslim Bodawma Quarter. Many people here trace their ancestry in whole or in part to Bengal, and indeed Sittwe has a Bangladesh Consulate, located in the north of town just east of the Buddhistic Museum. It's not of much interest or use to foreign travellers, however – overland travel to nearby Bangladesh is out of the question at present, and travel by sea, if permitted at all, will certainly be limited to locals. Also in Sittwe's Bengali quarter is the much-venerated **tomb of Babagyi**, a local Muslim *pir* or saint who died two centuries ago, and an undistinguished Hindu temple.

West of town, by the banks of the small Mayu River, stands Sittwe's main Buddhist *paya*, the **Atulamarazei Pyeloun Chantha Payagi**. Here the visitor can see a large seated Buddha image cast in bronze in the Rakhaing style. In the same location, the **Kyayouq Kyaung** boasts two *zedi*, one in Burmese style, the other belonging to the Sinhalese tradition.

Perhaps the main attraction of Sittwe, however, particularly during the early morning or towards dusk, is simply strolling along Strand Road by the banks of the Kaladan River. South of town along the waterfront is a recreation area known as **The Point**, where an old lighthouse has been converted into a look-out point. It's easy to imagine the great steamers coming and going between Sittwe and Calcutta and Yangon in times past. Whether the port will ever recover its past importance in the once thriving "country trade" of the Bay of Bengal and the Indian Ocean is another matter entirely. Much of the area remains off-limits to visitors, but less because of insurgency and insecurity than poor communications. In future the large, densely populated **Ramree Island ❽** and the more distant **Cheduba Island ❾** may be opened to provide isolated and tranquil retreats for travellers, but for now all beach-related activities in Rakhaing are concentrated south of **Taungup ❿**, the terminus for the road across the Arakan Yoma from Pyay.

The Burmese authorities deny the existence of Rakhaing's Rohingya Muslims as a separate people, insisting they are either Bengal migrants or Rakhaing converts to Islam.

Ngapali Beach

Visitors to Burma are usually drawn by the country's cultural and historic attractions. By comparison relatively few people are aware that one of Southeast Asia's most beautiful beaches is located along the southern Rakhaing coast – and that it is open to tourism. **Thandwe ⓫** is the central community of this beach district, and can be reached from Yangon by air far more easily than by road from Pyay. There's not a lot to see or do in town – Thandwe has a population of about 80,000, about 25 percent of whom are Rakhaing Muslims. While passable food and accommodation are available, most visitors will want to head straight out to the beach. About 10 km (6 miles) southwest of Thandwe, **Ngapali Beach ⓬** is very attractive and pretty much unspoiled. The sand is

BELOW: trishaw driver.

Map on page 296

Catamaran at Ngapali Beach. It is claimed that the name Ngapali derives from either an early Italian visitor homesick for Naples, or from the Rakhaing, meaning "alluring fish".

BELOW: dream beach at Ngapali.

white, and the strand broad and lined by swaying casuarina and palm trees. The swimming is good, and it is possible to surf during the southwest monsoon when the waves can reach reasonable heights. Ngapali is slowly developing, and new tourist facilities in the form of hotels, restaurants and bicycle hire businesses are appearing every year.

When you have tired of swimming and sunbathing, it's rewarding to hire a bicycle and visit the small fishing villages north and south of the beach. The resort is popular among Burmese, so advance hotel bookings, especially at the weekends, are advised. A few upmarket resorts have opened here recently, including the Amata Resort & Spa.

In ancient times, Thandwe may have been an important port of call for Indian merchants and seafarers on the way to or from the Malay Peninsula. It was then known as Dvaravati, which is a name taken from a city of *Jataka* myth: when attacked by enemies, the city could rise into the sky and hover until the siege had ended. The Buddha is said to have lived three of his 547 previous lives in Thandwe. Local pagodas enshrine the evidence: the tooth of a cobra in the **Andaw Pagoda**, the rib of a partridge in the **Nandaw Pagoda**, and a yak hair in the **Sandaw Pagoda**. Tradition says Gautama lived these incarnations along the path to enlightenment.

Approximately 130 km (80 miles) south of Thandwe isolated **Kanthaya** ⓭ is developing as a new beach resort, but still sees relatively few visitors, either Burmese or foreign. The nearest settlement is the small coastal town of Gwa, which is a five-hour drive from Thandwe or about eight hours from Yangon via Ngathaingchaung along a road which is reportedly in poor condition. If isolation is what you seek, Kanthaya might just be the place to try. ❑

Rakhaing Yoma Elephant Sanctuary

Burma, and more especially colonial Burma, is closely associated in most people's minds with teak forests and the great, intelligent beasts that work them – *Elephas maximus*, the Indian Elephant. Today elephants in Burma are most readily found in up-country teak forests, but they also exist in the wild, roaming the slopes of remote mountain ranges from the borders of Shan and Kachin State in the east to the Rakhaing Yoma in the west. Estimates put the total number of elephants in Burma at around 10,000, or about one-third of all those in Asia; of these, an astonishing 6,000 are thought to be engaged in the activity of teak-hauling, making Burma home to, by far, the largest herd of working elephants in the world.

The Burmese authorities have now established a sanctuary for wild elephants in the southern Rakhaing Yoma not far from Minbyin on the upper waters of the Thandwe River. The Rakhaing Yoma Elephant Sanctuary may be well off the beaten track, but in time and as communications develop in southern Rakhaing, it is likely to become an interesting attraction. For the present, as with most national parks and wildlife sanctuaries in the country, the elephant sanctuary is *de facto* (and probably *de jure*) off limits.

Working elephants extract over a million tons of fine teakwood and other hardwoods from the Burmese forests each year. The trees are cut by forestry workers and sawn into sections, after which powerful bull elephants begin hauling with harness and drag trains to the encouragement of shouts from their *uzi* or handlers, known also as *mahouts*. Trained elephants are amazingly adept. Using their heads, trunks, tusks and feet, they push, pull and otherwise manoeuvre logs of up to five tons to the banks of Burma's fast-flowing rivers. From here, the timber can be floated out of the forests and down to the sawmills.

Properly managed – as in Burma and in India's Andaman Islands – teak forestry can be a self-sustaining industry in which

elephants play a major role. They can haul and manoeuvre without damaging the environment in much smaller spaces than bulldozers or cranes. These skills ensure that today, and for the foreseeable future, Burma will remain one of the last places in Asia with a thriving elephant culture.

While many working elephants are bred in captivity, some are captured in the wild and trained. Each year, the Burmese Forestry Department determines how many of such elephants are to be taken from the wild under the Elephant Control Scheme. Capture is a dangerous process involving specially trained elephants called *kunkee*.

In times past the process was even more risky as elephants had to be lassoed; today, tranquilliser darts are used. A wild calf can usually be trained to basic levels in only a few months using a combination of "carrot" (tasty morsels of food, hypnotic singing and small kindnesses) and "stick" (sleep deprivation, confinement, limited food intake), but it takes around 20 years before an elephant is fully trained. ❑

RIGHT: bathing an elephant after a day's work.

SOUTHEASTERN BURMA

The southeast of Burma is the homeland of the Mon and contains the recently opened Kayin State

Tapering down the western side of the Gulf of Mottama (Martaban) to the Isthmus of Kra, Southeastern Burma is a long, narrow finger of land extending from Kayin and Mon State, through Tanintharyi (Tenasserim), almost to the Thai island of Phuket. In historical terms, the southeast is a marginal land, until recently peripheral to the Bamar centre, with distinct cultural, ethnic and historical ties to neighbouring Thailand and to the Malay-Indonesian world further to the south.

Long isolated from the outside world – essentially off-limits to overseas visitors since independence in 1948 – Tanintharyi has begun, slowly, to open to travellers. At present, the entire division is a delightful tropical backwater, perhaps fifty years removed from the relative affluence and openness of Thailand, geographically so close at hand, but politically and economically so very far removed. Yet Tanintharyi's very backwardness and isolation may yet become the region's best hope – a less despoiled, more pristine and more beautiful part of mainland Southeast Asia would be hard to find.

With judgement and care, the Tanintharyi Coast, and more especially totally undeveloped Myeik Archipelago, could become a major source of foreign exchange for Burma and its people. Unfortunately, there are few indications that wise and ecologically sustainable policies are currently at the forefront of Yangon's economic priorities for the region. For the present, access to Tanintharyi is strictly limited to the coastal regions, for the simple reason that much of the hinterland is still in open revolt against the Burmese authorities or troubled by banditry and smugglers. Yangon would like to keep a tight hold on the region – until the mid-18th century very much a part of Siam – but currently lacks the finances and foresight to develop its rich natural resources. The opening of a border crossing between Ranong, in Thailand, and Kawthaung has certainly improved international access to Tanintharyi, and provided access as well to foreign visitors from the Thai capital moving in with get-rich-quick schemes.

For the moment, however, the Tanintharyi Coast, and especially the old colonial town of Myeik, remain unspoiled. Beyond the coast it's a different matter. Communications are terrible, and neither the Burmese military nor their insurgent rivals would seek to welcome travellers here. The same is true of much of Kayin and Mon States – though the latter, home to a sophisticated, cultured and ancient people, as well as to the "Golden Rock" at Kyaiktyo and the sleepy Mon capital of Mawlamyaing – certainly has a great deal to offer the discerning visitor. ❑

PRECEDING PAGES: morning prayer at Kyaik-tiyo.
LEFT: a Buddhist monk.

MON AND KAYIN STATES

*Burma's troubled southeast regions – long off-limits
to foreign travellers – are finally opening up
to display their riches*

Map
on page
306

A thousand years ago, the town of **Bago**, just 80 km (50 miles) north of
Yangon, formed part of the ancient Mon Kingdom. Today, it's the capital
of Bago Division, and very much a part of the Bamar heartlands – though
a substantial minority of Mon still live in and around the town. Bago remains
the gateway to both Mon and Kayin States; however, just north of town the
road forks, with Route 2 leading northwards to Taungoo and Mandalay and
Route 8 leading eastwards via Waw to the mighty Sittoung (Sittang) River and
the frontiers of Mon State. For many years, both Mon and Kayin States were off-
limits to foreigners due to a combination of ethnic insurgency, common banditry
and poor communications. Both the Mon and more especially the Kayin – who
call themselves Karen, "Kayin" being nothing more than a Burmese mis-
pronunciation – were unhappy with coming under Bamar domination at the
time of independence in 1948.

The Kayin are a people renowned for their military prowess. During the colonial period the British employed Kayin and Kachin as the backbone of their
colonial army. Meanwhile, Christian missionaries, especially American Baptists,
were very active among the Kayin, winning many converts and indirectly
emphasising the differences between Kayin and Bamar peoples.

LEFT: the renowned
"Golden Rock".
BELOW: *mahout*
and elephant in
Mon State.

Ethnic conflict

In January 1948, when the British withdrew from
Burma, the stage was set for ethnic confrontation. In
simple terms, the Bamar Buddhist majority tended to
see the Kayin as lackeys of British Imperialism. For
their part the Kayin, who had fought bravely for the
British against the Japanese in World War II, were
nervous about coming under a Bamar Buddhist dominated government, and demanded their own state.
Nor were they entirely alone – the Thais, too, watched
anxiously as their traditional rival re-established its
independence and its hold over the long Thai-Burma
frontier. Old allies of the Kayin, acting on the basis of
the old axiom "my enemy's enemy is my friend",
Bangkok was prepared tacitly to support a low-scale
armed struggle which would weaken Yangon and
keep the troubled borderlands in friendly hands.

As a consequence, the Kayin were the first people
to rebel against Yangon rule. A largely forgotten but
vicious struggle has persisted to the present day. At
one time Kayin rebels held much of the Ayeyarwady
Delta and operated in the suburbs of Yangon itself.
Today, the once-powerful Karen National Liberation
Army (KNLA), armed wing of the Karen National
Union (KNU) has fragmented into different Buddhist
and Christian factions, while a tiny and undisciplined
splinter group led by a pair of 12-year-old twins and

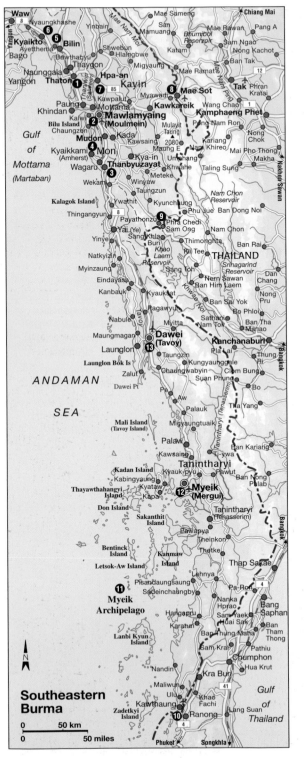

Southeastern Burma

0   50 km

0   50 miles

calling itself "God's Army", made the international headlines in 2000 when it seized first the Burmese Embassy in Bangkok, and subsequently a civilian hospital with almost 500 hostages in the Thai town of Petchaburi.

Despite this persistence, at the time of writing, the KNLA/KNU looks beaten. Burma's ruthless military, the *tatmawdaw*, have gradually pushed the Kayin back against the Thai frontier, while the borderlands of Thailand's own Mae Hong Son and Tak Provinces have taken in tens of thousands of refugees who live alongside Thailand's already substantial indigenous Karen population. Today, the Thai border between Ban Tha Song Yang and Mae Sot has become a virtual "Karen Land" in exile. Bo Mya, the corpulent Christian general who led the KNU from 1948 until 1999 is in semi-retirement, the Thai authorities while sympathetic to their old Karen allies are no longer prepared to offer substantive help, and the dream of Kayin independence is beginning to look exactly that – a dream.

The Mon, who are a lowland, wet-rice farming, Theravada Buddhist people just like the dominant Bamar, were slower to rebel. The New Mon State Party (NMSP), together with its armed wing, the Mon National Liberation Army (MNLA), never had the strength and cohesion of the KNU, and often found itself in a three-way armed struggle with the *tatmadaw* and the KNU as the latter fought to retain control of the lucrative cross-border trade with Thailand, most notably at Payathonzu (Three Pagodas Pass).

The MNLA still holds out against Yangon in a few scattered and isolated border regions mainly well beyond the frontiers of Mon State. Both the "forced labour" extension of the southern railway to Ye and the construction of a major gas pipeline across Mon State to Thailand are persistent sores which feed Mon separatist sentiment and arouse international concern. Nevertheless, despite the continuing human rights abuses by the Yangon authorities and a smouldering, low-key guerrilla war right on the Thai-Burma frontier, both Mon and Kayin States are today increasingly open to international travel. As of mid-2000, the whole of Mon State (except in the southern mountains east of Mudon and Ye) is safe for travel.

Kayin State is a shakier proposition, and still receives relatively few visitors. Nevertheless, the KNU has been driven from its last strongholds, and now operates mainly from bases further south in Tanintharyi Division, while – extraordinarily for such a rebellion-racked state, and a sure sign of Yangon's increasing confidence – border crossings are open for day tours from Thailand both at the Mae Sot-Myawadi frontier in Tak Province, and further south at Payathonzu-Phra Chedi Sam Ong in Kanchanaburi Province.

Mon State

Across the Sittoung (Sittang) begins the land of the Mon. This was Lower Burma's original cradle of civilisation, Suvannabhumi, the "golden land". It was probably **Thaton ❶** to which the great Indian King Ashoka sent two missionaries (Sona and Uttara) to spread the gospel of Theravada Buddhism in the 3rd century BC. In any case, it was Thaton which served as the first great capital of the Mon Empire, and Thaton which posed the greatest threat to Upper Burma. It was only after King Anawrahta of Bagan was victorious over Thaton's King Manuha in 1057 that Anawrahta established the First Burmese Empire. Although Thaton's influence waned from that point on, visitors to the ancient capital can still see some remains of the medieval fortifications – although modern Thaton was built on top of the old town.

Local legend maintains that the **Shwezayan Pagoda**, believed to contain four

Kayin Baptist church in Kabaung, a legacy of Christian missionaries, especially American Baptists, who were very active in Kayin.

BELOW: a young Kayin guerrilla.

ALLIES OF OLD – THE KAREN AND THE THAI

Just east of the Thai-Burma frontier town of Mae Sot, as the road to Tak climbs high towards Ton Krabak Yai National Park, a large gilded Buddha figure, shielded by Muchalinda, the seven-headed naga serpent, appears to the north of the road. Here, beneath a massive outcrop, is the shrine of Pho Phawo, a Karen general who defended the Tak frontier for Thailand's King Naresuan, and who lost his life fighting Burmese invaders over 400 years ago.

Every day, the shrine is a cacophony of sounds in these otherwise quiet hills. Fireworks account for much of this – great strings of red Chinese firecrackers exploding in volleys for 30 seconds at a time, sounding for all the world like gunfire. Most of the ruckus, however, comes from the horns of passing motorists – everyone, from truck drivers to chauffeurs, makes this traditional gesture of respect.

At almost any time family outings to the shrine are in progress, children laughing delightedly at the firecrackers, while husbands open bottles of whisky in honour of Pho Phawo. Meanwhile, their wives busy themselves lighting incense and arranging offerings of pigs' heads. It's just another day on the Tak frontier – but 400 years on, the old friendship between Karen and Thai has not been forgotten.

*Kyaikthanlan
Pagoda, the tallest
pagoda in
Mawlamyaing, offers
great views of the
city and the habour.*

BELOW:
the Sulati Mosque
in Mawlamyaing.

of the Buddha's teeth, dates to the 5th century BC. The **Thagyapaya Pagoda**, situated nearby, has three terraces, the uppermost terrace containing four large recesses with standing Buddha figures. Various terracotta glazed tiles, dating from the 11th and 12th centuries, illustrate the *Jataka* tales. Scenes from the 10 best known *Jataka* stories also decorate the **Kalyani Sima**, hall of ordination. Also worth seeing is the **Pitakat Taik**, or library.

"By the Old Moulmein Pagoda"

About 70 km (44 miles) south of Thaton lies **Mawlamyaing ❷** (Moulmein), the third largest city in Burma with a population of 220,000. It was British Burma's administrative centre between 1827 and 1852, but is best known today from Kipling's verse: "By the old Moulmein Pagoda, looking lazy at the sea..." The English writer was probably referring to the **Kyaikthanlan Pagoda ❹**, whose hilltop location offers breathtaking views over the city and its harbour, a centre for the export of rice and wood (especially teak). Just up the Thanlwin River – navigable for a short distance from Mawlamyaing and its sister town, **Mottama** (Martaban), across the river – there is a sawmill where the words of Rudyard Kipling again come to life: "Elephants a-pilin' teak..." Mawlamyaing has many beautiful pagodas. Among them is the **U Zina Pagoda ❸**, which houses four life-sized statues of the four images – an old man, a sick man, a dead man and an ascetic – which convinced young Siddhartha Gautama to devote his life to finding a means to ending human suffering.

Also in the vicinity of Mawlamyaing are two large caves. The **Cave of Payon** contains many Buddha figures among its stalagmites and stalactites. The **Cave of Kawgaun**, also known as the Cave of the Ten Thousand Buddhas, holds an

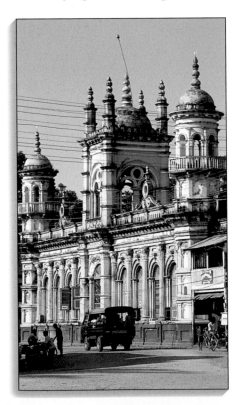

enormous number of Buddha figures that come in all shapes and sizes. Lying at a distance of about 65 km (40 miles) south of Mawlamyaing, near the colonial resort town of **Thanbyuzayat ❸**, is a large and well-kept war cemetery. Buried here are Allied prisoners-of-war who died constructing the World War II railway to Thailand for the Japanese. The Burmese government is currently developing a resort at **Kyaikkami ❹**, formerly known as Amherst, a coastal resort some 45 km (28 miles) south of Mawlamyaing. During the British colonial period, there was a bustling holiday centre here, the beach at **Setse** being particularly well known. The opening of this area to Western tourists depends, however, on the success of government troops in reducing rebel activity in southern Burma in the near future.

Forty-five km (28 miles) north of Thaton lies the village of **Ayetthema ❺**. Nearby are the ruins of an old city wall, which is believed to be the wall of the fort of **Taikkala** which stood at the original Mon settlement of Suvannabhumi. Also in the area is the **Kyaikthanlan Pagoda** with inscriptions dating to the time of King Kyanzittha in the 11th century.

To the south, standing on an octagonal base, is the conical **Tizaung Pagoda**, while a further 1.5 km (1 mile) south of this pagoda are the remains of another wall, this one standing 2 metres (6½ ft) high, with beautiful animal scenes chiseled into the rock.

The Golden Rock

About halfway between Thaton and Bago lies the town of **Kyaikto ❻**, famous for its pagoda situated east of the town at the end of a 10-km (6-mile) long footpath. This landmark is the Kyaik-tiyo Pagoda – the "Golden Rock." The small (5.5-metre/18-ft high) shrine is built on a gold-plated boulder atop a cliff, and it gives the viewer the sensation that it is about to crash down into the valley at any moment. Local Burmese will tell you that such a thing could never happen – the fine balance of the boulder is maintained by a hair of the Buddha preserved inside the pagoda.

According to legend, King Tissa, who lived in the 11th century, was the son of a *zawgyi* and a *naga* princess. He was given the Buddha's hair by an old hermit who had preserved it in his own hair-knot from centuries before. In giving King Tissa the hair, however, the hermit set one condition: the king had to find a rock which closely resembled the hermit's head, and on this rock he must build a pagoda to enshrine the hair relic. With the help of Thagyamin, king of the *nat*, Tissa located the perfect rock at the bottom of the sea. The rock was transported to the mountaintop by a ship – which subsequently turned to stone. Today, the legendary ship can be found a few hundred metres (about 1,000 ft) away from the Kyaik-tiyo, and is simply known as the Kyaukthanban, the "stone boat pagoda".

From base camp to pagoda

Until very recently, before the road that now leads most of the way up to the pagoda, only a few non-Burmese had ever made the pilgrimage to the **Kyaik-tiyo Pagoda**. The Burmese authorities, however, realising the tourist

Maps:
Area: 306
City: 309

Theravada Buddhist texts were traditionally recorded by both the Mon and the Bamar on parabaik, or folding palm-leaf manuscripts incised with a sharp instrument.

BELOW: pilgrims at Mount Kyaik-tiyo.

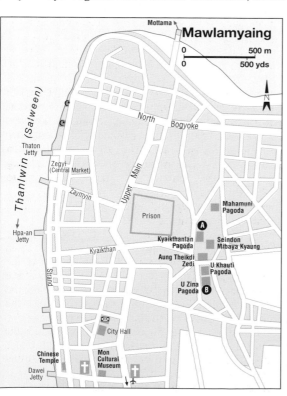

Mawlamyaing

The pilgrimage season at Kyaik-tiyo is between November and March when devotees from all over the country come to pray and meditate.

BELOW: sunrise at Kyaik-tiyo.

potential of the place, have had a hotel built and are now guiding tourists into the hills. Though it is more comfortable to drive up, walking up from Kinpun has its own charm. It is a fairly arduous walk – five hours from the Kinpun base camp near sea level to the pagoda at about 1,200 metres (4,000 ft) elevation. Most pilgrims carry a bedroll and spend the night at the *kyaung* near the pagoda. For the Burmese, the climb to Kyaik-tiyo is a soul-cleansing experience. It is a means of gaining merit, of offering respects to the *nat* of the region and of being reminded again and again of the Buddhist *dhamma*.

The millennium-old path leads through otherwise impenetrable bamboo jungle and along a seemingly interminable mountain ridge. There is an oasis halfway up the second hill, where a thoughtful businessman seeking merit has built several bamboo sheds over a clear spring; here pilgrims and other travellers can cool off in the refreshing water before continuing the trek. At various stages along the way, images have been conspicuously erected. They describe the chapters of the temple legend, integral to the pilgrims' appreciation of the trip. Once on the ridge, the going gets noticeably easier, and the Golden Rock can be seen in the distance; this seems to immediately relax the walker's strained limbs and reinvigorate his soul, which makes the journey's completion a much-easier task.

As tiring as the climb may be, even the sick and the old are not kept from reaching the golden boulder. Neither, for that matter, are the rich or the idle. Baggage will be carried from Kinpun to the temple for a small charge, and there are palanquins to carry persons unable – or unwilling – to trek on their own two feet. It is quite a sight to see a pair of 15-year-old boys marching up the steep mountain slopes, toting an overweight merchant who mutters, "*Ahmya*," which means, "Share with me the merit I gain by doing good things."

TISSA AND SHWE-NAN-KYIN

During the time that King Tissa was building the remarkable Kyaik-tiyo pagoda, he fell in love with the beautiful Shwe-nan-kyin, daughter of a highland chief. Tissa made her his queen, and brought her to his palace. Some time later, during pregnancy, she became sick, and concluded that only by making offerings to her family *nat* would she recover. Her family had not rejected their traditional beliefs even while accepting Buddhism, so with King Tissa's permission, her father and brother arrived to escort her home.

About halfway from the palace to the pagoda, a tiger – presumably sent by the offended family *nat* – sprang from the jungle. Father and brother instantly fled, and poor Shwe-nan-kyin, terrified, watched death approach. Then her eyes fell upon the golden Kyaik-tiyo shrine on the distant cliff-top. With her eyes fixed on the pagoda, she surrendered herself to whatever fate was to be hers. The tiger walked away. And Shwe-nan-kyin continued her journey to the platform of the pagoda.

Here she laid down and died peacefully, the beautiful truth of the Buddhist *dhamma* lodged in her mind. She is now the guardian *nat* of the Kyaik-tiyo pagoda, a spirit who radiates compassion.

Finally, there is the Kyaik-tiyo Pagoda itself at the highest point of the ridge. Seemingly perched on the top of the world, one cannot help but be awed by this religious wonder of the world balancing perfectly on a projecting boulder that even a few young boys can rock and move.

Kayin State

Although parts of Kayin State are now open to foreign travelers, the overall situation remains unclear. At some unspecified future time – perhaps not too far off, now that a bridge across the Taungyin River (known to the Thais as the Moei River) has opened linking Burmese Myawadi with Thai Mae Sot – the projected Pan Asian Highway will run through the heart of Kayin State, linking Bangkok with Yangon. For the present, however, Route 85 remains pitted and dangerous, well off the beaten track and closed to most foreigners.

The road to **Hpa-an** ❼, the capital of Kayin State, runs east from Thaton past the ancient Mon ruins at Ayetthema. A new bridge crosses the Thanlwin River and leads straight into town. It's also possible to reach Hpa-an, which only recently was officially opened to foreign visitors, by river boat from Mawlamyaing – a fascinating trip up the deep, narrow and treacherous Thanlwin River. Finally, a new bridge across the Gyaing River at Zathabyin, due east of Mawlamyaing, now permits access by road to Hpa-an from the Mon capital in just over an hour.

For the present it isn't worth considering travelling beyond Hpa-an to the east – even if this were permitted, there's little to see, the roads are in appalling condition, and there remains the constant danger of fighting between the *tatmawdaw* and the Karen rebels. Hpa-an itself has little to offer. A small but

Map on page 306

TIP

If you are not too fit, take your time making the ascent to the Golden Rock. It's better to stop briefly and frequently to catch your breath, especially during Burma's seriously hot season.

BELOW:
hilltop Buddha image at Kyaik-tiyo.

TIP

Although theoretically the Kyaik-tiyo can be rocked by a gentle push, don't try, even in jest! It's a highly venerated pagoda, and should be treated as such.

BELOW:
novice monks on the path leading to Kyaik-tiyo.

busy commercial centre, its people are an interesting mix of Bamar, Mon and Indian Muslim lowlanders. The Kayin tend to live out of town and especially in the hills to the east. There are no spectacular temples or outstanding monuments, and while the place is friendly enough there are no good reasons to go there. Of course, once the Pan Asian Highway opens all this will change – and fast. Hpa-an looks set to be a major transport hub and stopping off point between Bangkok and Yangon – but only when the road is upgraded (the Burmese are currently seeking a Thai loan for this purpose), and when political conditions permit.

Visiting Kayin State

One of the contradictory aspects of Kayin State is that, despite having been closed to foreigners and in a state of serious insurrection for decades, it has probably been visited by outsiders more frequently than any other part of forbidden Burma. The reason for this is the state's long common frontier with Thailand, the excellent communications linking its eastern frontier with Bangkok, and the warm relations which have long existed between the Thai authorities and the Kayin rebels – though this is fast fading as the Thais lose sympathy for the increasingly unrealistic cause of Kayin independence.

Until fairly recently, many of those visiting Kayin State from Thailand did so illegally, against the wishes of the Burmese authorities and with the tacit approval of the KNU, while the Thai border police sometimes turned a blind eye. One such excursion was via the isolated region where Burma and Thailand briefly share the **Thanlwin** (Salween) as a common frontier. Access is by Thai Route 1194 running west and south from Mae Sariang to **Mae Sam Laep** opposite the Burmese frontier, the only place in Thailand where it is possible to reach the Thanlwin River. The Thanlwin, rising high in the mountains of eastern Tibet, is one of the great rivers of Asia. But the river is unsuitable for any but the most rudimentary navigation, since it flows through narrow, deep and treacherous ravines for much of its length. In some ways, it remains Asia's least-known river, and for this reason alone a visit is well worthwhile.

At least one *songthaew* pick-up bus runs from Mae Sariang to Mae Sam Laep each morning. Until recently the journey took several hours and required much dismounting and pushing at dozens of stream crossings. The road has now been much improved and is surfaced for around two-thirds of the distance to Mae Sam Laep. At Mae Sam Laep, it is possible to hire long-tail boats for short trips up and down the Thanlwin – but now rarely across to the Burmese bank, which is firmly in the hands of the military government. Most people visit Mae Sam Laep as a day-trip, but those who wish to stay can make arrangements to lodge with the headman for about US$2 per person. Swimming in the Thanlwin isn't advised – it's cold (a reminder of the high Tibetan snowfields of its birth), deep and swift flowing, with dangerous eddies and undertows.

Further south, across the Taungyin (Moei) River in the area opposite the Thai town of Tha Song Yang, the former KNU capital of **Manerplaw** could once be visited illegally from Thailand with the blessing of both the KNU and the local border police obtained in advance. No longer – Manerplaw fell to the Burmese army in January 1995, and is now very much a place to stay clear of.

Map on page 306

The Thai frontier

Further south, however, the situation has improved. The important Thai frontier town of Mae Sot is now linked to the Burmese frontier town of **Myawadi ❽** by bridge, and despite some continuing tension between the Thai and Burmese armies in this tense border area, day trips to Myawadi – but no further into Kayin State – are now permitted by Yangon.

Most visitors to Mae Sot check into a hotel and then head straight out for the Burmese border. It's only around 7 km (4 miles) to the banks of the Taungyin (Moei) River, and the rooftops and temples of Myawadi, the Burmese frontier town on the far side of the river, are readily visible. Visitors can cross over on payment of US$5 to explore Myawadi and purchase Burmese handicrafts, cigarettes, sarongs and foodstuffs.

Cheroot (the pungent Burmese cigar) for sale at a colourful stall.

Here, all manner of clothing, medicines, local alcohols, imported cigarettes, handicrafts and woodwork from Burma are for sale, as well as – if you know your stuff – jade, rubies, zircon and other semi-precious stones. Burmese *longyi* make comfortable house clothing, and are very reasonably priced. Watch out, too, for the bundles of fat, green Burmese *cheroot* – a good photo opportunity, even if you don't smoke. In future, Myawadi is likely to become the most important land crossing into Burma across any of its international frontiers – but only when land entry is legalised and regularised, and when the road to Hpa-an has been seriously upgraded. The KNU/KLIA, though battered, is not yet broken, and its leadership, too, may have something to say in the matter.

BELOW: mandarin oranges at a street stall.

Finally, further south from Myawadi and about 110 km (66 miles) southeast of Thanbyuzayat, the small town of **Payathonzu ❾** is the last point in Kayin State currently open to foreign visitors – but again, only via Thailand. Best reached from Sangkhlaburi in Thailand's Kanchanaburi Province, it is visited mainly as a day trip by local Thais.

Payathonzu has a bustling handicraft market and weekends see hundreds of Thais and a handful of Westerners swarm in to hunt for bargains. On sale are woodcarvings, furniture, precious stones, jewellery, clothes and various souvenirs. You can also stock up on alcohol and cigarettes, but be aware that there is a Thai customs post one kilometre along the road to Sangkhlaburi. Prices are generally low, but bargaining is still a must.

The Thai side of the border is marked by a famous landmark, the **Phra Chedi Sam Ong**. These are three small chedis, which make a very popular backdrop for taking photographs. The border is open daily from 6am to 6pm. To get there other than by car, take a bus from Bangkok's Southern Bus Terminal to Kanchanaburi (130 km/81 miles). There, change to a bus or van to Sangkhlaburi (225 km/140 miles). From Sangkhla it's a 15-km (9-mile) ride by *songthaew* (a converted pick-up truck) to the border post. ❑

MYEIK REGION

*The remote, historically fascinating port of Myeik,
with its neighbouring archipelago of unspoilt islands,
is slowly becoming accessible to visitors*

Map
on page
306

Yangon

The Tanintharyi (Tenasserim) Coast, and especially the region around the old port city of Myeik (Mergui), is culturally rich and spectacularly beautiful. Yet despite its proximity to neighbouring Thailand, it has long been off the beaten track. In recent years, it has begun, gradually, to open up. It's possible to take a slow and rusty passenger steamer from Yangon, and even (with luck) to travel south from Mawlamyaing by road to Yai (Ye). Travel by land between Ye and Dawei (Tavoy), the first town of any size in Tanintharyi, is still fraught with difficulty, however. Kayin rebels – including the notorious splinter group "God's Army" – are still active along the mountainous Burmese-Thai frontier, while the predominantly Mon population around Thanbyuzayat remain restive and discontented. This is a politically sensitive zone, where gas from the Yadana field in the Bay of Bengal comes ashore to enter Thailand by pipeline. It's also the area transversed by the controversial Yai-Dawei railroad, which opponents of the Yangon military regime claim has been constructed by forced labour. All in all, northern Tanintharyi is a region best avoided, at least for the present, and almost all of the few adventurous foreign visitors to Burma's remote peninsular south make the journey by air between Yangon and Myeik.

An interesting alternative to this approach, which is likely to become more popular as the attractions of Myeik and its attendant archipelago become known, is to enter Burma via Kawthaung (formerly Victoria Point), just across the wide, slow-flowing Pakchan Estuary from the Thai city of Ranong. This is quite easily done. Boats leave Ranong's Saphan Pla jetty on a regular basis – there's a short stop to complete Thai immigration formalities – and then the boat proceeds to Kawthaung's Myoma Jetty. At present, most travellers using this method to enter Burma visit as day trippers, but increasing numbers of travellers are turning up at Kawthaung with a 28-day visa for Burma and are allowed to travel onwards – sometimes by boat but almost always by air – to Myeik and points beyond in the Burmese heartlands. For the present, travel north from Kawthaung by road is forbidden, though in time this will surely change.

LEFT:
house surrounded
by palm trees.
BELOW:
Myeik town centre.

Thai relations

Kawthaung ❿ is an unremarkable frontier town, dominated by Thai trade, with many locals bilingual in Burmese and Thai, and Thai baht welcome everywhere – certainly more welcome than Burmese kyat. There's not a lot to see if you're coming from Thailand, just a poorer and more run-down version of Ranong. If, on the other hand, you are coming the other way – south from Myeik by terrible roads or rust-bucket country boats, then it must seem a wealthy

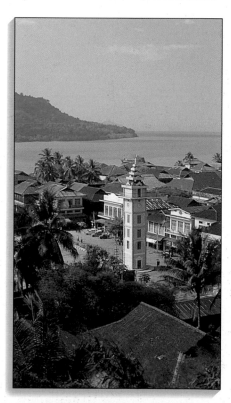

place indeed. To the south of the harbour lies **Cape Bayinnaung**, a promontory called after the Burmese king of the same name who invaded Thailand several times via this route during the 16th century. A statue of this legendary warrior clad in battle armour and flourishing a sword at the nearby Thai coast serves to remind Thai visitors that Burma wasn't always as "down and out" as it is today.

Day trippers to Kawthaung don't need a Burmese visa, but will find little to do beyond wandering the busy waterfront, buying cheap souvenirs, or chartering a boat to visit the offshore islands. Unspectacular accommodation is available at two or three small hotels in Kawthaung, while the offshore Andaman Club resort offers upmarket surroundings for visiting Thais intent upon golf, duty-free shopping and gambling – casinos are illegal in neighbouring Thailand.

For most visitors, then, it's out to the airport and on to **Myeik**. This historic port was once at the centre of Thailand's trade with India via the Bay of Bengal. Between 1350 and 1750, Mergui – as the town was then known – came under Thai control and functioned as Ayutthaya's major link with the Indian Ocean. Goods were unloaded at Myeik, or further up the navigable Tanintharyi River at the port of Tanintharyi, then pulled upriver in canoes or on rafts to the upper reaches of the Ngawun Chaung before taken across the Mawdaung Pass and down to Prachuap Khiri Khan. Here, they were loaded onto small vessels, before being sent up the Gulf of Thailand to Ayutthaya via the Chao Phraya River.

The decline and fall of the Tanintharyi trade

While the Portuguese conquest of Malacca contributed to the expansion of trans-peninsular trade in the 16th and early 17th centuries, subsequent mercantile competition from other European nations, notably the Dutch and the British,

"I have heard it said throughout the East Indies that the closer a people lives to Burma the more lively and intelligent it is." De La Loubère, French Ambassador to Siam (1685).

BELOW: snack seller with *thanaka* make-up.

began to undermine the profitability of trans-peninsular trade with Ayutthaya. Another factor detrimental to the Tanintharyi trade was the rise of the Greek adventurer Constant Phaulkon at the Court of King Narai of Siam. Phaulkon was hostile to the Muslim merchants controlling Thailand's commerce with the Bay of Bengal, and, under his influence, the "Moors" were displaced.

In 1863, the Englishman Samuel ("Siamese") White was appointed Shahbandar or Harbourmaster of Mergui at Phaulkon's insistence, and for the next few years trade suffered disruption at the hand of White and his fellow adventurers, who seized their chance to amass personal wealth at the expense of local commerce. White's misrule was to lead to the outbreak of war between Thailand and Golconda, the two principal participants in the Tanintharyi trade, in 1685. Two years later, the Mughal Emperor Aurangzeb subdued Golconda, reducing its eponymous capital and chief port to the status of a fishing village. Next, in 1765, the Burmese armies of King Hsinbyushin moved southwards, seizing Dawei, Myeik and Kawthaung, severing the area permanently from Thailand. Finally, in 1826, the area was annexed by the British, denying the Thais any chance of reconquest, and ensuring that Tanintharyi would remain forever part of Burma.

The Myeik Archipelago

One of the most scenic and charming island groups in Southeast Asia is the **Myeik (Mergui) Archipelago ⑪**. Comprising more than 800 islands off the south Tanintharyi Coast, it is home to the Moken, sea gypsies who, until recently, were notorious for their piracy. Like the Bajao of the Sulu Sea, they live on small boats, the countless bays of the archipelago offering shelter and food.

Map on page 306

"A very ill man and a great Interloper and a great Enemy of this Kingdom in general." The Honourable East India Company's opinion of Samuel "Siamese" White (circa 1687).

BELOW: preparing to fish.

LINKING THE BAY OF BENGAL AND THE SOUTH CHINA SEA

Records of an important trade route in the Thanintharyi region date back at least as far as the 3rd century AD, when Chinese sources record the conquest of "Tiensun" by Fu-nan, a powerful kingdom of the lower Mekong valley. By the fifth century, the former had become an important centre of the trans-peninsular trade with India, partly because of its strategic location across Fu-nan's lines of communication with the Bay of Bengal, and partly because of an increase in piracy around the Straits of Malacca. Thanintharyi's real importance as a trans-peninsular route was only to emerge, however, as a result of the southward migration of the Tai peoples into the Chao Phraya around AD 1200.

Siamese control over the north of the Malay Peninsula began around AD 1280, when Mon chronicles indicate a southward expansion by the Sukhothai Kingdom into the Thanintharyi area. The Siamese Kingdom then moved south, with the founding of a dynastic capital at Ayutthaya in 1350–51. The central polity of the expanding Thai state was now within 400 km (250 miles) of the Myeik and the Bay of Bengal, providing a catalyst for trans-peninsular trade. Within 25 years, the Siamese had laid the foundations of a township at Thanintharyi, and trade with Ayutthaya had begun to flourish.

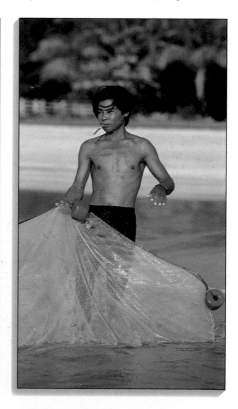

A boat undergoing repairs. Myeik has been an important sea port since the 16th century.

The Japanese are currently engaged in the lucrative business of pearl fishing in the Myeik Archipelago. Other unusual products of this island group include sea cucumbers and swifts' nests, which are harvested for exotic bird's nest soup. The latter are found in cathedral-like limestone caves and accessible only at low tide.

Picturesque Myeik

The onshore district capital is the town of **Myeik** ⑫ (Mergui), a short way from the mouth of the Tanintharyi River. A small offshore island helps to enclose Myeik's sheltered harbour. On it, and visible from the city's centre, lies Burma's third largest **Shwethalyaung** (reclining Buddha) lazily watching the town.

Myeik still holds the charm of an eastern colonial city in the 1930s. Nothing much has changed since then, except that modern goods, smuggled in from across Thailand, fill the stands of the teeming market. Up on the hill, next to the government rest house, is the place where the Mergui massacre took place in the 17th century and the famed "haunted house" of Maurice Collis, historian, novelist and colonial governor, still stands on the ridge.

Unfortunately, the vicinity of Myeik is almost inaccessible to outsiders today. It is a major centre for the Burmese-Thailand smuggling trade, and the Yangon government has been forced to take extreme security measures. Myeik itself, however, remains an isolated ocean-side Shangri-La. Certainly Myeik is isolated and tranquil. The **Theindawgyi Pagoda**, a classic Mon-style cube-form temple, is lined with well-executed interior mosaic and high-quality bronze Buddha images. While it may be the town's most celebrated *paya*, **Payagyi Road** ("Big Pagoda Road") is literally lined with monasteries, including Theinwa Kyaung,

BELOW:
Theindawgyi Pagoda.

Atulawka Marazein, Nyaung Yeiktha and Shwetaung. Further out, on the edge of town, **Kuthein Nayon Kyaung** is a temple built in Mon style with characteristic square shrines – several of the Buddha images here are believed to have come from Thailand, and may date back to the time before 1765 when Myeik was a part of the Kingdom of Siam.

Besides temples, Myeik is remarkable for its fine harbour and the views from the waterfront across nearby **Pataw Padet Island**, described in Collis' writings on Myeik as "Cat and Mouse Island" due to the two distinct hillocks at either end of the isle. Pataw Padet and Myeik harbour are the gateway to the extensive and unspoilt Myeik Archipelago – or rather, they will become so when this remote corner of southeast Burma opens up more fully. When visiting the Myeik waterfront, the visitor should keep an eye open for a stone slab set in the footpath. This is all that remains of the tombstone of Mary Povey White, wife of Samuel "Siamese" White. For a long time the site of Mary's tomb disappeared, but the indefatigable Maurice Collis was out strolling one day when he noticed a washerwoman pounding clothes with what appeared to be an inscribed piece of stone. Collis deciphered the worn-away writing, and was amazed to discover the slab was part of the tombstone of Mary White – the former colonial administrator is responsible for the stone having been set in its present position.

Most visitors to Myeik will arrive and leave by air from Yangon or Kawthaung. It is also possible to fly north to the isolated port of **Dawei ⓭**, which can also be reached by sea, but not yet by land. There's not a lot to see or do here, but the town has a wonderful vernacular architecture, a Raj-era marketplace, and the usual assortment of teashops and pagodas. ❑

Map on page 306

TIP

The Tanintharyi Coast is, as yet, remarkably unpolluted and unexposed to tourism. Don't miss the fresh seafood available at Kawthaung, Myeik and Dawei and dress conservatively when swimming.

BELOW:
Maungmagan Beach near Dawei.

CONTENTS

Getting Acquainted

The Place...............................322
Climate..................................323
Government & Economy........323

Planning the Trip

Visas and Passports..............323
Customs Regulations............324
Health & Insurance................324
Tourist Offices.......................325
Money Matters......................325
What to Wear.........................326
Photography..........................326
Public Holidays......................326
Getting There.........................326
Tour Operators......................327

Practical Tips

Media & Postal Services........328
Telecommunications.............328
Tipping..................................329
Security & Crime....................329
Tourist Information................329
Business Hours......................329
International Organisations....329
Religious Services.................329
Consulates & Embassies.......329
Medical Treatment................330
Travelling with Kids...............330
Business Travellers...............330
Travellers with Disabilities.....330
Etiquette................................330

Getting Around

General Conditions................332
From the Airport....................332
Domestic Travel.....................332
Tourist Information................335
Tour Packages......................336

Where to Stay

Hotels...................................337

Where to Eat

What to Eat............................344
Where to Eat.........................344
Drinking Notes......................345
Teashops..............................346

Nightlife

General..................................347
Discos, Bars & Pubs.............347
Cinemas in Yangon...............348

Culture

Pagodas & Temples..............348
The Six Buddhist Synods.......349
Monasteries..........................349
The Mudras..........................350
Libraries...............................350

Sports

General..................................351
Spectator Sports..................351
Outdoor Activities.................352

Shopping

Markets.................................353
Arts & Crafts.........................353

Language

Ana-deh................................354
Survival Burmese.................354

Further Reading

General Interest & Travel.......356
General History.....................356
European Contact..................356
The British Colonial Era.........357
World War II...........................357
Contemporary Burma............357
Ethnic Minorities..................358
Religion................................358
Arts & Culture.......................358

Getting Acquainted

The Place

Area: The Union of Myanmar, a change in name in 1989 from Union of Burma, has a total land area of 678,500 sq km (261,970 sq miles) making it about equal to the combined size of France and Great Britain.

Location: The country extends from 28°30' to about 10°20' N latitude. Its borders are shared with Bangladesh, the Chinese province of Yunnan, Thailand and Laos; the Andaman Sea (or the Indian Ocean being the larger body of water) are on the western, southern and southwestern peripheries with a total coastline of about 2,800 km (1,740 miles).

Population: Burma has seven minority-dominated states: Rakhaing (Arakan), Chin, Kachin, Kayin (Karen), Kayah (Karenni), Mon and Shan. There are seven divisions populated mainly by Bamar (Burman): Ayeyarwady (Irrawaddy), Magway (Magwe), Mandalay, Bago (Pegu), Yangon (Rangoon), Sagaing and Tanintharyi (Tenasserim).

Burma has a population of 52.8 million (2004 estimate), of whom 80 percent are rural dwellers and 20 percent urban. The annual population growth rate is 1.84 percent. Life expectancy is 57 years; infant mortality rate is 77 per 1,000 (2002 figures).

Language: The Burmese language is a member of the Tibeto-Burman language family, which is in turn a subgroup of Sino-Tibetan. While 80 percent of Burma's diverse peoples speak this language, there remain more than 100 distinct languages and dialects spoken in different parts of the country. The great variation in cultural histories of the ethnic groups can be seen in their languages.

The Burmese language is thought to have originated in the Bamar's ancestral central Asian homeland. The language spread rapidly among Burma's Thai (Shan) and Mon-Khmer peoples during the 19th century, when the last Mon Empire had declined and the Ayeyarwady Delta was opened to rice cultivation, attracting many hill Kayin.

Religion: Burma is primarily a Buddhist country with close to 90 percent of the population following Theravada Buddhism; the rest of the population is split among Muslim, Hindu and Christian minorities.

Time Zone: Burma Standard Time is 6 hours and 30 minutes ahead of Greenwich Mean Time. If you come from Bangkok, you would have to set your watch back half-an-hour upon arrival in Yangon.

Currency: Burma's official currency is the kyat (pronounced "chat"). Hotel rooms, air tickets and Myanma Railways tickets are now priced in US dollars, so you'll need to bring enough US currency to cover these expenses. For just about everything else you will have to use kyat *(see page 325)*.

Weights & Measures: Burma has retained many of the old weights and measures in use during the British colonial period.
1 viss (peith-tha) = 1,633 grams
/3.6 lbs
1 tical = 16.33 grams
1 cubit (tong) = 0.457 metres
/18 inches

National Flag

The Burmese national flag is red in colour with a dark blue canton in the top left corner. Within the blue field are a white pinion and ears of paddy rice, surrounded by 14 white stars. The pinion represents industry, the rice symbolises agriculture, and the stars correspond to the 14 administrative states and divisions of Burma. The three colours of the flag represent decisiveness (red), purity and virtue (white) and peace and integrity (blue). The state flag was adopted in 1974.

1 span (htwa) = 0.23 metres
/9 inches
1 furlong = 201 metres/659 feet
1 lakh = 100,000 (units)
1 crore = 100 lakh
The tin, or basket, is used to measure quantities of agricultural export goods. The kilogram equivalent differs for rice, sesame, and other goods.
Electricity: In Burma, the standard electrical current is 230-volt, 50 hertz.

Climate

Like all countries in South and Southeast Asia's monsoonal region, Burma's year is divided into three seasons. The Southwest Monsoon brings rains beginning in May, which are most intense between June and August. This is a time of high

Burmese alphabet, script and numbers

The Burmese script has a different origin than the spoken Burmese. It derives from the Pallava languages of south India, and has strong similarities with the Telugu script. The Mon adopted these scripts during their interactions with Theravada Buddhist priests from South India in the 6th century, and the Bamar absorbed it after King Anawrahta's conquest of the Mon capital of Thaton in the 11th century.

The Burmese alphabet consists of 44 letters: 32 consonants, eight vowels and four diphthongs. It is written and read from left to right, top to bottom.

The Burmese numerical system, although written in typically Burmese script, is based upon the Arabic and decimal systems in common use in the West.

humidity – especially in the coastal and delta regions – and of daily afternoon/evening showers, as monsoonal winds carry the moisture in from the Indian Ocean. The central inland region is drier than other parts of the country, but is also subject to much rain during this time. Travel during the rainy season can quite often be interrupted due to flooded roads and railway lines; it is made even more difficult as this information is not always made available through the media.

In October, the rains let up. From November through to May the Northeast Monsoon brings dry weather. The "cool season" (November–February) is the most pleasant time to visit Burma. The average temperature along the Ayeyarwady plain, from Yangon to Mandalay, is between 21°C and 28°C (70°F and 82°F), although in the mountains in the north and east, the temperature can drop below freezing and snow can fall.

During the months of March and April, Burma has its "dry season". Temperatures in the central Burma plain, particularly around Bagan (Pagan), can climb to 45°C (113°F).

The annual rainfall along the coasts of Rakhaing (Arakan) and Tanintharyi (Tenasserim) ranges from 300 to 500 cm (120 to 200 in). The Ayeyarwady Delta gets about 150 to 200 cm (60 to 100 in), while the central Burma region, between Mandalay and Bagan and the surrounding areas, averages 50 to 100 cm (20 to 40 in) of rain each year. In the far north, the melting snows of the Himalayan foothills keep rivers fed with water.

Government

The most significant event in politics of the past 15 years took place in 1990 when the first free elections were held in 30 years. Nobel laureate Aung San Suu Kyi's NLD (National League for Democracy) won the first free election in 30 years by a majority of about 80 percent. The military-led "State Peace and Development Council" (SPDC) responded by raiding NLD headquarters and arresting key members. Since then, SPDC has been fighting a war of attrition with the NLD. Several attempts have since been made to adopt a new constitution for the Union of Myanmar (in Burmese, Myanmar Naing-Ngan). Should that ever happen, a newly elected People's Assembly (*Hluttaw*) will convene. Until then, the SPDC headed by Senior General Than Shwe, rules by decree.

Economy

Burma's gross national product (GNP) is US$74 billion (2003 estimates), or a per capita GNP of US$1,800. It is growing by about 5 percent yearly. The 1989 opening of Burma to foreign investment and privatisation of many state industries boosted the official economy considerably, but an underground trade in smuggled consumer goods is still quite significant. Income from tourism contributes to the country's foreign currency reserves but large-scale movements are hindered by a lack of infrastructure and potential tourists' reaction to Burma's poor human rights record.

Planning the Trip

Visas & Passports

Visitors to Burma must present a valid passport and a tourist or business visa obtained at one of Burma's overseas embassies or consulates. An entry visa for tourists (EVT) is valid for 28 days. These visas can now be easily extended for another four weeks at the Yangon immigration office. It is also possible to obtain a multiple-journey entry visa for those operating a business in Burma. A visa for a longer stay, a so called stay permit, can be issued for a duration of up to one year and extended upon application; there is also a visa that permits multiple entries during the period of one year. Stay permits must be endorsed by the Foreign Investment Commission or the ministry concerned. Visas can be obtained online at www.visa.gov.mm.

Children above seven years of age, even when included on their parents' passport, must have their own visas.

Burmese Calendar

The Burmese calendar subscribes to both the solar and the lunar months, thus requiring an intercalary 30-day 13th month every second or third year.

Tourists should keep this in mind when planning their visit, and consult the Myanmar embassy to synchronise their schedule with the Burmese calendar. Visits should ideally be timed to coincide with the full moon, so you can witness the many festivities held at this time of the month.

OFFICIAL REGISTRATION

Officially, as a foreign tourist, you must register either with the immigration authorities or police whenever you move around the country. This obligation is automatically fulfilled by staying overnight at any tourist hotel. When staying overnight at a monastery or private home you must register with the police to avoid complications for you and your hosts. Many new regions have been opened since 1994. Some can be visited by individuals without problems, others require the company of a registered tourist guide. Most travel agencies can arrange such trips including permit, transport and guide; but the costs add up.

Departure Tax

There is a US$10 airport departure tax, payable in dollars at the check-in counter.

Customs

Tourists are allowed duty-free import of limited quantities of tobacco – 400 cigarettes, 100 cigars, or 250 gm (8 oz) of pipe tobacco as well as two litres of alcoholic beverage, and a half-litre bottle of perfume or eau de cologne and articles for personal use. In detail this includes the following items, although the local customs is really interested in valuables such as jewellery and items which could be sold:

Items accepted for import into Burma:
- 1 camera and accessories with 3 rolls of film
- 1 tape recorder
- 1 portable radio
- 1 video cassette recorder
- 1 portable computer
- 24 diskettes
- 1 pair of field glasses
- 1 set of golf clubs
- 1 portable typewriter
- personal jewellery
- 1 electric shaver
- 1 hair dryer
- 1 pocket calculator
- personal effects in actual use
- two tennis rackets
- medicine for personal use
- 1 travelling blanket
- 1 portable musical instrument
- 20 records/12 unrecorded tapes
- 1 unrecorded video tape
- professional/technical equipment for personal use

Items in excess of the numbers shown above can be brought in at the discretion of the official in charge provided they are for personal use. Bringing more film does not present a problem either. You will be required to fill out a customs form declaring your camera(s) (still and video), jewellery, tape recorder, radio, computer and similar effects.

Another form listing all items you are expected to have on you upon departure will be attached to your passport; this is to ensure that you haven't sold any of these items on Burma's black market. Contrary to the regulation in force during the 1970s and 1980s you are now permitted to bring in your video camera.

Items prohibited from import into Burma:
Counterfeit currency
Pornography
Narcotic and psychotropic substances
Playing cards
Goods bearing the reproduction of the flag of the Union of Myanmar
Goods bearing the emblem of the Buddha or pagodas of Myanmar
Toy guns and remote control toys
Firearms
Live animals/birds

FOREIGN CURRENCIES

Foreigners may bring in as much foreign currency as they wish. Amounts in excess of US$2,000 or its equivalent must be declared on the Foreign Exchange Declaration Form (FED). However, the import and export of Burmese kyat is forbidden, and the export of foreign currency is limited to the amount declared upon entry.

After having your customs declaration stamped and if you have no goods to declare, you can pass through the "Green Channel". If you have any doubts, use the "Red Channel".

Formalities both on arrival and departure are now quite easy as long as you do not lose the various forms you have been given upon entry.

Artefacts of archaeological interest cannot be taken out of the country, nor can any precious stones – unless they've been purchased from the Tourist Department Stores, the airport duty-free shop, or with special government permission. There is no enforced restriction on the export of souvenirs of genuine tourist interest. For inquiries, call the Customs House in Yangon tel: 01 284 533.

Prohibited Exports

- Stone-Age implements and artefacts
- Fossils
- Ancient coins
- Bronze and clay pipes
- Palm leaf manuscripts and *Parabaike* (folding manuscripts)
- Inscribed stones and bricks
- Inscribed gold and silver plates and other inscribed objects
- Historical documents
- Religious images and statues
- Carvings or sculptures of bronze, stone, stucco and wood
- Frescoes and fragments of frescoes
- Burmese regalia and paraphernalia

Health & Insurance

Health officials require certification of immunisation against cholera, and against yellow fever if you arrive within nine days after leaving or transiting an affected area. Proof of smallpox vaccination is no longer required.

All visitors to Burma should take appropriate anti-malarial precautions before entering the country, and should continue to take medication throughout their stay. The risk is highest at altitudes below 1,000 m (3,000 ft) between May and December. Many upcountry hotels have mosquito nets, but any hole makes them worthless. Bring your own mosquito net and carry mosquito coils to burn while you sleep.

Perhaps the two most common hazards to visitors are sunburn and intestinal problems. The best way to prevent sunburn, especially if you're not used to the intense tropical sun, is to stay under cover whenever possible at midday and if you do go out, wear a hat or carry an umbrella. You'll see many Burmese, especially women and children, with yellow thanaka-bark powder applied to their faces to help screen out the sun. If you find yourself sweating a lot and feeling weak or dizzy, sit down (in the shade) and take some salt, either in tablet form or by mixing salt in a soft drink or tea.

Nearly every Westerner (especially first-timers) travelling in Asia and eating local food comes down with diarrhoea. This can be uncomfortable and inconvenient. A good solution is to carry charcoal or Lomotil tablets. Better still, stay away from unfamiliar foods wherever possible.

Health standards in much of Burma are still relatively low. Don't ever drink water unless you know it has been boiled or is sold in sealed bottles. All fruit should be carefully peeled before being eaten, and no raw vegetables should be eaten. Amoebic dysentery is a danger to those who are not careful.

It is best to discuss your travel plans with your personal physician with regard to recommended immunisation (tetanus, hepatitis, typhoid) and the specific anti-malarial drug needed. If you require any medication, it is best to bring along a sufficient supply.

For longer stays in Burma and if your travels should take you to outlying areas, consider bringing your own medical kit as your specific prescription or drug may not be available.

TRAVEL INSURANCE

Travel insurance gives you the peace of mind that – in the case of unforeseen circumstances – you will be compensated for any loss of property and expenses incurred from the interruption and cancellation of trips, and for medical and other emergencies as spelled out in the specific policy.

What travel insurance usually includes are cover for damaged and lost luggage – although most airlines *do* pay compensation against such claims; loss of deposit (for travel arrangements) – and compensation for flight delay and cancellation. Insurance policies also carry provision for hospitalisation and emergency evacuation to the nearest locality for proper treatment.

Tourist Offices

MTT (Myanmar Travels & Tours) is supposedly the country's official "tourist promotion" office, but it maintains no offices abroad. Burma's diplomatic representatives have information of interest to tourists, although little is available in terms of brochures and maps.

Burma has overseas embassies or consulates in the following countries: Australia, the USA, Canada, France, Germany, Italy, the UK, Hong Kong, Laos, Singapore and Thailand.

Burmese Embassies Abroad

Australia, 22 Arkana Street, Yarralumla, ACT 2600. Tel: 02 6273 3811.
France, 06 rue de Courcelles, 75008 Paris. Tel: 01 4225 5695.
Italy, Via Vincenzo Bellini 20m Interno 1. Tel: 06 854 9374.
Singapore, 15 St. Martin's Drive, S'pore 257996.
Tel: 65 6735 0209.
Thailand, 132 Thanon Sathon Neua, Bangkok 10500.
Tel: 02 233 7250.
UK, 19A Charles Street, London W1X 8ER. Tel: 020 7629 6966.
USA, 2300 'S' St NW, Washington DC 20008. Tel: 202 332 9044.

Money Matters

Until recently all foreign visitors to the country were required to buy US$200 worth of Foreign Exchange Certificates (FECs) upon entry, which could be used to pay for hotel rooms and air tickets or exchanged for kyat through licensed money-changers. In 2003, however, the government did away with the FEC system.

Today, the official rate of exchange is artificially pegged at about six kyats to US$1. However, no one pays any attention to this rate, and instead use the free market exchange rate – currently between 700 and 1,100 kyats for US$1.

Along with FECs, Burma has abolished licensed money-changers so your best bet is to buy kyats from hotels, travel agencies or trustworthy shopkeepers. Avoid money-changers on the street wherever possible, and don't hand over your money before having counted the kyats.

Kyats can be used to pay for meals, souvenirs, tips, bus and car transportation and occasionally (in the outlying districts) for accommodation. But you will still need US dollars to pay for hotel rooms in the main cities, as well as airline and rail tickets.

US dollars are the best currency to have, although some places will accept pounds sterling. Other hard currencies such as the Euro and Japanese yen can only be changed at very disadvantageous rates.

You can draw US dollar advances on your Visa or MasterCard at the Foreign Trade Bank (in Yangon, it's on Barr Street; in Mandalay, on B Road at 82nd Street).

Kyat Denominations

Kyats are issued in denominations of 1, 5, 10, 15, 20, 45, 50, 90, 100, 200, 500 and 1,000 notes.

Travellers' Cheques

The following travellers' cheques are accepted: MasterCard, American Express, Bank of Tokyo, Citibank, Visa, Bank of America, National Westminster Bank, First National City Bank, Swiss Bankers and Commonwealth Bank of Australia.

Credit Cards

Visa, American Express and MasterCard are only accepted at Myanmar Travels & Tours, all the major hotels, at airline offices and at the Yangon Duty Free Shop.

Service Charge & Tax

International-standard hotels levy a government tax and a service charge of 10 percent each; some restaurants impose a 10 percent government tax only.

What to Wear

Dress in Burma is casual but neat. Unless you are conducting business in Yangon, you won't be expected to wear a tie anywhere. Long trousers for men and a dress or long skirt for women, lightweight and appropriate to the prevailing climatic conditions, is the generally accepted mode of dress for visitors. Quick-drying clothes are a good idea for visits during the rainy season or Thingyan (the "water festival"). There is no law against shorts or short skirts, but this type of clothing is not welcomed by the Burmese.

A sweater or jacket should be carried if you plan a visit to the hill stations or Shan Plateau, especially in the cool season. Open footwear, such as sandals, is acceptable, but remember to remove footwear when entering religious institutions. An umbrella would be a worthwhile investment during the rainy season.

Photography

You can now get film nearly everywhere, though slide film is scarce outside Yangon. There are also a few efficient film developing shops in Yangon and Mandalay where you can have your film developed within an hour. If you are interested in secondhand classic camera models in working condition you may get lucky in Yangon's stores.

Burmese are extremely photogenic – bring twice the amount of film you think you may need. Hand-carry all film (exposed and unexposed) and don't let it pass though x-ray machines, particularly at provincial airports. When travelling it is essential to guard your equipment and film against excessive heat and dust. Always use a UV-filter to protect your lenses and (when necessary) a polarisation filter to reduce some reflective glare and enhance the blue of the sky. The best times for outdoor photography are the morning and late afternoon.

Getting There

BY AIR

Most of Burma's visitors arrive at Yangon's **Mingaladon Airport**. Situated 19 km (12 miles) northwest of the capital, it is where most scheduled international flights arrive. Others have begun to arrive in Mandalay from Chiang Mai, Thailand. There are plans to make the new **Mandalay International Airport** eventually a regional hub of Indochina. The largest number of international flights connect Yangon and Bangkok. **Thai Airways** (www.thaiair.com) and Burma's international carrier, **Myanmar Airways International** (MAI; www.maiair.com), each have two roundtrip flights daily. MAI also operates daily flights to Singapore, two flights a week to Hong Kong, two a week to Kuala Lumpur and one per week to Dhaka. **Silk Air** (www.silkair.com) flies daily from Singapore, **Malaysian Airlines**

Public Holidays

All offices are closed on the following days:
● **4 January** Independence Day commemorates the date in 1948 that Burma left the British Commonwealth and became a sovereign independent nation.
● **12 February** Union Day marks the date in 1947 that Aung San concluded an agreement with Burma's ethnic minorities at Panglong in the Shan State.

The Union of Myanmar (Burma) flag, which has been carried by runners to each of Burma's state capitals, is returned to Yangon amid the roar of hundreds of thousands of people from all over the nation.
● **2 March** Peasants' Day honours the working population.
● **27 March** Resistance (Tatmadaw) Day commemorates the World War II struggle against Japan. It is celebrated with parades and fireworks. Ironically, Burma spent most of the war on the Japanese side fighting Allied forces, but switched allegiance in early 1945.
● **1 May Workers'/May Day** The working people's holiday.

● **19 July** Martyrs' Day is a memorial to Burma's founding father, Aung San, and his cabinet who were assassinated in 1947. Ceremonies take place at the Martyrs' Mausoleum, Yangon.
Non-Buddhist religious holidays: Minority groups celebrate holidays not on the Burmese calendar: the Hindu festival Dewali in October, the Islamic observance of Bakri Idd with changing dates, the Christian holidays of Christmas and Easter, and the Kayin (Karen) New Year Festival on or about 1 January.

(MAS; www.mas.com.my) has two roundtrip flights from Kuala Lumpur, **Biman** of Bangladesh (www.bimanair.com) flies once a week from Chittagong via Yangon to Bangkok and back. **Air Mandalay** (www.air-mandalay.com), a private domestic airline, operates a biweekly service between Yangon and Chiang Mai. **Air China** (CAAC; www.china-airlines.com) has a weekly flight between Yangon and Kunming (Yunnan). Newcomers are **Druk Airlines** (Bhutan; www.drukair.com.bt) and ANA (All Nippon Airways of Japan; www.ana.co.jp), connecting their respective countries. Travellers from the US, Australia and Europe probably will find it easiest to reach Burma via Bangkok or Singapore. Some 80 international airlines connect these cities with other world capitals.

BY LAND

Burma's frontiers have long been closed to overland international travel, primarily due to the continuing rebellions by various ethnic groups in the border areas. It is, however, possible to visit Tachilek and Kyaingtong (Kengtung) in Shan State from Mae Sai in northern Thailand.

For a day trip the visa is available at the border post. Similarly, the island of Kawthaung (the former Victoria Point) in the Myeik (Mergui) archipelago can be reached from Ranong in southern Thailand. On the Burma-Yunnan frontier border posts have been opened at Lwe-ge from where organised group tours can go to Bhamo, Muse, Namkham and Kunlon.

Organised groups are also permitted to continue up to Lashio. The Thai and Burmese governments have constructed a bridge across the Moei River between Mae Sot and Myawaddy but so far travel is still not permitted between the two countries except for the visit to a casino within sight of the bridge. If the present development plan is carried through, it should eventually

be possible to travel by car from Singapore through Burma to India or China and on to Europe.

Tour Operators

Tour Operators in the UK

Silverbird Travel (tailor-made tours)
4 Northfields Prospect, Putney Bridge Road, London SW18 1PE.
Tel: 020 8875 9090
e-mail: sales@silverbird.co.uk
www.silverbird.co.uk

Trans-Indus (tailor-made and package tours)
Northumberland House, 11 The Pavement, Popes Lane, Ealing, London W5 4NG.
Fax: 020 8840 5327
e-mail: enquiries@transindus.co.uk
www.transindus.co.uk

Tour Operators in Europe

Indochina Services
Enzianstr. 4a/D-82319, Starnberg, Germany.
Tel: 8151 770222
Fax: 8151 770229
www.indochina-services.com

Tour Operators in the US

Asia Transpacific Journeys
(tailor-made and package tours)
2995 Center Green Court, Boulder, Colorado 80301.
Tel: 1 800 642 2742; 1 303 443 6789
Fax: 1 303 443 7078
e-mail: Travel@AsiaTranspacific.com
www.asiatranspacific.com

Airline Offices in Yangon

Air China: 13/23 Shwe Kanayei Housing, Narnattaw Road.
Tel: 01 500 054
Air Mandalay: 146 Dhammazedi Road. Tel: 01 525 344
Austrian Airlines: La Pyayt Wun Plaza, Suite 808, 37 Signal Pagoda Road. Tel/Fax: 01 371 383
Biman Bangladesh Airlines: 106-108 Pansodan Street.
Tel: 01 240 922
Druk Airlines: 52 Phyapon Street. Tel: 01 524 904
Indian Airlines: 127 Sule Pagoda Road. Tel: 01 254 758

Arriving by Sea

Several cruise lines feature a stopover in Yangon harbour on their itineraries.

Indochina Services
870 Market Street, Suite 923, San Francisco, CA 94102 USA.
Tel: 415 434 4015
Fax: 434 4145
e-mail: americas@is-americas.com
www.indochina-services.com

Diving Operators

Dive Asia
Tel: 076 330 598 (Thailand)
www.diveasia.com
Santana Diving & Canoeing
Tel: 076 294 220 (Thailand)
www.santanaphuket.com
South East Asia Liveaboards
Tel: 076 340 406 (Thailand)
Fax: 076 340 586
www.seal-asia.com

Meditation Study in Yangon

Chamnyay Yeiktha Meditation Centre, 655-A-Kaba Aye Paya Lan.
Tel: 01 661 479
Fax: 01 667 050
www.chanmyay.org
Panditarama Meditation Centre (Shwe Taung Gon Sasana Yeiktha), 80/A Shwetaauggyaw Lan (Thanlwin Lan).
Tel: 01 535 448
e-mail: panditarama@mptmail.net.mm

Malaysia Airlines: Central Hotel, 335-357 Bogyoke Aung San Road.
Tel: 01 241 001
Mandarin Airlines: 353-355 Bo Aung Kyaw Street.
Tel: 01 240 399
Myanmar Airways International: 08-02 Sakura Tower, 339 Bogyoke Aung San Road. Tel: 01 255 440
SilkAir: 2nd Floor, Sakura Tower, 339 Bogyoke Aung San Road.
Tel: 01 255 287
Thai Airways International: Sakura Tower, 339 Bogyoke Aung San Road. Tel: 01 255 499

Practical Tips

Media

NEWSPAPERS & MAGAZINES

The daily English language newspaper, *The New Light of Myanmar*, mostly filled with government announcements, is available on newsstands and in all hotels. *The International Herald Tribune* and other international newspapers are sometimes available at hotel newsstands, along with weekly news magazines. Used magazines can be purchased inexpensively from street vendors.

RADIO & TELEVISION

Radio: The only radio stations permitted in Burma are those affiliated with the state-owned Radio Myanmar. Radio Myanmar broadcasts intermittently between 7am and 9pm daily at AM 576 and FM 104. English-language news comes on for 45 minutes at 8.30am and for 90 minutes at 1.30pm. Military-owned Myawaddy Radio is similar. A newer station, Yangon City FM 89, broadcasts news, music and entertainment 8 to 10am and 2 to 6pm daily.

Visitors carrying shortwave radios will be able to pick up BBC Radio (www.bbc.co.uk) and Voice of America (VOA, www.voanews.com). The shortwave frequencies change according to the time of day; see their respective websites for further detail.

Television: One state-owned network, Myanmar Television (MRTV, Channel 3), and one military-owned-and-operated network, Myawaddy TV (Channel 6), sent telecasts at various times of the day between 7am and 10.30pm to 109 re-transmission stations covering most areas around the country. The government also telecasts Myanmar TV International (MRTV3 and MRTV4) via satellite to those households in Burma and neighbouring countries with satellite service.

Luxury hotels in Yangon usually offer satellite television reception, with private broadcasts from nearby India, Thailand, Malaysia or China.

Postal Services

The Yangon General Post Office (Tel: 01 285 499) is located on Strand Road at the corner of Bo Aung Gyaw Street and is open 7.30am–6pm Monday to Friday. All other post offices in Burma are open 9.30am–4.30pm Monday to Friday, and 9.30am– 12.30pm Saturday. They are closed Sunday and public holidays.

The only exception is the Mingaladon (Yangon) Airport mail sorting office. It is open round-the-clock daily, including Sunday and holidays, for receipt and dispatch of foreign mail. Ordinary letters and postcards will be accepted here at any time. Registered letters can be taken at the airport postal counter only during normal government working hours.

Commemorative stamps are occasionally issued. All can be purchased at Yangon's GPO.

Useful Phone Numbers

Immigration, Yangon: 01 286 434
Customs, Yangon: 01 284 533
Fire, Yangon: 191/192
Police, Yangon: 199
Ambulance, Yangon: 256 122, 281 722 (Ext 286 – for emergency general; Ext 269 – for emergency-injury)
Airport: 01 662 811
Myanmar Railways: 01 274 027, 202 175
Ministry of Hotels & Tourism (MTT): 01 254 098, 282 075
Tourist Information: 01 202 240

Telecommunications

The country code for Burma is 95, the code for Yangon is 1 (01 when dialling in the country). Burma has direct satellite links to seven countries: Japan, Hong Kong, Singapore, Thailand, India, UK and Australia. Siemens of Germany has installed additional satellite communication lines that have brought telecommunication connections up to Western standards. International-class hotels offer in-room IDD telephone and fax service to foreign countries.

Enquiries/Complaints

If you encounter problems with any of the communications systems, direct your queries to the Myanmar Posts and Telecommunications, 43 Bo Aung Gyaw Street, Tel: 285 499 or the enquiries/complaints hotline: tel: 277 209

Area codes:
Yangon: 01
Bago: 052
Chauk: 061
Hinthada: 044
Pa-an: 035
Lashio: 082
Loikaw: 083
Kyaingtong: 084
Magway: 063
Mandalay: 02
Mawlamyaing: 032
Meiktila: 064
Minbu: 065
Monywa: 071
Myingyan: 066
Myitkyina: 074
Pakokku: 062
Pathein: 042
Pyay: 053
Pyinmana: 067
Pyin-U-Lwin: 085
Sagaing: 072
Sittwe: 043
Taunggyi: 081
Taungoo: 054
Thanlyin: 065

When dialling from outside the country omit the 0 in the area code. IDD (International Direct Dialling) is easily available in major Yangon and Mandalay hotels and at kiosks; costs are based on US$ rates plus a service fee. From the smaller towns it may be possible to call Yangon but not overseas.

The Central Telegraph Office (Tel: 01 281 133), located one block east of the Sule Pagoda on Mahabandoola Street, is open from 8am to 9pm Monday to Saturday, and from 8am to 8pm Sunday and public holidays.

MOBILE PHONES

There is no international roaming facility for mobile phones in Burma. Phones brought in from outside the country are subject to temporary confiscation at the airport, to be returned upon departure. Visitors to Burma can rent mobile phones by the week or by the month at rates well above the world market.

INTERNET & E-MAIL ACCESS

Some hotels, tour operators and private companies have access to e-mail. The cost for sending and receiving messages is US$1 per 5 kb. Internet access is not available except by making a long-distance call to your service provider.

Tipping

Tipping is not a common practice in Burma, but it is becoming less unusual in Yangon at major tourist hotels. International-class hotels

Business Hours

- **Government offices/post offices** 9.30am–4.30pm Mon–Fri, 9.30am–12.30pm Sat
- **Myanma Airways** 9.30am–4.30pm Mon–Fri
- **Banks** 10am–2pm weekdays
- **Central Telegraph Office** 8am–9pm weekdays, 8am–8pm Sunday and holidays.
- **Myanmar Travels & Tours** information counter 8am–8pm seven days a week.
- **Restaurants** Most close by 10pm, although some tea and coffee shops will stay open later.
- **Stores** open between 8 and 9am and close at about 6pm.

and some restaurants add a service charge of 10 percent plus government tax to your bill.

Security & Crime

Visitors who confine themselves to seeing the sights will find the country and its cities among the safest to travel in. The government frowns upon foreigners involving themselves in political activities and will also do everything to keep them from getting into "closed areas". Keep your personal belongings safe at all times.

Tourist Information

Myanmar Travels & Tours (MTT) has offices in Yangon, Mandalay, Bagan, Taunggyi, Muse, Tachilek and Kawthaung which increasingly have become of little use to the traveller

other than selling airline and rail tickets. Private entrepreneurs have taken over much of the business.

International Organisations

United Nations Children's Fund (UNICEF), 330, 6 & 7th Floor, Yangon International Hotel, Ahlone Road, Yangon. Tel: 01 212 086.
United Nations Development Program (UNDP), 6 Natmauk Road, Yangon. Tel: 01 542 910.
United Nations Drug Control Program, Myanmar (UNDCP), 262–264, 6th floor, Dagon Centre, Pyay Road, Yangon. Tel: 01 512 647.
World Health Organisation (WHO), 330, 7th Floor, Yangon International Hotel, Ahlone Road, Yangon. Tel: 01 511 076.
FAO, Myanmar Agriculture Service Insein Road, Yangon. Tel: 01 641 672.

Religious Services

The following list of non-Buddhist places of worship in Yangon is indicative:
Roman Catholic
St Mary Cathedral, 372 Bo Aung Kyaw Street. Tel: 01 245 647.
St Augustine's Church, 64 Inya Road. Sunday masses at 7 and 9.30am. Tel: 01 530 620.

Anglican
Cathedral of the Holy Trinity, 446 Bogyoke Aung San Street. Sunday services: 8am, evensong 5pm. Tel: 01 272 326.

Consulates and Embassies in Yangon

Australia, 88 Strand Road. Tel: 01 251 809/10.
Bangladesh, 56 Kaba Aye Pagoda Road. Tel: 01 549 556/7.
Canada, see Australia.
China, 1 Pyidaungsu Yeiktha Road. Tel: 01 221 280/1.
France, 102 Pyidaungsu Yeiktha. Tel: 01 212 523.
Germany, 32 Natmauk Street. Tel: 01 548 951.

India, 545/547 Merchant Street. Tel: 01 282 550.
Lao PDR, A1, Diplomatic Quarters, Taw Win Road. Tel: 01 222 482.
Malaysia, 82 Pyidaungsu Yeiktha Road. Tel: 01 220 248.
Nepal, 17 Natmauk Road. Tel: 01 545 880.
Pakistan, A-4 Diplomatic Quarters, Pyay Road. Tel: 01 222 881.
Singapore, 326 Pyay Road.

Tel: 01 525 688.
Sri Lanka, 34 Taw Win Street. Tel: 01 222 812.
Thailand, 437 Pyay Road. Tel: 01 533 082.
United Kingdom, 80 Strand Road. Tel: 01 281 700.
United States, 581 Merchant Street. Tel: 01 282 055.
Vietnam, 6 Wingbar Road. Tel: 01 548 905.

Methodist
Methodist-English Church,
65 Alanphaya. Tel: 01 284 165.
Sunday school 8.30 to 9.30am,
morning service 9.45am,
Methodist youth fellowship 3.30 to
4.30pm Sunday.

Baptist
Immanuel Church, corner of
Mahabandoola and Barr streets.
Tel: 01 250 079. Sunday school
8am, Sunday worship 5pm.

Armenian
**St John the Baptist Armenian
Church**, 113 Bo Aung Gyaw Street
at the corner of Merchant Street.
Sunday service 9 to 10.30am.

Jewish
There is a synagogue on 26th
Street in Yangon. Tel: 01 275 062.

Muslim
Khoja Mosque, Shwebontha Street.
Shia Mosque, 30th Street.
Sunni Mosque, Shwebontha Street.

Hindu
Hindu Temple, Anawratha Street,
near to Thein Ghyi Zei market.
Sri Sri Durga Temple, 307 Bo Aung
Gyaw Street.
Sri Sri Siva Krishna Temple, 141
Pansodan Street. Open daily 8 to
11am and 4 to 8pm.

Sikh
Sikh Temple, 256 Thein Byu Road.

Pharmacies

Yangon has several pharmacies,
all with 24-hour counters:
May Pharmacy, 542 Merchant
Street.
AA Pharmacy, 142 Sule Pagoda
Road.
Global Network, 155 Sule
Pagoda Road.
  Outside Yangon, pharmacies
are few and far between.

Medical Treatment

In the event that you get sick despite
all your precautions, there are

several hospitals in Yangon that
can cater for foreigners' medical
needs. These include the following
places:
AEA International Clinic, Inya Lake
Hotel, Kaba Aye Paya Road.
Tel: 01 667 879.
Kandawgyi Clinic, Natmauk Road.
Tel: 01 530 083.
**Pacific Medical Centre & Dental
Surgery**, 81 Kaba Aye Pagoda
Road. Tel: 01 548 022.
  Upcountry, in the event of an
emergency, the best bet is the
nearest military hospital.

Women Travellers

Women travelling alone will find
themselves rarely hassled when
compared to other countries in
the region. Still, single women
may find it more comfortable to
travel with a companion. There
are no restrictions on wearing
shorts when visiting temples in
Bagan particularly those in ruins
or that have been reconstructed.
However, brief shorts or skirts,
or skimpy clothing is frowned
upon and women would probably
feel more comfortable wearing
long trousers or an over-the-knee
skirt. The traditional *longyi* that
the Burmese wear is a good
alternative.

Travelling with Kids

Travelling in Burma is never easy
(unless you stay at The Strand and
move around by air only). The mode
of transport and the climate require
patience and some degree of
stamina. Having said that, the
Burmese love children and will do
everything to make them
comfortable, to the extent of taking
them off parents' hands. Other than
that, there are no facilities intended
specifically for the benefit or
amusement of children.

Business Travellers

While Burma was "Socialist Burma"
all businesses were nationalised, but
in 1989, restrictions were relaxed

considerably. The government
encourages small private
businesses, joint ventures and even
100 percent foreign ownership of
factories. The former 11 "trade
corporations" have now become
"State-owned Economic Enterprises"
run by different ministries.
  For those who want to set up
joint ventures in Burma, the
government has published a
booklet, *Guide to Foreign
Investment in Myanmar*, that can be
ordered at UMFIC, 653/691,
Merchant Street, Yangon. It
contains a wealth of interesting
information about the new state of
the economy since the socialist
system was abolished.

Addresses
**The Union of Myanmar Federation
of Chambers of Commerce and
Industry**, 74/86 Bo Son Pet Street,
Pabedan Township. Tel: 01 270
749; 504/506 Merchant Street,
Kyanktada Township. Tel: 01 246
495.
International Business Centre, 88
Pyny Road, Ward 10, Hlaing. Tel: 01
455 044.
  Hotels catering for the business
traveller have business service
centres on their premises.

Travellers with Disabilities

Disabled travellers may find it
difficult to travel around in Burma as
there are very few establishments
with facilities catering for the
handicapped or those confined in
wheelchairs. If you are travelling
through Thailand to Burma, contact
Disabled Peoples International, 78/2
Tivanon Road, Pak Kret, Nonthaburi
11120. Tel: 66 2583 3021.

Etiquette

BURMESE NAMES

Unlike Western culture, there are no
family names in Burmese usage.
Men and women, parents and
children, married couples and single
people cannot be differentiated by
their names. Women keep their

maiden names upon marriage, and a child can have a name which bears no relation to his parents' names.

A Burmese has a name of one, two or three syllables, given to him (or her) shortly after birth at a naming ceremony. Parents consult an authority in astrology and supernatural knowledge – perhaps a monk, a soothsayer or a spiritual medium – in selecting the name. While this practice does not follow Buddhist doctrine, it is customary throughout the country.

Burmese can change their name as often as they like. If they feel success will be brought to a new enterprise or a change of fortune will be made by doing so, a change of name will be made. Small children are often given unpleasant names to ward off illness and evil; when they have grown up, they change their names to something more pleasant. Only by way of address can one tell the gender or social status of a Burmese.

For example, a Burmese named Kau Reng, if a man, might be addressed as "U Kau Reng", "Ko Kau Reng" or "Maung Kau Reng." The title "U" says that the person being addressed is a superior in social or official position, or in age. "Ko" is commonly used among men of similar standing in addressing each other. "Maung" generally is used with persons who are younger or of an inferior status; it also is commonly used among children and teenage boys. Sometimes the dual title "Ko Maung" is used if the Burmese has a monosyllabic name.

A woman named Kau Reng would be addressed as either "Daw Kau Reng" or "Ma Kau Reng". "Daw" implies social status or greater age; it can suggest that the woman is married, although this is not necessarily so. "Ma" is applicable to Burmese women regardless of social status, and is the most commonly used female title, even for married women. It is very discourteous to address any woman in Burma without the use of one of these titles.

Within the family circle, there are other titles with finer shades of meaning. Wives often address their husbands as "Eing Ga Lu" or "Ein Thar" ("Good man of the house"). An elder brother is called "Ko Ko". An uncle is "U Lay", "U Gyi" or "Ba

Burmese Friends

It is particularly difficult for a Burmese to address a Westerner only by his Christian name, even when they are close friends. Thus Ko Kau Reng will never call his friend "Ronnie", but will address him as "Ko Ronnie" or "Maung Ronnie". Similarly, Nancy would be called "Ma Nancy". Ko Kau Reng expects that he, too, will be similarly addressed.

Gyi". Similar terms of affection are directed towards women. "Ma Ma" and "A Ma Gyi" refer to an elder sister; "Daw Daw" is for aunt.

Superiors are often addressed "Ah Ko Gyi," "Ko Gyi" or "Saya" (teacher). "Saya" is also used in reference to medical doctors. Monks are called "Sayadaw" ("Venerable"), "Ashin" ("Reverend") or "Kodaw" ("Your Reverence"), the latter used most frequently by a layman addressing a monk. Military officers are addressed as "Bo".

TEMPLE ETIQUETTE

A Buddhist place of worship is unlike a similar place in the West. You might find a devout Buddhist in deep meditation on any temple platform, but you might also see whole families eating their lunches in front of a Buddha image. You will see lines of monks walking slowly around the stupa, but you also may observe hordes of children happily running around. The temple ground is where every Burmese village or city neighbourhood congregates in the evening. But don't let the "everydayness" fool you. This is sacred ground, and there are certain rules you must keep in order to show your respect.

Throughout Burma, wherever you enter religious grounds, you must remove your shoes (or sandals) and socks. Proper clothing should also be worn at a temple: especially, no short skirts for women, and no brief shorts. Theravada Buddhists have a strong "anti-flesh" attitude, an equally strong desire for virtue, and a refined awareness of beauty.

If you watch the pious Buddhists who climb to the terrace surrounding a stupa, or who wander through the passageways leading around a temple's central cella, you will notice that they always turn to their left. By keeping the sanctuary on the right, they follow a universal "law", moving in the same direction as the sun across the sky.

At the Shwedagon Pagoda and other shrines with planetary posts on their terraces, the pilgrim walks from one season to another. By visiting monuments to the last four Buddhas, he walks through different worlds and different times. This reminds him of his smallness compared to the universe, and awakens in him pure Theravadin spirit. He may stop at planetary posts corresponding to his birthday and the current weekday; he may pause (especially at older shrines) to study the terracotta friezes describing the Buddha's former lives; he might make an offering of flowers or candles at a Buddha image, and perhaps wash it for additional merit. You will hear him murmur the "Three Gems": "I take refuge in the Buddha, I take refuge in the Dhamma, I take refuge in the Sangha."

No Shrine Souvenirs

Pagodas and temples are usually beautifully decorated, and most Burmese show great pride if you are inspired to photograph their shrine. But photos should be your only souvenirs. Although many Buddhist structures seem to have a surplus of small Buddha statues that no one appears to care about, these are still venerated images. Leave them alone.

Getting Around

General Conditions

Travel around the country may tax your patience and – if you go by road or rail – your derrière. Rail and road infrastructure is either antiquated or non-existent and the means of conveyance are equally "tired". There has been a noticeable improvement, though, in vehicles available for travel within the bigger cities and towns and in long-distance travel.

In Burma, it is not the distance that you should concern yourself with but rather the road conditions in the particular area in question. Average speeds achievable on road or rail are well below those in neighbouring countries. Many roads are pot-holed while others are mere dirt tracks.

From The Airport

There are two ways to get from **Mingaladon Airport** to downtown Yangon, a distance of 19 km (12 miles). You have the option of getting a "limousine" (actually just a better-looking taxi) for US$5–8 to anywhere in the city, payable in advance at the counter. Otherwise taxi drivers will besiege you in a bid to drive you into the city. Once huge middle-of-the-century conveyances are now second-hand imports of more recent vintages, without taxi-meters. Travel to Yangon should not cost more than the equivalent of US$3. If you book a room through the hotel desk at the airport, transport into town is usually arranged free of charge. On departure, the fare from Yangon to the airport usually can be paid in local currency.

Domestic Travel

BY AIR

Three different domestic airlines ply a network of air routes to 37 localities within Burma. Privately owned **Air Mandalay** (AM) serves several domestic destinations and offers Western standard service, check-in procedures and flight safety. The newer **Yangon Airways** (YA) is similar. Government-owned **Myanma Airways** (UB) consists of ageing Fokker F-28 jets and Fokker F-27 turboprop planes; it has a reputation for unreliable service and a questionable safety record and cannot be recommended. A new domestic carrier, **Air Bagan** (AB), began operating in late 2004 and offers services between Yangon and Bagan, Mandalay, Heho and Thandwe. Like Air Mandalay, the airline uses Franco-Italian ATR aircraft. Myanma Airways is not a member of the International Air Transport Association (IATA) and is therefore not bound to honour tickets sold overseas. Air Mandalay, Yangon Airways and Air Bagan tickets can be purchased in Bangkok, or through many travel agents in Yangon or Mandalay. Myanma Airways tickets may only be purchased at offices of Myanma Airways or Myanmar Travels & Tours.

Nowadays, very few foreigners use Myanma Airways, whose flights are often fully booked. On Myanma Airways, it's always possible that you might get bumped from your seat on the plane. Air Mandalay, Yangon Airways and Air Bagan tend

Official Priority

The Burmese government runs an unofficial but nevertheless rigid priority list which can disrupt flight bookings right up to the last minute. Burmese VIPs, of course, have priority. Behind them, in order, come tour parties, individual foreign visitors, foreign expatriate residents, and – last and least – native residents of Burma.

Buying Air Tickets

Domestic flight schedules of **Yangon Airways** can be checked at www.yangonair.com while **Air Mandalay**'s is found at www.airmandalay.com and **Air Bagan** at www.airbagan.com. Travel agents sometimes sell domestic air tickets below their recommended published fares. But note that travel agents accept cash payment only, while airlines can accept credit cards. *See page 327 for airline contact numbers and page 336 for a list of travel agents in Yangon.*

to keep more strict flight schedules than Myanma Airways, and in-flight service is much better as well.

BY RIVER/SEA

Burma's rivers provide more than 8,000 km (5,000 miles) of navigable routes, and as a result, shipping is the most important means of transport for people and goods throughout much of the country.

Rivers

The Ayeyarwady (Irrawaddy) River, Burma's lifeline, is navigable from its delta to Bhamo throughout the year, and all the way to Myitkyina during the rainy season. When water levels drop (any time after mid-January) shifting sandbanks make adherence to any schedule difficult and ships do run aground (without any danger to its passengers, though).

The Twante Canal links the Ayeyarwady to Yangon. The Chindwin (Chindwinn) River – the Ayeyarwady's most important tributary, joining it a short distance above Bagan – is navigable in shallow-bottomed boats for 792 km (492 miles) from Yesagyo to Hkamti.

In the east, the Thanlwin (Salween) River is suitable for shipping only as far as 89 km (53 miles) from its mouth near Mawlamyaing to Shwegun. Strong currents funnelling through its narrow chasm block further progress.

In Rakhaing (Arakan), the Kaladan River and the Saing Tin are the most important routes for river transport.

The Kaladan is navigable for 177 km (110 miles) from Sittwe (Akyab) to Paletwa, and the Saing Tin for 129 km (80 miles) from Sittwe to Buthidaung.

Popular River Routes

The most travelled river route for tourists is the stretch of the Ayeyarwady between Mandalay and Bagan.

A local slowboat leaves Mandalay at 5am, arriving in Bagan (Pagan) in 25–28 hours with an overnight stop in Pakokku. You can travel deck class on the boat, sharing open quarters with monks, soldiers, nursing mothers, chicken and fruit baskets; or you can step up to the "first class" section – a salon in the prow of the upper deck with four wooden benches and a table. Either way, kit yourself out with a blanket or sleeping bag, especially during the winter months, and with mosquito netting or repellent during the summer months.

Two modern and faster express boats, *Shwe Kein Nayi* 1 & 2, sail the same route daily except Sunday and Wednesday, leaving at 6am from both Mandalay and Bagan for the 9-hour journey. For all bookings, contact the **Inland Waterways Transport** office (for foreigners) near the Kaingdan Jetty in Yangon (tel: 01 284 055); and in Mandalay near the Gawein Jetty on 35th Street, tel: 02 86035.

If you have the money to burn, book yourself on the *Road to Mandalay* (operated by Orient-Express Trains & Cruises), which sails the Ayeyarwady between Mandalay and Bagan in great splendour. Five-and six-night itineraries spending three and four nights respectively aboard the luxury ship are offered. There are 66 air-conditioned cabins and the ship is oufitted with a pool, library and boutique apart from restaurants and a bar. Guests are pampered with gourmet cuisine and

service *par excellence*. An extensive shore excursion programme is included in the fare.

The *Road to Mandalay* cruise season runs late September to April. Contact **Orient-Express Trains & Cruises** in Yangon, tel: 01 296 680, www.orient-express.com.

A smaller cruise boat, the *Irrawaddy Princess*, runs on a regular basis between Bagan and Mandalay. Contact **Barani Cruise & Trading** in Yangon, tel: 01 220 949, e-mail: barani-cruise@mptmail.net.mm.

A third option for the Mandalay-Bagan stretch is on board either the 24-cabin *Pandaw II* or 39-cabin *Pandaw III*, newly-built river steamers that recall the experience of river travel during colonial times. Operated by the London-based Irrawaddy Flotilla Company (IFC), both vessels have comfortable cabins with attached bathrooms. There are overnight as well as 2-night cruises from Mandalay to Bagan and vice versa. All meals and shore excursions to interesting villages and attractions are included in the fare. Stops are also made at schools and monasteries that the IFC help to sponsor.

A longer 4-night cruise (Royal Burma) on board the smaller 16-cabin *Pandaw I* is ideal for those with more time. This option travels north of Mandalay to places like Mingun, Ava and Amarapura before making the journey to Bagan. Travelling on board the charming old-world *Pandaw I* – originally built in 1947 and now completely refurbished – is an experience not to be missed. The *Pandaw I* also operates the 5-night Middle Burma Exploration from Bagan to Pyay

(Prome) stopping by little-known towns and villages along the way.

The ultimate adventure trip on the river however is the 10-night cruise up the untamed Chindwin, one of Burma's most scenic rivers, to the remote northern outpost of Mawlaik. Another equally long cruise travels through the third and second defiles, a constantly changing riverscape north to Bhamo, the ancient gateway to China. For all the above options, contact the **Irrawaddy Flotilla Company** at its Yangon office, tel: 01 244 256 or check its website: www.pandaw.com.

Myo Yee at **Zone Express Tours**, 145, 74th Street, Mandalay, tel: 02 61151, also owns a 110-foot (33 metre) boat that can be chartered for trips to Bhamo.

A short popular ferry trip for tourists is the one up the Ayeyarwady from Mandalay to Mingun. Boats leave from Mandalay's B Road Jetty several times daily for the one-hour voyage.

The **Myanmar Five Star Line** (MFSL) manages the country's overseas and coastal routes with a fleet of 21 vessels, only eight of which take passengers. Of interest are the services linking Yangon with Thandwe, Kyaukpyu, Sittwe in Rakhaing and Dawei, Myeik and Kawthaung in Tanintharyi. Its Yangon office is at the corner of Merchant Road and Theinbyu Street (tel: 01 295 279).

BY TRAIN

Myanmar Railways has a network of more than 4,500 km (2,800

Refreshments on Train Journeys

Long-distance rail travellers in Burma will find vendors selling fruit, curries, grilled chicken on bamboo skewers, fried small birds and even whole ducks (at 200 kyats a piece) and soft drinks and beer through the windows of the train at every stop. Some vendors persist until the next stop.

Burmese trains don't have diners, with the exception of the daytime Yangon–Mandalay express. Therefore, you would be well advised to bring your own food and beverages unless you want to go "local", or else survive on the fruit and nuts that are constantly offered for sale.

miles) of track. Yangon's Central Railway Station, of course, is the nation's hub. By day and night, express trains, mail trains and local trains depart on journeys of varying lengths.

Ordinary (second class) and Upper Class (first class) seating is available on all trains. Upper Class seats cost almost three times that of Ordinary Class. Sleepers are not readily available for overnight trips. Foreigners can purchase their tickets through **Myanmar Travels & Tours** *(see page 335)* or at the **railway station** (Tel: 01 274 027), advisably 24 hours in advance, if possible.

Yangon to Mandalay

For the main train route most often used by tourists, the 716-km (445-mile) **Yangon-Mandalay Line** uses reasonably comfortable Korean and Chinese coaches. This is the country's most acceptable railway and can be recommended for the scenes of Burmese village life it offers from its windows. Passengers must be willing to put up with a little discomfort, and often much delay (the train often arrives in Mandalay four or more hours late); however, the journey conforms roughly to European expectations.

Yangon to Mandalay

There are six (one daytime and five overnight) services daily between Yangon and Mandalay. Schedules are not always strictly adhered to. Problems of climatic, technical or bureaucratic nature often cause long delays in rail journeys. Although the Yangon–Mandalay service is the most reliable in Burma, most visitors now use the faster and more reliable – and cheaper – air-conditioned express bus services operating between the two cities.

More expensive but also better than the government-run train is a private express train, **Dagon Mann** (Tel: 01 249 024), which reserves

several sleeping berths and upper-class seats for foreigners on its daily Yangon–Mandalay service.

From Mandalay, there are train connections to the hill station of Pyin U Lwin (Maymyo), 61 km (38 miles) east, from where you are now permitted to continue across the famous Gokteik viaduct to Kyaukme and Lashio. Other rail trips of interest to tourists might include the following:

Yangon to Thazi

Yangon to Thazi takes 12 hours minimum. Local trains connect Thazi with Shwenyaung, the nearest rail terminus to Taunggyi and Inle Lake. A better choice, though, is to continue by bus which travels west to Bagan from Thazi or east to Inle Lake. Passengers can disembark from the Yangon–Mandalay express in Thazi, but boarding the main line in Thazi might be more difficult: it is usually full.

Visitors to Taungoo can disembark from trains on the Yangon–Mandalay line.

Yangon to Mottama

The journey from Yangon takes up to 12 hours to reach Mottama (Martaban), from where a ferry across the Thanlwin River carries travellers to Mawlamyaing on the opposite bank. Stops can also be made in Kyaiktiyo (for Kyaikto Pagoda) or Thaton on this line. This, all previously mentioned lines and others, pass through Bago, and day trippers can embark there as well, though they may find themselves waiting for seriously delayed trains.

Bagan can be reached by train, via Pyinmana, departing Yangon daily at 10.35pm. The journey takes about 20 hours.

Train Novels

For one foreigner's experience in bucking the Burma Railways Corporation and before rail travel to the Gokteik viaduct and Lashio was permitted, read Paul Theroux's famous account: *The Great Railway Bazaar*.

Yangon's Local Trains

Yangon City has a suburban local train service which connects to the national routes. Of greatest interest to the visitor is the Circular Line, running both clockwise and anti-clockwise through Yangon Central Station to Insein and Mingaladon in the north, and stopping at all smaller stations en route. The journey takes about three hours to complete, but should be avoided during rush hours. Tickets are very inexpensive.

Mandalay to Myitkyina

The trip between Mandalay and Myitkyina is a journey reserved for hard-core travellers. Even upper class coaches are in a state of disrepair. A train leaves Mandalay three times daily at 1.50pm, 4.40pm and 5.45pm and takes a very minimum of 25 hours. En route stops of interest to the traveller are at Naba (for Katha, an Ayeryarwady embarkation point for river trips to Bhamo or Mandalay) and Hopin (for Indawgyi Lake).

BY BUS & COACH

Government Bus Transport

Public bus travel aboard government-owned **Road Transport Company** vehicles tend to be long and tedious. Many roads are poor, vehicles are overcrowded, and in the event a bus breaks down, it can be hours before mechanical assistance becomes available.

From Yangon, buses run the 80 km (50 miles) to Bago on a regular half-hourly basis. The terminal is on 18th Street, near the Chinese quarter west of downtown.

Yangon city is served by an extensive network of local buses which connect Yangon with the new satellite towns that were created after 1989.

Visitors to Mandalay can reach the ancient capitals of Amarapura and Inwa (Ava) by taking the No. 8 bus south from the city.

Private Bus Service

Several companies run comfortable air-conditioned buses from Yangon to Mandalay, Bagan, Taunggyi/Inle Lake for the approximate equivalent of US$10. Fares to Pyay and Mawlamyaing cost about US$5. These companies operate from one station, the **Highway Bus Centre** at the intersection of Pyay and Station roads, southwest of Mingaladon Airport. Some also maintain ticket offices opposite the Central Railway Station.

Travel from Yangon to other major tourist destinations is overnight and you can choose between several companies. Some travellers prefer bus to train, it's less than a quarter of the price (as you can pay in kyats) and the arrival times are more reliable than that of trains. Regular stops for food and refreshments are also made.

Among the companies providing reliable service and vehicles are:
Leo Express – tel: 01 249 512
Sun Moon Express – tel: 01 642 903
Transnational Express – tel: 01 249 671

Horse-drawn Cabs

In Burma's dry central plain, especially in the areas of Mandalay and Bagan, there are many horse-drawn cabs, or *myint hlei*. They are slow moving, but are well-suited for sightseeing trips. In smaller towns and villages, high-wheeled ox carts are often counted upon for transportation.

City Transport

Bicycle trishaws *(sai-kaa)* or motorised three-wheelers *(thoun bein)* are the most popular means of getting around the streets of the larger cities – less so in Yangon where taxis have taken over. Easily available and cheap, they take their passengers anywhere they want to go in the city for US$1 or less per trip. For longer trips in the vicinity of Yangon, Mandalay and other large population centres, jeep collectives or "pick-ups" *(kaa)* – similar to the Thai *songthaew* – do yeomen's work

carrying large numbers of riders. They don't follow a set schedule; instead, they take off whenever the last seat is taken. For journeys from Yangon to Bago and from Mandalay to Pyin U Lwin, this is a cheap, fast means of transport.

Driving

Driving in Myanmar is best left to the locals; in fact, until recently, there were no car rental agencies in the country. Hiring a car with driver is an increasingly popular way of travelling around Burma. Typically the hire charge for an air-conditioned Japanese-made minibus in reasonably good condition, along with a driver, is US$50 per diem for five days or less, US$45 per diem for more than five days.

TAXIS

Cab drivers wait in front of all the big tourist hotels in Yangon, anxious to carry visitors to their destinations; their vehicles nowadays are either second-hand Japanese cars or retired Singapore taxis.

Taxis are not metered although they charge by the trip. Ask at your hotel or guesthouse for the proper fare, which shouldn't exceed US$1 within the city. Rates for a full day's charter run is about US$20 within Yangon; a little more if the driver speaks good English, and about US$25 for a day trip into the countryside (Bago or Thanlyin). Taxis are by far the best way to explore the countryside surrounding Yangon, especially if one is able or willing to share the fare with other passengers.

Tourist Information

Since 1991, dozens of private officially recognised tour operators have set up business in Yangon, Mandalay and elsewhere. They are more flexible than Myanmar Travels & Tours *(see box)*, and are quite eager to please.

Tourism Office

There is a limited amount of literature on Burma and no official overseas tourist offices. Burma embassies abroad have brochures and leaflets, and specialist tour operators can supply helpful details, but the best source of information is **Myanmar Travels & Tours** (MTT), which is part of the government tourist board. Though it provides little in the way of brochures, it sells tours and can arrange various types of transport around Burma. Head office: 77–91 Sule Pagoda Road, Yangon. Tel: 01 374 281, 378 376.
e-mail: mtt.mht@mptmail.net.mm
www.myanmars.net/mtt
Within Burma, there is also:
Myanmar Tourism Promotion Board (MTPB), Traders Hotel, 223 Sule Pagoda Road, Yangon. Tel: 01 242 828, ext. 6482, Fax: 01 242 800.
www.myanmar-tourism.com
In addition, you may wish to check the following websites:
www.myanmar.com
www.shwenet.com
www.myanmars.net

Travel to certain areas requires hiring the services of an approved tour operator. Other areas are strictly off-limits. The "official list" (MTT still uses one published in 1996) distinguishes between areas open to individuals (I) and those restricted to package tours (P). Updates from recent travel experiences are included.

Areas listed as open may be closed to tourists with no explanation given; other destinations such as Mogok are in an "on-again, off-again" mode. Travel to some cities that are technically "open" is also restricted to travel within a certain perimeter; Bhamo is an example.

Official list of places that may be visited:
Yangon Division, Mandalay Division (except Mogok), Bago Division, Magway Division and Ayeyarwady Division – open.

Tour Operators in Yangon

A list of Yangon-based tour operators follows:

Abercrombie & Kent
64, B-2 Shwe Gon Plaza
Tel: 01 542 949/542 902
Fax: 01 542 992
e-mail: tun@mptmail.net.mm
www.abercrombieandkent.com

Ainda Travel Associates Limited
10 Highland Avenue, Mayangon
Tel: 01 660 266; Fax: 01 544 014
e-mail: ainda@mptmail.net.mm

Asian Trails Tour Ltd.
73 Pyay Road
Tel: 01 211 212/727 422
Fax: 01 211 670
e-mail: res@asiantrails.com.mm
www.asiantrails.com

Columbus Travels and Tours
586 Strand Road
Tel: 01 229 245; Fax: 01 229 246

e-mail: columbus@mptmail.net.mm
www.travelmyanmar.com

Diethelm Travel
I Inya Road
Tel: 01 527 110/527 117
Fax: 01 527 135
e-mail: leisure@diethelm.com.mm
www.diethelm-travel.com

Euro-Asie Voyage
177, 51st Street
Tel: 01 297 934; Fax: 01 297 943
e-mail:
euroasievoyage@mptmail.net.mm

Exotissimo
#0303 Sakura Tower
339 Bo Gyoke Aung San Street
Tel: 01 255 266; Fax: 01 255 428
e-mail: myanmar@exotissimo.com
www.exotissimo.com

Golden Express Ltd
97B, Wardan Street

Tel: 01 226 779; Fax: 01 227 636
e-mail: getours@mptmail.net.mm

Insight Myanmar
85–7 Thein Byu Street
Tel: 01 297 798; Fax: 01 295 599
e-mail: insight@mptmail.net.mm

Santa Maria Travels & Tours
195-B 32nd Street, Panbedan
Township
Tel: 01 254 625; Fax: 01 297 946
e-mail: santamaria@mptmail.net.mm

Tour Mandalay
2nd floor, Pearl Centre, Kaba Aye Road
Tel: 01 540 271; Fax: 01 540 220
e-mail: info@tourmandalay.com

Woodland Travels
422/426 Strand Road
Tel: 01 202 071; Fax: 01 202 076
e-mail:
woodlandtravels@mptmail.net.mm
www.woodlandgroups.com

Sagaing Division: Monywa, Kyaukka, Butalin, Twin Taung (Hills), Pho Win Taung, Yinmarpin, Yeshantwin, Alaungdaw Kathapa, Kale, Homalin, Khamti – open.
Kachin State: Mohnyin, Hopin, Indawgyi, Mogaung, Myitkyina, Putao, and Bhamo (I) – Putao (P).
Northern Shan State: Up to Lashio (I), to the Chinese border (Muse, Namkham) from Lashio and Kutkai (P). Coming from China enter Muse, Namkham, Kyu Koke or Kunlon through Lashio (P).
Southern Shan State: Kyaingtong, Tachilek, Kalaw, Pindaya, Inle Lake and Taunggyi, and recently Kekku (I).
Coming from Mae Sai, Thailand: Up to Kyaingtong (I).
Coming from China: Up to Kyaingtong and Tachilek via Mai Lar and up to Tachilek via Wun Pon Jetty (P).
Kayah State: Loikaw (P).
Rakhaing State: Sittwe, Myohaung, Taungkoke, Thandwe, Ngapali and Gwa. Nga Tine Chaung-Gwa motorway and Pyay Taungkoke motorway (I).
Kayin State: Up to Pa-an and Hlaing Bwe (I).
Mon State: Kyaiktiyo, Thaton, Belugyun, Kyaikmaraw, Thanpyu, Zayat and Kyaikkami (I).

Tanintharyi Division: Dawei, Maungmakan, Lanpi Island, Myeik, Kawthaung (I). Zadetgyi Island entirely off-limits.
Chin State: southern Chin (P); northern Chin off limits.
Gem mines area: Mogok (P), Hpakant, Mai Shoo and Pearl Island off-limits.

Tour Packages

A typical 15-day tour covers the following:
Bangkok–Yangon–Mandalay–Pyin U Lwin–Mandalay–Bagan–Kalaw–Pindaya Caves–Lake Inle–Taunggyi–Thazi–Yangon–Bangkok. The economy price would be around US$2,000. The cost for an 8-day trip which includes Mandalay and Bagan would be in the region of US$1,000.

As an individual traveller to Burma you have much more flexibility. You can take in as many sights as possible or you can dawdle in one or two locations. Generally speaking, while groups may have an easier time travelling in Burma, the individual will be better able to absorb the "lost, old-time travel feeling" of which Somerset Maugham's stories are a

reminder. Financially, the individual's trip won't be as costly as that of the group traveller. By far the most enjoyable way of travelling is in a small group of four to six people in a minibus accompanied by a guide.

ENTRANCE FEES

Since April 1989, the Burmese have copied the Chinese custom of charging tourists all sorts of fees to sites of religious and other importance. For the sacred Shwedagon or the Maha Muni Pagoda, Burmese enter freely since it is a place of worship, foreigners, however, have to pay between US$3–5. At museums, foreigners pay up to US$5 while locals pay a handful of kyats. The ticket is good for the day. Lesser pagodas and those in outlying districts are free of charge, but you are sometimes expected to make a donation. On special occasions, the donations may even make you the subject of public praise over the pagoda's loudspeaker system.

Where to Stay

Hotels

Starting from a low 25,000 visitors per annum in the 1980s, by the end of the '90s, Burma tourism had grown to an estimated 250,000 a year. The hotel building boom of the 90s has calmed down somewhat but at any time of year except December to February, there is usually an excess of rooms available. For the savvy traveller, this may present an opportunity to ask for better-than-advertised rates.

Hotels and guesthouses are required to post rates in US dollars, although much lower kyat rates may be available for Burmese nationals. In the case of some of the remaining government-owned hotels, rates can be high compared to those of similar standards offered in the rest of Southeast Asia. With increased competition from the private sector, however, all hotel rates tend to follow what the market can bear.

Since the 1989 change to a free market economy, most hotels in the country are now privately owned. Most charge between US$20 and US$80 for a double room, and are often affiliated to some of the private tour organisations. Representatives of tour agencies and private hotels normally meet all flight arrivals at the airport.

YANGON & AYEYARWADY DELTA

Yangon
The Strand
92 Strand Road
Tel: 01 243 377; Fax: 01 289 880
e-mail:
reservations@thestrand.com.mm

www.ghmhotels.com
This hotel is in a class of its own not only in price, but also in its tasteful décor and appointments. Originally built in 1903 by the Sarkies brothers and completely renovated in 1993, it reflects the epoch of the 1920s and '30s. It has 52 guest rooms, including 32 suites, and a business centre. The Strand Grill, an elegant evening restaurant, and the Strand Café serve Burmese, Southeast Asian and Continental fare. The Strand Bar offers a full range of drinks in a club-like atmosphere. The Strand's restaurants and bar provide rewarding experiences. **$$$$**

Price Guide

A very approximate guide to current room rates for a standard double per night is:
$$$$ Luxury = US$200 and above
$$$ Expensive (by Burmese standards) = US$80 and above
$$ Moderate = US$20 and above
$ Budget = US$20 and below

Dusit Inya Lake Resort
Kaba Aye Pagoda Road
Tel: 01 662 857; Fax: 01 665 537
e-mail: inyalake.dusit.com
inyalake.dusit.com
Built by the Russians in 1961, completely renovated and modernised in 1995, and now owned by a Thai hotel group, the Inya Lake offers a complete range of facilities including a swimming pool, tennis courts, fitness centre, putting green, barber shop, beauty salon and conference facilities. **$$$**
Grand Plaza Parkroyal Yangon (formerly Sofitel Plaza)
33 Alan Paya Lan
Tel: 01 250 388; Fax: 01 252 478
www.grandplaza.yangon.parkroyal hotels.com
Located north of the centre of Yangon and containing 312 rooms, this hotel was recently refurbished and rebranded. The décor features lots of rattan, wood and Burmese art. Along with a business centre,

disco/bar, swimming pool and fitness centre, there are Chinese and Japanese restaurants. **$$$**
The Governor's Residence (formerly Pansea Yangon)
35 Taw Win Road
Tel: 01 229 860; Fax: 01 228 260
e-mail: yangon@pansea.com
www.pansea.com
A beautiful 49-room hotel set in spacious grounds. The superb Mandalay Restaurant is known for its French and Asian cuisines. **$$$**
Hotel Nikko Royal Lake Yangon
40 Natmauk Road
Tel: 01 544 500; Fax: 01 544 400
e-mail: nikko@nikkoyangon.com.mm
www.nikkoyangon.net
Overlooking Kandawgyi Lake, this 303-room hotel is geared towards the business traveller with facilities that include internet access, business centre and secretarial services. Excellent Japanese restaurant. Swimming pool and fitness centre. **$$$**
The Kandawgyi Palace
Kanyeiktha Road
Tel: 01 249 255; Fax 01 280 412
e-mail: kphotel@mptmail.net.mm
www.kandawgyipalace.com
At the lake shore. Located on the site of the former Museum of Natural History and the Orient Boat Club, the Kandawgyi Palace Hotel was renovated in 1996. Facilities include a fitness centre, swimming pool and business centre. **$$$**
Savoy Hotel
129 Dhammazedi (near Shwedagon Pagoda)
Tel: 01 526 289; Fax: 01 542 891
e-mail: savoy.ygn@mptmail.net.mm
www.savoy-myanmar.com
This is a lovely hotel with 36 rooms, including suites, all of which are tastefully decorated. On the premises are a good restaurant, swimming pool, and business centre. **$$$**
Season of Yangon
Opposite Mingaladon Airport
Tel: 01 666 699; Fax: 01 663 375
Used frequently by business travellers, this hotel is adjacent to the airport and contains 121 rooms. Facilities include a fitness centre, business centre and swimming pool. **$$$**

Mid-range Hotels

In the price range of US$20 and slightly above there is an ever-increasing range of accommodation in Yangon; many are converted residences with just a small number of rooms of varying sizes; the better ones offer IDD phone service.

Sedona Hotel
1 Kaba Aye Pagoda Road
(near Inya Lake)
Tel: 01 666 900; Fax: 01 666 911
e-mail: rsv@sedona.com.mm
www.sedonahotels.com
The Sedona has a business centre, fitness centre with sauna, swimming pool and a lively pub/disco. **$$$**

Summit Parkview
350 Ahlone Road
Tel: 01 211 888; Fax: 01 227 992
e-mail: summit@summityangon.com
www.summityangon.com
One of the first modern hotels in Yangon, this recently renovated hotel contains 140 rooms and serviced apartments. Its facilities include a swimming pool, health club, coffee shop and a shopping arcade including an art gallery. Popular with business travellers and Japanese visitors. Some rooms face Shwedagon Pagoda which is magnificent at night. **$$–$$$**

Traders Hotel
223 Sule Pagoda Road
Tel: 01 242 828; Fax: 01 242 800
e-mail: thyn@shangri-la.com
www.shangri-la.com
Elegant décor with Oriental touches, four excellent restaurants and bar establishments; business centre with e-mail facility; gym, sauna, pool. Contains 407 rooms and serviced apartments. **$$$**

Aurora Inn
37 Thirimingalar, off Pyay Road
Tel: 01 525 961; Fax: 01 525 221
Less than 10 rooms, but all decorated in the style of old Burmese houses with lots of local artefacts. Chez Sylvie offers French cuisine. **$$**

Central Hotel
335-357 Bogyoke Aung San Road
Tel: 01 241 001; Fax: 01 248 003
e-mail: central.ygn@mptmail.mm
Rather uninspiring décor, but with rooms that are larger than normal. Restaurant, coffee shop, lounge. 82 rooms. **$$**

Comfort Inn
4 Shwe Lin Street
Tel: 01 533 377; Fax: 01 524 256
Located in spacious grounds which include a putting green. Comfortable rooms; breakfast included; provides transfers to the airport. **$$**

Mya Yeik Nyo Royal Hotel
Off Kaba Aye Pagoda Road
Tel: 01 548 310; Fax: 01 548 318
Two-storey building built by the British to house the offices of the Irrawaddy Flotilla Company. Great views of Shwedagon Pagoda from its grounds. **$$**

Thamada Hotel
37 Kaba Aye Pagoda Road
Tel: 01 243 639/43
Fax: 01 245 001
This older moderate class hotel is located opposite the Yangon railway station. Popular with both business and leisure travellers. **$$**

Three Seasons Hotel
83/85 52nd Street
Tel: 01 293 304; Fax: 01 297 946
e-mail: phyuaung@mptmal.net.mm
Quiet, family-run inn with friendly, personalised service and choice of Western or Burmese breakfast. All rooms are air-conditioned and have a fridge. **$$**

Yoma Hotel
146 Bogyoke Aung San Street
Tel: 01 297 725; Fax: 01 297 957
Popular with business travellers on a budget. E-mail available. 20 rooms. **$$**

Price Guide

A very approximate guide to current room rates for a standard double per night is:
$$$$ Luxury = US$200 and above
$$$ Expensive (by Burmese standards) = US$80 and above
$$ Moderate = US$20 and above
$ Budget = US$20 and below

Yoma Hotel 2
24A Inya Lake Road
Tel: 01 531 065; Fax: 01 526 945
Related to Yoma Hotel. Also a popular choice among business travellers for much the same reasons. **$$**

May Shan Guest House
115/117 Sule Pagoda Road
Tel: 01 283 599
This guesthouse run by a young Burmese family is a stone's throw away from Sule Pagoda and the Thai Airways International Office.

Yangon YMCA Hostel
265 Mahabandoola Road
Tel: 01 294 128, Fax: 01 296 848
e-mail: yangonymca@mptmail.mm
Recently expanded to include 25 basic but comfortable rooms with shared bath, 49 with private bath. Rates include breakfast. Women guests welcome. Free transport to and from the airport and luggage storage facilities are available. **$**

DELTA REGION

Pathein (Bassein)
Myint Wa Kyun Paw Guest House
44 Mingyi Road
Tel: 042 22131
Centrally located with small, clean rooms, some with air-conditioning and bath. **$–$$**

Pathein Hotel
Monywa-Ye Road
Tel: 042 21162
Quite a distance from town and set in spacious grounds. The rooms on the top floor have air-conditioning, TV and fridge. **$–$$**

Letkhokkon
Letkhokkon Beach Hotel
Tel: 01 224 346 (Yangon)
30 simple beach chalets facing the beach. The restaurant serves good seafood. **$$**

Chaungtha
Chaungtha Beach Hotel
Tel: 042 22587 or 01 225 913 (Yangon)
60 rooms in wooden chalets with air-con and TV. **$$**

Chaungtha Oo Beach
Tel: 01 254 708 (Yangon office)

Chalets on the beach. A bit run-down but beach location makes up for less-than-perfect conditions. **$$**
See Seim Hotel
Tel: 042 22909
On the beach. Clean rooms with fans and attached bath. Family rooms also available. **$**

Ngwe Saung
Palm Beach Resort
9 Ngwe Saung (Silver Beach)
Pathein, Ayeyawaddy Division
Tel: 01 511 937 or 01 536 255 (Yangon)
Fax: 01 504 528
www.thepalmbeachresort.com
Located about a 5-hour drive from Yangon, the hotel sits on 9 miles of beautiful white sand beach. The resort has 31 charming and spacious cottages built in traditional style but equipped with modern facilities. Pool, restaurants, bar and a spa are also found on-site. Inquire with Diethelm Travel (www.diethelm-travel.com) about packages that include river ferry (on board the Delta Queen) and coach transportation to the resort. **$$$**

Bargaining

If you're planning to stay in budget or moderately priced accommodation, try to get a discount on your room rate, especially if you're travelling off-season. Top-end hotels won't offer discounts unless they're advertised but it's always worth asking if the hotel looks quiet.

BAGO DIVISION

Bago (Pegu)
Emperor Motel
8/2 Min Street
Tel: 052 21297
A simple but clean and modern hotel with a friendly and informative management. **$–$$**
Shwewartun Hotel
Yangon-Mandalay Road
Tel: 052 21263
40 clean rooms, both fan-cooled and air-conditioned. Overpriced, but the restaurant is reasonable. **$–$$**

Shwe See Sein Motel
345 Bayinnaung Lane
Tel: 052 22118
Near the bus station, with room and bungalow accommodation available. **$**

Taungoo
Myanmar Beauty Guest House
Tel: 054 21270
This is a very pleasant complex of three guesthouses: one in town and two at the edge of town, run by a doctor's family. The owners are very helpful in arranging excursions to elephant camps and the surrounding area. **$**

Pyay
Mingalar Garden Resort
Aung Chan Thar Quarter
Aung Lan Road
Tel: 053 25493, 25518
Fax: 053 22716
Facing a lake and surrounded by beautiful gardens, this resort is perfect for a relaxing and quiet stay while in Pyay. **$$**
Pyay Hotel
Strand Road
Tel: 053 21890
Good location near the river, but overpriced. Rooms are either economy (without own bath) or double with own bath, fan and air-conditioning. Breakfast included in room rates. **$–$$**
Sweet Golden Land Motel
12 Nawaday Road
Tel: 053 22526
Bungalows in pleasant setting about 20 minutes walk from the town centre. Accommodation is clean and spacious. Owners will arrange tours and day trips. Has its own restaurant. **$–$$**

MANDALAY & ENVIRONS

Mandalay
Mandalay City Hotel
26tj Street betweem 82nd and 83rd streets
Tel: 02 36146
e-mail: mdycityhotel@myanmar.com.mm
Managed by Yangon's Summit Parkview, with 64 fully outfitted

rooms aimed at the business traveller. **$$$**
Mandalay Hill Resort (formerly Novotel Mandalay)
9 Kwin (416B), 10th Street
Tel: 02 35638; Fax: 02 35639
e-mail: MDYHILL@mptmail.net.mm
www.mandalayhillresort.com.mm
206 rooms; high-rise hotel at base of Mandalay Hill. Café, restaurant, disco, outdoor performance theatre, large pool, tennis courts. Room rates include breakfast. **$$$**
Mandalay Swan Hotel
Corner of 26th Road and 68th streets facing Mandalay Palace
Tel: 02 31619; Fax: 02 35677
e-mail: mdyswan@mptmail.net.mm
The restored former Mandalay Hotel, with comfortable 106 rooms ranging from economy to suites. Coffee shop, restaurant, pool and tennis courts. **$$–$$$**
Sedona Hotel Mandalay
Corner of 26th and 66th streets
Tel: 02 36488; Fax: 02 36499
e-mail: bc.shm@sedona.com.mm
www.sedonahotels.com
247 rooms. Great location opposite southeast corner of Mandalay Palace with view of Mandalay Hill. Easily the best hotel in town; pool, fitness centre, business centre with e-mail facility. All room rates include breakfast. **$$$**
Emerald Land Inn
14th Street between 87th and 88th streets
Tel: 02 26990; Fax: 02 35645
Comfortable hotel in a garden setting located in a residential area northwest of the Mandalay Palace. Restaurant, bar and pool **$$**
Myit Phyar Ayer Hotel
80th Street between 33rd and 34th
Tel: 02-27242, Fax: 02-35646
e-mail: mpahotel@mdy.net.mm
High-rise establishment with 42 well-furnished rooms and attractive lobby area. **$$**
Universe Hotel
83rd Street between 27th and 28th
Tel: 02 33246, Fax: 02 33245
Popular with groups; rooftop restaurant/bar with music. Clean rooms, some with air-conditioning and own bath. Room rates include breakfast and transfer to airport or train station. **$$**

AD–1 Hotel
Corner of 87th and 28th streets,
near the Eindawya Pagoda
Tel: 02 34505
One of the best budget hotels.
Clean rooms with fans and showers
or with air-conditioning. Breakfast
included in the room rate **$**

Dynasty Hotel
304 81st Street, between 24th and
25th streets
Tel: 02 35801
Inexpensive air-conditioned rooms,
satellite TV in the lobby, breakfast
included. **$**

Garden Hotel
174 83rd Street, corner of 25th
and 83rd streets
Tel: 02 27657
Rooms with either private or
common bath. All rooms have air-
conditioning, TV, fridge. Breakfast
included in the room rate. **$–$$**

Nylon Hotel
Corner of 25th and 83rd streets
Tel: 02 33460
Clean rooms with choice of fan and
common bath or air-conditioning,
fan, TV and private bath. In good
location. Very popular choice. **$**

AROUND MANDALAY

Monywa
Monywa Hotel
Bogyoke Aung San Road
Tel: 071 21549
20 wooden chalets divided into
rooms with fridge, air-conditioning
and attached hot-water bath. More
expensive rooms have TV. The
outdoor bar and surrounding
gardens are very pleasant. Room
rates include breakfast. **$–$$**

Pyin-U-Lwin (Maymyo)
Gandamar Myaing Hotel
corner of Lanthanyar and Myopaq
streets
Tel: 085 22007
Brick-built, mock-Tudor two-storey
mansion. Economy rooms have
cold-water showers; standard rooms
have attached bath. **$$**

Nan Myaing Hotel
Mandalay-Lashio Road
Tel: 085 22118
Tudor-style half-timbered building.

Price Categories

A very approximate guide to
current room rates for a standard
double per night is:
$$$$ Luxury = US$200 and
above
$$$ Expensive (by Burmese
standards) = US$80 and above
$$ Moderate = US$20 and
above
$ Budget = US$20 and below

Has 30 cosy rooms with fireplaces
and wooden floors. Breakfast is
included in the room rate. **$$**

Royal Parkview Hotel
107 Eindaw Road
Tel: 085 21210
Comfortable 20-room hotel near
town and golf course. Rooms have
with fridge, satellite TV. Good
restaurant found in-house. **$$**

Dahlia Motel
105 Eindaw Road
Tel: 085 22255
Good value economy rooms and
standard rooms with bath, TV and
fans – all rooms have hot water.
Quite far from the town centre, but
transfers can be arranged free of
charge. Room rate includes
breakfast. **$**

Thiri Myaing Hotel (Candacraig)
Anawrahta Road
Tel: 085 22047
This is the most classic hotel in
town with colonial-style rooms with
wooden balconies overlooking the
grounds. Old-world atmosphere with
an open fire (for a fee) in the
spacious sitting room and British
dishes on the menu at the
restaurant. 12 dormitory to
standard rooms. **$/$$**

BAGAN REGION

Bagan Archaeological Zone
Bagan Thiripyitsaya Sakura Hotel
Tel: 062 70289; Fax: 062 60033
e-mail: thiri@myanmar.com.mm
www.bagan-thiripyitsaya-sakura-
hotel.com
Overlooking the Ayeyarwady River;
68 rooms and 8 riverside suites,
amidst 24 acres of landscaped

gardens. An excellent older
establishment, well located with
great river views. Restaurant
serving Burmese cuisine; bar;
swimming pool, conference
facilities. **$$$–$$$$**

Bagan Hotel
Tel: 062 70145; Fax: 062 70313
e-mail: baganhotel@myanmars.net
110 rooms, on the river near
Gawdawpalin Pagoda and Bagan
Archaeological Museum; air-
conditioned rooms, satellite TV and
IDD telephones. Pretty gardens,
good value and well located. **$$$**

Aye Yar Hotel
Near Bupaya
Tel: 062 70027; Fax: 062 70055
This moderate older hotel has 80
rooms, some in a brick building,
others in wooden chalets, all with
air-con and fridge. Formerly known
as Irra Inn, it is located on the
banks of the Ayeyarwady near
Bupaya Pagoda. **$$**

Thazin Garden Hotel
22 Thazin Road
Tel: 062 70020
Fax: 01 512 715 (Yangon)
e-mail:
thazingarden@mptmail.net.mm
Charming hotel in a quiet location.
Low-rise wood-panelled rooms
furnished with Burmese artefacts
are located amid well tended
gardens. Restaurant serving
Burmese and Western fare. Staff
are very helpful and go out of their
way to make you feel welcome. **$$**

Thande Hotel
Tel: 062 70144; Fax: 062 70143
Old Bagan, near Archaeological
Museum overlooking the river; 42
rooms and attractive bungalow units.
Dining room and bar. Breakfast
included in room rate. **$–$$**

Around Bagan
In the budget category there is
much choice in both the Nyaung U
and Bagan Myothit (New Bagan)
areas:

Ruby True Hotel
Myat Lay Road, New Bagan
Tel: 062 70262, 70354
Fax: 062 70263
e-mail: winrth@mptmail.net.mm
Great location in the heart of the
New Bagan area. Easy access to

most of the key temples and pagodas. Comfortable rooms decorated with local flavour. **$$**

Bagan Central Hotel
15/16 Kha Yay Street, New Bagan
Tel: 062 70141
Particularly good value for a mid-range hotel. Room and bungalow accommodation with air-conditioning, fridge and baths. Pleasant courtyard. **$–$$**

Golden Express Hotel
Wetkyi-In
Tel: 062 70101, 01 226 779 (Yangon)
One of the earliest modern "tourist" hotels near New Bagan in the village of Wetkyi-In. Has 20 chalets spread out in a spacious compound; swimming pool. **$–$$**

No Breakfast Please

Most room rates for hotel rooms in Burma include breakfast. If you're travelling on a really tight budget it's worth asking for the room rate without breakfast and then eating somewhere else for less.

Golden Village Inn
Nyaung U
Tel: 062 70088
Bungalow-style rooms with balconies, free transport from railway station. **$**

New Heaven Hotel
Tel: 062 70061
Formerly two hotels which merged into one, same owner as Golden Village Inn; each hotel complex still maintains its own entrance and compound. Accommodation in chalets with balcony. Friendly and helpful staff; has bikes for hire. **$**

Silver Moon Hotel
New Bagan
Tel: 062 70161
Clean and quiet standard bungalow rooms with air-conditioning, television and fridge. Room rates include breakfast. **$**

Mount Popa
Popa Mountain Resort
Tel: 062 69168; Fax: 062 69169
www.woodlandgroups.com

Luxurious mountain resort set in National Park with views of the Taungzalat Monastery. Stunning architecture reminiscent of a Balinese resort and beautifully presented chalet-style rooms. Facilities include swimming pool; terrace restaurant and bar. The resort also offers activities including trekking, horse riding and birdwatching. **$$$**

Zay Yar Thein Guest House
Tel: 062 69128
Moderately priced with clean and spacious rooms. Breakfast is included in the room rate. **$–$$**

Meiktila
Meiktila Hotel
Yangon–Mandalay Road
Tel: 064 21892
26 rooms, superior and chalet all with air-conditioning and attached toilet. Clean and unpretentious. Room rate includes breakfast. **$–$$**

Wunzin Hotel
Nandaw Gone Qtr
Tel: 064 21848
Fine view of the lake. 30 rooms, standard, with/without air-conditioning and suites. **$–$$**

Honey Hotel
Pan Chan Street (near the lake)
Tel: 064 21588
Converted mansion with large rooms all with air-conditioning and a choice of a hot-water shower or shared bath. Breakfast available. **$**

SHAN & KAYAH STATES

Nyaungshwe – Inle Lake
Inle Lake View Resort
Kaungdaing
Tel: 081 29332; 01 253 850 (Yangon)
Fax: 081 23656
www.inlelakeviewresort.com
Overlooks the tranquil Inle Lake and with the mountains as a backdrop, this hotel is only a 40-minute drive from the airport. Comfortable and spacious rooms furnished with Burmese artefacts. Good restaurant and bar. **$$$**

Inle Princess Resort
Magyizin Village
Tel: 081 29055; 01 211 226

(Yangon)
Fax: 081 29363; 01 211 226 (Yangon)
www.inleprincessresort.com
Charming chalets on stilts on the eastern shore of the Inle Lake with Shan mountain range as backdrop. A 20-minute drive or 30-minute boat ride from Nyaungshwe. **$$$**

Golden Island Cottages
Nampan
Tel: 081 29390; 01 549 019 (Yangon)
Fax: 01 559 756 (Yangon)
Located on the eastern lake shore, individual bamboo and hardwood cottages on stilts with balconies. Restaurant serves Chinese, Pa-O and Shan dishes. **$$**

Paradise-on-the-Lake Hotel
Mine Thauk Village
Tel: 081 24142, 22009, 23586
Fax: 081 22009
Charming hotel built on stilts right on Inle Lake and affording beautiful views of both the sunrise and sunset. Has 50 spacious bungalows constructed of thatch and wood and a good restaurant serving Asian and Western dishes. Convenient boat transfers to nearby Nyaungshwe town are also available. **$$**

Royal Orchid Hotel
Kaungdaing
Tel: 081 23182
On the lake shore, 20 bungalows with great views and private facilities. **$$**

Golden Express Hotel
19 Phaungtawpyin Road, Nyaungshwe
Tel: 081 21374
11 rooms. Located in town; various room categories. **$–$$**

Inle Regal Resort
Nyaungshwe
Tel: 081 29312; 01 664 592 (Yangon)
www.myanmartravelinformation.com/inleregal
Large wooden bungalows, all with lake views. **$–$$**

Evergreen Hotel
East of Mingala Market
Yongyi Street, Nyaungshwe
Tel: 081 23594
Popular two-storey hotel with basic and standard rooms. **$**

Four Sisters Inn
Nyaungshwe
Tel: 081 29190
Quiet guesthouse; rooms with fans and showers. Famous for its delicious communal meals. Bike hire can be arranged. **$**

Joy Hotel
Kanthar Quarter, Nyaungshwe
Tel: 081 29083
Situated along a narrow, quiet canal, has basic rooms in main building and five more in newer block. Range of rooms and facilities. **$**

Taunggyi
Aye Thar Yar Golf Resort
Tel: 081 24245/7
www.ayetharyargolfresort.com
Newer resort with a golf course at its doorstep. Excursions can be arranged to the ancient pagoda complex of Kakku, the Inle Lake, the Pindaya caves and other sites. **$$$**

Paradise Hotel
157 Khwa Nyo Road
Tel/Fax: 081 22009
Functional but fairly nice rooms. **$$**

Taunggyi Hotel
Off Shu Myaw Khin Road
Tel: 081 21127
Hillside location with a bit of the old colonial ambience. 56 spacious rooms with hot-water showers. Popular restaurant and bar. **$$**

Kalaw
Kalaw Hotel
84A University Road
Tel: 081 51091, 50039
Peaceful setting outside of town. Aging Tudor-style bungalows with good vistas. 43 rooms with a range of facilities and rates. **$$**

Pine Hill Resort
151 U Min Road
Tel: 081 50079, 50303
Fax: 081 50078
Very comfortable bungalow-style hotel with 30 units and view of the hills. Good restaurant serving Burmese and Indian fare. **$$**

Pine View Inn
Tatkatho Street, 10th Qtr.
Tel: 081 50185, 50020
Friendly small establishment near Kalaw Hotel with spacious rooms. Breakfast is included. **$$**

Off the Beaten Track

It is advisable for visitors travelling off the beaten track or going trekking to carry a sleeping bag or a sleeping cover, as monasteries will usually make floor space available for a night or two. Many towns that served as regional administrative centres during the period of British rule have "circuit houses". Then as now, these are primarily reserved for travelling state officials. However, if the tourist has been granted official permission to travel outside the normal tourist areas, there is a good chance of finding overnight accommodation at these inns.

Winner Hotel
Pyi Taung Su Road
Tel: 081 50025
Comfortable rooms in a three-story building in town. **$–$$**

Eastern Paradise Motel
15 Thirimingalar Street, 5th Qtr.
Clean, quiet and comfortable budget rooms with private facilities. **$**

Kyaingtong (Kengtung)
Kyainge Tong Hotel
Tel: 084 21323
12 moderately priced rooms, MTT-operated. Night-time entertainment features a Shan band playing traditional music; guests are encouraged to take to the floor with female dancers in traditional dress. **$$**

Private Hotel
5 Airport Road
Tel: 084 21438
Comfortable one-storey hotel near the airport. **$–$$**

Harry's Guest House
132 Mai Yang Lan, Kanaburi
Tel: 084 21418
Clean budget rooms. The owner was a trekking guide in Thailand. **$**

Pindaya
Conqueror Hotel
Tel: 081 23257
www.conquerorhotel.com
Comfortable hotel with faux-Burmese stylings at the foot of Shwe

U Min Pagoda. Duplex bungalows with TV and fridge. Restaurant serving Shan and Burmese food. Staff will help book tours to places of interest nearby. **$$**

Pindaya Inle Inn
Mahabandoola Street
Tel: 081 21347, 23709
www.inleprincessresort.com
New lodgings with 36 wood-and-bamboo-thatch chalets surrounded by landscaped gardens. Restaurant, bar. Close to the caves. **$–$$**

Pindaya Hotel
Shwe U Min Pagoda Road
Tel: 081 21347
Clean and comfortable two-storey building with 45 rooms. Overlooking the lake. Good restaurant. **$**

Lashio
Lashio Motel
Mandalay-Lashio Road
Tel: 082 21702
46 clean, spacious rooms with views of the hills, air-conditioning and TV, fridge, toilet and attached shower. Up-market restaurant. **$–$$**

New Asia Hotel
San Gaung Street
Tel: 082 21622
Modern hotel. Most rooms have an attached bath but there are also cheaper options. **$**

KACHIN STATE

Myitkyina
Sumpra Hotel
Tel: 074 22298
Comfortable bungalows located on river bank, but out of town. Friendly staff. **$$**

Pantsun Hotel
Tel: 074 22748/49

Licenced Hotels

Officially, hotels and guesthouses that accept foreign guest must have permission from the government in the form of a licence, usually displayed in the reception area. To gain a licence the establishment must have at least five rooms and charge room rates in dollars.

Centrally located. Functional hotel but lacks charm. **$**

Mrauk-U & Chin
Mrauk-U Hotel
Tel: 043 23060
Government-owned hotel with air-conditioning, Chinese restaurant. Breakfast is included in the room rate. **$$**
Nawarat Hotel
near Nyaungpin Market
Tel: 051 703 885; 01 220 649 (Yangon)
Newer private hotel with air-con rooms, restaurant and bar. **$$**

Sittwe
Sittwe Hotel
Tel: 043 21939
On the beach. Government-owned establishment set in a large compound offering large rooms with air-conditioning. **$$**
Prince Guest House
27 Main Road
Tel: 043 21395
Centrally located, offering basic single and double rooms with fans and shared bathroom. **$**

Ngapali
Amata Resort & Spa
Ngapali Beach
Tel: 01 542 535
Fax: 01 549 885 (Yangon)
www.amataresort.com
New luxurious resort with extensive spa treatments available. Twenty nicely designed cabanas of varying size, all equipped with satellite TV, IDD phone, outdoor shower and e-mail access. Swimming pool, free airport shuttle.
Bayview Beach Resort
Ngapali Beach
Tel: 01 504 471 (Yangon)
Fax: 01 526 292 (Yangon)
www.bayview-myanmar.com
Situated on the northern end of beautiful Ngapali Beach, this resort has 33 tastefully furnished rooms with private terrace and large sundecks. Full range of facilties: swimming pool, spa, watersports, restaurants and bars. **$$$**
Sandoway Resort
Ngapali Beach
Tel: 043 42233

www.sandowayresort.com
Designed by an Italian architect and using local materials like teak wood, stone and marble, this elegant resort is *the* place to stay. Thirty spacious cottages set either in gardens or facing the broad expanse of Ngapali beach. **$$$**
Silver Beach Hotel
Ngapali Beach
Tel: 01 294 587
Modest resort on Ngapali Beach next to the Bayview Beach Resort. Cottages have private verandahs and most have views of the sea. Restaurant and bar. **$$**

Price Categories

A very approximate guide to current room rates for a standard double per night is:
$$$$ Luxury = US$200 and above
$$$ Expensive (by Burmese standards) = US$80 and above
$$ Moderate = US$20 and above
$ Budget = US$20 and below

MON & KAYIN STATE

Kyaiktiyo
Golden Rock Hotel
On the slope of Mount Kyaikto, about 1.2km from the top
Tel: 035 701 741
e-mail: grh@mptmail.net.mm
48 well-furnished rooms, restaurant/bar. **$–$$**
Kyaikto Hotel
Top of Mount Kyaikto
Tel: 01 663 341, 663 351
e-mail: onyx@mptmail.net.mm
12 basic rooms, near the Golden Rock, overpriced, intermittent running water. Bungalows and A-frame huts lack charm but the panoramic views more than compensate. **$–$$**
Mountain View Motel
At foothill of Mount Kyaikto
Tel: 01 524 613 (Yangon)
Comfortable rooms or bungalow-style accommodation. Good restaurant; breakfast included. **$–$$**

Mawlamyaing (Moulmein)
Mawlamyaing Hotel
Strand Road
Tel: 032 22560, 24650
24 attractive and spacious rooms in duplex bungalows with air-conditioning, mini-fridge, and local TV. A bit on the expensive side, evidently to take advantage of its location near the seafront and Shampoo Island. **$$**
Ngwe Moe Hotel
Corner of Kyaikthoke Pagoda Road and Strand Road
Tel: 032 24703, 24704, 25553
A newer and comfortable hotel with 24 rooms. **$$**
Thanlwin Hotel
541 Lower Main Road, Bo Gone Qtr., close to bus terminal
Tel: 032 21976, 21518
15 rooms; delightful old merchant's house with spacious rooms with four-poster beds and mosquito netting. Harks back to the old colonial days. **$–$$**

MYEIK REGION

Kawthaung
Andaman Club
Thatay island
Tel: 01 956 4354 (Yangon)
Fax: 02 285 6408 (Bangkok)
Resort with casino and a Jack Nicklaus-designed golf course. Accessible via a 15-minute jetboat ride from the Andaman Club jetty near Ranong, Thailand. Burmese tourist visa is easily obtainable at the border in Kawthaung. Good food. Guests are allowed to buy wines at resort's duty-free shop for consumption in the dining outlets. **$$$–$$$$**
Kawthaung Motel
Bosonpet Road
Tel: 09 22611; 01 272723
Overpriced rooms for the standards offered but only one of two hotels in town available to foreigners. **$$**
Honey Bear Hotel
Strand Road, near the Myoma Jetty
Tel: 01 229 6190
Offers better standards than the Kawthaung, with 39 clean rooms with air-conditioning and cold-water showers. **$–$$**

Where to Eat

What to Eat

Chinese, Indian and European food – and, of course, typical Burmese cuisine – are available at restaurants throughout the country. Reservations are seldom needed. Restaurants, except those located in the larger hotels, tend to close early in the evening. Burmese take their main meal at lunchtime and usually have an early dinner, around 6pm. Below is a categorised list of food items and their respective English translations widely available on any Burmese restaurant menu.

Soups

Ah Nyar Hin Cho. Upper Burmese lentil soup.
Chin Ye Hin. Spicy fish soup.
Bu Thee Hin Khar. Clear soup with vermicelli and gourd.
Kin Mone Ywet Hin Khar. Clear soup with herbal leaves.

Appetisers

Pa Zun nga paung kyaw. Deep fried prawns with onions.
Ginn Thoke. Pickled ginger salad with fried condiments.
Nga Paung Kyaw. Deep fried beansprouts with fish.
Bu Thee Kyaw. Fried gourd in batter.
Ah Kyaw Sone. Selection of deep fried appetisers.

Salads

(Caution is advised here as many ingredients are raw or slightly marinated only.)
Pe Thee Thoke. Long bean salad.
Dha – wei Tha – nat Sone. Mixed vegetable salad (Dawei speciality).
Pa Zun Thoke. Prawn salad.
Myin Khwar Ywet Thoke. Herbal leaves salad.

Ngar Phe Thoke. Pounded fish salad.
Kyet Thar Thoke. Burmese chicken salad.

Vegetables

Ah Sone Kyaw. Mixed-fried vegetables.
The Sone Hin. Vegetables in curry sauce.
Kha Yan Thee Hnat. Eggplant curry with shrimps.
Mho Ne Ka Zun Ywet Kyaw Chet. Mushrooms with watercress.

Curries

Kyet Tha Hin. Chicken Curry.
Wet Tha Hin Lay. Pork Curry.
Ah Mae Tha Hnat. Beef Curry.
Ngar See Pyan. Fish Curry with tomatoes.
Bae Tha Hin. Duck Curry.
Pa Zun Ne Ahloo Hin. Prawn Curry and potatoes.

Seafood

Ngar Doke Kha. Red snapper with garlic and parsley.
Pa Zun Oh Kat. Shrimp with chili.
Nga Su See. Yangon fish fillet.
Mawlamyine Nga Thalauk Paung. Fish steamed in lemongrass, ginger and garlic.

Meat dishes

Wet Tha A Sat Kyaw. Pork with chillies and onions.
Sin Gaw Hut. Minced meat sautéed with mint and ginger.
Kyet Tha Cho Chet. Chicken with basil.

Desserts

Rakhaing Nget Pyaw Paung. Steamed banana with coconut milk.
Mote Kyar Sae. Sticky rice, lotus seeds and syrup.
Thaku Pyin. Sago with coconut milk.

Where to Eat

YANGON

Burmese and Shan food

There are street stalls selling Burmese food at numerous locations throughout Yangon. Listed below are some of the best restaurants in the city:

Aung Thuka
17A 1st Street (between Shwegondine Street and Dhammazedi Road)
Tel: 01 525 194
One of the most famous local eateries. Reasonably priced and clean. Easy to order as all you have to do is point at the array of cooked food in clay pots to indicate your choice. **$**
Danubyu Daw Sawyi
194 29th Street
Tel: 01 275 397
Modern looking restaurant, serving traditional Burmese dishes. Good place to go for breakfast as it serves noodles and other local snacks. **$**
Green Elephant
519A Pyay Road
Tel: 01 531 231
Recommended; serves very good Burmese food in air-conditioned atmosphere. The *pennywort* salad is excellent. Popular with both visitors and locals. **$–$$**
Hla Myanmar Htamin Zai
27 5th Street
Simple restaurant offering a wide variety of Burmese and Shan dishes displayed in pots, plus some Chinese and Indian food. **$**
Maw Shwe Li
(Shan) W. Anawratha Road between 3rd and 4th streets
Very popular with locals; serves good, cheaply priced Shan food though it's a bit out of the way. **$**
Strand Grill and Strand Café
At The Strand
Tel: 01 243 377

Price Categories

Eating out in Burma is, with a few exceptions, inexpensive. Most meals for two people cost under US$10. More expensive restaurants in Yangon and Mandalay quote prices and charge in US dollars; all other restaurants accept local currency.
$$$$ Very expensive (US$30 and above)
$$$ Expensive (US$20–30)
$$ Moderate (US$10–20)
$ Budget (Under US$10)

The Grill is one of the most elegant restaurants in Yangon. Both the Grill and the Café have similar menus which offer excellent Burmese dishes, among others. The Grill is open only for dinner while the Café serves lunch and dinner at slightly lower prices too (open 6.30am to 11pm). The café also serves a high tea between 2 and 5pm. **$$–$$$$**

Chinese food

Palace Restaurant
84, 37th Street at City Central Plaza
One of the oldest Chinese restaurants in Yangon and still a safe choice. **$**

Panda Restaurant
205 Warden Street
Tel: 01 221 152
Dependable and inexpensive Chinese cuisine. **$**

Singapore Kitchen
524 Strand
Tel: 01 226 297
Excellent. Seafood is particularly fresh as the fish of your choice is taken straight from the tanks on display. Outdoor dining in good weather; stays open until late. **$$**

Shan Kan
U Wisaya Road, near Kandawmingalar Park
Tel: 01 244 336
Large Hong Kong-style restaurant, very popular and good. **$–$$**

Shwe Inya
Inya Road, on Inya Lake
Tel: 01 536 688
Banquet-style Chinese with lake views. **$–$$**

Thai food

Sabai Sabai
232 Dhammazedi Road
Tel: 01 544 724
Authentic Thai food served in wooden Thai-style building. **$–$$**

Sala Thai
56 Sayasan Road
Tel: 01 548 661
Good Thai food at reasonable prices. **$$–$$$**

Silom Village
69 Pyay Road (6½ mile)
Tel: 01 525 403
Atmospheric outdoor dining, good Thai cuisine. **$$–$$$**

Indian food

The Indian quarter of Yangon has many small restaurants and food stalls. Listed below are the best-known restaurants:

Bharat
356 Mahabandoola Street
Tel: 01 281 519
Smallish restaurant with marble-top tables. Serves South Indian food. **$**

Golden City Chetty Restaurant
170 Sule Pagoda Road
Tel: 01 275 447
Brightly lit, inexpensive South India with *dosas* a specialty. **$**

New Delhi Restaurant
262 Anawrahta Street, between 29th and Shwebontha streets
Tel: 01 251 867
Wide range of North and South Indian dishes available. Longer opening hours than most Indian restaurants. **$**

Tandoor
26 Wizaya Plaza, U Wizaya Road

Price Categories

$$$$ Very expensive (US$30 and above)
$$$ Expensive (US$20–30)
$$ Moderate (US$10–20)
$ Budget (Under US$10)

Tel: 01 241210
The place to go for North Indian specialities. **$**

Western food

50th Street Bar & Grill
9/13 50th Street, Botataung
Tel: 01 298 096
Colonial atmosphere; popular with the expat community and locals. Serves good pizza and pasta. Bar stays open until late. **$$$**

Bar-B-Q Hut
Bogyoke Aung San Park
Tel: 01 533 720
Pleasant outdoor lakeside dining at reasonable prices. **$–$$**

Chez Sylvie
Aurora Hotel, off Pyay Road
Tel: 01 525 961
French set lunch and dinner menu. Indoor and garden dining. Open for lunch and dinner. **$$$$**

Le Planteur
16 Sawmaha Street, off Natmauk
Tel: 01 549 389
Serves very good French-Swiss food with smoked ham and salami. The house punch is excellent. **$$$$**

L'Opera
20 Thukhawaddy Road, near Inya Lake
Tel: 01 566 662
Excellent Italian food, though on the expensive side. Offers home-made pasta and pizza. **$$$$**

Japanese food

Donburiya
112 Pansodan Street
Tel: 01 280 528
Open 24 hours. Offers good Japanese noodle dishes. **$**

Yakiniku
357 Shwebontha Street
Tel: 01 274 738
Specialising in Japanese grill.

Drinking Notes

Most of the better hotels offer fully stocked bars with both domestic and imported beer, wine and liquor (charged in US dollars). The best hotel bars in Yangon are those at Traders Hotel, The Strand, Inya Lake Hotel and Kandawgyi Palace Hotel. The 50th Street Bar & Grill in Yangon has the most congenial bar atmosphere in the city.

In Mandalay only the Novotel and Sedona hotels offer full bar service but the city is full of places, many of them outdoors near the Ayeryarwady, selling beer by the glass or pitcher.

In addition to local beer (Mandalay and Myanmar labels), there is also rum, whisky and gin made in Burma, of which Mandalay Rum is the most potable one. Throughout the Delta region and Central Myanmar (the plains of Bagan) lightly fermented palm juice (toddy) is drunk.

Teashops in Yangon

Mya Sabe Café, 71 Pansodan Street.
Paris Bakery House, branches on Insein Road, Mahabandoola Street and Sule Pagoda Road.
Sei Taing Kya Teashop, the most popular with branches around town.
Theingi Shwe Yee Tea House, 265 Seikkantha. Tel: 01 289 542, one of Yangon's cleanest classic teashops.

DELTA REGION

Pathein (Bassein)

Shwezinyaw Restaurant
24/25 Shwezedi Road
Serves Indian and Burmese food. Open from 8am–9pm. **$**
Zee Bae Inn
Merchant Street
Air-conditioned restaurant serves Chinese food. Opens 9am and closes around 7 or 8 pm. **$**

BAGO DIVISION

Bago

555 Hotel & Restaurant
On Bago's main avenue, serving good Burmese, Chinese, European and Indian food. **$**
Triple Diamond Restaurant
Popular and cheap eating place next door to the 555 Hotel & Restaurant in Bago. **$**

Taungoo

Sawasdee Restaurant
On the main road
Chinese, Thai and Indian dishes. Outdoor dining area available; open from 7am to 10pm. **$**

BAGAN

European and Burmese food

Everqueen Restaurant
Bagan Archaeological Zone
Nice outdoor garden setting; breezy at night. Tucked along a sandy road before the old city gate. Offers good fish dishes. **$**
Sarabha Restaurant
Bagan Archaeological Zone

Teashops in Bagan

Aung Mya Thi, Myinkaba.
Bagan Café, New Bagan.
Nay Pyi Taw, New Bagan.
Yar Kyaw, New Bagan.
Toe Toe, Old Bagan.

Offers a choice of indoor and outdoor dining. **$**
Bagan Thiripyitsaya Sakura Hotel
Bagan Archaeological Zone
Tel: 062 70285; Fax: 062 70286
Serves food that cannot be faulted.
$$$$
Bagan Hotel
Bagan Archaeological Zone
Tel: 062 70146; Fax: 062 70313
Upmarket hotel with café offering a good selection of dishes. **$$$$**

Burmese food

Aye Yeik Thar Yar, Nyaung U; offers views of Shwezigon Pagoda. **$**
Nation, Nyaung U. Facing Shwezigon Pagoda. Also serves Chinese food. Friendly staff. **$**
River View, New Bagan; pleasant location overlooking the river. **$$**

MANDALAY

Burmese food

Pyi Gyi Mon Royal Barge
Tel: 02 26779
Replica of the floating Karaweik restaurant in Yangon and located in the southeastern corner of the moat at Mandalay Palace. Burmese and Chinese dishes; puppet show at dinner. **$$$**
Tu Tu
27th Street, between 74th and 75th streets
Very popular at lunch, one of the more authentic places for Burmese cuinese. **$–$$**
Sakantha Restaurant
24 72nd Street, between 27th and 28th streets
Tel: 02 21066
Good food justifies the higher than average prices. Setting is pleasant as its dining room looks out onto a garden. **$–$$**

Shan food

Lashio Lay Restaurant, 23rd Street between 83rd and 84th Streets. Very tasty and spicy Shan food and a few vegetarian dishes. It's easy to order as dishes are on display. **$**
Thai Yai Restaurant, 84th and 23rd streets.
Shan and Thai food served. Open from 6am to 10pm. **$**

Chinese food

Honey Garden Restaurant
70th and 29th streets
Tel: 02 24098
Certainly at the top end of Chinese restaurants in Mandalay. Excellent food; outdoor dining. Open from 9am to 10pm. **$$**
Mann Restaurant
83rd Street between 25th and 26th streets
Popular with visitors and noted for

Teashops

Teashops or teahouses are very Burmese institutions. They may be housed in a building like any other restaurant or operate in the open. They are popular with the Burmese as a place to gather and to snack. Mini tables and stools are the norm and customers drink tea or coffee from doll-size cups and glasses. Snacks served are typically *eikyakwe* (made from deep-fried flour dough), stuffed buns, samosas and Burmese pastries.

Burmese tea is generally very sweet as condensed milk is used and sugar is also added. If you prefer a less sweet concoction, ask for the sugar to be left out. Burmese coffee is unfiltered and you drink it only after the grounds have settled. Again, condensed milk and sugar are added; black coffee is not served unless it is specified.

Teashops are the first places to open in towns and villages (some as early as 5am) and a good place for breakfast if you have to set off early. They also stay open till late – up to 11pm or so.

being one of Mandalay's better Chinese restaurants. **$$**

Min Min
83rd Street between 26th and 27th streets
Chinese-Muslim food served by a Chinese-Muslim family originally from Yunnan Province in China. Clean and friendly; reasonable prices. **$**

European food
Barman Beer Bar (BBB)
76th Street between 26th and 27th
Tel: 02 25623
Pleasant atmosphere. Air-conditioned dining room. Chinese, Indian and Burmese food also available. Open daily from 7am to 11pm. **$**

Vegetarian food
Marie-Min Vegetarian Restaurant
27th Street, between 74th and 75th streets
Clean. Wide array of Indian-style and Western-style dishes. Great place to meet fellow travellers and exchange information. Open 8am to 10pm. **$**
Punjab Food House, near corner of 80th and 27th Streets
Good curries. Open 8.30am to 7.30pm. **$**

Snack Shops

Golden Land Cold Drink, on 80th Street between 32nd and 33rd streets. Serves great lassi drinks.
Nylon Ice Cream Bar, 176 83rd Street between 25th and 26th. Many flavours available.

PYIN U LWIN

European food
Thiri Myaing Hotel (Candacraig)
Anawrahta Road, 6th Qtr.
Tel: 085 22047
Its famous Beef Wellington is still served. Roast chicken is also available. **$**

Price Categories

$$$$ Very expensive (US$30 and above)
$$$ Expensive (US$20–30)
$$ Moderate (US$10–20)
$ Budget (Under US$10)

Chinese food
Lay Ngoon Restaurant
Mandalay-Lashio Road
Popular restaurant serving Cantonese dishes. **$**
Shanghai Restaurant
Mandalay-Lashio Road
Another good place specialising in Shanghainese food. **$**

Indian food
Aung Padamya Restaurant
28 Thu Min Galar, Zaythit Road
Located near Shan Market.
Delicious Indian curries from 11am–6am. **$**

Other Places

Besides typical Burmese snack shops and restaurants you will find – depending on the specific area – Chinese or Indian eateries in even small towns throughout the country.

NYAUNGSHWE – INLE LAKE

Hu Pin
Well-known Chinese restaurant next to the hotel of the same name. Friendly owner. Excellent lake fish. Open from 8am to 7pm. **$**
Four Sisters Inn
Daily menu of Shan vegetarian dishes to (sometimes) musical accompaniment by one of the sisters. **$**

Nightlife

General

Evening entertainment in Yangon and Mandalay is limited to cultural performances at the National Theatre (Myaung Kyaung Street, Yangon) and dinner shows featuring either female singers or cultural performances.

The latter, showing condensed or excerpted versions of Burmese classical dance, can be seen in Yangon at the **Lone Ma Lay** (Off Natmauk Road, Kandawgyi, tel: 01 550 357), the **Dolphin Seafood Restaurant** (Kan Yeik Thar Road, tel: 01 250 240) and several other restaurants on the banks of Kandawgyi Lake including the state-owned **Karaweik Restaurant** (on Kandawgyi Lake).

In Mandalay, similar dinner shows are available at **Pyi Gyi Mon Restaurant** with performances of the Mandalay Marionettes at 7pm. Performances of **Mandalay Marionettes** also at 65th Street between 26th and 27th streets, tel: 02 38718 at 8.30 pm. On a smaller, more intimate scale you can enjoy a demonstration of classical dances with humorous commentary at the **Moustache Brothers** (39th Street between 80th and 81st).

Discos, Bars and Pubs

Yangon
Spectrum Disco Fun Pub
Grand Plaza Parkroyal Yangon (formerly Sofitel Plaza)
33 Alan Paya Lan
Tel: 01 250 388
This complex in the hotel's basement remains one of the hottest live music clubs in town featuring touring DJs and

occasional live music, plus private karaoke rooms.

Hot Shot
The Kandawgyi Palace
Kanyeiktha Road
Tel: 01 242 613
The Kandawgyi's disco, co-run by Thais, has been gaining favour lately. Cover charge.

Club Pioneer
Yuzana Garden Hotel
44 Alan Paya Road
Tel: 01 240 995
One of the most popular discos in town, especially on weekends.

Mr. Guitar Café
22 Sayasan Road
Tel: 01 701 270
Folk music bar with live performances from 7pm to midnight. Atmospheric, cozy place which also serves European and local food.

Paddy O' Malley's
Sedona Hotel
1 Kaba Aye Pagoda Road (near Inya Lake)
Tel: 01 666 900
Yangon's first Irish-style pub.

Silver Oak Café
83/91 Bo Aung Kyaw Street
Tel: 01 256 930
Tucked away in back of Ko Ko Beauty Salon, two blocks from The Strand, this friendly live music club caters to a mixed gay and straight clientele.

19th Street
This narrow street in the old town center is lined with beer terraces, bars and barbecue joints where both foreigners and locals meet for and inexpensive evening out.

Casinos

Although gambling is considered illegal in Burma, three establishments have opened up in border areas:

Andaman Resort on Thahtay Khun (near Thailand's Ranong), one at Myawadi across the border from Mae Sot (Thailand) and the Paradise Resort (at the Golden Triangle of Laos, Burma and Thailand).

Theatre

The best place to view a Burmese *pwe* is on the city street or pagoda grounds at festival times. If your visit does not coincide with a festival, however, there are two public theatres in Yangon and smaller establishments in Mandalay which have various performances:

The National Theatre, Myoma Kyaung Lan, Yangon.
Open-Air Theatre, Lanmadaw (Godwin) Road, Yangon.
Mandalay Marionettes, Burmese puppet theatre, 66th Street, between 26th and 27th streets, Mandalay.
Moustache Brothers, dance and comedy presentation, 39th Street, Mandalay.

Cinemas in Yangon

The Burmese love movies. There are more than 50 "cinema halls" in Yangon, about a third of them in the downtown area. In addition to Burmese language films, the Motion Picture Corporation shows carefully selected foreign features on a regular basis, including movies from India, North America, Europe, and Japan.

The **Thamada** cinema (5 Alan Paya Road, tel: 01 246 962) is the most comfortable and presents English-language and other foreign films on a regular basis. The **American Cinema** (14 Taw Win Road) shows free performances of American films every Monday at noon. Others you may wish to try for the "experience" are:

Bayint, 321 Bogyoke Aung San Street.
Nay Pyi Daw, 242-248 Sule Pagoda Road.
Shae Saung, Sule Pagoda Road.
Waziya, 327 Bogyoke Aung San Street.

Culture

Pagodas & Temples

There are two main types of Buddhist monuments in Burma: pagodas and temples. A pagoda consists of a stupa and its surrounding enclosure. The stupa (also known as a *zedi*, the Burmese pronunciation of the Pali *cetiya*) is a monument of commemoration containing a Buddhist relic chamber beneath (or sometimes above) the bell-shaped central structure. Burmese stupas are generally built on several terraces; these are passages on which devotees should walk in a clockwise direction.

The term "temple" is applied to Buddhist structures in Burma only because a more specific terminology does not exist in

The Eras

Burmese date their years by four different systems. Most frequently seen is one calendar based on the Christian, but you may see any of these other three as well:

The **Buddhist Era** began in 543 BC with the death of Gautama. According to this system, the Christian year 2004 is the Buddhist year 2547.

The **Pyay (Prome) Era** began in 78 AD. A large amount of epigraphical data of interest to archaeologists is dated by this system. The year 1992 is 1914 of the Prome Era.

The **Bagan (Pagan) Era** is considered to have begun in 638 AD. Linked to Burmese royalty, it is rarely in use today. The year 1354 of the Bagan Era parallels 1992 of the Christian Era.

English. In Theravada Buddhism a temple is not a place of worship of a higher being; the Buddha is not a god, and Theravada Buddhism in its pure form does not recognise any form of divine worship. The temple is instead seen as a place of meditation. The Burmese word is *ku*, derived from the Pali *guha*, which roughly translated means "cave". This word also reflects the cultural heritage of the edifice – these buildings were formerly constructed as artificial caves used by monks where there were no overhanging slopes.

The main element of a *ku* is that it is dark and cool inside. This feature characterises the Mon-style ("hollow cube") Bagan temples, into which only a little light is able to enter through the perforated stone windows. The Bamar-style ("central pillar") temples are totally different: they were built with huge entrances and two tiers of windows to make the interiors bright and airy.

One can trace the development of the "central pillar" type from the stupas. During festivals, it was the custom to stretch huge awnings from the stupa to the surrounding wall of the enclosure to offer protection from rain and sun. As a result, a covered walkway surrounds the central sanctuary. When this was copied in solid materials, it gave the impression that the upper part of a stupa had been built on the temple roof. The same principle applies to the multi-storied Bamar-style temples.

The "hollow cube" type of temples are not actually hollow inside; they may seem to be so, but the majority have a central supporting pillar. From the outside, their pointed, bell-shaped domes resemble Gothic buildings. But the temples of Bagan could not be more different. Instead of spanning the greatest possible space, the Buddhist temple interiors consist of a multitude of walls enclosing narrow passageways and chambers, thereby satisfying the *ku*'s original purpose as a sanctuary for inner peace and meditation. The exterior of these temples – white, and invariably decorated with a gold finial – represent Mount Meru and the devout Buddhist's striving for a spiritual goal via the ever-valid *dharma* (or *dhamma*), the law of life.

The Six Buddhist Synods

Theravada and Mahayana Buddhists are not in complete agreement about the dates of the Buddha's life. While Mahayana reckons his birth at 556 BC and his death at 476 BC, Theravada chronicles specify the years 623 BC to 543 BC. The latter date is the starting point for the Buddhist calendar valid in Southeast Asia.

Whichever calendar may be correct, the First Synod took place three months after Gautama Buddha's death and entry into *nirvana*. It was held in the Satta Panni Cave in Rajagriha in the present-day Indian state of Bihar.

The Second Synod was convened in Vesali in northern Bihar not long after. King Ashoka convened the Third Synod – the last joint meeting between the divided sects – in 253 BC in Pataliputra. Then the two schools of thought went their separate ways.

The Fourth Synod, summoned by King Kanishka, took place in 78 AD in northern India. Theravadins later denied the validity of this synod, maintaining that the Fourth Synod took place in Lanka (Sri Lanka) between 29 and 13 BC.

The Fifth Synod, at which the entire text of the *Tipitaka* (Buddhist scripture) was committed to stone tablets for the first time, was held in Mandalay in 1871–72 *(see Mandalay chapter)*.

Modern legend has it that Prime Minister U Nu, who in the early 1950s took a pilgrimage to Buddhism's most important religious sites, had a vision while sitting under the Bodhi tree in Bodhgaya, India. He saw that on the 2,500th anniversary of Gautama's death – a date that would also represent the halfway point of the Buddha's 5,000-year world regency – faithful Buddhists from all over the world would meet in Burma to hear the message of peace and light in a world of hate and war.

Monasteries

If the temples and pagodas of Burma haven't exhausted you, and you're still enthused about exploring more Buddhist buildings in Yangon before departure from Burma, the Burmese government has compiled a list of "impressive monasteries" in Yangon. Many of them feature ornate woodcarving and fine Buddhist artefacts. Visitors should make it a point to obtain permission to enter the monasteries from their respective *sayadaw*, or abbots.

Aletawya Kyaungtaik, Dhamma Zedi (Boundary) Street.

Bagaya Kyaungtaik, Bagaya Road, Kemendine.
Bahan Kyaungtaik, Bahan.
Kyaunggyi Kyaungtaik, Kemendine.
Mingun Tawyar, Inyamyaing (Louis) Street.
Mya Theindan Kyaungtaik, Kemendine.
Naw-man Kyaungtaik, Pazundaung.
Ngadatkyi Kyaungtaik, Nagadatkyi Road.
Payagyi Kyaungtaik, Schwegondine Road.

Pazundaung Kyaungtaik, Pazundaung.
Pyinnya Ramika Maha, Theinbyu Road.
Salin Kyaungtaik, Lower Kemendine Road.
Shin Ah-deiksa-wuntha Kyaungtaik, Pazundaung.
Theinbyu Kyaungtaik, Theinbyu Road.
U-Kyin Kyaungtaik, Bagaya Road, Kemendine.
Weluwun Kyaungtaik, Kemendine.
Zeyawaddy Kyaungtaik, Kemendine.

Upon his return to Burma, U Nu ordered work be started immediately on the Maha Pasana Guha artificial cave. It was completed in 1954, three days before the official opening of the Sixth Synod on 17 May, the day on which the Theravada Buddhists celebrate the birth of the Buddha. The synod, which recited, interpreted and amended the Tipitaka, lasted for two years.

The Mudras

Just as temples and pagodas are created in different styles, so are Buddha images *(see picture story on Buddha Images page 96–7).* The various *asana* (body postures) and *mudra* (hand positions) have symbolic meanings, each of considerable importance to students of Buddhism. These positions or postures are thousands of years old. As religion and art form is an inseparable unity in Burmese life, they constitute the basis of dance and of the *yok thei pwe,* or marionette theatre.

In addition to the *asana (see box above),* there are six different *mudras,* each conveying a clear message. These are demonstrated in the following:

The Bhumisparsa Mudra

In this *mudra,* the left hand lies palm upwards on Buddha's lap, and the right hand rests palm downwards across his right knee, with the fingertips touching the ground below. This is the most common mudra; it shows the Buddha calling upon Mother Earth to stand witness to his moment of enlightenment.

According to the Buddha legend, Mara, the god of destruction, tried to subdue the Buddha by sending his army of demons to attack the Buddha as he meditated under the Bodhi tree, and by sending his three daughters – Desire, Pleasure and Passion – to tempt the Buddha. But the Buddha called upon Vasumdarhi, the Earth goddess, to bear witness that he had found perfect knowledge. With this, the ground began to shake, and Mara took flight.

Asana – the Body Postures of the Buddha

There are four basic *asana* (body postures) in which a Buddha image might appear:

The standing posture depicts the descent of the Buddha from the Tavatimsa heaven where, according to legend, he travelled to preach the Buddhist doctrine to his mother.

The walking posture represents the Buddha's taming of the Nalagiri elephant.

The seated posture is the most common. It can represent any of three events: the Buddha calling upon Mother Earth to stand witness to his enlightenment; his preaching of the Sermon of the Wheel of the Law; or the Buddha in deep meditation.

There are three different seated postures: legs crossed with both soles out of sight; legs crossed with soles turned upwards and resting on thighs in the lotus position; and legs upright in almost a European style of sitting.

The Buddha might also be in a reclining posture. If his head is pointed north, the position depicts his death and transition into nirvana. If his head is pointed any direction but north, he is sleeping.

The Dhyana Mudra

This position, said to represent many events in the life of the Buddha, has the palm of his right hand placed flat in the palm of the left, with both hands laid in his crossed legs. Objects placed in the palms, or figures standing to the side of an image in this position, specify which event is being depicted.

The Dharmacakra Mudra

In this *mudra,* both of the Buddha's hands are held in front of his breast. The tips of the middle finger and thumb of the left hand are joined with the tips of the index finger and thumb of the right hand to form a circle. This gesture recalls the Buddha's first sermon (at Sarnath, India); the hand sign is said to start the Wheel of the Law into motion.

The Abhaya Mudra

This posture, found only in a standing Buddha, has the figure's right hand raised and the left pointed downwards. It represents the promise of tranquillity, protection and fearlessness given by the Buddha to his followers. It is also a reminder of the attempted assassination of the Buddha by his cousin Devadatta, who sent the Nalagiri elephant against him.

The Varada Mudra

The arms of the standing Buddha are half out-stretched in front of the body in this pose. The palms are opened out, and the tips of the fingers point downwards. This *mudra* depicts the bestowal of the Buddha's blessing on his Buddhist followers.

The Abhaya & Varada Mudras

The Buddha's right hand is in the raised position of the *Abhaya Mudra,* and his left hand is out-stretched as in the *Varada Mudra.* This posture signifies protection and blessing, and at the same time recalls the Buddha's descent to earth after preaching in the Tavatimsa heaven.

All makers of Buddha images in Burma today must follow the specific *mudras* outlined here, as well as other strict rules. A list of 108 characteristics which all Buddha images must exhibit are laid down in the Digha Nikaya, found in the Buddhist scriptures.

Libraries

Sarpay Beikman Public Library, 529 Merchant Street at the corner of 37th Street. It has more than 11,000 English-language books among its 35,000 volumes. Of particular interest are the contemporary Burmese language books translated into English.

University Central Library, located on the Yangon University campus, is Burma's largest library. Some 170,000 books in Burmese, English and many other languages are kept here.

The library at the International **Institute of Advanced Buddhistic Studies**, Kaba Aye Pagoda, has a large selection as well. Among its holdings are more than 10,000 volumes in English. The collection also includes about 9,000 sets of ancient palm-leaf manuscripts and 2,412 museum objects.

The **National Library** in the Yangon City Hall houses a rather interesting collection of rare books and palm-leaf manuscripts.

There are libraries in the **United States Embassy**, 581 Merchant Street, and at the **British Embassy**, 80 Strand Road. Both embassies carry current magazines as well as a variety of books.

In addition, the **Information and Broadcasting Department** operates 110 libraries and reading rooms through the country. Many of them, especially in major towns, have English-language literature. The department's headquarters in Yangon, near the Strand Hotel on Pansodan Street, has a wide selection of newspapers and periodicals, as well as official publications of the government.

Sport

General

Sports are a popular diversion in Burma. Soccer is often played at Aung San Stadium in Yangon, and on small fields throughout the country. More typically Burmese, however, are the sports of *chinlon* (volleyball-like game played with a rattan ball) and *bando* (traditional Burmese kickboxing).

Spectator Sports

BURMESE BOXING

To the unfamiliar Westerner, Burmese boxing appears to be a needlessly vicious sport. Boxers may use any parts of their bodies in attacking their opponents, and a match is won by whoever draws first blood on his opponent. But there are specific rules and courtesies which keep a match from getting out of hand, and musical accompaniment by a Burmese *saing-waing* (percussion orchestra), lends an air of unreality to the event. *(See box on page 351).*

You can see boxing matches in Mandalay at the training facility on 76th Street between 27th and 28th streets. Boxing matches are held throughout the country at temple festivals. Classes in Burmese boxing for beginners take place at the YMCA in Yangon (tel: 01 294 128) on Tuesday, Thursday and Saturday from 7 to 9am. Classes for more experienced students take place on Monday, Wednesday and Friday from 3 to 5pm. The Institute of Myanmar Traditional Advanced Boxing also holds classes at 4pm on Saturday at the Yangon University.

CHINLON

Chinlon is Burma's national game. Said by some to have originated in ancient Pyay in the 7th century, its object is to keep a rattan ball in the air for as long as possible, using no part of the body except the feet and knees. The game is played in similar fashion throughout Southeast Asia (where it is known as *takraw* or *sepak takraw*). Although the game is played for fun throughout the country once the heat of the day has subsided, the All-Myanmar Chinlon Association has set up rules for team play that is increasing in status. A team of six players stand within a boundary circle 6.5 metres (21 ft) in diameter, passing the ball back and forth among themselves.

Points are scored according to the difficulty of the footwork used and the skill with which it is executed; specific point values are assigned to certain "strokes." Points are subtracted if the ball hits the ground or if a player steps outside the boundary circle. The *chinlon*, or rattan ball, is made of six rattan vines flattened, interwoven and dried, forming a circular ball with holes about an inch and a half apart. The standard-size ball is 40 cm (16 in) around.

Golf Courses

Golf courses can be found in all major locations throughout the country. For information contact **Myanmar Golf Association** at Pyay Road, 9 mile, Yangon. Tel: 01 661 702.

SPORTS CLUBS

The following private clubs in Yangon will generally welcome visitors: **Kandawgyi Swimming Pool**, on Kandawgyi Lake. Tel: 01 551 327. **Kokine Swimming Club**, 23 Sayasan Road. Tel: 01 542 749. **National Swimming Pool**, U Wisara Road. Tel: 01 278 550. **City Golf Resort**, Thirimingala Street, Mile 10, Insein. Tel: 01 641 342.

Myanmar Golf Association, Pyay Road, Mile 10. Tel: 01 661 702.
Yangon Golf Club, Danyingon Road, Insein, Tel: 01 635 563.
Dagon Golf Club, Kha Yae Pin Road, Mingalardon. Tel: 01 636 112.
Yangon Sailing Club, 132 Inya Road. Tel: 01 531 298.
Myanmar Yachting Federation, 132 Inya Road, Tel: 01 531 298.

Fitness Centres

The Traders (tel: 01 242 828), **Summit Parkview** (tel: 01 211 888), **Nikko** (tel: 01 544 500) and **Sedona** (tel: 01 666 900) hotels all have good fitness centres free for guests or open to the public for various fees. In dependent fitness centres include:
Hard Body, Tha Htone Road. Tel: 01 701 387.
Lido Fitness Centre, 1 Kaba Aye Pagoda Road. Tel: 01 666 900.
Miss Myanmar, 223-A Shwegondaing Street. Tel: 01 556 455.

Outdoor Activities

HIKING

In the past few years hiking has become popular in several areas: Kalaw, Inle Lake and – to a lesser extent – Hsipaw. Operators in Kalaw offer a range of trips, from day treks in the vicinity to multi-day hikes as far as Pindaya and even Inle Lake. Nights invariably are spent at monasteries and with hilltribe villagers. In Nyaungshwe, (Inle Lake) half- and full-day hikes can easily be arranged.

RUNNING

The **Yangon Hash House Harriers** (tel: 01 515 011 or contact the Traders Hotel tel: 01 242 828) meet every Saturday at 3pm at the Yangon Sailing Club, 132 Inya Road. The pace of the run is slow, and many people walk the distance around central Yangon, which takes about 30 to 45 minutes. Two other runs of 3km/2 miles and 6km/4 miles are organised between the Traders Hotel to the Zoological Garden every Sunday.

CYCLING

Due to popular demand, bicycles are available for rent at most locations where young travellers congregate. The environs of Bagan, Mandalay and Nyaungshwe are particularly suitable. Bikes for hire are not necessarily the latest models on the market, but they come very cheap. Almost any guesthouse can get you one. It is of course possible to bring in your own mountain bike.

CLIMBING & SKIING

Climbing is only possible in Myanmar's far north and so far only very few individuals have been able to do it. Plans were under discussion at one time to attract skiers to the same area.

DIVING

Without question, Myanmar, especially the Myeik (Mergui) archipelago, holds lots of promise (see Diving Operators page 327).

HOT-AIR BALLOONING

It's possible to fly over the ancient ruins of Bagan in a hot-air balloon. Flights take place at sunrise or sunset and last for about 45 minutes. For details contact:
Balloons Over Bagan, Sedona Hotel, Yangon. Tel/fax: 01 652 809; www.balloonsoverbagan.com; alternatively head for the sales desk at the **Bagan Hotel**, Bagan Archaeological Zone. Tel: 062 70145/6; Fax: 062 70313.

A Burmese Boxing Match

The following description of Burmese boxing is taken from Forward magazine (1 August, 1964), as quoted by author Helen Trager in her book We, The Burmese:

"The head is used for butting, either to stop an opponent's rush or to soften him up while holding him fast in a tight grip. The hands are used not only for hitting but also for holding. The elbows are used to parry an opponent's blow or to deliver one in the opponent's side. The knees are used for hitting an opponent who is held fast, or they may be used to deliver blows while the boxers are apart. The feet may trip an opponent or at least keep him off balance, or they may be used to stop an opponent's rush with a well-executed flying kick.

"These tactics are commonly employed by Burmese boxers. To deliver the blows effectively, however, the boxer has to master his footwork, which is also considered important in another branch of art of self-defence, Thaing. A Burmese boxer has to know where to place his feet, how to advance, how to retreat, from what position to jump into the attack, and how best to evade the blows of the opponent. In close combat the Burmese boxer has to be well acquainted with techniques of wrestling.

"...To safeguard the boxers from accidents, there are rules against scratching, biting, pulling hair, and hitting or kicking an opponent in the groin. The fingernails and toenails of boxers have to be kept properly trimmed. A boxer who is down may not be kicked or hit in any way...

"The match is decided at the sign of blood. Each boxer is allowed to wipe away the blood three times before he is declared the loser. A match may also be decided when one of the boxers is too hurt to continue although he may not be bleeding."

Shopping

Markets

Burma's *zei* (markets) and bazaars are the most interesting and most reasonable places to shop for native arts and crafts.

Yangon

In Yangon, the **Bogyoke Aung San Market** (known during British times as Scott Market) is open from 9.30am to 4.30pm Monday to Saturday. It is the place where most tourists do their last shopping before leaving the country. Some of the shops in the market with a large selection and reasonable prices are listed here – don't forget to bargain:
Lacquerware, Daw Chit Khin Lacquerware, Shop 43, East (C) Block.
Jade, Colourful Jade Store, Shop 42, West "D" Arcade.
Mother of Pearl, Myanmar Variety Store, Shop 75, Center Arcade.
Silverware, William Tan, Shop 33, Main Line.

There are **open-air markets** across Bogyoke Aung San Street from the Bogyoke Market; at the corner of St John's Road and Pyay Road; and east of the Botataung Pagoda. The **Theingi Zay Indian Market** is just off Anawrahta Street. The biggest and oldest market in Yangon, it sells household wares, textiles and traditional medicine and herbs. The **Thirimingala Market** in Ahlone Township at the northern end of Strand Road sells fresh fruit, vegetables and meat and provides some good photo opportunities. There's also a **Chinese Market** at the corner of Mahabandoola Street and Lanmadaw Road. There are also separate **night markets** which set up on specified streets after dark; the best ones are in Yangon's Chinese and Indian quarters.

Mandalay

Mandalay's **Zegyo Market** (at 84th Street between 26th and 27th streets and 27th and 28th streets) opens early in the morning and remains open until dark. This markets sells more or less everything. The **Kaingdan Market** fruit and vegetable market is found by walking a couple of blocks west from the Zegyo. The cheapest market for household goods is in Chinatown between 29th and 33rd streets.

The **night market** is on 84th Street between 26th and 28th.

Arts & Crafts

Yangon

The entrances to the **Shwedagon Pagoda** – as is the case in many other well-known pagodas throughout the country – are also bazaars – of some length, in fact, covering both sides of the stairways. The bazaar at the east entrance is possibly the most interesting; among the items frequently sold are puppets, drums, masks, toys, brassware and metal goods, including swords. The bazaar at the pagoda's south entrance is notable for wood and ivory carvings. (Caution: many countries ban the import of ivory.) Woodcarvings are also sold in quantity and quality at the New Carving Shop, 20 University Avenue.

For other types of handicrafts and art work, try the following:
J's Irrawaddy Dream, 59 Taw Win Road. Tel: 01 221 695. Textiles, clothing, lacquerware and handicrafts.
Myanmar Gallery of Contemporary Art, 5 Kaba Aye Pagoda Road. Tel: 01 548 058.
Orient Art Gallery, 1 Kaba Aye Pagoda Road. Tel: 01 666 900.
Sun Myanmar Elephant House, Sein Kyaw Road, Dawbon Township. Tel: 01 579 709.
Lokanat Art Galleries, 62 Pansodan Street. Tel: 01 282 196.
Zawgyi House, 372 Bogyoke Aung San Road. Tel: 01 256 355.

Mandalay

Mandalay has a good selection of arts and crafts shops.
The MMK traditional Store, 84th Street between 33rd and 34th streets. Tel: 02 25226. Best place to buy silk and cotton clothing and longyis and accessories.
Sein Myint Artist, 42 Sanga University Road. Tel: 02 26553. Sells *kalagas* and has an interesting gallery with paintings and carvings.
Manaw Myay, 1 30th Street, between 77th and 78th streets. Tel: 02 32737. Unique shop selling Kachin and Lisu clothing and handicrafts.
Mann Swe Gon Handicrafts, 27th street between 72nd and 73rd streets. Good selection of local handicrafts.
Yadanapura Art Centre, 78th Street. This government-run enterprise has a good selection of quality handicrafts and jewellery.

Bagan

The best shopping for lacquerware is done in New Bagan, the residential area about 8 km (5 miles) from the Bagan archaeological zone.

OTHER SHOPS IN YANGON

Jewellery & Gems

Banner Gems, Dusit Inya Lake Hotel. Tel: 01 662 866; branch: Gem Museum (Booth No. 20), Kaba Aye Pagoda Road. Tel: 01 650 489.
Myanmar VES Joint Venture Co. Ltd., 66 Kaba Aye Pagoda Road. Tel: 01 661 902.
Top Gems, 11 Front Row, Bogyoke Aung San Market. Tel: 01 245 706.
Golden Owl, Jewellery and Gem Laboratory, 724 Merchant Street. Tel: 01 281 863.

Art

Golden Valley Art Centre, 54 D, Golden Valley. Tel: 01 533 830.
Heaven Art Gallery, 104 Bogyoke Aung San Road. Tel: 01 290 829.

Bargaining

Bargaining is a way of life in Burma. Except for top-of-the-range hotels, department stores and restaurants, you should be able to get a few kyats off the "fixed price" of most things. Even room prices are negotiable. Offer half the asking price and work your way up and expect to settle for a bit less than 50 percent of the original rate. Bartering is also an accepted means of transaction at market stalls; stall holders are happy to take jeans, watches and T-shirts as payment for goods.

Summit, 27/3 Golden Valley, Bahan. Tel: 01 510 954.
Traditional Arts and Sculpture Sales Shop, 188 to 192, East Wing Bogyoke Aung San Market.
 If you are looking for a special producer or distributor, look in the Myanmar Business Directory.

Antiques & Furniture
Augustine`s Antique Shop, 23A Thirimingalar Road.
Tel: 01 705 969.
Green Elephant, 519A Pyay Road. Tel: 01 531 231.
Hla Gabar, S-4, 4th floor, Banyar Dala Street. Tel: 01 200 747.
Charlie Antiques, 17 Kaba Aye Pagoda Road.
 There are gift and souvenir shops at all the major hotels.

Booksellers
Innwa Book Store, 232 Sule Pagoda Road, carries an acceptable selection of English language books and magazines. Paperbacks and foreign journals can generally be found at two shops operated by the Paper, Stationery, Books and Photographic Stores Trading. They are at 232 Sule Pagoda Road and 98 Pansodan Street. It also has shops selling general literature (corner of Merchant and Pansodan streets) and medical literature (181/189 Sule Pagoda Road).

Myanmar Book Centre, 477 Pyay Road; good selection of books and magazines on Burmese history including otherwise hard to find titles. It also has a branch at the public library at 529 Merchant Street.
 Two outstanding used book shops in Burma: In Yangon, book collectors should seek out the **Bagan Bookshop**, 100, 37th Street; and in out-of-the-way Taunggyi, a charming surprise is the **Myoma Book Stall**, 390 Main Road. Book lovers will also find it worthwhile to browse through the many bookstalls set up along main streets in both Yangon and Mandalay. In Yangon, book vendors have their shops and stalls on Bogyoke Aung San Street and on side streets west of Sule Pagoda Road, where original and photocopied, long-sought out-of-print books can often be found.

Beauty Parlours
Vilas Beauty Salon, several locations including: 64, Latha Street. Tel: 01 272 302.
 Several of the major hotels including Summit Parkview (L'Espace) have beauty parlours of high standard.

Language

Ana-deh

Every language contains expressions which don't lend themselves to translation. Burmese is no exception. The essence of Burmese courtesy stresses encouraging the other person to agree with you. Not imposing on others is the basic principle of "ana-deh." The venerable Judson dictionary explains the term well as, "to be deterred by feelings of respect, delicacy, constraint, or by fear of offending." While all these feelings exist in Western countries, the concept as a single idea does not or else there would be a word for it (such as in the Thai language where "kreng chai" means "ana-deh")."
 "Ana-deh" must be learned and felt inwardly. It is true art to meet another person at a halfway point where neither side will lose face in the confrontation.
 In the Westerner's dealings with Burmese authorities, he will often encounter this "ana-deh" approach to problems, coupled with a marked aversion to making a decision that will cause someone difficulty (such as turning down a visa extension application). In some cases, it can lead to considerable delays. Westerners must be patient and try to understand what other forces are influencing the individuals concerned.

Survival Burmese

The Burmese language is tonal, like Chinese and Thai. The way in which a word is pronounced affects its meaning: a single syllable, given different stress, may carry several distinctly different meanings. Tones exist in English, but only to convey connotation. A gruffly uttered "No" (close to the falling tone) indicates one shouldn't even think of asking again while a "No" with the rising tone makes the exclamation a question which might not mean no at all.

In fact tones by themselves rarely obstruct survival communication. In a restaurant, for example, when trying to order pork curry (*we'tha: hin:*), if you accidentally utter *"we tha: hin:"* (loud meat curry) you will quite likely get your pork. Other factors such as correct pronunciation of the vowels and consonants and having the proper rhythm are also important.

In the following list of words and phrases, the following accent marks are used: (no mark) – low even tone (:) – long falling tone (.) – short falling tone (') – glottal stop or creaky tone. The (') sign at the end indicates a glottal stop (like a final "t" but softer). The only way to know exactly how they sound is to have a native speaker say them for you to hear.

An "h" beginning a word indicates aspiration: "hk" is like the English "k" in Kate whereas "k" is closer to the "k" in skate. Sounds such as "hm" "hn" resemble "m" and "n" but without the "breathiness." "Ng" is a sound not found at the beginning of English words. It does occur frequently in the middle of words such as "ringing" or "singing". Practice by first saying the whole word and the gradually cutting off the first two letters until you are saying "nging".

Health

Dentist *thwa: sa ya wun*
Doctor *sa ya wun*
Hospital *hsei: yone*
Pharmacy *hse: zain*
Where is the...? *...beh hma leh:*
Call the doctor. *sa ya wun ko pei: ba*
I am ill. *nei lo. ma kaun: bu:*

CONVERSATION

How are you? *nei kaun: dha la:*
I am well *nei kaun: ba deh*
I am not well *nei thei' ma kaun: bu:*
How're you doing? (informal) *beh lo leh:*
That's good *kaun: deh*
I like it *chai' teh*
Do you understand? *na: leh la:*
I understand *na: leh ba deh*
I do not understand *na: ma leh bu:*
Yes *ho' keh.*
Yes (politely by male) *ho'keh.hka mya.*
Yes (politely by female) *ho'keh shin'*
Yes (answering a call politely by male) *hka-mya.*
Yes (answering a call politely by female) *hka-shin'*
That's true *ho' ba deh*
That's right *hman ba deh*
No, that's not so *ma ho' ba bu:*
Please repeat *pan pyaw: ba oun:*
Speak clearly *shin: shin: pyaw: ba*
Why? *ba pyi' lo. leh:*
Never mind *nei ba zei*
It doesn't matter *kei'sa. ma shi. ba bu:*
What is it? *ba leh:*

Do you know Burmese? *bama lo ta. dha la:*
Only a little *neh: neh: pa: pa: ba beh:*
I speak very well *kaun: kaun: ta. ba deh*
Are you English? *ein:galeik. lumyo: la:*
No, I'm not English *ein:galeik. lu myo: ma ho' bu:*
Where do you come from? *beh ga. la dha leh:*
I come from America *ameiri.kan ga. ba*
Goodbye *thwa: meh*
Take care *kaun: kaun: thwa:*

ACCOMMODATION

Is there a hotel near here? *di na: hma ho-te shi. la:*
Can I see the room? *a-kan chi. ba ya zei*
Single room *ta yau' hkan:*
Double room *hna yau'.hkan:*

DINING

What do you want to eat? *ba sa: chin dha leh:*
Is there...? *...shi. dha la:*
I'll eat... *...sa: meh*
Pork curry *weh. tha: hin:*
Chicken curry *cheh. tha: hin:*
Beef curry *a-meh: hin:*
Fish curry *nga: hin:*
Shrimp curry *bazun hin:*
Noodles with curry *kau' hswe:*
Vegetables *hin: dhi:*
Fruit *thi' thi:*
Fermented tea leaf salad *la peh. thou.*

Numbers

one	*ti'*	**twelve**	*hseh.hni'*	**fifty**	*nga:zeh*
two	*hni'*	**thirteen**	*hseh.thone:*	**sixty**	*hchau' hseh*
three	*thone:*	**fourteen**	*hseh.lei:*	**seventy**	*hkun-na-hseh*
four	*lei:*	**fifteen**	*hseh.nga:*	**eighty**	*hyi' hseh*
five	*nga:*	**sixteen**	*hseh.hcau'*	**ninety**	*ko:zeh*
six	*hchau'*	**seventeen**	*hseh.hkun*	**one hundred**	*ta-ya*
seven	*hkun/hkun–ni'*	**eighteen**	*hseh.hyi'*	**one thousand**	*ta htaun*
eight	*hyi'*	**nineteen**	*hseh.ko:*	**ten thousand**	*ta thaun:*
nine	*ko:*	**twenty**	*hna-hseh*	**hundred thousand**	*ta thein:*
ten	*ta-hseh/hseh*	**thirty**	*thone:zeh*	**one million**	*ta than:*
eleven	*hseh.ti'*	**forty**	*lei:zeh*	**ten million**	*ta ga dei*

Fermented noodles with
fish broth *mo: hin: ka:*
What do you want to drink? *ba
thau' chin dha le?*
I don't want to drink. *ma thau'
chin bu:*
I'll drink... *...thau' meh*
Coffee *ka pi*
Black tea with milk and sugar *la
peh. yei.*
Plain green tea *la peh. yei jan:*
Hot water *yei nwei:*
yei *Water.*
bi ya *Beer*
hin: jo *Hot soup.*

DIRECTIONS AND PLACES

Where is the...? *...beh hma leh:*
Where are you going? *be go thwa:
ma lo le:*
Railway Station *mi: ya ta: buda
yone*
Theatre *yo' shin yone*
Hotel *ho teh*
Post Office *sa dai'*
Bank *ban*

TIME

When will you go? *beh do. thwa:
ma leh:*
What time will it start? *beh ah-
chein sa. ma leh:*
One o'clock *ta na yi*
Two o'clock *hna na yi*
Airplane *lei yin byan*
Train *mi: ya ta:*
The bus will leave. *bas. ka: twe.
me*
Trishaw. *hsai'ka:*

SHOPPING

How much is it? *be lau' le:*
Lower your price. *sho. ba ohn:*
The price is too high. *zei: mya: deh*
Lower some more. *hta. sho. ba
ohn:*
Expensive *zei: chi: deh*
OK/good *kaun: ba bi*

Further Reading

General Interest & Travel

Abbott, Gerry. **The Traveller's
History of Burma**. Stories of early
European travellers. Orchid Press
Bangkok.
Bixler, Norma. **Burma: A Profile.**
New York: Praeger, 1971. A well
written general survey.
Burma Research Society. 50th
Anniversary Publication (two
volumes). Yangon: 1961. Highlights
of 50 years of scholarly writings.
Collis, Maurice. **Lords of the
Sunset**. New York: Dodd Mead,
1938. A tour of the Shan States.
Henderson, John W., and others.
Area Handbook for Burma.
Washington, DC: American
University Foreign Area Studies,
1971. An overview.
Keyes, Charles F. **The Golden
Peninsula: Culture and Adaptation
in Mainland Southeast Asia**. New
York: Macmillan, 1977. An
anthropologist studies changes in
the region's Buddhist societies.
Kipling, Rudyard. **Letters From the
East**. London: 1889. The author's
travels through Asia.
Lewis, Norman. **Golden Earth**.
Eland Books, London.
Maugham, Somerset. **The
Gentleman in the Parlour**. Garden
City, NY: Doubleday, Doran & Co.,
1930. Subtitled: A Record of a
Journey From Yangon to Haiphong.
Nash, Manning. **The Golden Road
to Modernity: Village Life in
Contemporary Burma**. New York:
Wiley, 1965. A study of peasant
agricultural society.
Scott, Sir James G. **Burma: From
the Earliest Day to the Present Day**.
New York: Alfred A. Knopf, 1924.
Shway Yoe (Sir J.G. Scott). **The
Burman: His Life and Notions**.
London: Macmillan, 1882. Two
volumes. A gold mine of cultural
information from a 19th Century
British colonial official.

Theroux, Paul. **The Great Railway
Bazaar: By Train Through Asia**.
New York: Random House, 1975.
Amusing account of the author's
railway adventures.
Trager, Helen G. **We the Burmese**.
New York: Praeger, 1969. Burmese
life and culture through its people's
eyes.

General History

Bennett, Paul J. **Conference Under
the Tamarind Tree**. New Haven,
Conn.: Yale University Southeast
Asian Studies, 1971. Three essays
on Burmese history.
Cady, John F. **A History of Modern
Burma**. Ithaca, NY: Cornell University
Press, 1958. The standard history of
Burma since the 18th Century.
Hall, D.G.E. **Burma**. London:
Hutchinson's University Library,
1960. A brief but complete history.
Harvey, Godfrey E. **History of Burma**.
London: Longmans, Green, 1925.
Reprinted 1967. A detailed treatment
from ancient times to 1824.
Htin Aung. **A History of Burma**. New
York: Columbia University Press,
1967. A Burmese view of the
nation's history.
Humble, Richard. **Marco Polo**. New
York: GP Putnam's Sons, 1975.
Easy-reading survey of the travels of
Marco Polo.
Phayre, Sir Arthur P. **History of
Burma**. London: Trübner, 1883.
Reprinted 1967. The first formal
history of Burma by a Westerner.

European Contact

Anderson, John M.D. **English
Intercourse With Siam in the 17th
Century**. London: Kegan Paul,
Trench, Trübner, 1890.
Cox, Hiram. **Journal of a Residence
in the Burmhan Empire, and more
particularly at the Court of
Amarapoorah**. London: John Warren
and G. & WB Whittaker, 1821.
Establishes a pattern of anti-
Burmese writing by British authors.
Symes, Michael. **An Account of the
Embassy to the Kingdom of Ava
sent by the Governor-General of
India in 1795**. London: W. Bulmer,
1800. Keen observations on all

aspects of Burmese life.

Symes, Michael. **Journal of his Second Embassy to the Court of Ava in 1802**. London: George Allen and Unwin, 1955.

The British Colonial Era

Anderson, John M.D. **Mandalay to Moulmein**. London: Macmillan, 1876. Reprinted 1979. Subtitled: A narrative of the two expeditions to western China of 1868 and 1875 under Col. Edward B. Sladen and Col. Horace Browne. Good data about Shan and Kachin areas.

Bruce, George. **The Burma Wars, 1824–1886**. London: Hart-Davis MacGibbon, 1973. A review of the three Anglo-Burmese wars.

Hall, Gordon L. **Golden Boats from Burma**. Philadelphia: Macrae Smith, 1961. The life of Ann Hasseltine Judson, the first American woman in Burma.

Htin Aung. **The Stricken Peacock**. Den Haag: Martinus Nijhoff, 1965. Anglo-Burmese relations between 1752 and 1948.

Moscotti, Albert D. **British Policy in Burma, 1917–1937**. Honolulu: University Press of Hawaii, 1974.

Orwell, George. **Burmese Days**. London: Secker and Warburg, 1934. Bittersweet novel about British colonial rule.

World War II

Collis, Maurice. **Last and First in Burma**. London: Faber and Faber, 1956. An account of the country during and after the war.

Fellowes-Gordon, Ian. **Amiable Assassins: The Story of the Kachin Guerrillas of North Burma**. London: Robert Hale, 1957. Freedom fighters take on Japanese invaders.

Jesse, Tennyson. **The Story of Burma**. London: Macmillan, 1946. A wartime account.

Morrison, Ian. **Grandfather Longlegs**. London: Faber and Faber, 1946. The biography of Major H.P. Seagrim, who stayed behind Japanese lines in Burma.

Nu, Thakin. **Burma Under the Japanese**. London: Macmillan,

1954. An important account of the occupation.

Seagrave, Gordon S. **Burma Surgeon**. New York: W.W. Norton, 1943. An important work about the life of a wartime doctor.

Slater, Robert. **Guns Through Arcady: Burma and the Burma Road**. Madras, India: Diocesan Press, 1943. An account of events leading to the Japanese invasion.

Slim, W.J. **Defeat Into Victory**. London: Cassell, 1956. A good autobiographical account of the war, by the British military leader.

Stilwell, Joseph. **The Stilwell Papers**. Edited and arranged by Theodore H. White. New York: William Sloane Associates, 1948. "Vinegar Joe" in his own words.

Takeyama, Michio. **Harp of Burma**. Tokyo: Charles E. Tuttle, 1966. First published in Japanese in 1949. Poignant novel about the Japanese experience in wartime Burma.

Tuchmann, Barbara W. **Stilwell and the American Experience in China, 1911–1945**. New York: Macmillan, 1971. A very important history and biography.

Bibliographies

Aung Thwin. **Southeast Asia Research Tools: Burma**. Honolulu: University of Hawaii Asian Studies Program, 1979.

Trager, Frank N. **Burma: A Selected and Annotated Bibliography**. New Haven, Conn.: Human Relations Area Files Press, 1973. The most complete bibliography available.

Contemporary Burma

Aung San Suu Kyi. **Freedom from Fear & Other Writings**. Viking, London and New York, 1991. A collection of essays by and about the Nobel Peace Prize winner.

Aung San Suu Kyi. **Burma and India**. New Delhi, 1990.

Butwell, Richard. **U Nu of Burma**. Stanford, Calif.: Stanford University Press, 1963. Second edition, 1969. Political biography.

Lintner, Bertil. **Aung San Suu Kyi**

and Burma's Unfinished Renaissance. Bangkok, 1990.

Lintner, Bertil. **Burma In Revolt: Opium and Insurgency since 1948**. Westview Press, 1994.

Lintner, Bertil. **The Rise and Fall of the Communist Party of Burma**. Ithaca, 1990.

Lintner, Bertil. **Outrage**. Hong Kong, 1989.

Maung Maung, editor. **Aung San of Burma**. Den Haag: Martinus Nijhoff, 1962. Collected writings by and about the nation's founding father.

Maung Maung. **Burma and General Ne Win**. Bombay, India: Asia Publishing House, 1969. A Burmese interpretation of the nationalist movement.

McCoy, Alfred W. **The Politics of Heroin in Southeast Asia**. New York: Harper & Row, 1972. A fascinating expose of the web of international involvement in the Golden Triangle.

Mya Than Tin, editor. **Encounters on the Road to Mandalay**. White Orchid, Bangkok, 1995. A collection of recent interviews with ordinary Burma citizens.

Naw, Dr. Angelene. **Aung San**. Silkworm Books, Chiang Mai, 1999. Press, 1984.

Nu, U. **U Nu: Saturday's Son**. New Haven, Conn.: Yale University Press, 1975. The former prime minister's autobiography.

Pye, Lucian W. **Politics, Personality and Nation Building: Burma's Search for Identity**. New Haven, Conn.: Yale University Press, 1962. An analysis of events in postwar Burma.

Sargent, Inge. **Twilight over Burma – My Life as a Shan Princess**. University of Hawaii Press, Honolulu, 1994. Written by the Austrian wife of the last *sawbwa* (prince) of Hsipaw.

Silverstein, Josef. **Burma: Military Rule and the Politics of Stagnation**. Ithaca, NY: Cornell University Press, 1977. An analysis of Ne Win's politics.

Silverstein, Josef, compiler. **The Political Legacy of Aung San**. Ithaca, NY: Cornell University Press, 1972.

Silverstein, Josef. **Independent Burma at Forty Years: Six Assessments**. Ithaca, 1989.

Steinberg, David. **The Future of Burma – Crisis and Choice in Myanmar**. New York, 1990

Tin Maung Latt. **City of Yangon**. Modernization Record, Yangon, 1990

Tinker, Hugh. **The Union of Burma**. London: Oxford University Press, 1967. Fourth edition. A study of Burma's first years of independence.

Ethnic Minorities

Cochrane, Wilbur W. **The Shans**. Yangon: Government Printing Office, 1915. Reprinted 1978. A missionary's account.

Colquhoun, Archibald R. **Amongst the Shans**. New York: Scribner and Welford, 1885. Reprinted 1970. Of historical interest.

Enriquez, C.M.D. **A Burmese Arcady**. London: Seeley, Service, 1923. Reprinted 1978. An account of the Burmese hill tribes.

Leach, Edmund R. **Political Systems of Highland Burma**. Cambridge, Mass: Harvard University Press, 1954. A study of Kachin social structure. An anthropological classic.

Lehman, Frederick Y. **The Structure of Chin Society**. Urbana, Ill.: University of Illinois Press, 1963. Contemporary anthropological study.

Milne, Leslie. **Shans at Home**. London: Murray, 1910. Reprinted 1970. Descriptive account.

Scott, Sir James G. **Burma: A Handbook of Practical Information**. London: Daniel O'Connor, 1921. Third edition. Reference book on ethnic minorities.

Smith, Martin. **Burma – Insurgency & the Politics of Ethnicity**. Zed Press, London, 1996. The best researched of recent books on Burma's rebellious ethnic groups.

Yegar, Moshe. **The Muslims of Burma**. Wiesbaden: O. Harrassowitz, 1972.

Religion

Bigandet, Father Paul A. **The Life or Legend of Gautama, the Buddha of the Burmese**. Two volumes. London: Kegan Paul, Trench, Trübner, 1911. Reprinted 1978.

Bode, Mabel Haynes. **The Pali Literature of Burma**. London: Royal Asiatic Society, 1909. Reprinted 1965.

Fraser-Lu, Sylvia. **Burmese Crafts, Past and Present**. Oxford University Press, 1994.

Htin Aung. **Folk Elements in Burmese Buddhism**. London: Oxford University Press, 1962.

King, Winston L. **A Thousand Lives Away: Buddhism in Contemporary Burma**. Oxford, England: Bruno.

Lester, Robert C. **Theravada Buddhism in Southeast Asia**. Ann Arbor, Mich.: University of Michigan Press, 1973. Good basic survey.

Mendelson, E. Michael. **Sangha and State in Burma**. Ithaca, NY: Cornell University Press, 1975. Relations between the government and Buddhist monks.

Ray, Nihar-ranjan. **An Introduction to the Study of Theravada Buddhism in Burma**. Calcutta: University of Calcutta Press, 1946. Reprinted in 1978. Historical treatment.

Rodrigue, Yves. **Nat-Pwe: Burma's Supernatural**. Sub-Culture Kiscadale Publications, 1992.

Sarkisyanz, Emmanuel. **Buddhist Backgrounds of the Burmese Revolution**. Den Haag: Martinus Nijhoff, 1965.

Smith, Donald E. **Religion and Politics in Burma**. Princeton, NJ: Princeton University Press, 1965. Excellent study of the impact of Buddhism on the nationalist movement.

Spiro, Melford E. **Burmese Supernaturalism**. Englewood, NJ: Prentice-Hall, 1967. Expanded edition, 1977. A fascinating study.

Warren, Henry Clarke. **Buddhism in Translations**. Cambridge, Mass.: Harvard University Press, 1896. Reprinted 1953, 1962, 1976. Perhaps the best translation of the most important Buddhist scriptures.

Arts & Culture

Allott, Anna, ed. **A Traveller's Literary Companion to South-East Asia**. In Print Publishing, Brighton, 1994.

Allott, Anna. **"Burmese Literature"**

in A Guide to Eastern Literatures, edited by David M. Lang. New York: Praeger, 1971.

Brandon, James R. **Guide to Theater in Asia**. Honolulu: The University Press of Hawaii, 1976. What to see, where to go.

Falconer, John et al. **Myanmar Style: Art, Architecture and Design of Burma**. Periplus Editions, Singapore, 1998. A photographic survey of major design components in both traditional and contemporary Burmese design.

Frederic, Louis. **The Art of Southeast Asia**. New York: 1965.

Griswold, Alexander B. **The Art of Burma, Korea, Tibet**. New York: Methuen, 1964.

Htin Aung. **Burmese Drama**. Calcutta: Oxford University Press, 1937.

Htin Aung. **Burmese Folk Tales**. Calcutta: Oxford University Press, 1948.

Htin Aung. **Burmese Monks' Tales**. New York: Columbia University Press, 1966.

Khin Myo Chit. **The 13-Carat Diamond and Other Stories**. Yangon: Sarpay Lawka, 1969.

Lustig, Friedrich von. **Burmese Classical Poems**. Yangon: Yangon Gazette, 1966.

Myint Thein. **Burmese Folk Songs**. Oxford, England: Asoka Society, 1969.

Strachan, Paul. **Pagan: Art and Architecture of Old Burma**. Kiscadale Publications, 1988.

Win Pe, Richard. **Modern Burmese Poetry**. Thawda Press, Yangon, 1989.

Other Insight Guides

Companion volumes to the present title cover the Southeast Asian region comprehensively and include *Bali, Bangkok, Laos & Cambodia, Indonesia, Java, Malaysia, Singapore, Southeast Asia, Thailand* and *Vietnam*.

ART & PHOTO CREDITS

Picture Spreads

INSIGHT GUIDE
BURMA

Cartographic Editor **Zoë Goodwin**
Production **Linton Donaldson**
Design Consultants
Carlotta Junger, Graham Mitchener
Picture Research **Hilary Genin**

Map Production Cosmographics
© 2005 Apa Publications GmbH & Co.
Verlag KG (Singapore branch)

Index

a

accommodation listings 337–43
agriculture and forestry 47, 288, 289, 293
  bamboo 50
  coconuts 241, 279
  fish farms 145
  rice 27, 37, 45, 49–50, 145, 151, 161, 164, 279
  sugar 237
  tanaq-hpeq 257, 258
  taunggya (slash-and-burn) cultivation 50
  tea 257
  timber 47, 50, 115, 163, 165–6, 264, 299
  tobacco 238, 313
Alaungpaya 24, 120, 155, 157
Alaungsithu 22, 220–21
Amarapura 25, 102, 103, 111, 173, 189–91
  Kyauktawgyi Pagoda 103, 189, 192
  Maha Gandha Monastery 190
  Nagayon shrine 103
  Patodawgyi Pagoda 190
  Shwe-kyet-yet Pagoda 191
  Shwe-kyet-kya Pagoda 191
  Thanbyedan Fort 191
  U Bein Bridge 191
Ananthasurya 236–7
Ananthathurya 237
Anaukhpetlun 24, 155, 159
Anawrahta 22, 70–71, 101, 129, 154, 162, 213–15, 225, 231, 232, 307
Andaman Sea 45, 47, 147
architecture
  temple 99–103, 229
  British colonial 119, 121, 127, 203, 257
Aris, Michael 41
arts and crafts 85–9
  see also **museums and galleries, shopping**
  bronze casting and metalwork 86–8, 96–7, 190
  embroidery 89
  gold leaf 86, 183, 187
  lacquerware 85, 86
  in Mandalay 175
  marionettes 88
  in Mingun 198

"opium weights" 87–8, 89
  paintings 88–9
  pottery 145, 147, 149
  Shwi Hninsi Gold Leaf (Mandalay) 187
  textiles 86, 89, 189, 253, 293
  umbrellas 146, 147
  woodcarving 88, 293
arts, performance 91–5
  see also **festivals and events**
  dance-drama 91, 92–3
  Karaweik Restaurant (Yangon) 140
  Maha Gita 95
  Moustache Brothers (Mandalay) 186
  music 92, 94–5
  National Theatre 91
  popular music 92
  pwe 77, 91, 92, 93
  pya zat 91
  travelling theatre troupes 91–2
  yok thei pwe (puppet theatre) 90, 93, 94
  zat gyi 91
Aungban 258
Aungdet 281
Aung San 28, 29, 34, 35–6, 138–9
Aung San Suu Kyi 19, 39, 40, 41
Ayetthema 308
  Kyaikthanlan Pagoda 308
  Taikkala fort ruins 308
  Tizaung Pagoda 308
  Ayutthaya 24

b

Bagan (Pagan) Archaeological Zone 15, 22, 23, 45, 102, 111, 187, 213–33
  see also **Myinkaba, Nyaung U**
  Abyadana Temple (Myinkaba) 233
  Ananda Temple 22, 96, 101, 216, 217–19
  Ananda Temple Festival 78, 219
  Bagan Archaeological Museum 217
  Bagan Moat 225
  Bupaya Pagoda 225–6
  desecration of temples 218
  Dhammayangi Temple 221–2
  Gawdawpalin Temple 220
  Gubyaukgyi Temple 228
  Gubyaukgyi Temple (Myinkaba) 231–2
  Myazedi Stone 232
  Gubyauknge Temple 228
  Hmyathat Cave temple (Nyaung U) 230

Htilominlo Temple 97, 222–3
  Kondawgyi Temple (Nyaung U) 231
  Kubyaukkyi Temple 227
  Kyanzittha Cave temple (Nyaung U) 228, 229
  Kyaukgu Temple (Nyaung U) 230
  Mahabodhi Temple 224
  Manuha Temple (Myinkaba) 232, 233
  Mimalaung Kyaung 226
  Mingalazedi Pagoda 223
  Mingalazedi Pagoda (Myinkaba) 231
  Myinkaba Pagoda (Myinkaba) 232
  Nagayon Temple (Myinkaba) 233
  Nanpaya Temple (Myinkaba) 223, 233
  Nathlaung Kyaung 226–7
  Ngakywenadaung Pagoda 227
  Pahtothamya Temple 226
  Pebinkyaung Pagoda 224–5
  Pitakat Taik 223–4
  Sapada Pagoda (Nyaung U) 229–30
  Sarabha Gateway 223
  Seinnyet Ama Temple 233
  Seinnyet Nyima Pagoda 233
  Shinbinthalyaung 222
  Shinbinthalyaung Reclining Buddha 222
  Shwegugyi Temple 220–21
  Shwesandaw Pagoda 222
  Shwezigon Pagoda (Nyaung U) 22, 216, 228, 229, 230
  Shwezigon Pagoda Festival (Nyaung U) 220
  Somingyi Monastery 233
  Thamiwhet Cave temple (Nyaung U) 230
  Thandawgya Image 220
  Thatbyinnyu Temple 219–220
  Thatkyamuni Temple (Nyaung U) 231
  Upali Thein 227–8
Bagan Myothit (New Bagan) 216–7, 235
Bagan Plain 211–43
Bago (Pegu) 15, 23, 24, 111, 115, 151–60, 305
  Hinthagone Hill 157
  Hinthagone Pagoda 157
  Kalyani Sima 157–8
  Kyaikpun Pagoda 160
  Mahazedi Pagoda 159, 160
  Shwegugale Pagoda 160
  Shwemawdaw Pagoda 151, 154, 156, 157

Shwethalyaung Buddha 158
Bago Division 151–67
see also individual place names
Bago Yoma forest 165–6
Bagyidaw 21, 25
Ba Maw 29, 35
Bay of Bengal 148
beaches and resorts 49, 111,
147–8, 275, 295
Andaman Club resort
(Kawthaung) 316
Kanthaya 298
Maungmagan Beach (Dawei) 319
Ngapali Beach 297–8
Setse beach (Kyaikkami) 308
Thandwe 277, 298
Beikthano 101, 167
Bo Mya 39, 306
Bayinnaung 24, 155, 156, 159,
165
Bhamo 23, 45, 111, 265
Eikkhawtaw stupa 265
Shwekyaynar stupa 265
Thein Maha Chedi 265
Binnyagyan 129
Bodawpaya 25, 63, 155, 156,
182, 189, 197, 199–201, 280
"Burma Road" 28, 249, 259
business hours 328
business travellers 330
Byatta 206
Byinnya U 129, 154

c

calendar 323
Cape Bayinnaung 316
Chauk 239
Chaungtha 148
Pagoda Festival 148
Chennault 32
children, travelling with 330
Chin State 275, 286–92
see also individual place names
Chindits 31
climate and seasons 45–6, 47, 64,
173, 203, 323
monsoons 46, 49, 64, 77, 279,
295, 298, 323
Collis, Maurice 318, 319
crime 329
see also **drugs**
bandits 303
smuggling 49, 55, 292, 303, 318
currency *see* **money matters**
customs regulations 324–5
export of antiques 230, 284, 324

d

Dawei (Tavoy) 15, 47, 319
Maungmagan Beach 319
de Brito y Nicote, Philip 24, 130,
157, 160, 163
Delta Region 115, 145–8
see also individual place names
Dhammazedi 129, 154, 155,
156, 157
Dhannavati 285
Diamond Island 147
di Varthema, Ludovico 48
drugs 53–7, 287
opium 47 53–7, 173, 249, 256

e

eating out listings 344–7
economy 27, 37–8, 40, 323
education 67
elephants, working 49, 115, 163,
166, 169, 265, 266, 287, 299,
305, 308
see also **wildlife**
emergency telephone numbers 328
etiquette 62, 330–31
in religious buildings 136,
177, 331

f

Falam 275, 292
festivals and events 76–9
Ananda Temple Festival (Bagan)
78
Bawgyo Pagoda Festival (Hsipaw)
258, 259
Buddhist Lent 77
Chaungtha Pagoda Festival 148
Chinese New Year 79
Divali (Hindu "Festival of Lights")
79
Festival of the Spirits (Mount
Popa) 240
Htamein (rice harvest festival) 76
'Id al-Fitr (end of Ramadan) 79
Kachin Manao 79, 262–3
Kason (Buddha's birthday) 76–7
Kyundaw island festivals 267
Manao Festival (Myityina) 78
Maulid al-Nabi (Prophet
Mohammed's birthday) 79
Mount Popa Festival (Nayon) 78
nat festivals 78
pagoda festivals 78
Phaung Daw U Festival (Inle
Lake) 78
Poy Sang Long 69

Shan Festival (Kyaukme) 78
Shwedagon Pagoda Festival
(Yangon) 78, 79
Shwe Myitzu Pagoda Festival
(Indawgyi Lake) 265
Taungbyon Festival (Wagaung)
78, 205
Taungbyon Spirit Festival
(Taungbyon) 205
Tawthalin (boat-races) 78
Tazaungdaing Festival (Pyay) 166
Tazaungmone (Weaving Festival)
77, 78
Thadingyut (Festival of Lights) 78
Thadingyut Light Festival
(Sagaing) 196
Thadingyut (Festival of Lights)
(Ywama) 253–4
Thingyan (New Year's Day) water
festival 76
Thingyan Festival (Inwa) 192
Wagaung ("Draw-a-Lot") festival
77
Fitch, Ralph 103, 120
"Flying Tigers" 32
food and drink 80–83
festival food 76
plum wine 204
further reading 356–8

g

galon 28
Gawwein 271
gems and precious minerals 48,
67, 249, 258
Gems and Pearls Emporium 48
gold mining and panning 261,
264, 271
gems fair and auction (Yangon)
141–2
mining areas 48, 204, 258, 261,
264, 265, 271
Yangon Duty-Free Shop 128
geography 45–50, 322
getting around 332–6
see also **transport**
restricted areas 295, 303, 307,
308, 311, 313, 315, 327,
335–6
getting there 326
overland access from Thailand
312–3, 315, 327
**Glass Palace Chronicle of the
Kings of Burma** 21, 217, 223
Gokteik Viaduct 207, 258
"Golden Triangle" 53–7
Gulf of Mottama (Martaban) 47,
50, 119, 303

h

Halin (Halingyi) 21, 101, 167, 205, 271
Harvey, G.E. 64
health 325
  medical treatment 330
  mosquitoes 281, 325
history 21–41, 119–20, 153–5, 161–4, 175–6, 199–201, 277–81, 305–7
  anti-government demonstrations 38, 39
  Burmese constitution 288
  Chinese involvement 55, 265
  civil war 261, 266
  "dyarchy reform" 28
  European involvement 23–35, 160, 317
  British 24, 27–35, 130, 164, 176, 288, 295, 305, 308, 317
  Dutch 24
  French 24
  Portuguese 23–4, 159, 160, 162–3, 279
  First Anglo-Burmese War 25, 120, 193, 200, 281, 295
  First Burmese Empire 22–3, 154, 157, 187, 278, 307
  Government of Burma Act (1935) 28
  Independence 35
  post-independence militarisation 37–40
  Mongol invasion 23, 154, 162, 216
  nationalisation of businesses 38
  nationalism 28
  Second Anglo-Burmese War 25, 120, 130
  Second Burmese Empire 23, 154, 155, 163
  Third Anglo-Burmese War 33
  Third Burmese Empire 24
  Treaty of Yandabo (1826) 25
  World War II 29–35, 36, 151, 177, 261, 305, 308
Hlegu 151
Hmawza 166, 167
Hopin 264
Hopong 255
Hpa-an 311
Hpakant 265
Hsinbyushin 24, 130, 317
Hsipaw 207, 258, 259
Htaukkyant 151
  British War Cemetery 32, 151
  Hlwga Wildlife Park 151–2
human rights issues 15, 306–7

i

Indawgyi Lake 111, 249, 264–5
  Shwe Myitzu Pagoda 264–5
  Shwe Myitzu Pagoda Festival 265
industry
  brewing 160
  cotton ginning and spinning 238
  minerals 50
  natural gas 50, 239
  gem stone mining 48
  marble 271
  oil 50, 160, 239
Inle Lake 47, 249, 251, 253, 257
  Phaung Daw U Festival 78
Insein 143
  Ah Lain Nga Sint Pagoda
international organisations 329
internet and email services 329
Inwa (Ava) 23, 24, 102, 111, 191–4
  Adoniram Judson Memorial 193
  Bayaga Kyaung 194
  Gaung Say Daga 192
  Htilaingshin Pagoda 193
  Inwa Bridge 193, 194
  Inwa Fort 193–4
  Lawkatharaphy Pagoda 193
  Leitutgyi Pagoda 193
  Maha Aungmye Bonzan Monastery 192, 193
  Nanmyin Watchtower 192
  Thingyan Festival 192
Inywa 269
Isthmus of Kra 47, 303

k

Kabaung 307
  Kayin Baptist church 307
Kabuang 166
Kabwet 271
Kachin State 173, 261–71
  see also individual place names
Kalaw 47, 249, 257–8
Kalemyo 205
Kanishka 178
Kanthaya 298
Katha 267
Kawthaung 315–16
  Andaman Club resort 316
Kayah State 249, 259
  see also individual place names
Kayin (Karen) State 27, 249, 305–7, 311–13
  see also individual place names
Kekku 256
Kengtung 255–6
Khapland, SS 293

Khun Sa 256
Kipling, Rudyard 119, 143, 308
Kaung Daing 252
  hot sulphur springs 252
  Inlay Kaung Daing Hotel 252
Kublai Khan 23, 154, 213, 216, 265
Kyaikkami 308
  Setse beach 308
Kyaikto 101, 111, 309
  Golden Rock 304, 309
  Kyaik-tiyo Pagoda 309–11, 312
Kyanzittha 22, 213, 214–16, 233
Kyaukka 202
Kyaukme 207, 258
Shan Festival 78
Kyaukmyaung 270
Kyaukpadaung 239
Kyauktan Pagoda 150, 162, 164, 165
Kyauktaw 285
Kyetshar 166
Kyundaw island 267

l

Lake Taungthaman 190–91
  Kyauktawgyi Pagoda 191
  U Bein Bridge 191
language 15, 21, 22, 61, 68, 232, 289, 293, 322, 353–5
Lashio 47, 111, 96, 207, 258, 259
Launggyet 284
Lawpita Falls 259
Ledo Road 31
leg-rowing 251, 254
Letkhokkon 147
libraries 350–51
Loikaw 259

m

Machembo 264
  Muladashi suspension bridge 264
Mae Sam Laep (Thailand) 312
Mae Sot (Thailand) 307, 313
  shrine of Pho Phawo 307
Magway 243
Maha Muni Buddha 96, 97, 181, 181–2, 183, 277, 280, 285, 287
Maha Nandamu caves 204
Male 270
Mandalay 25, 45, 78, 103, 111, 173–87, 207, 271
  airport 173
  Atumashi Kyaung 180
  boat trip Ayeyarwady River 186–7
  Buffalo Point 185
  Craft workshops 86–7, 183, 185–6, 187

Diamond Jubilee Clock 184
Eindawya Pagoda 183
Maha Muni Pagoda 96, 97,
181–2, 183
Mandalay Fort and museum 177
Mandalay Hill 25, 175, 177,
178–80, 271
Kuthodaw Pagoda 180
Kyauktawgyi Pagoda 179
Sandamuni Pagoda 179–80
Shweyattaw Buddha 178
South Stairway 179
Moustache Brothers 186
National Museum and National
Library 184
Pyigyimon restaurant 176
Royal Palace 31, 103, 175,
176, 177
Setkyathiha Pagoda 183
Shwi Hninsi Gold Leaf 187
Shwe In Bin Kyaung 182, 183
Shwekyimyint Paya 97
Shwe Nandaw Kyaung 180
U-Bein bridge 172
Zegyo Market 175, 183, 184
Manerplaw 312–3
Manrique, Father Sebastiao 280
Manuha 231, 307
Ma-ubin 148, 167
Maugham, Somerset 103, 129, 131
Maung Maung 39
Mawlamyaing (Moulmein) 15, 45
47, 64, 111, 308
Cave of Kawgaun 308
Cave of Payon 308
Kyaikthanlan Pagoda 308
Sulati Mosque 308
Uzina Pagoda 308
media 328
medical treatment see health
Meiktila 242–3
Meiktila Lake 242
Meiktila Dam 200
Merrill, Frank 32
"Merrill's Marauders" 30, 32
Mindon, King, of Mandalay 18, 25,
33, 103, 130, 173, 175–6, 179
Mingun 103, 198–202, 271
Hsinbyume, or Myatheindan
Pagoda 200, 201
Mingun Bell 198, 199
Mingun (Mantara Gyi) Pagoda
103, 188, 199, 200–201
Pondawpaya Pagoda 201
Settawya Pagoda 201
Minnanthu 236–8
Lemyethna Temple 236–7
Nandamannya Temple 237–8
Payathonzu Temple 237

Sulamani Temple 236
Minsawmun 281
Mogaung 264
Mogok 48, 204, 258, 271
ruby, sapphire and jade mines 48
monasteries 348
money matters 322, 325–6
black market currency exchange
122, 322, 325
credit cards 128, 326
foreign currency payments 125,
128, 322
import and export of currency 324
Mon State 305–11
see also individual place names
Monywa 202
Thanboddhay Temple 202
Mottama (Martaban) 23, 154, 308
mountains and hill ranges
Arakan 287
Chin Hills 45, 205, 285–6,
287–8
Himalayas 31, 45, 47, 261
Hkakabo Razi 47, 264, 266
Kachin Hills 45, 46, 47, 263
Mangain Taung ridge 269
Naga Hills 31, 45, 288, 293
Nat-Myet-Hna-Taung 266
Patkai Hills 46, 287
Pegu Yoma range 242
Popa 235, 239–40, 241, 242
Rakhaing Hills 45
Sagyin 271
Santsung range 31
Taunggyi 254
Taungkwe 259
Victoria 49, 187, 287, 295
Mount Popa 235, 239–40, 241, 242
Mahagiri Nat shrine 240
Popa monastery 240
Mrauk U (Myohaung) 23, 102, 111,
274, 275, 276, 277, 278–84
Andaw Paya Temple 282
Dukkanthein 282
Laymyetnha Temple 282
Royal Palace ruins 281
Shittaung Temple 281, 282
Shwetaung Pagoda 282
Muse 259
museums and galleries
archaeological museum
(Pakhangyi) 238
Bagan Archaeological Museum
(Bagan) 217
Buddhistic Museum (Sittwe) 296
Curio Museum (Shwedagon
Pagoda, Yangon) 138
galleries in Yangon 141
Gems Museum (Yangon) 141

Hmawza Archaeological Museum
(Hmawza) 167
lacquer school and museum
(Myinkaba) 231
National Museum (Yangon) 128
National Museum and National
Library (Mandalay) 184
Rakhaing State Cultural Museum
(Sittwe) 296
Toungoo museum (Toungoo) 165
Myadaung 269
Myaungmya 148
Myawadi 313
Myeik (Mergui) 303, 315, 316, 318
Kuthein Nayon Kyaung 319
Pataw Padet Island 319
Payagyi Road ("Big Pagoda
Road") 318–9
Shwethalyaung 318
Theindawgyi Pagoda 318
Myeik (Mergui) Archipelago 15,
47, 49, 111, 303, 315–19
see also individual place names
Myingyan 187, 238
Myinkaba (Myinpagan) 231–3
lacquer school and museum 231
Myitkyina 47, 111, 261–3
Manao Festival 78, 262–3
mythology and legends
Bawgyo Pagoda images 259
hamsa (mythological duck) of
Bago 153
Indawgyi Lake 265
in the theatre 93
Jataka 93
Kaba Aye (Yangon) 142
Kyaik-tiyo Pagoda 309
King Tissa 309, 311
Kyaikpub Pagoda (Bago) 160
Kayanzittha 233
Lake Myitta Kan 196
Mahagiri Nat 240–41
Maha Muni 181
Mandalay Hill 175
Mount Popa 239–40
Ramayana 93
Sanda Moke Khit 178–9
Sri Ksetra 167

n–o

Namkham 259
Namtu 258
Nantaungmya 223
Narapathisithu 226, 259
Naratheinka 226
Narathihapate 23
Narathu 221–2
national holidays 78–9

Nayon
 Mount Popa Festival 78
Ne Win 36, 37, 38–40, 62
nightlife 347–8
Northeastern Burma 249–71
 see also individual place names
Northwest Coast 295–8
 see also individual place names
Northwestern Burma 275–99
 see also individual place names
Ngapali Beach 14, 277, 294, 297–8
Nyaung U 22, 187, 216, 228–31
Old Bagan 270

p

Padah-Lin Caves 258
Pagan 191
Pakhangyi 238
 archaeological museum 238
Pakokku 187, 238
Paletwa 286
Pan Asian Highway 311, 312
Panchakalyani 214
Parrot's Beak rock 266
Pathein (Bassein) 15, 45, 145–7
 parasol workshops 147
 St Joseph's Convent 147
 St Peter's Cathedral 146–7
 Settayaw Pagoda 146
 Shwemokhtaw Pagoda 146
 Shwezigon Pagoda 146
 Twenty-Eight Pagoda 146
Payathonzu 160, 306, 313
 Shwegugyi Pagoda 160
people 21–4, 35–6, 61–6, 68–9
 Bamar (Burman) 21, 24, 37, 49,
  56, 61–2, 68, 99
 Chin 64, 68, 285–6, 288–91
 Chinese community 66, 69, 121
 Ghurka 69
 Indian community 65, 120, 161
 Inthas 249, 251–2
 Kachin 38, 47, 63, 68, 261
 Kayah 38, 50, 63
 Kayin (Karen) 37, 38, 40, 63,
  68, 69, 146, 166, 290, 307
 Lisu 47, 68
 Moken 317
 Mon 21–3, 38, 50, 64–5, 68,
  101, 153, 306, 315
 Naga 64, 289, 293
 Padaung 63, 252–3, 256, 259
 Palaung 68, 257
 Panthays 54
 Pyu 21, 166, 277–8
 Rakhaing 23, 38, 61, 63–4, 68,
  146
 Shan 23, 38, 62, 68, 255

 Tai 21
 Talaing see **Mon**
 Taungyo 257–8
 Wa 64
 women's rights 67
Phaulkon, Constant 317
photography 326
Pindale 197
Pindaya 257–8
Pindaya Cave 249, 257, 258
place name changes 15, 39, 46
political and military organisations
 All Burma Student Movement 28,
  36–7
 Anti-Fascist People's Freedom
  League (AFPFL) 35–6, 37
 Burma Socialist Program Party
  (BSPP) 36, 39
 Chin National Army (CAN) 291
 Chin National Front (CNF) 291
 Communist Party of Burma (CPB)
  242, 265
 Democratic Alliance of Burma
  (DAB) 39
 "God's Army" 40, 305–6, 315
 Kachin Independence Army
  (KIA) 291
 Kachin Independence
  Organisation (KIO) 40, 291
 Karen National Liberation Army
  (KNLA) 305
 Karen National Union (KNU) 305
 Mon National Liberation Army
  (MNLA) 306
 National Council of Nagaland
  (NSCN) 293
 National Democratic Front
  (NDF) 291
 National League for Democracy
  (NLD) 39, 41, 323
 National United Liberation Front
  (NULF) 38
 New Mon State Party (NMSP) 306
 People's Volunteer Organisation
  (PVO) 35
 Pigidaungsu (Union) Party 38
 Pyidawtha (Eight-Year Plan) 37
 Pyithu Hluttaw 39–40
 Revolutionary Council 38
 Shan Independence Army 62
 "Socialist Republic of the Union
  of Burma" 38–9
 State Law and Order Restoration
  Council (SLORC) 39
 State Peace and Development
  Council (SPDC) 36, 40, 323
politics 323
Polo, Marco 211
population 45, 322

 of Amarapura 189
 of Bago 151
 of Mandalay 175
 of Pathein 145
 of Yangon 119
postal services 328
public holidays 326
Putao 263–4
 Myoma market 264
 rope bridge 264
Pwasaw 235–6
 Dhammayazika Pagoda 236
Pyay (Prome) 15, 21, 115, 166,
 167, 271
 Shwesandaw Pagoda 166
 Tazaungdaing Festival 166
Pyin-U-Lwin (Maymyo) 15, 47, 173,
 202–4, 207
 Botanical Garden 203
 horse-drawn carriages 203–4
 Jamh Mosque 203
 Thiri Myaing hotel 203
Pyusawti 225

r

rainforests 50
Rajakumar 231–2
Rakhaing (Arakan) 15, 49, 102,
 275, 277
 see also individual place names
**Rakhaing Yoma Elephant
 Sanctuary** 299
Rangoon see **Yangon**
Razadarit 154
Razagyi 279
religion 322, 348–51
 see also **festivals and events**
  Buddhism 21, 22, 25, 38, 50,
   63, 64, 70–72, 119, 157,
   177–8, 194–5, 213, 225,
   230, 277, 290, 307, 309,
   348–51
  Christianity 24, 63, 161, 163,
   164, 263, 290, 293, 305
  folk religion and animism 71,
   206, 241–2, 278,
   289–90, 293
  Hindu 65, 161, 226–7
  Islam 63, 64, 65, 66, 277,
   280, 297
  Mount Meru 70, 100
  Naga cult 152–3
  religious services 329–330
  shin-pyu 67, 72, 73, 194–5
  temple architecture 99–103
  Tipitaka 25, 180, 225
rivers 15
 Ayeyarwady (Irrawaddy) 15, 22,

27, 31, 45, 49, 111, 115, 120, 145–8, 175, 185, 186, 187, 191, 194, 198, 211, 213, 225, 235, 260, 261–2, 265, 266–71
Bago 151
Chao Phraya 316
Chindwin 46, 49, 202, 238–9
Hlaing see Yangon
Kaladan 275, 277, 281, 285, 287, 295–7
Lomro 277
Malihka 261, 266
Mehka 261, 266
Mekong 31, 47
Mogaung 266
Mula 264
Myinkaba 232
Myitnge 191–2
Myittha 287
Ngawun Chaung 316
Pathein (Ngawun) 147
Sakoya Chaung 296
Sittoung (Sittang) 49, 307
Shweli 269
Tanintharyi 316–7
Taungyin (Moei) 311, 313
Thanlwin (Salween) 15, 31, 47, 308, 311, 312
Yangon 119, 120, 125, 147, 164

S

Sagaing 47, 111, 173, 194–8
Aungmyelawka Pagoda 197
Datpaungzu Pagoda 197
Hsinmyashin Pagoda 196
Htupayon Pagoda 196–7
Kaunghmudaw Pagoda 195, 196
Lake Myitta Kan 196
Myipaukgyi Pagoda 197–8
Ngadatgyi Pagoda 197
Pa Ba Kyaung 198
Shwe Ume Kyaung 197
Sun U Ponya Shin Pagoda 195, 197
Thadingyut Light Festival 196
Tilawkaguru Cave 197
U Min Kyaukse Pagoda 197
U Min Thonze Pagoda 197
Sale 239
San Yu 39
Sapada 230
Sargent, Inge 254
Sawlu 215
Saw Maung 37, 39
Saya San 28
Scott, Sir James George 30, 33, 254

Sein Lwin 39
Shan Plateau 45, 46, 47
Shan State 173, 249, 251–9
see also individual place names
Shin Arahan 22, 213–14, 215, 219
Shinsawpu 129, 154–5
shopping listings 352–3
Shway Yoe see Scott, Sir James George
Shwebo 173, 204–5, 271
Shwedaung 166
Shwemyetmhan Pagoda 166
Shwegu 267
Shwe Min Phone 257
Shwenyaung 251
Sinkan 266
Singu 130, 271
Sinpyumashin 33
Sirigutta Hill 277, 285
Yattara Bell 277, 285, 287
Sittwe (Akyab) 275, 277, 278, 281, 295, 296–7
Atulamarazei Pyeloun Chantha Payagi 297
Buddhistic Museum 296
Cheduba Island 297
Jama' Masjid 297
Kyayouq Kyaung 297
Rakhaing State Cultural Museum 296
Ramree Island 297
The Point 297
tomb of Babagyi 297
Slim, William 30
Sokkate 232
Southeast Burma 303–19
see also individual place names
sport 351–2
Stilwell, Joseph Warren ("Vinegar Joe") 29–30, 32
Sumprabhum 264
Supayalat 33, 176
Syriam (Thanhlyn) 24, 120

t

Tabinshweti 23, 24, 155
Tachilek 256
Tada-u 194
Tagaung 111, 167, 270
shrine of the Tagaung Nat 270
Tanintharyi (Tenasserim) 15, 46, 47, 303, 315, 319
Taungbyon 205
Taungbyon Spirit Festival 205
Taungbyon Brother Lords 205–6
Taungdwingyi 167
Taunggyi 30, 47, 249, 254–5
Taunggyi Museum 249, 255

Wish Granting Pagoda 255
Taungkwe Zedi 259
Taungoo (Toungoo) 24, 115, 165
Lay Kyaung Kandawgyi lake 165
Toungoo museum 165
Myasigon Pagoda 165
Shwesandaw Pagoda 165
Taungup 295, 297
Taungup Pass 295
Ta Yaw 257
telephones 328
useful numbers 328
Temple, Sir Richard
The Thirty-seven Nats 20, 21
Thabeikkyn 270
Thadominbya 192
Thalun 159
Thamuddarit 225
Thanbyuzayat 308
Allied war cemetery 308
Thandwe 298, 314
see also Ngapali Beach
Andaw Pagoda 298
Nandaw Pagoda 298
Sandaw Pagoda 298
Thang, John Kaw Kim 291
Thanlyin (Syriam) 160–64
Church of the Sacred Heart of Jesus 164
Kyaik-Khauk Pagoda 164
People's Brewery 160
Portuguese Church 163
Tharrawaddy 130
Thaton 307–8
Kalyani Sima 308
Pitakat Taik 308
Shwezayan Pagoda 307–8
Thagyapaya Pagoda 308
Thayekhittaya (Sri Ksetra) 21, 45, 101, 166, 167
Bebe Temple 167
East Zegu Temple 167
Leimyethna Temple 167
Payagyi Pagoda 166–7
Payama Pagoda 167
Theroux, Paul 121, 207
Thibaw 27, 33, 176, 180
Thiripyitsaya Village 235
Anauk (or Eastern) Petleik 235
Ashe (or Western) Petleik 235
Lawkananda Pagoda 235
Thiri-thu-dhamma 279
Thonganbwa 197, 218
Tigyaing 269
time differences 322
tipping 329
Tombo 167
Ton Krabak Yai National Park 307
tourism 47, 261, 275

eco-tourism 165–6
restricted areas 295, 303, 307, 308, 311, 313, 315, 327, 335–6
tourist information 325, 329
tour operators 335–6
traditions and customs 67
nahtwin 67
shin-pyu 67, 72, 73
thanaka 61, 65, 160, 244–5, 286
traditional costume 62, 63, 67, 68–9, 88, 189, 244–5, 285–6, 293
transport 168–9
air travel within Burma 243, 251, 332
bus and coach travel 120, 168, 243, 334–5
rail 167, 169, 204, 207, 243, 265, 333–4
river boats and ferries 111, 115, 125, 126, 145, 146, 148, 167, 186–7, 198, 243, 264, 266, 267, 268, 277, 281, 284, 311, 332–3
Pandaw III river boat 186, 243
Road to Mandalay cruise ship 186, 243
taxis 335
trishaws 147, 283, 297, 335
trekking 249, 257, 262, 352
etiquette 62
Twante 145, 167
potteries 145, 147
Shwe San Daw Pagoda 145
Snake Temple 145
Twante Canal 145
Twinn Hills crater lake 202

u–v

Union of Myanmar 15
U Nu 28, 35, 36–8, 142, 143
U Saw 36, 139
Vasali 284–5
visas and passports 315, 316, 323–4

w

Wagaung
Taungbyon Festival 78, 205
Wareru 154
Wetwun 207
White, Mary Povey 319
White, Samuel ("Siamese") 317
wildlife 50
Elephant Control Scheme 299

elephants 267, 299
Hlwaga Wildlife Park (Htaukkyan) 151–2
leopards 292
Rakhaing Yoma Elephant Sanctuary 299
turtles 147
Yangon Zoological Gardens (Yangon) 141
Wingate, Orde Charles 30–31
women travellers 330

y

Yandabo 187
Yangon (Rangoon) 15, 39, 45, 115–43
see also **Insein**
Aung San Statue 140
Bogyoke Aung San Market 127
Bogyoke Aung San Park 140
Botataung Pagoda 125
Chinatown 126
Chinese Market 126
City Hall 123
gems fair and auction 141–2
Gems Museum 141
Horticultural Garden 141
Htaukkyan cemetery 29
Independence monument 123
Indian quarter 126
Inya Lake 141
Kaba Aye Pagoda 141, 142, 143
Kandawgyi (Royal Lake) 78, 140
Karaweik Restaurant 140
Koehtatgyi Pagoda 141
Kyaukhtatgyi Pagoda 139
Mahabandoola Garden 123
Maha Pasana Guha 143
Maha Wizaya Pagoda 138
Martyrs' Mausoleum 138–9
Me La Mu Pagoda 143
Monul Street 120
National Museum 128
Ngahtathyi 139
nightlife 121
parks 139–40
river traffic and boat trips 125, 126, 148
shopping 127–8
Shwedagon Pagoda 21, 27, 28, 98, 100, 119, 124, 129–38
Assembly Hall 134–5
Chinese Community's Tazaung 133–4
Chinese Merchants' Tazaung 134
Commemorative Column 134
Curio Museum 138
Dhammazedi Stones 131, 137–8

Eastern Stairway 131
Guardian Nat of the Shwedagon 134
Hamsa Tagundaing 138
Kannaze Tazaung 136
Maha Gandha Bell 130, 134
Maha Tissada Bell 136, 137
Naungdawgyi Pagoda 137
Northern Stairway 131
Pagoda of the Eight Weekdays 134
Pigeon Feeding Square 138
Planetary Posts 133, 134, 137, 138
Rakhaing (Arakan) Tazaung 134
Replica of the Apex of the Pagoda 137
Replica of the hti 137
Sandawdwin Tazaung 136
Shin Itzagona Tazaung 137
Southern Stairway 131
Statue of King Okkalapa 134
Statues of Me La Mu and Sakka 134
Tawa Gu Buddha 137
Tazaung with Buddha's Footprint 135–6
Temple of the Gautama Buddha 136
Temple of the Kakusandha Buddha 137
Temple of the Kassapa Buddha 134
Temple of the Konagamana Buddha 133
Two Pice Tazaung 131, 134
U Nyo Tazaung 138
Western Stairway 131
Wish Fulfilling Place 135
Wonder Working Buddha Image 135
Zediyingana Society library 136
Shwedagon Pagoda Festival (Yangon) 78, 79
Sri Kali Temple 126
Strand Hotel 123, 125
Sule Pagoda 122, 123
teahouses 122
Theingyi Zei (Indian Market) 126
Yangon Duty-Free Shop 128
Yangon Zoological Gardens 141
Yattara Bell 277, 285, 287
Yaunghwe 251–3
Ywama 253–4
Ywama Festival of Lights 253–4
handicrafts market 253, 254
Phaung Daw U Pagoda 253
Ywataung 86, 196

A
B
C
D

F
G
H
I
J
a
b
c
d
e
f
g
h
i
j
k